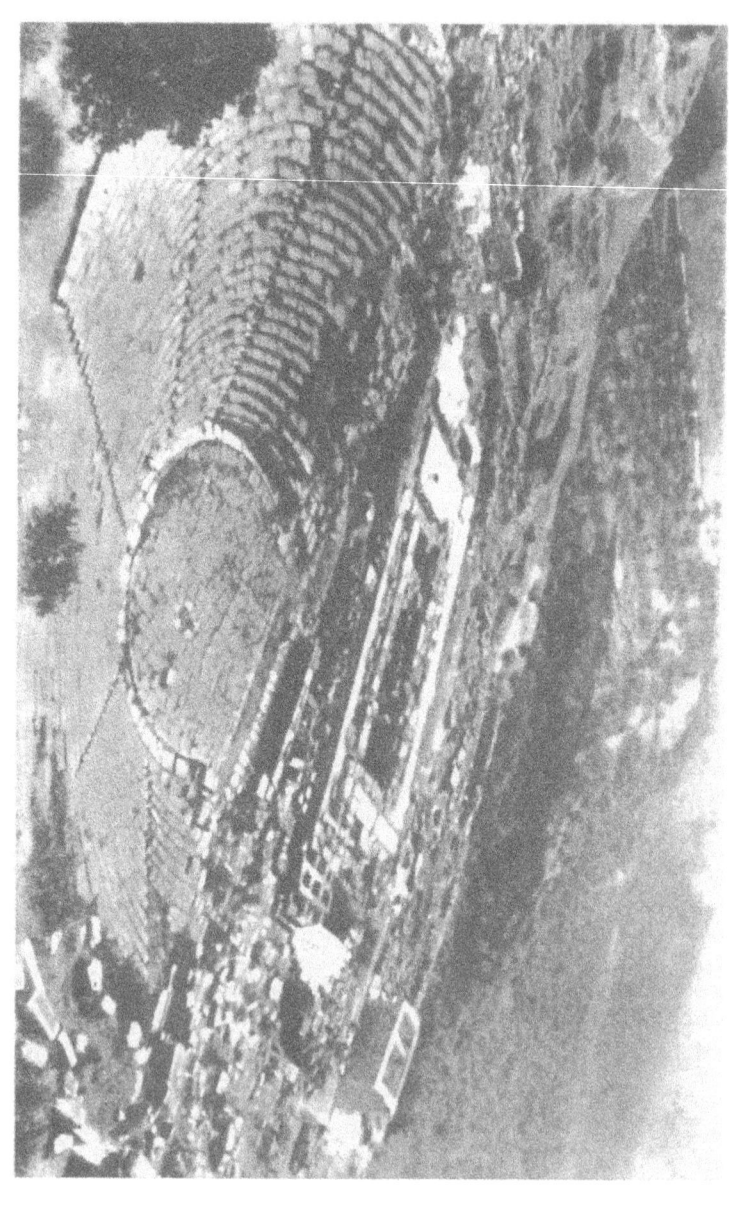

THE HARVARD CLASSICS
EDITED BY CHARLES W. ELIOT, LL.D.

Nine Greek Dramas

By Æschylus, Sophocles,
Euripides *and* Aristophanes

TRANSLATIONS BY E. D. A. MORSHEAD
E. H. PLUMPTRE · GILBERT MURRAY
AND B. B. ROGERS

With Introductions and Notes
Volume 8

CONTENTS

THE HOUSE OF ATREUS (Æschylus)   PAGE
- AGAMEMNON 7
- THE LIBATION-BEARERS 76
- THE FURIES 122
  TRANSLATED BY E. D. A. MORSHEAD

PROMETHEUS BOUND (Æschylus) 166
  TRANSLATED BY E. H. PLUMPTRE

ŒDIPUS THE KING (Sophocles) 209
ANTIGONE (Sophocles) 255
  TRANSLATED BY E. H. PLUMPTRE

HIPPOLYTUS (Euripides) 303
THE BACCHÆ (Euripides) 368
  TRANSLATED BY GILBERT MURRAY

THE FROGS (Aristophanes) 439
  TRANSLATED BY B. B. ROGERS

THE HOUSE OF ATREUS
BEING
THE AGAMEMNON, THE LIBATION-BEARERS, AND THE FURIES OF ÆSCHYLUS

TRANSLATED BY
E. D. A. MORSHEAD

PROMETHEUS BOUND
OF ÆSCHYLUS

TRANSLATED BY
E. H. PLUMPTRE

INTRODUCTORY NOTE

OF THE life of Æschylus, the first of the three great masters of Greek tragedy, only a very meager outline has come down to us. He was born at Eleusis, near Athens, B.C. 525, the son of Euphorion. Before he was twenty-five he began to compete for the tragic prize, but did not win a victory for twelve years. He spent two periods of years in Sicily, where he died in 456, killed, it is said, by a tortoise which an eagle dropped on his head. Though a professional writer, he did his share of fighting for his country, and is reported to have taken part in the battles of Marathon, Salamis, and Platæa.

Of the seventy or eighty plays which he is said to have written, only seven survive: "The Persians," dealing with the defeat of Xerxes at Salamis; "The Seven against Thebes," part of a tetralogy on the legend of Thebes; "The Suppliants," on the daughters of Danaüs; "Prometheus Bound," part of a trilogy, of which the first part was probably "Prometheus, the Fire-Bringer," and the last, "Prometheus Unbound"; and the "Oresteia," the only example of a complete Greek tragic trilogy which has come down to us, consisting of the "Agamemnon," the "Choëphoræ" ("The Libation-Bearers"), and the "Eumenides" ("The Furies").

The importance of Æschylus in the development of the drama is immense. Before him tragedy had consisted of the chorus and one actor; and by introducing a second actor, expanding the dramatic dialogue thus made possible, and reducing the lyrical parts, he practically created Greek tragedy as we understand it. Like other writers of his time, he acted in his own plays, and trained the chorus in their dances and songs; and he did much to give impressiveness to the performances by his development of the accessories of scene and costume on the stage. Of the four plays here reproduced, "Prometheus Bound" holds an exceptional place in the literature of the world. As conceived by Æschylus, Prometheus is the champion of man against the oppression of Zeus; and the argument of the drama has a certain correspondence to the problem of the Book of Job. The Oresteian trilogy on "The House of Atreus" is one of the supreme productions of all literature. It deals with the two great themes of the retribution of crime and the inheritance of evil; and here again a parallel may be found between the assertions of the justice of God by Æschylus and by the Hebrew prophet Ezekiel. Both contend against the popular idea that the fathers have eaten sour grapes and the children's teeth are set on edge; both maintain that the soul that sinneth, it shall die. The nobility of thought and the majesty of style with which these ideas are set forth give this triple drama its place at the head of the literary masterpieces of the antique world.

THE HOUSE OF ATREUS
BEING
THE AGAMEMNON, THE LIBATION-BEARERS, AND THE FURIES OF ÆSCHYLUS

AGAMEMNON

DRAMATIS PERSONÆ

A Watchman	**Chorus**	**Clytemnestra**
A Herald	**Agamemnon**	**Cassandra**
	Ægisthus	

The Scene is the Palace of Atreus at Mycenæ. In front of the Palace stand statues of the gods, and altars prepared for sacrifices.

A Watchman

I PRAY the gods to quit me of my toils,
   To close the watch I keep, this livelong year;
   For as a watch-dog lying, not at rest,
Propped on one arm, upon the palace-roof
Of Atreus' race, too long, too well I know
The starry conclave of the midnight sky,
Too well, the splendours of the firmament,
The lords of light, whose kingly aspect shows—
What time they set or climb the sky in turn—
The year's divisions, bringing frost or fire.

And now, as ever, am I set to mark
When shall stream up the glow of signal-flame,
The bale-fire bright, and tell its Trojan tale—
Troy town is ta'en: such issue holds in hope
She in whose woman's breast beats heart of man.

Thus upon mine unrestful couch I lie,
Bathed with the dews of night, unvisited

By dreams—ah me!—for in the place of sleep
Stands Fear as my familiar, and repels
The soft repose that would mine eyelids seal.
And if at whiles, for the lost balm of sleep,
I medicine my soul with melody
Of trill or song—anon to tears I turn,
Wailing the woe that broods upon this home,
Not now by honour guided as of old.

But now at last fair fall the welcome hour
That sets me free, whene'er the thick night glow
With beacon-fire of hope deferred no more.
All hail!   [*A beacon-light is seen reddening
                              the distant sky.*
Fire of the night, that brings my spirit day,
Shedding on Argos light, and dance, and song,
Greetings to fortune, hail!

Let my loud summons ring within the ears
Of Agamemnon's queen, that she anon
Start from her couch and with a shrill voice cry
A joyous welcome to the beacon-blaze,
For Ilion's fall; such fiery message gleams
From yon high flame; and I, before the rest,
Will foot the lightsome measure of our joy;
For I can say, *My master's dice fell fair—
Behold! the triple sice, the lucky flame!*
Now be my lot to clasp, in loyal love,
The hand of him restored, who rules our home:
Home—but I say no more: upon my tongue
Treads hard the ox o' the adage.
                                   Had it voice,
The home itself might soothliest tell its tale;
I, of set will, speak words the wise may learn,
To others, nought remember nor discern.
    [*Exit. The chorus of old men of Mycenæ enter, each
      leaning on a staff. During their song Clytemnestra
      appears in the background, kindling the altars.*

AGAMEMNON

Chorus

Ten livelong years have rolled away,
Since the twin lords of sceptred sway,
By Zeus endowed with pride of place,
The doughty chiefs of Atreus' race,
 Went forth of yore,
To plead with Priam, face to face,
 Before the judgment-seat of War!

A thousand ships from Argive land
Put forth to bear the martial band,
That with a spirit stern and strong
Went out to right the kingdom's wrong—
Pealed, as they went, the battle-song,
 Wild as the vultures' cry;
When o'er the eyrie, soaring high,
In wild bereavèd agony,
Around, around, in airy rings,
They wheel with oarage of their wings,
But not the eyas-brood behold,
That called them to the nest of old;
But let Apollo from the sky,
Or Pan, or Zeus, but hear the cry,
The exile cry, the wail forlorn,
Of birds from whom their home is torn—
On those who wrought the rapine fell,
Heaven sends the vengeful fiends of hell.

Even so doth Zeus, the jealous lord
And guardian of the hearth and board,
Speed Atreus' sons, in vengeful ire,
'Gainst Paris—sends them forth on fire,
Her to buy back, in war and blood,
Whom one did wed but many woo'd!
And many, many, by his will,
The last embrace of foes shall feel,

And many a knee in dust be bowed,
And splintered spears on shields ring loud,
Of Trojan and of Greek, before
That iron bridal-feast be o'er!
But as he willed 'tis ordered all,
And woes, by heaven ordained, must fall—
Unsoothed by tears or spilth of wine
Poured forth too late, the wrath divine
Glares vengeance on the flameless shrine.

And we in gray dishonoured eld,
Feeble of frame, unfit were held
To join the warrior array
That then went forth unto the fray:
And here at home we tarry, fain
Our feeble footsteps to sustain,
Each on his staff—so strength doth wane,
And turns to childishness again.
For while the sap of youth is green,
And, yet unripened, leaps within,
The young are weakly as the old,
And each alike unmeet to hold
The vantage post of war!
And ah! when flower and fruit are o'er,
  And on life's tree the leaves are sere,
  Age wendeth propped its journey drear,
As forceless as a child, as light
And fleeting as a dream of night
Lost in the garish day!

But thou, O child of Tyndareus,
  Queen Clytemnestra, speak! and say
  What messenger of joy to-day
Hath won thine ear? what welcome news,
That thus in sacrificial wise
E'en to the city's boundaries
Thou biddest altar-fires arise?

Each god who doth our city guard,
And keeps o'er Argos watch and ward
　From heaven above, from earth below—
The mighty lords who rule the skies,
The market's lesser deities,
　To each and all the altars glow,
Piled for the sacrifice!
And here and there, anear, afar,
Streams skyward many a beacon-star,
Conjur'd and charm'd and kindled well
By pure oil's soft and guileless spell,
Hid now no more
Within the palace' secret store.

O queen, we pray thee, whatsoe'er,
　Known unto thee, were well revealed,
That thou wilt trust it to our ear,
　And bid our anxious heart be healed!
That waneth now unto despair—
Now, waxing to a presage fair,
Dawns, from the altar, Hope—to scare
From our rent hearts the vulture Care.

List! for the power is mine, to chant on high
　The chiefs' emprise, the strength that omens gave!
List! on my soul breathes yet a harmony,
　From realms of ageless powers, and strong to save!

How brother kings, twin lords of one command,
　Led forth the youth of Hellas in their flower,
Urged on their way, with vengeful spear and brand,
　By warrior-birds, that watched the parting hour.

Go forth to Troy, the eagles seemed to cry—
　And the sea-kings obeyed the sky-kings' word,
When on the right they soared across the sky,
　And one was black, one bore a white tail barred.

High o'er the palace were they seen to soar,
   Then lit in sight of all, and rent and tare,
Far from the fields that she should range no more,
   Big with her unborn brood, a mother-hare.

And one beheld, the soldier-prophet true,
   And the two chiefs, unlike of soul and will,
In the twy-coloured eagles straight he knew,
   And spake the omen forth, for good and ill.

(Ah woe and well-a-day! but be the issue fair!)

Go forth, he cried, and Priam's town shall fall.
   Yet long the time shall be; and flock and herd,
The people's wealth, that roam before the wall,
   Shall force hew down, when Fate shall give the word.

But O beware! lest wrath in heaven abide,
   To dim the glowing battle-forge once more,
And mar the mighty curb of Trojan pride,
   The steel of vengeance, welded as for war!

For virgin Artemis bears jealous hate
   Against the royal house, the eagle-pair,
Who rend the unborn brood, insatiate—
   Yea, loathes their banquet on the quivering hare.

(Ah woe and well-a-day! but be the issue fair!)

For well she loves—the goddess kind and mild—
   The tender new-born cubs of lions bold,
Too weak to range—and well the sucking child
   Of every beast that roams by wood and wold.

So to the Lord of Heaven she prayeth still,
   "Nay, if it must be, be the omen true!
Yet do the visioned eagles presage ill;
   The end be well, but crossed with evil too!"

Healer Apollo! be her wrath controll'd,
  Nor weave the long delay of thwarting gales,
To war against the Danaans and withhold
  From the free ocean-waves their eager sails!

She craves, alas! to see a second life
  Shed forth, a curst unhallowed sacrifice—
'Twixt wedded souls, artificer of strife,
  And hate that knows not fear, and fell device.

At home there tarries like a lurking snake,
  Biding its time, a wrath unreconciled,
A wily watcher, passionate to slake,
  In blood, resentment for a murdered child.

Such was the mighty warning, pealed of yore—
  Amid good tidings, such the word of fear,
What time the fateful eagles hovered o'er
  The kings, and Calchas read the omen clear.

(In strains like his, once more,
Sing woe and well-a-day! but be the issue fair!)

   Zeus—if to The Unknown
     That name of many names seem good—
   Zeus, upon Thee I call.
     Thro' the mind's every road
   I passed, but vain are all,
     Save that which names thee Zeus, the Highest One,
       Were it but mine to cast away the load,
   The weary load, that weighs my spirit down.

   He that was Lord of old,
In full-blown pride of place and valour bold,
   Hath fallen and is gone, even as an old tale told!
   And he that next held sway,

By stronger grasp o'erthrown
Hath pass'd away!
And whoso now shall bid the triumph-chant arise
To Zeus, and Zeus alone,
He shall be found the truly wise.
'Tis Zeus alone who shows the perfect way
Of knowledge: He hath ruled,
Men shall learn wisdom, by affliction schooled.

In visions of the night, like dropping rain,
Descend the many memories of pain
Before the spirit's sight: through tears and dole
Comes wisdom o'er the unwilling soul—
A boon, I wot, of all Divinity,
That holds its sacred throne in strength, above the sky!

And then the elder chief, at whose command
The fleet of Greece was manned,
Cast on the seer no word of hate,
But veered before the sudden breath of Fate—

Ah, weary while! for, ere they put forth sail,
Did every store, each minish'd vessel, fail,
While all the Achæan host
At Aulis anchored lay,
Looking across to Chalcis and the coast
Where refluent waters welter, rock, and sway;
And rife with ill delay
From northern Strymon blew the thwarting
blast—
Mother of famine fell,
That holds men wand'ring still
Far from the haven where they fain would be!—
And pitiless did waste
Each ship and cable, rotting on the sea,
And, doubling with delay each weary hour,
Withered with hope deferred th' Achæans' warlike
flower.

But when, for bitter storm, a deadlier relief,
And heavier with ill to either chief,
Pleading the ire of Artemis, the seer avowed,
  The two Atridæ smote their sceptres on the plain,
And, striving hard, could not their tears restrain!
And then the elder monarch spake aloud—
  Ill lot were mine, to disobey!
  And ill, to smite my child, my household's love
    and pride!
  To stain with virgin blood a father's hands, and
    slay
  My daughter, by the altar's side!
  'Twixt woe and woe I dwell—
  I dare not like a recreant fly,
And leave the league of ships, and fail each true ally;
  For rightfully they crave, with eager fiery mind,
  The virgin's blood, shed forth to lull the adverse
    wind—
  God send the deed be well!

  Thus on his neck he took
  Fate's hard compelling yoke;
Then, in the counter-gale of will abhorr'd, accursed,
  To recklessness his shifting spirit veered—
  Alas! that Frenzy, first of ills and worst,
With evil craft men's souls to sin hath ever stirred!

  And so he steeled his heart—ah, well-a-day—
    Aiding a war for one false woman's sake,
      His child to slay,
    And with her spilt blood make
An offering, to speed the ships upon their way!

  Lusting for war, the bloody arbiters
Closed heart and ears, and would nor hear nor heed
    The girl-voice plead,
  Pity me, Father! nor her prayers,
    Nor tender, virgin years.

So, when the chant of sacrifice was done,
  Her father bade the youthful priestly train
Raise her, like some poor kid, above the altar-stone,
  From where amid her robes she lay
    Sunk all in swoon away—
Bade them, as with the bit that mutely tames the steed,
  Her fair lips' speech refrain,
Lest she should speak a curse on Atreus' home and
  seed,

  So, trailing on the earth her robe of saffron dye,
With one last piteous dart from her beseeching eye
  Those that should smite she smote—
  Fair, silent, as a pictur'd form, but fain
To plead, *Is all forgot?*
How oft those halls of old,
Wherein my sire high feast did hold,
  Rang to the virginal soft strain,
    When I, a stainless child,
  Sang from pure lips and undefiled,
    Sang of my sire, and all
His honoured life, and how on him should fall
  Heaven's highest gift and gain!
And then—but I beheld not, nor can tell,
  What further fate befel:
But this is sure, that Calchas' boding strain
  Can ne'er be void or vain.
This wage from Justice' hand do sufferers earn,
  The future to discern:
And yet—farewell, O secret of To-morrow!
  Foreknowledge is fore-sorrow.
Clear with the clear beams of the morrow's sun,
  The future presseth on.
Now, let the house's tale, how dark soe'er,
  Find yet an issue fair!—
So prays the loyal, solitary band
  That guards the Apian land.

*[They turn to Clytemnestra, who leaves
the altars and comes forward.*

O queen, I come in reverence of thy sway—
For, while the ruler's kingly seat is void,
The loyal heart before his consort bends.
Now—be it sure and certain news of good,
Or the fair tidings of a flatt'ring hope,
That bids thee spread the light from shrine to shrine,
I, fain to hear, yet grudge not if thou hide.

Clytemnestra

As saith the adage, *From the womb of Night
Spring forth, with promise fair, the young child Light.*
Ay—fairer even than all hope my news—
By Grecian hands is Priam's city ta'en!

Chorus

What say'st thou? doubtful heart makes treach'rous ear.

Clytemnestra

Hear then again, and plainly—Troy is ours!

Chorus

Thrills thro' my heart such joy as wakens tears.

Clytemnestra

Ay, thro' those tears thine eye looks loyalty.

Chorus

But hast thou proof, to make assurance sure?

Clytemnestra

Go to; I have—unless the god has lied.

Chorus

Hath some night-vision won thee to belief?

Clytemnestra

Out on all presage of a slumb'rous soul!

Chorus

But wert thou cheered by Rumour's wingless word?

Clytemnestra

Peace—thou dost chide me as a credulous girl.

Chorus

Say then how long ago the city fell?

Clytemnestra

Even in this night that now brings forth the dawn.

Chorus

Yet who so swift could speed the message here?

Clytemnestra

From Ida's top Hephæstus, lord of fire,
Sent forth his sign; and on, and ever on,
Beacon to beacon sped the courier-flame.
From Ida to the crag, that Hermes loves,
Of Lemnos; thence unto the steep sublime
Of Athos, throne of Zeus, the broad blaze flared.
Thence, raised aloft to shoot across the sea,
The moving light, rejoicing in its strength,
Sped from the pyre of pine, and urged its way,
In golden glory, like some strange new sun,
Onward, and reached Macistus' watching heights.
There, with no dull delay nor heedless sleep,
The watcher sped the tidings on in turn,
Until the guard upon Messapius' peak

Saw the far flame gleam on Euripus' tide,
And from the high-piled heap of withered furze
Lit the new sign and bade the message on.
Then the strong light, far flown and yet undimmed,
Shot thro' the sky above Asopus' plain,
Bright as the moon, and on Cithæron's crag
Aroused another watch of flying fire.
And there the sentinels no whit disowned,
But sent redoubled on, the hest of flame—
Swift shot the light, above Gorgopis' bay,
To Ægiplanctus' mount, and bade the peak
Fail not the onward ordinance of fire.
And like a long beard streaming in the wind,
Full-fed with fuel, roared and rose the blaze,
And onward flaring, gleamed above the cape,
Beneath which shimmers the Saronic bay,
And thence leapt light unto Arachne's peak,
The mountain watch that looks upon our town.
Thence to th' Atrides' roof—in lineage fair,
A bright posterity of Ida's fire.
So sped from stage to stage, fulfilled in turn,
Flame after flame, along the course ordained,
And lo! the last to speed upon its way
Sights the end first, and glows unto the goal.
And Troy is ta'en, and by this sign my lord
Tells me the tale, and ye have learned my word.

Chorus

To heaven, O queen, will I upraise new song:
But, wouldst thou speak once more, I fain would hear
From first to last the marvel of the tale.

Clytemnestra

Think you—this very morn—the Greeks in Troy,
And loud therein the voice of utter wail!
Within one cup pour vinegar and oil,

And look! unblent, unreconciled, they war.
So in the twofold issue of the strife
Mingle the victor's shout, the captives' moan.
For all the conquered whom the sword has spared
Cling weeping—some unto a brother slain,
Some childlike to a nursing father's form,
And wail the loved and lost, the while their neck
Bows down already 'neath the captive's chain.
And lo! the victors, now the fight is done,
Goaded by restless hunger, far and wide
Range all disordered thro' the town, to snatch
Such victual and such rest as chance may give
Within the captive halls that once were Troy—
Joyful to rid them of the frost and dew,
Wherein they couched upon the plain of old—
Joyful to sleep the gracious night all through,
Unsummoned of the watching sentinel.
Yet let them reverence well the city's gods,
The lords of Troy, tho' fallen, and her shrines;
So shall the spoilers not in turn be spoiled.
Yea, let no craving for forbidden gain
Bid conquerors yield before the darts of greed.
For we need yet, before the race be won,
Homewards, unharmed, to round the course once more.
For should the host wax wanton ere it come,
Then, tho' the sudden blow of fate be spared,
Yet in the sight of gods shall rise once more
The great wrong of the slain, to claim revenge.
Now, hearing from this woman's mouth of mine,
The tale and eke its warning, pray with me,
Luck sway the scale, with no uncertain poise,
For my fair hopes are changed to fairer joys.

Chorus

A gracious word thy woman's lips have told,
Worthy a wise man's utterance, O my queen;
Now with clear trust in thy convincing tale

I set me to salute the gods with song,
Who bring us bliss to counterpoise our pain.
                    [*Exit Clytemnestra.*

Zeus, Lord of heaven! and welcome night
Of victory, that hast our might
  With all the glories crowned!
On towers of Ilion, free no more,
Hast flung the mighty mesh of war,
  And closely girt them round,
Till neither warrior may 'scape,
Nor stripling lightly overleap
The trammels as they close, and close,
Till with the grip of doom our foes
  In slavery's coil are bound!

Zeus, Lord of hospitality,
In grateful awe I bend to thee—
  'Tis thou hast struck the blow!
  At Alexander, long ago,
  We marked thee bend thy vengeful bow,
But long and warily withhold
The eager shaft, which, uncontrolled
And loosed too soon or launched too high,
Had wandered bloodless through the sky.

Zeus, the high God!—whate'er be dim in doubt,
  This can our thought track out—
The blow that fells the sinner is of God,
  And as he wills, the rod
Of vengeance smiteth sore. One said of old,
  The gods list not to hold
  A reckoning with him whose feet oppress
  The grace of holiness—
An impious word! for whensoe'er the sire
  Breathed forth rebellious fire—
What time his household overflowed the measure
  Of bliss and health and treasure—

His children's children read the reckoning plain,
  At last, in tears and pain.
On me let weal that brings no woe be sent,
  And therewithal, content!
Who spurns the shrine of Right, nor wealth nor power
  Shall be to him a tower,
To guard him from the gulf: there lies his lot,
  Where all things are forgot.
Lust drives him on—lust, desperate and wild,
  Fate's sin-contriving child—
And cure is none; beyond concealment clear,
  Kindles sin's baleful glare.
As an ill coin beneath the wearing touch
  Betrays by stain and smutch
Its metal false—such is the sinful wight.
  Before, on pinions light,
Fair Pleasure flits, and lures him childlike on,
  While home and kin make moan
Beneath the grinding burden of his crime;
  Till, in the end of time,
Cast down of heaven, he pours forth fruitless prayer
  To powers that will not hear.

  And such did Paris come
  Unto Atrides' home,
And thence, with sin and shame his welcome to repay,
  Ravished the wife away—
And she, unto her country and her kin
Leaving the clash of shields and spears and arming ships,
And bearing unto Troy destruction for a dower,
  And overbold in sin,
Went fleetly thro' the gates, at midnight hour.
  Oft from the prophets' lips
Moaned out the warning and the wail—Ah woe!
Woe for the home, the home! and for the chieftains, woe!
  Woe for the bride-bed, warm
Yet from the lovely limbs, the impress of the form

AGAMEMNON

   Of her who loved her lord, a while ago!
      And woe! for him who stands
Shamed, silent, unreproachful, stretching hands
   That find her not, and sees, yet will not see,
      That she is far away!
And his sad fancy, yearning o'er the sea,
      Shall summon and recall
Her wraith, once more to queen it in his hall.
      And sad with many memories,
The fair cold beauty of each sculptured face—
      And all to hatefulness is turned their grace,
Seen blankly by forlorn and hungering eyes!
      And when the night is deep,
Come visions, sweet and sad, and bearing pain
      Of hopings vain—
Void, void and vain, for scarce the sleeping sight
      Has seen its old delight,
When thro' the grasps of love that bid it stay
      It vanishes away
On silent wings that roam adown the ways of sleep.

      Such are the sights, the sorrows fell,
About our hearth—and worse, whereof I may not tell.
      But, all the wide town o'er,
Each home that sent its master far away
      From Hellas' shore,
Feels the keen thrill of heart, the pang of loss, to-day.
      For, truth to say,
The touch of bitter death is manifold!
Familiar was each face, and dear as life,
      That went unto the war,
But thither, whence a warrior went of old,
      Doth nought return—
Only a spear and sword, and ashes in an urn!
      For Ares, lord of strife,
Who doth the swaying scales of battle hold,
War's money-changer, giving dust for gold,

Sends back, to hearts that held them dear,
Scant ash of warriors, wept with many a tear,
Light to the hand, but heavy to the soul;
   Yea, fills the light urn full
   With what survived the flame—
Death's dusty measure of a hero's frame!

Alas! one cries, and yet alas again!
Our chief is gone, the hero of the spear,
   And hath not left his peer!
Ah woe! another moans—*my spouse is slain,*
   The death of honour, rolled in dust and blood,
Slain for a woman's sin, a false wife's shame!
   Such muttered words of bitter mood
Rise against those who went forth to reclaim;
   Yea, jealous wrath creeps on against th' Atrides'
     name.

And others, far beneath the Ilian wall,
Sleep their last sleep—the goodly chiefs and tall,
Couched in the foeman's land, whereon they gave
Their breath, and lords of Troy, each in his Trojan
     grave.

Therefore for each and all the city's breast
   Is heavy with a wrath supprest,
As deep and deadly as a curse more loud
   Flung by the common crowd;
And, brooding deeply, doth my soul await
   Tidings of coming fate,
Buried as yet in darkness' womb.
For not forgetful is the high gods' doom
   Against the sons of carnage: all too long
Seems the unjust to prosper and be strong,
   Till the dark Furies come,
And smite with stern reversal all his home,
   Down into dim obstruction—he is gone,
And help and hope, among the lost, is none!

AGAMEMNON

O'er him who vaunteth an exceeding fame,
    Impends a woe condign;
The vengeful bolt upon his eyes doth flame,
    Sped from the hand divine.
This bliss be mine, ungrudged of God, to feel—
    To tread no city to the dust,
Nor see my own life thrust
Down to a slave's estate beneath another's heel!

Behold, throughout the city wide
Have the swift feet of Rumour hied,
    Roused by the joyful flame:
But is the news they scatter, sooth?
Or haply do they give for truth
    Some cheat which heaven doth frame?
A child were he and all unwise,
    Who let his heart with joy be stirred,
To see the beacon-fires arise,
    And then, beneath some thwarting word,
    Sicken anon with hope deferred.
The edge of woman's insight still
    Good news from true divideth ill;
Light rumours leap within the bound
That fences female credence round,
But, lightly born, as lightly dies
The tale that springs of her surmise.

Soon shall we know whereof the bale-fires tell,
The beacons, kindled with transmitted flame;
Whether, as well I deem, their tale is true,
Or whether like some dream delusive came
The welcome blaze but to befool our soul.
For lo! I see a herald from the shore
Draw hither, shadowed with the olive-wreath—
And thirsty dust, twin-brother of the clay,
Speaks plain of travel far and truthful news—
No dumb surmise, nor tongue of flame in smoke,

Fitfully kindled from the mountain pyre;
But plainlier shall his voice say, *All is well,*
Or—but away, forebodings adverse, now,
And on fair promise' fair fulfilment come!
And whoso for the state prays otherwise,
Himself reap harvest of his ill desire!

Enter Herald

O land of Argos, fatherland of mine!
To thee at last, beneath the tenth year's sun,
My feet return; the bark of my emprise,
Tho' one by one hope's anchors broke away,
Held by the last, and now rides safely here.
Long, long my soul despaired to win, in death,
Its longed-for rest within our Argive land:
And now all hail, O earth, and hail to thee,
New-risen sun! and hail our country's God,
High-ruling Zeus, and thou, the Pythian lord,
Whose arrows smote us once—smite thou no more!
Was not thy wrath wreaked full upon our heads,
O king Apollo, by Scamander's side?
Turn thou, be turned, be saviour, healer, now!
And hail, all gods who rule the street and mart,
And Hermes hail! my patron and my pride,
Herald of heaven, and lord of heralds here!
And Heroes, ye who sped us on our way—
To one and all I cry, *Receive again*
With grace such Argives as the spear has spared.

Ah, home of royalty, belovèd halls,
And solemn shrines, and gods that front the morn!
Benign as erst, with sun-flushed aspect greet
The king returning after many days.
For as from night flash out the beams of day,
So out of darkness dawns a light, a king,
On you, on Argos—Agamemnon comes.
Then hail and greet him well! such meed befits

Him whose right hand hewed down the towers of Troy
With the great axe of Zeus who righteth wrong—
And smote the plain, smote down to nothingness
Each altar, every shrine; and far and wide
Dies from the whole land's face its offspring fair.
Such mighty yoke of fate he set on Troy—
Our lord and monarch, Atreus' elder son,
And comes at last with blissful honour home;
Highest of all who walk on earth to-day—
Not Paris nor the city's self that paid
Sin's price with him, can boast, *Whate'er befal,
The guerdon we have won outweighs it all.*
But at Fate's judgment-seat the robber stands
Condemned of rapine, and his prey is torn
Forth from his hands, and by his deed is reaped
A bloody harvest of his home and land
Gone down to death, and for his guilt and lust
His father's race pays double in the dust.

Chorus

Hail, herald of the Greeks, new-come from war.

Herald

All hail! not death itself can fright me now.

Chorus

Was thine heart wrung with longing for thy land?

Herald

So that this joy doth brim mine eyes with tears.

Chorus

On you too then this sweet distress did fall——

Herald

How say'st thou? make me master of thy word.

Chorus

You longed for us who pined for you again.

Herald

Craved the land us who craved it, love for love?

Chorus

Yea, till my brooding heart moaned out with pain.

Herald

Whence thy despair, that mars the army's joy?

Chorus

Sole cure of wrong is silence, saith the saw.

Herald

Thy kings afar, couldst thou fear other men?

Chorus

Death had been sweet, as thou didst say but now.

Herald

'Tis true; Fate smiles at last. Throughout our toil,
These many years, some chances issued fair,
And some, I wot, were chequered with a curse.
But who, on earth, hath won the bliss of heaven,
Thro' time's whole tenor an unbroken weal?
I could a tale unfold of toiling oars,
Ill rest, scant landings on a shore rock-strewn,
All pains, all sorrows, for our daily doom.
And worse and hatefuller our woes on land;
For where we couched, close by the foeman's wall,
The river-plain was ever dank with dews,
Dropped from the sky, exuded from the earth,
A curse that clung unto our sodden garb,
And hair as horrent as a wild beast's fell.

Why tell the woes of winter, when the birds
Lay stark and stiff, so stern was Ida's snow?
Or summer's scorch, what time the stirless wave
Sank to its sleep beneath the noonday sun?
Why mourn old woes? their pain has passed away;
And passed away, from those who fell, all care,
For evermore, to rise and live again.
Why sum the count of death, and render thanks
For life by moaning over fate malign?
Farewell, a long farewell to all our woes!
To us, the remnant of the host of Greece,
Comes weal beyond all counterpoise of woe;
Thus boast we rightfully to yonder sun,
Like him far-fleeted over sea and land.
The Argive host prevailed to conquer Troy,
And in the temples of the gods of Greece
Hung up these spoils, a shining sign to Time.
Let those who learn this legend bless aright
The city and its chieftains, and repay
The meed of gratitude to Zeus who willed
And wrought the deed. So stands the tale fulfilled.

Chorus

Thy words o'erbear my doubt: for news of good,
The ear of age hath ever youth enow:
But those within and Clytemnestra's self
Would fain hear all; glad thou their ears and mine.

Re-enter Clytemnestra

Last night, when first the fiery courier came,
In sign that Troy is ta'en and razed to earth,
So wild a cry of joy my lips gave out,
That I was chidden—*Hath the beacon watch*
Made sure unto thy soul the sack of Troy?
A very woman thou, whose heart leaps light
At wandering rumours!—and with words like these
They showed me how I strayed, misled of hope.

Yet on each shrine I set the sacrifice,
And, in the strain they held for feminine,
Went heralds thro' the city, to and fro,
With voice of loud proclaim, announcing joy;
And in each fane they lit and quenched with wine
The spicy perfumes fading in the flame.
All is fulfilled: I spare your longer tale—
The king himself anon shall tell me all.

Remains to think what honour best may greet
My lord, the majesty of Argos, home.
What day beams fairer on a woman's eyes
Than this, whereon she flings the portal wide,
To hail her lord, heaven-shielded, home from war?
This to my husband, that he tarry not,
But turn the city's longing into joy!
Yea, let him come, and coming may he find
A wife no other than he left her, true
And faithful as a watch-dog to his home,
His foemen's foe, in all her duties leal,
Trusty to keep for ten long years unmarred
The store whereon he set his master-seal.
Be steel deep-dyed, before ye look to see
Ill joy, ill fame, from other wight, in me!

Herald

'Tis fairly said: thus speaks a noble dame,
Nor speaks amiss, when truth informs the boast.
                                          [*Exit Clytemnestra.*

Chorus

So has she spoken—be it yours to learn
By clear interpreters her specious word.
Turn to me, herald—tell me if anon
The second well-loved lord of Argos comes?
Hath Menelaus safely sped with you?

Herald

Alas—brief boon unto my friends it were,
To flatter them, for truth, with falsehoods fair!

Chorus

Speak joy, if truth be joy, but truth, at worst—
Too plainly, truth and joy are here divorced.

Herald

The hero and his bark were rapt away
Far from the Grecian fleet? 'tis truth I say.

Chorus

Whether in all men's sight from Ilion borne,
Or from the fleet by stress of weather torn?

Herald

Full on the mark thy shaft of speech doth light,
And one short word hath told long woes aright.

Chorus

But say what now of him each comrade saith?
What their forebodings, of his life or death?

Herald

Ask me no more: the truth is known to none,
Save the earth-fostering, all-surveying Sun.

Chorus

Say by what doom the fleet of Greece was driven?
How rose, how sank the storm, the wrath of heaven?

Herald

Nay, ill it were to mar with sorrow's tale
The day of blissful news. The gods demand
Thanksgiving sundered from solicitude.

If one as herald came with rueful face
To say, *The curse has fallen, and the host*
Gone down to death; and one wide wound has reached
The city's heart, and out of many homes
Many are cast and consecrate to death,
Beneath the double scourge, that Ares loves,
The bloody pair, the fire and sword of doom—
If such sore burden weighed upon my tongue,
'Twere fit to speak such words as gladden fiends.
But—coming as he comes who bringeth news
Of safe return from toil, and issues fair,
To men rejoicing in a weal restored—
Dare I to dash good words with ill, and say
How the gods' anger smote the Greeks in storm?
For fire and sea, that erst held bitter feud,
Now swore conspiracy and pledged their faith,
Wasting the Argives worn with toil and war.
Night and great horror of the rising wave
Came o'er us, and the blasts that blow from Thrace
Clashed ship with ship, and some with plunging prow
Thro' scudding drifts of spray and raving storm
Vanished, as strays by some ill shepherd driven.
And when at length the sun rose bright, we saw
Th' Ægæan sea-field flecked with flowers of death,
Corpses of Grecian men and shattered hulls.
For us indeed, some god, as well I deem,
No human power, laid hand upon our helm,
Snatched us or prayed us from the powers of air,
And brought our bark thro' all, unharmed in hull:
And saving Fortune sat and steered us fair,
So that no surge should gulf us deep in brine,
Nor grind our keel upon a rocky shore.

So 'scaped we death that lurks beneath the sea,
But, under day's white light, mistrustful all
Of fortune's smile, we sat and brooded deep,
Shepherds forlorn of thoughts that wandered wild,

O'er this new woe; for smitten was our host,
And lost as ashes scattered from the pyre.
Of whom if any draw his life-breath yet,
Be well assured, he deems of us as dead,
As we of him no other fate forebode.
But heaven save all! If Menelaus live,
He will not tarry, but will surely come:
Therefore if anywhere the high sun's ray
Descries him upon earth, preserved by Zeus,
Who wills not yet to wipe his race away,
Hope still there is that homeward he may wend.
Enough—thou hast the truth unto the end.

Chorus

Say from whose lips the presage fell?
Who read the future all too well,
   And named her, in her natal hour,
   Helen, the bride with war for dower?
'Twas one of the Invisible,
   Guiding his tongue with prescient power.
On fleet, and host, and citadel,
   War, sprung from her, and death did lour,
When from the bride-bed's fine-spun veil
She to the Zephyr spread her sail.

Strong blew the breeze—the surge closed o'er
The cloven track of keel and oar,
   But while she fled, there drove along,
   Fast in her wake, a mighty throng—
Athirst for blood, athirst for war,
   Forward in fell pursuit they sprung,
Then leapt on Simois' bank ashore,
   The leafy coppices among—
No rangers, they, of wood and field,
But huntsmen of the sword and shield.

Heaven's jealousy, that works its will,
Sped thus on Troy its destined ill,

Well named, at once, the Bride and Bane;
And loud rang out the bridal strain;
But they to whom that song befel
   Did turn anon to tears again;
Zeus tarries, but avenges still
   The husband's wrong, the household's stain!
He, the hearth's lord, brooks not to see
Its outraged hospitality.

Even now, and in far other tone,
Troy chants her dirge of mighty moan,
   Woe upon Paris, woe and hate!
   Who wooed his country's doom for mate—
This is the burthen of the groan,
   Wherewith she wails disconsolate
The blood so many of her own
   Have poured in vain, to fend her fate;
Troy! thou hast fed and freed to roam
A lion-cub within thy home!

A suckling creature, newly ta'en
From mother's teat, still fully fain
   Of nursing care; and oft caressed,
   Within the arms, upon the breast,
Even as an infant, has it lain;
   Or fawns and licks, by hunger pressed,
The hand that will assuage its pain;
   In life's young dawn, a well-loved guest,
A fondling for the children's play,
A joy unto the old and gray.

But waxing time and growth betrays
The blood-thirst of the lion-race,
   And, for the house's fostering care,
   Unbidden all, it revels there,
And bloody recompense repays—
   Rent flesh of kine its talons tare:

A mighty beast, that slays and slays,
    And mars with blood the household fair,
A God-sent pest invincible,
A minister of fate and hell.

Even so to Ilion's city came by stealth
    A spirit as of windless seas and skies,
A gentle phantom-form of joy and wealth,
    With love's soft arrows speeding from its eyes—
Love's rose, whose thorn doth pierce the soul in
        subtle wise.

Ah, well-a-day! the bitter bridal-bed,
    When the fair mischief lay by Paris' side!
What curse on palace and on people sped
    With her, the Fury sent on Priam's pride,
By angered Zeus! what tears of many a widowed
        bride!

Long, long ago to mortals this was told,
    How sweet security and blissful state
Have curses for their children—so men hold—
    And for the man of all-too prosperous fate
Springs from a bitter seed some woe insatiate.

Alone, alone, I deem far otherwise;
    Not bliss nor wealth it is, but impious deed,
From which that after-growth of ill doth rise!
    Woe springs from wrong, the plant is like the
        seed—
While Right, in honour's house, doth its own likeness
        breed.

Some past impiety, some gray old crime,
    Breeds the young curse, that wantons in our ill,
Early or late, when haps th' appointed time—
    And out of light brings power of darkness still,
A master-fiend, a foe, unseen, invincible;

A pride accursed, that broods upon the race
    And home in which dark Atè holds her sway—
Sin's child and Woe's, that wears its parents' face;
    While Right in smoky cribs shines clear as day,
And decks with weal his life, who walks the righteous
    way.

From gilded halls that hands polluted raise,
    Right turns away with proud averted eyes,
And of the wealth men stamp amiss with praise,
    Heedless, to poorer, holier temples hies,
And to Fate's goal guides all, in its appointed wise.

    Hail to thee, chief of Atreus' race,
    Returning proud from Troy subdued!
    How shall I greet thy conquering face?
    How nor a fulsome praise obtrude,
    Nor stint the meed of gratitude?
    For mortal men who fall to ill
    Take little heed of open truth,
    But seek unto its semblance still:
    The show of weeping and of ruth
    To the forlorn will all men pay,
    But, of the grief their eyes display,
    Nought to the heart doth pierce its way.
    And, with the joyous, they beguile
    Their lips unto a feignèd smile,
    And force a joy, unfelt the while;
    But he who as a shepherd wise
        Doth know his flock, can ne'er misread
    Truth in the falsehood of his eyes,
    Who veils beneath a kindly guise
        A lukewarm love in deed.
    And thou, our leader—when of yore
    Thou badest Greece go forth to war
    For Helen's sake—I dare avow
    That then I held thee not as now;

That to my vision thou didst seem
Dyed in the hues of disesteem.
I held thee for a pilot ill,
And reckless, of thy proper will,
Endowing others doomed to die
With vain and forced audacity!
Now from my heart, ungrudgingly,
To those that wrought, this word be said—
Well fall the labour ye have sped—
Let time and search, O king, declare
What men within thy city's bound
Were loyal to the kingdom's care,
And who were faithless found.

> [*Enter Agamemnon in a chariot, accompanied by Cassandra. He speaks without descending.*

Agamemnon

First, as is meet, a king's All-hail be said
To Argos, and the gods that guard the land—
Gods who with me availed to speed us home,
With me availed to wring from Priam's town
The due of justice. In the court of heaven
The gods in conclave sat and judged the cause,
Not from a pleader's tongue, and at the close,
Unanimous into the urn of doom
This sentence gave, *On Ilion and her men,
Death:* and where hope drew nigh to pardon's urn
No hand there was to cast a vote therein.
And still the smoke of fallen Ilion
Rises in sight of all men, and the flame
Of Atè's hecatomb is living yet,
And where the towers in dusty ashes sink,
Rise the rich fumes of pomp and wealth consumed.
For this must all men pay unto the gods
The meed of mindful hearts and gratitude:
For by our hands the meshes of revenge

Closed on the prey, and for one woman's sake
Troy trodden by the Argive monster lies—
The foal, the shielded band that leapt the wall,
What time with autumn sank the Pleiades.
Yea, o'er the fencing wall a lion sprang
Ravening, and lapped his fill of blood of kings.

Such prelude spoken to the gods in full,
To you I turn, and to the hidden thing
Whereof ye spake but now: and in that thought
I am as you, and what ye say, say I.
For few are they who have such inborn grace,
As to look up with love, and envy not,
When stands another on the height of weal.
Deep in his heart, whom jealousy hath seized,
Her poison lurking doth enhance his load;
For now beneath his proper woes he chafes,
And sighs withal to see another's weal.

I speak not idly, but from knowledge sure—
There be who vaunt an utter loyalty,
That is but as the ghost of friendship dead,
A shadow in a glass, of faith gone by.
One only—he who went reluctant forth
Across the seas with me—Odysseus—he
Was loyal unto me with strength and will,
A trusty trace-horse bound unto my car.
Thus—be he yet beneath the light of day,
Or dead, as well I fear—I speak his praise.

Lastly, whate'er be due to men or gods,
With joint debate, in public council held,
We will decide, and warily contrive
That all which now is well may so abide:
For that which haply needs the healer's art,
That will we medicine, discerning well
If cautery or knife befit the time.

Now, to my palace and the shrines of home,
I will pass in, and greet you first and fair,
Ye gods, who bade me forth, and home again—
And long may Victory tarry in my train!

> [*Enter Clytemnestra, followed by maidens bearing purple robes.*

Clytemnestra

Old men of Argos, lieges of our realm,
Shame shall not bid me shrink lest ye should see
The love I bear my lord. Such blushing fear
Dies at the last from hearts of humankind.
From mine own soul and from no alien lips,
I know and will reveal the life I bore,
Reluctant, through the lingering livelong years,
The while my lord beleaguered Ilion's wall.

First, that a wife sat sundered from her lord,
In widowed solitude, was utter woe—
And woe, to hear how rumour's many tongues
All boded evil—woe, when he who came
And he who followed spake of ill on ill,
Keening *Lost, lost, all lost!* thro' hall and bower.
Had this my husband met so many wounds,
As by a thousand channels rumour told,
No network e'er was full of holes as he.
Had he been slain, as oft as tidings came
That he was dead, he well might boast him now
A second Geryon of triple frame,
With triple robe of earth above him laid—
For that below, no matter—triply dead,
Dead by one death for every form he bore.
And thus distraught by news of wrath and woe,
Oft for self-slaughter had I slung the noose,
But others wrenched it from my neck away.
Hence haps it that Orestes, thine and mine,
The pledge and symbol of our wedded troth,

Stands not beside us now, as he should stand.
Nor marvel thou at this: he dwells with one
Who guards him loyally; 'tis Phocis' king,
Strophius, who warned me erst, *Bethink thee, queen,
What woes of doubtful issue well may fall!
Thy lord in daily jeopardy at Troy,
While here a populace uncurbed may cry,
"Down with the council, down!" bethink thee too,
'Tis the world's way to set a harder heel
On fallen power.*
                    For thy child's absence then
Such mine excuse, no wily afterthought.
For me, long since the gushing fount of tears
Is wept away; no drop is left to shed.
Dim are the eyes that ever watched till dawn,
Weeping, the bale-fires, piled for thy return,
Night after night unkindled. If I slept,
Each sound—the tiny humming of a gnat,
Roused me again, again, from fitful dreams
Wherein I felt thee smitten, saw thee slain,
Thrice for each moment of mine hour of sleep.

All this I bore, and now, released from woe,
I hail my lord as watch-dog of a fold,
As saving stay-rope of a storm-tossed ship,
As column stout that holds the roof aloft,
As only child unto a sire bereaved,
As land beheld, past hope, by crews forlorn,
As sunshine fair when tempest's wrath is past,
As gushing spring to thirsty wayfarer.
So sweet it is to 'scape the press of pain.
With such salute I bid my husband hail!
Nor heaven be wroth therewith! for long and hard
I bore that ire of old.
                    Sweet lord, step forth,
Step from thy car, I pray—nay, not on earth
Plant the proud foot, O king, that trod down Troy!

Women! why tarry ye, whose task it is
To spread your monarch's path with tapestry?
Swift, swift, with purple strew his passage fair,
That justice lead him to a home, at last,
He scarcely looked to see.
                      For what remains,
Zeal unsubdued by sleep shall nerve my hand
To work as right and as the gods command.

Agamemnon

Daughter of Leda, watcher o'er my home,
Thy greeting well befits mine absence long,
For late and hardly has it reached its end.
Know that the praise which honour bids us crave,
Must come from others' lips, not from our own:
See too that not in fashion feminine
Thou make a warrior's pathway delicate;
Not unto me, as to some Eastern lord,
Bowing thyself to earth, make homage loud.
Strew not this purple that shall make each step
An arrogance; such pomp beseems the gods,
Not me. A mortal man to set his foot
On these rich dyes? I hold such pride in fear,
And bid thee honour me as man, not god.
Fear not—such footcloths and all gauds apart,
Loud from the trump of Fame my name is blown;
Best gift of heaven it is, in glory's hour,
To think thereon with soberness: and thou—
Bethink thee of the adage, *Call none blest
Till peaceful death have crowned a life of weal.*
'Tis said: I fain would fare unvexed by fear.

Clytemnestra

Nay, but unsay it—thwart not thou my will!

Agamemnon

Know, I have said, and will not mar my word.

Clytemnestra
Was it fear made this meekness to the gods?

Agamemnon
If cause be cause, 'tis mine for this resolve.

Clytemnestra
What, think'st thou, in thy place had Priam done?

Agamemnon
He surely would have walked on broidered robes.

Clytemnestra
Then fear not thou the voice of human blame.

Agamemnon
Yet mighty is the murmur of a crowd.

Clytemnestra
Shrink not from envy, appanage of bliss.

Agamemnon
War is not woman's part, nor war of words.

Clytemnestra
Yet happy victors well may yield therein.

Agamemnon
Dost crave for triumph in this petty strife?

Clytemnestra
Yield; of thy grace permit me to prevail!

Agamemnon
Then, if thou wilt, let some one stoop to loose
Swiftly these sandals, slaves beneath my foot:

And stepping thus upon the sea's rich dye,
I pray, *Let none among the gods look down
With jealous eye on me*—reluctant all,
To trample thus and mar a thing of price,
Wasting the wealth of garments silver-worth.
Enough hereof: and, for the stranger maid,
Lead her within, but gently: God on high
Looks graciously on him whom triumph's hour
Has made not pitiless. None willingly
Wear the slave's yoke—and she, the prize and flower
Of all we won, comes hither in my train,
Gift of the army to its chief and lord.
—Now, since in this my will bows down to thine,
I will pass in on purples to my home.

Clytemnestra

A Sea there is—and who shall stay its springs?
And deep within its breast, a mighty store,
Precious as silver, of the purple dye,
Whereby the dipped robe doth its tint renew.
Enough of such, O king, within thy halls
There lies, a store that cannot fail; but I—
I would have gladly vowed unto the gods
Cost of a thousand garments trodden thus
(Had once the oracle such gift required),
Contriving ransom for thy life preserved.
For while the stock is firm the foliage climbs,
Spreading a shade, what time the dog-star glows;
And thou, returning to thine hearth and home,
Art as a genial warmth in winter hours,
Or as a coolness, when the lord of heaven
Mellows the juice within the bitter grape.
Such boons and more doth bring into a home
The present footstep of its proper lord.
Zeus, Zeus, Fulfilment's lord! my vows fulfil,
And whatsoe'er it be, work forth thy will!

[*Exeunt all but Cassandra and the Chorus.*

Chorus

Wherefore for ever on the wings of fear
   Hovers a vision drear
Before my boding heart? a strain,
  Unbidden and unwelcome, thrills mine ear,
    Oracular of pain.
Not as of old upon my bosom's throne
   Sits Confidence, to spurn
    Such fears, like dreams we know not to discern.
Old, old and gray long since the time has grown,
   Which saw the linkèd cables moor
The fleet, when erst it came to Ilion's sandy shore;
   And now mine eyes and not another's see
    Their safe return.

   Yet none the less in me
The inner spirit sings a boding song,
   Self-prompted, sings the Furies' strain—
    And seeks, and seeks in vain,
    To hope and to be strong!

Ah! to some end of Fate, unseen, unguessed,
   Are these wild throbbings of my heart and breast—
    Yea, of some doom they tell—
    Each pulse, a knell.
   Lief, lief I were, that all
To unfulfilment's hidden realm might fall.

  Too far, too far our mortal spirits strive,
   Grasping at utter weal, unsatisfied—
  Till the fell curse, that dwelleth hard beside,
  Thrust down the sundering wall. Too fair they blow,
   The gales that waft our bark on Fortune's tide!
   Swiftly we sail, the sooner all to drive
   Upon the hidden rock, the reef of woe.

Then if the hand of caution warily
  Sling forth into the sea
Part of the freight, lest all should sink below,
From the deep death it saves the bark: even so,
  Doom-laden though it be, once more may rise
  His household, who is timely wise.

  How oft the famine-stricken field
Is saved by God's large gift, the new year's yield!
    But blood of man once spilled,
  Once at his feet shed forth, and darkening the
      plain,—
  Nor chant nor charm can call it back again.

    So Zeus hath willed:
Else had he spared the leech Asclepius, skilled
  To bring man from the dead: the hand divine
Did smite himself with death—a warning and a sign.

  Ah me! if Fate, ordained of old,
Held not the will of gods constrained, controlled,
    Helpless to us-ward, and apart—
    Swifter than speech my heart
Had poured its presage out!
Now, fretting, chafing in the dark of doubt,
  'Tis hopeless to unfold
Truth, from fear's tangled skein; and, yearning to
    proclaim
  Its thought, my soul is prophecy and flame.

      Re-enter Clytemnestra

  Get thee within, thou too, Cassandra, go!
  For Zeus to thee in gracious mercy grants
  To share the sprinklings of the lustral bowl,
  Beside the altar of his guardianship,
  Slave among many slaves. What, haughty still?
  Step from the car; Alcmena's son, 'tis said,

Was sold perforce and bore the yoke of old.
Ay, hard it is, but, if such fate befal,
'Tis a fair chance to serve within a home
Of ancient wealth and power. An upstart lord,
To whom wealth's harvest came beyond his hope,
Is as a lion to his slaves, in all
Exceeding fierce, immoderate in sway.
Pass in: thou hearest what our ways will be.

Chorus

Clear unto thee, O maid, is her command,
But thou—within the toils of Fate thou art—
If such thy will, I urge thee to obey;
Yet I misdoubt thou dost nor hear nor heed.

Clytemnestra

I wot—unless like swallows she doth use
Some strange barbarian tongue from oversea—
My words must speak persuasion to her soul.

Chorus

Obey: there is no gentler way than this.
Step from the car's high seat and follow her.

Clytemnestra

Truce to this bootless waiting here without!
I will not stay: beside the central shrine
The victims stand, prepared for knife and fire—
Offerings from hearts beyond all hope made glad.
Thou—if thou reckest aught of my command,
'Twere well done soon: but if thy sense be shut
From these my words, let thy barbarian hand
Fulfil by gesture the default of speech.

Chorus

No native is she, thus to read thy words
Unaided: like some wild thing of the wood,
New-trapped, behold! she shrinks and glares on thee.

Clytemnestra

'Tis madness and the rule of mind distraught,
Since she beheld her city sink in fire,
And hither comes, nor brooks the bit, until
In foam and blood her wrath be champed away.
See ye to her; unqueenly 'tis for me,
Unheeded thus to cast away my words.
                              [*Exit Clytemnestra.*

Chorus

But with me pity sits in anger's place.
Poor maiden, come thou from the car; no way
There is but this—take up thy servitude.

Cassandra

Woe, woe, alas! Earth, Mother Earth! and thou
Apollo, Apollo!

Chorus

Peace! shriek not to the bright prophetic god,
Who will not brook the suppliance of woe.

Cassandra

Woe, woe, alas! Earth, Mother Earth! and thou
Apollo, Apollo!

Chorus

Hark, with wild curse she calls anew on him,
Who stands far off and loathes the voice of wail.

Cassandra

Apollo, Apollo!
God of all ways, but only Death's to me,
Once and again, O thou, Destroyer named,
Thou hast destroyed me, thou, my love of old!

Chorus

She grows presageful of her woes to come,
Slave tho' she be, instinct with prophecy.

Cassandra

Apollo, Apollo!
God of all ways, but only Death's to me,
O thou Apollo, thou Destroyer named!
What way hast led me, to what evil home?

Chorus

Know'st thou it not? The home of Atreus' race:
Take these my words for sooth and ask no more.

Cassandra

Home cursed of God! Bear witness unto me,
   Ye visioned woes within—
The blood-stained hands of them that smite their kin—
The strangling noose, and, spattered o'er
With human blood, the reeking floor!

Chorus

How like a sleuth-hound questing on the track,
Keen-scented unto blood and death she hies!

Cassandra

Ah! can the ghostly guidance fail,
Whereby my prophet-soul is onwards led?
Look! for their flesh the spectre-children wail,
Their sodden limbs on which their father fed!

Chorus

Long since we knew of thy prophetic fame,—
But for those deeds we seek no prophet's tongue.

Cassandra

God! 'tis another crime—
Worse than the storied woe of olden time,
Cureless, abhorred, that one is plotting here—
A shaming death, for those that should be dear!
  Alas! and far away, in foreign land,
  He that should help doth stand!

Chorus

I knew th' old tales the city rings withal—
But now thy speech is dark, beyond my ken.

Cassandra

O wretch, O purpose fell!
Thou for thy wedded lord
The cleansing wave hast poured—
A treacherous welcome!
                    How the sequel tell?
Too soon 'twill come, too soon, for now, even now,
  She smites him, blow on blow!

Chorus

Riddles beyond my rede—I peer in vain
Thro' the dim films that screen the prophecy.

Cassandra

God! a new sight! a net, a snare of hell,
Set by her hand—herself a snare more fell!
  A wedded wife, she slays her lord,
  Helped by another hand!
                    Ye powers, whose hate
Of Atreus' home no blood can satiate,
Raise the wild cry above the sacrifice abhorred!

Chorus

Why biddest thou some fiend, I know not whom,
Shriek o'er the house? Thine is no cheering word.

Back to my heart in frozen fear I feel
My waning life-blood run—
The blood that round the wounding steel
Ebbs slow, as sinks life's parting sun—
Swift, swift and sure, some woe comes pressing on!

Cassandra

Away, away—keep him away—
The monarch of the herd, the pasture's pride,
Far from his mate! In treach'rous wrath,
Muffling his swarthy horns, with secret scathe
She gores his fenceless side!
Hark! in the brimming bath,
The heavy plash—the dying cry—
Hark—in the laver—hark, he falls by treachery!

Chorus

I read amiss dark sayings such as thine,
Yet something warns me that they tell of ill.
O dark prophetic speech,
Ill tidings dost thou teach
Ever, to mortals here below!
Ever some tale of awe and woe
Thro' all thy windings manifold
Do we unriddle and unfold!

Cassandra

Ah well-a-day! the cup of agony,
Whereof I chant, foams with a draught for me.
Ah lord, ah leader, thou hast led me here—
Was't but to die with thee whose doom is near?

Chorus

Distraught thou art, divinely stirred,
And wailest for thyself a tuneless lay,
As piteous as the ceaseless tale

Wherewith the brown melodious bird
Doth ever Itys! Itys! wail,
Deep-bowered in sorrow, all its little lifetime's day!

Cassandra

Ah for thy fate, O shrill-voiced nightingale!
Some solace for thy woes did heaven afford,
Clothed thee with soft brown plumes, and life apart
     from wail—
But for my death is edged the double-biting sword!

Chorus

What pangs are these, what fruitless pain,
   Sent on thee from on high?
Thou chantest terror's frantic strain,
Yet in shrill measured melody.
How thus unerring canst thou sweep along
The prophet's path of boding song?

Cassandra

Woe, Paris, woe on thee! thy bridal joy
Was death and fire upon thy race and Troy!
   And woe for thee, Scamander's flood!
   Beside thy banks, O river fair,
   I grew in tender nursing care
   From childhood unto maidenhood!
Now not by thine, but by Cocytus' stream
And Acheron's banks shall ring my boding scream.

Chorus

   Too plain is all, too plain!
A child might read aright thy fateful strain.
   Deep in my heart their piercing fang
   Terror and sorrow set, the while I heard
   That piteous, low, tender word,
Yet to mine ear and heart a crushing pang.

Cassandra

Woe for my city, woe for Ilion's fall!
  Father, how oft with sanguine stain
Streamed on thine altar-stone the blood of cattle, slain
  That heaven might guard our wall!
  But all was shed in vain.
Low lie the shattered towers whereas they fell,
And I—ah burning heart!—shall soon lie low as well.

Chorus

Of sorrow is thy song, of sorrow still!
  Alas, what power of ill
Sits heavy on thy heart and bids thee tell
In tears of perfect moan thy deadly tale?
Some woe—I know not what—must close thy piteous wail.

Cassandra

List! for no more the presage of my soul,
Bride-like, shall peer from its secluding veil;
But as the morning wind blows clear the east,
More bright shall blow the wind of prophecy,
And as against the low bright line of dawn
Heaves high and higher yet the rolling wave,
So in the clearing skies of prescience
Dawns on my soul a further, deadlier woe,
And I will speak, but in dark speech no more.
Bear witness, ye, and follow at my side—
I scent the trail of blood, shed long ago.
Within this house a choir abidingly
Chants in harsh unison the chant of ill;
Yea, and they drink, for more enhardened joy,
Man's blood for wine, and revel in the halls,
Departing never, Furies of the home.

They sit within, they chant the primal curse,
Each spitting hatred on that crime of old,
The brother's couch, the love incestuous
That brought forth hatred to the ravisher.
Say, is my speech or wild and erring now,
Or doth its arrow cleave the mark indeed?
They called me once, *The prophetess of lies,
The wandering hag, the pest of every door*—
Attest ye now, *She knows in very sooth
The house's curse, the storied infamy.*

Chorus

Yet how should oath—how loyally soe'er
I swear it—aught avail thee? In good sooth,
My wonder meets thy claim: I stand amazed
That thou, a maiden born beyond the seas,
Dost as a native know and tell aright
Tales of a city of an alien tongue.

Cassandra

That is my power—a boon Apollo gave.

Chorus

God though he were, yearning for mortal maid?

Cassandra

Ay! what seemed shame of old is shame no more.

Chorus

Such finer sense suits not with slavery.

Cassandra

He strove to win me, panting for my love.

Chorus

Came ye by compact unto bridal joys?

Cassandra

Nay—for I plighted troth, then foiled the god.

Chorus

Wert thou already dowered with prescience?

Cassandra

Yea—prophetess to Troy of all her doom.

Chorus

How left thee then Apollo's wrath unscathed?

Cassandra

I, false to him, seemed prophet false to all.

Chorus

Not so—to us at least thy words seem sooth.

Cassandra

Woe for me, woe! Again the agony—
Dread pain that sees the future all too well
With ghastly preludes whirls and racks my soul.
Behold ye—yonder on the palace roof
The spectre-children sitting—look, such things
As dreams are made on, phantoms as of babes,
Horrible shadows, that a kinsman's hand
Hath marked with murder, and their arms are full—
A rueful burden—see, they hold them up,
The entrails upon which their father fed!

For this, for this, I say there plots revenge
A coward lion, couching in the lair—
Guarding the gate against my master's foot—
My master—mine—I bear the slave's yoke now,
And he, the lord of ships, who trod down Troy,
Knows not the fawning treachery of tongue

Of this thing false and dog-like—how her speech
Glozes and sleeks her purpose, till she win
By ill fate's favour the desirèd chance,
Moving like Atè to a secret end.
O aweless soul! the woman slays her lord—
Woman? what loathsome monster of the earth
Were fit comparison? The double snake—
Or Scylla, where she dwells, the seaman's bane,
Girt round about with rocks? some hag of hell,
Raving a truceless curse upon her kin?
Hark—even now she cries exultingly
The vengeful cry that tells of battle turned—
How fain, forsooth, to greet her chief restored!
Nay then, believe me not: what skills belief
Or disbelief? Fate works its will—and thou
Wilt see and say in ruth, *Her tale was true.*

Chorus

Ah—'tis Thyestes' feast on kindred flesh—
I guess her meaning and with horror thrill,
Hearing no shadow'd hint of th' o'er-true tale,
But its full hatefulness: yet, for the rest,
Far from the track I roam, and know no more.

Cassandra

'Tis Agamemnon's doom thou shalt behold.

Chorus

Peace, hapless woman, to thy boding words!

Cassandra

Far from my speech stands he who sains and saves.

Chorus

Ay—were such doom at hand—which God forbid!

Cassandra

Thou prayest idly—these move swift to slay.

Chorus
What man prepares a deed of such despite?

Cassandra
Fool! thus to read amiss mine oracles.

Chorus
Deviser and device are dark to me.

Cassandra
Dark! all too well I speak the Grecian tongue.

Chorus
Ay—but in thine, as in Apollo's strains,
Familiar is the tongue, but dark the thought.

Cassandra
Ah ah the fire! it waxes, nears me now—
Woe, woe for me, Apollo of the dawn!

Lo, how the woman-thing, the lioness
Couched with the wolf—her noble mate afar—
Will slay me, slave forlorn! Yea, like some witch,
She drugs the cup of wrath, that slays her lord
With double death—his recompense for me!
Ay, 'tis for me, the prey he bore from Troy,
That she hath sworn his death, and edged the steel!
Ye wands, ye wreaths that cling around my neck,
Ye showed me prophetess yet scorned of all—
I stamp you into death, or e'er I die—
Down, to destruction!
                    Thus I stand revenged—
Go, crown some other with a prophet's woe.
Look! it is he, it is Apollo's self
Rending from me the prophet-robe he gave.

God! while I wore it yet, thou saw'st me mocked
There at my home by each malicious mouth—
To all and each, an undivided scorn.
The name alike and fate of witch and cheat—
Woe, poverty, and famine—all I bore;
And at this last the god hath brought me here
Into death's toils, and what his love had made,
His hate unmakes me now: and I shall stand
Not now before the altar of my home,
But me a slaughter-house and block of blood
Shall see hewn down, a reeking sacrifice.
Yet shall the gods have heed of me who die,
For by their will shall one requite my doom.
He, to avenge his father's blood outpoured,
Shall smite and slay with matricidal hand.
Ay, he shall come—tho' far away he roam,
A banished wanderer in a stranger's land—
To crown his kindred's edifice of ill,
Called home to vengeance by his father's fall:
Thus have the high gods sworn, and shall fulfil.
And now why mourn I, tarrying on earth,
Since first mine Ilion has found its fate
And I beheld, and those who won the wall
Pass to such issue as the gods ordain?
I too will pass and like them dare to die!

[*Turns and looks upon the palace door.*

Portal of Hades, thus I bid thee hail!
Grant me one boon—a swift and mortal stroke,
That all unwrung by pain, with ebbing blood
Shed forth in quiet death, I close mine eyes.

Chorus

Maid of mysterious woes, mysterious lore,
Long was thy prophecy: but if aright
Thou readest all thy fate, how, thus unscared,
Dost thou approach the altar of thy doom,
As fronts the knife some victim, heaven-controlled?

Cassandra

Friends, there is no avoidance in delay.

Chorus

Yet who delays the longest, his the gain.

Cassandra

The day is come—flight were small gain to me!

Chorus

O brave endurance of a soul resolved!

Cassandra

That were ill praise, for those of happier doom.

Chorus

All fame is happy, even famous death.

Cassandra

Ah sire, ah brethren, famous once were ye!
   [*She moves to enter the house, then starts back.*

Chorus

What fear is this that scares thee from the house?

Cassandra

Pah!

Chorus

What is this cry? some dark despair of soul?

Cassandra

Pah! the house fumes with stench and spilth of blood.

Chorus

How? 'tis the smell of household offerings.

Cassandra

'Tis rank as charnel-scent from open graves.

Chorus

Thou canst not mean this scented Syrian nard?

Cassandra

Nay, let me pass within to cry aloud
The monarch's fate and mine—enough of life.
Ah friends!
Bear to me witness, since I fall in death,
That not as birds that shun the bush and scream
I moan in idle terror. This attest
When for my death's revenge another dies,
A woman for a woman, and a man
Falls, for a man ill-wedded to his curse.
Grant me this boon—the last before I die.

Chorus

Brave to the last! I mourn thy doom foreseen.

Cassandra

Once more one utterance, but not of wail,
Though for my death—and then I speak no more.

Sun! thou whose beam I shall not see again,
To thee I cry, Let those whom vengeance calls
To slay their kindred's slayers, quit withal
The death of me, the slave, the fenceless prey.

Ah state of mortal man! in time of weal,
A line, a shadow! and if ill fate fall,
One wet sponge-sweep wipes all our trace away—
And this I deem less piteous, of the twain.

[*Exit into the palace.*

Chorus

Too true it is! our mortal state
With bliss is never satiate,
And none, before the palace high
And stately of prosperity,
Cries to us with a voice of fear,
Away! 'tis ill to enter here!

Lo! this our lord hath trodden down,
By grace of heaven, old Priam's town,
    And praised as god he stands once more
    On Argos' shore!
Yet now—if blood shed long ago
Cries out that other blood shall flow—
His life-blood, his, to pay again
The stern requital of the slain—
Peace to that braggart's vaunting vain,
    Who, having heard the chieftain's tale,
    Yet boasts of bliss untouched by bale!

[*A loud cry from within.*

Voice of Agamemnon

O I am sped—a deep, a mortal blow.

Chorus

Listen, listen! who is screaming as in mortal agony?

Voice of Agamemnon

O! O! again, another, another blow!

Chorus

The bloody act is over—I have heard the monarch's cry—
Let us swiftly take some counsel, lest we too be doomed
    to die.

One of the Chorus

'Tis best, I judge, aloud for aid to call,
"Ho! loyal Argives! to the palace, all!"

Another

Better, I deem, ourselves to bear the aid,
And drag the deed to light, while drips the blade.

Another

Such will is mine, and what thou say'st I say:
Swiftly to act! the time brooks no delay.

Another

Ay, for 'tis plain, this prelude of their song
Foretells its close in tyranny and wrong.

Another

Behold, we tarry—but thy name, Delay,
They spurn, and press with sleepless hand to slay.

Another

I know not what 'twere well to counsel now—
Who wills to act, 'tis his to counsel how.

Another

Thy doubt is mine: for when a man is slain,
I have no words to bring his life again.

Another

What? e'en for life's sake, bow us to obey
These house-defilers and their tyrant sway?

Another

Unmanly doom! 'twere better far to die—
Death is a gentler lord than tyranny.

Another

Think well—must cry or sign of woe or pain
Fix our conclusion that the chief is slain?

Another

Such talk befits us when the deed we see—
Conjecture dwells afar from certainty.

Leader of the Chorus

I read one will from many a diverse word,
To know aright, how stands it with our lord!

> [*The scene opens, disclosing Clytemnestra, who comes forward. The body of Agamemnon lies, muffled in a long robe, within a silver-sided laver; the corpse of Cassandra is laid beside him.*

Clytemnestra

Ho, ye who heard me speak so long and oft
The glozing word that led me to my will—
Hear how I shrink not to unsay it all!
How else should one who willeth to requite
Evil for evil to an enemy
Disguised as friend, weave the mesh straitly round him,
Not to be overleaped, a net of doom?
This is the sum and issue of old strife,
Of me deep-pondered and at length fulfilled.
All is avowed, and as I smote I stand
With foot set firm upon a finished thing!
I turn not to denial: thus I wrought
So that he could nor flee nor ward his doom.
Even as the trammel hems the scaly shoal,
I trapped him with inextricable toils,
The ill abundance of a baffling robe;
Then smote him, once, again—and at each wound
He cried aloud, then as in death relaxed

Each limb and sank to earth; and as he lay,
Once more I smote him, with the last third blow,
Sacred to Hades, saviour of the dead.
And thus he fell, and as he passed away,
Spirit with body chafed; each dying breath
Flung from his breast swift bubbling jets of gore,
And the dark sprinklings of the rain of blood
Fell upon me; and I was fain to feel
That dew—not sweeter is the rain of heaven
To cornland, when the green sheath teems with grain.

Elders of Argos—since the thing stands so,
I bid you to rejoice, if such your will:
Rejoice or not, I vaunt and praise the deed,
And well I ween, if seemly it could be,
'Twere not ill done to pour libations here,
Justly—ay, more than justly—on his corpse
Who filled his home with curses as with wine,
And thus returned to drain the cup he filled.

Chorus

I marvel at thy tongue's audacity,
To vaunt thus loudly o'er a husband slain.

Clytemnestra

Ye hold me as a woman, weak of will,
And strive to sway me: but my heart is stout,
Nor fears to speak its uttermost to you,
Albeit ye know its message. Praise or blame,
Even as ye list,—I reck not of your words.
Lo! at my feet lies Agamemnon slain,
My husband once—and him this hand of mine,
A right contriver, fashioned for his death.
Behold the deed!

Chorus

Woman, what deadly birth,
What venomed essence of the earth

Or dark distilment of the wave,
  To thee such passion gave,
Nerving thine hand
To set upon thy brow this burning crown,
  The curses of thy land?
Our king by thee cut off, hewn down!
  Go forth—they cry—*accursèd and forlorn,*
    To hate and scorn!

Clytemnestra

O ye just men, who speak my sentence now,
The city's hate, the ban of all my realm!
Ye had no voice of old to launch such doom
On him, my husband, when he held as light
My daughter's life as that of sheep or goat,
One victim from the thronging fleecy fold!
Yea, slew in sacrifice his child and mine,
The well-loved issue of my travail-pangs,
To lull and lay the gales that blew from Thrace.
That deed of his, I say, that stain and shame,
Had rightly been atoned by banishment;
But ye, who then were dumb, are stern to judge
This deed of mine that doth affront your ears.
Storm out your threats, yet knowing this for sooth,
That I am ready, if your hand prevail
As mine now doth, to bow beneath your sway:
If God say nay, it shall be yours to learn
By chastisement a late humility.

Chorus

  Bold is thy craft, and proud
Thy confidence, thy vaunting loud;
Thy soul, that chose a murd'ress' fate,
  Is all with blood elate—
    Maddened to know
The blood not yet avenged, the damnèd spot
  Crimson upon thy brow.

AGAMEMNON

But Fate prepares for thee thy lot—
Smitten as thou didst smite, without a friend,
   To meet thine end!

Clytemnestra

Hear then the sanction of the oath I swear—
By the great vengeance for my murdered child,
By Atè, by the Fury unto whom
This man lies sacrificed by hand of mine,
I do not look to tread the hall of Fear,
While in this hearth and home of mine there burns
The light of love—Ægisthus—as of old
Loyal, a stalwart shield of confidence—
As true to me as this slain man was false,
Wronging his wife with paramours at Troy,
Fresh from the kiss of each Chryseis there!
Behold him dead—behold his captive prize,
Seeress and harlot—comfort of his bed,
True prophetess, true paramour—I wot
The sea-bench was not closer to the flesh,
Full oft, of every rower, than was she.
See, ill they did, and ill requites them now.
His death ye know: she as a dying swan
Sang her last dirge, and lies, as erst she lay,
Close to his side, and to my couch has left
A sweet new taste of joys that know no fear.

Chorus

  Ah woe and well-a-day! I would that Fate—
    Not bearing agony too great,
  Nor stretching me too long on couch of pain—
    Would bid mine eyelids keep
The morningless and unawakening sleep!
    For life is weary, now my lord is slain,
      The gracious among kings!
Hard fate of old he bore and many grievous things,

And for a woman's sake, on Ilian land—
Now is his life hewn down, and by a woman's hand!

    O Helen, O infatuate soul,
    Who bad'st the tides of battle roll,
    O'erwhelming thousands, life on life,
    'Neath Ilion's wall!
And now lies dead the lord of all.
    The blossom of thy storied sin
    Bears blood's inexpiable stain,
    O thou that erst, these halls within,
    Wert unto all a rock of strife,
      A husband's bane!

Clytemnestra

Peace! pray not thou for death as though
Thine heart was whelmed beneath this woe,
Nor turn thy wrath aside to ban
The name of Helen, nor recall
How she, one bane of many a man,
Sent down to death the Danaan lords,
To sleep at Troy the sleep of swords,
And wrought the woe that shattered all.

Chorus

Fiend of the race! that swoopest fell
  Upon the double stock of Tantalus,
Lording it o'er me by a woman's will,
  Stern, manful, and imperious—
    A bitter sway to me!
    Thy very form I see,
  Like some grim raven, perched upon the slain,
Exulting o'er the crime, aloud, in tuneless strain!

Clytemnestra

Right was that word—thou namest well
The brooding race-fiend, triply fell!

From him it is that murder's thirst,
Blood-lapping, inwardly is nursed—
Ere time the ancient scar can sain,
New blood comes welling forth again.

Chorus

Grim is his wrath and heavy on our home,
    That fiend of whom thy voice has cried,
Alas, an omened cry of woe unsatisfied,
    An all-devouring doom!

Ah woe, ah Zeus! from Zeus all things befal—
    Zeus the high cause and finisher of all!—
Lord of our mortal state, by him are willed
    All things, by him fulfilled!

Yet ah my king, my king no more!
What words to say, what tears to pour
    Can tell my love for thee?
The spider-web of treachery
She wove and wound, thy life around,
    And lo! I see thee lie,
And thro' a coward, impious wound
    Pant forth thy life and die!
A death of shame—ah woe on woe!
A treach'rous hand, a cleaving blow!

Clytemnestra

My guilt thou harpest, o'er and o'er!
I bid thee reckon me no more
    As Agamemnon's spouse.
The old Avenger, stern of mood
For Atreus and his feast of blood,
    Hath struck the lord of Atreus' house,
And in the semblance of his wife
    The king hath slain.—
Yea, for the murdered children's life,
    A chieftain's in requital ta'en.

Chorus

Thou guiltless of this murder, thou!
  Who dares such thought avow?
Yet it may be, wroth for the parent's deed,
The fiend hath holpen thee to slay the son.
  Dark Ares, god of death, is pressing on
  Thro' streams of blood by kindred shed,
  Exacting the accompt for children dead,
For clotted blood, for flesh on which their sire did feed.

  Yet ah my king, my king no more!
  What words to say, what tears to pour
    Can tell my love for thee?
  The spider-web of treachery
  She wove and wound, thy life around,
    And lo! I see thee lie,
  And thro' a coward, impious wound
    Pant forth thy life and die!
  A death of shame—ah woe on woe!
  A treach'rous hand, a cleaving blow!

Clytemnestra

I deem not that the death he died
  Had overmuch of shame:
For this was he who did provide
  Foul wrong unto his house and name:
His daughter, blossom of my womb,
He gave unto a deadly doom,
Iphigenia, child of tears!
And as he wrought, even so he fares.
Nor be his vaunt too loud in hell;
For by the sword his sin he wrought,
And by the sword himself is brought
  Among the dead to dwell.

AGAMEMNON

Chorus

    Ah whither shall I fly?
For all in ruin sinks the kingly hall;
Nor swift device nor shift of thought have I,
    To 'scape its fall.
A little while the gentler raindrops fail;
I stand distraught—a ghastly interval,
Till on the roof-tree rings the bursting hail
Of blood and doom. Even now fate whets the steel
On whetstones new and deadlier than of old,
    The steel that smites, in Justice' hold,
    Another death to deal.
O Earth! that I had lain at rest
And lapped for ever in thy breast,
Ere I had seen my chieftain fall
Within the laver's silver wall,
Low-lying on dishonoured bier!
And who shall give him sepulchre,
And who the wail of sorrow pour?
Woman, 'tis thine no more!
A graceless gift unto his shade
Such tribute, by his murd'ress paid!
Strive not thus wrongly to atone
The impious deed thy hand hath done.
Ah who above the godlike chief
Shall weep the tears of loyal grief?
Who speak above his lowly grave
The last sad praises of the brave?

Clytemnestra

    Peace! for such task is none of thine.
    By me he fell, by me he died,
    And now his burial rites be mine!
    Yet from these halls no mourners' train
        Shall celebrate his obsequies;

Only by Acheron's rolling tide
His child shall spring unto his side,
  And in a daughter's loving wise
Shall clasp and kiss him once again!

Chorus

Lo! sin by sin and sorrow dogg'd by sorrow—
  And who the end can know?
The slayer of to-day shall die to-morrow—
  The wage of wrong is woe.
While Time shall be, while Zeus in heaven is lord,
  His law is fixed and stern;
On him that wrought shall vengeance be outpoured—
  The tides of doom return.
The children of the curse abide within
  These halls of high estate—
And none can wrench from off the home of sin
  The clinging grasp of fate.

Clytemnestra

Now walks thy word aright, to tell
This ancient truth of oracle;
But I with vows of sooth will pray
To him, the power that holdeth sway
  O'er all the race of Pleisthenes—
Tho' dark the deed and deep the guilt,
With this last blood my hands have spilt,
  I pray thee let thine anger cease!
I pray thee pass from us away
  To some new race in other lands,
There, if thou wilt, to wrong and slay
  The lives of men by kindred hands.

For me 'tis all sufficient meed,
Tho' little wealth or power were won,
So I can say, *'Tis past and done.*

AGAMEMNON

The bloody lust and murderous,
The inborn frenzy of our house,
Is ended, by my deed!

[*Enter Ægisthus.*

Ægisthus

Dawn of the day of rightful vengeance, hail!
I dare at length aver that gods above
Have care of men and heed of earthly wrongs.
I, I who stand and thus exult to see
This man lie wound in robes the Furies wove,
Slain in requital of his father's craft.
Take ye the truth, that Atreus, this man's sire,
The lord and monarch of this land of old,
Held with my sire Thyestes deep dispute,
Brother with brother, for the prize of sway,
And drave him from his home to banishment.
Thereafter, the lorn exile homeward stole
And clung a suppliant to the hearth divine,
And for himself won this immunity—
Not with his own blood to defile the land
That gave him birth. But Atreus, godless sire
Of him who here lies dead, this welcome planned—
With zeal that was not love he feigned to hold
In loyal joy a day of festal cheer,
And bade my father to his board, and set
Before him flesh that was his children once.
First, sitting at the upper board alone,
He hid the fingers and the feet, but gave
The rest—and readily Thyestes took
What to his ignorance no semblance wore
Of human flesh, and ate: behold what curse
That eating brought upon our race and name!
For when he knew what all-unhallowed thing
He thus had wrought, with horror's bitter cry
Back-starting, spewing forth the fragments foul,

On Pelops' house a deadly curse he spake—
As darkly as I spurn this damnèd food,
So perish all the race of Pleisthenes!
Thus by that curse fell he whom here ye see,
And I—who else?—this murder wove and planned;
For me, an infant yet in swaddling bands,
Of the three children youngest, Atreus sent
To banishment by my sad father's side:
But Justice brought me home once more, grown now
To manhood's years; and stranger tho' I was,
My right hand reached unto the chieftain's life,
Plotting and planning all that malice bade.
And death itself were honour now to me,
Beholding him in Justice' ambush ta'en.

Chorus

Ægisthus, for this insolence of thine
That vaunts itself in evil, take my scorn.
Of thine own will, thou sayest, thou hast slain
The chieftain, by thine own unaided plot
Devised the piteous death: I rede thee well,
Think not thy head shall 'scape, when right prevails,
The people's ban, the stones of death and doom.

Ægisthus

This word from thee, this word from one who rows
Low at the oars beneath, what time we rule,
We of the upper tier? Thou'lt know anon,
'Tis bitter to be taught again in age,
By one so young, submission at the word.
But iron of the chain and hunger's throes
Can minister unto an o'erswoln pride
Marvellous well, ay, even in the old.
Hast eyes, and seest not this? Peace—kick not thus
Against the pricks, unto thy proper pain!

Chorus

Thou womanish man, waiting till war did cease,
Home-watcher and defiler of the couch,
And arch-deviser of the chieftain's doom!

Ægisthus

Bold words again! but they shall end in tears.
The very converse, thine, of Orpheus' tongue:
He roused and led in ecstasy of joy
All things that heard his voice melodious;
But thou as with the futile cry of curs
Wilt draw men wrathfully upon thee. Peace!
Or strong subjection soon shall tame thy tongue.

Chorus

Ay, thou art one to hold an Argive down—
Thou, skilled to plan the murder of the king,
But not with thine own hand to smite the blow!

Ægisthus

That fraudful force was woman's very part,
Not mine, whom deep suspicion from of old
Would have debarred. Now by his treasure's aid
My purpose holds to rule the citizens.
But whoso will not bear my guiding hand,
Him for his corn-fed mettle I will drive
Not as a trace-horse, light-caparisoned,
But to the shafts with heaviest harness bound.
Famine, the grim mate of the dungeon dark,
Shall look on him and shall behold him tame.

Chorus

Thou losel soul, was then thy strength too slight
To deal in murder, while a woman's hand,
Staining and shaming Argos and its gods,
Availed to slay him? Ho, if anywhere

The light of life smite on Orestes' eyes,
Let him, returning by some guardian fate,
Hew down with force her paramour and her!

Ægisthus

How thy word and act shall issue, thou shalt shortly understand.

Chorus

Up to action, O my comrades! for the fight is hard at hand.
Swift, your right hands to the sword hilt! bare the weapon as for strife——

Ægisthus

Lo! I too am standing ready, hand on hilt for death or life.

Chorus

'Twas thy word and we accept it: onward to the chance of war!

Clytemnestra

Nay, enough, enough, my champion! we will smite and slay no more.
Already have we reaped enough the harvest-field of guilt:
Enough of wrong and murder, let no other blood be spilt.
Peace, old men! and pass away unto the homes by Fate decreed,
Lest ill valour meet our vengeance—'twas a necessary deed.
But enough of toils and troubles—be the end, if ever, now,
Ere thy talon, O Avenger, deal another deadly blow.
'Tis a woman's word of warning, and let who will list thereto.

Ægisthus

But that these should loose and lavish reckless blossoms of the tongue,
And in hazard of their fortune cast upon me words of wrong,
And forget the law of subjects, and revile their ruler's word——

Chorus

Ruler? but 'tis not for Argives, thus to own a dastard lord!

Ægisthus

I will follow to chastise thee in my coming days of sway.

Chorus

Not if Fortune guide Orestes safely on his homeward way.

Ægisthus

Ah, well I know how exiles feed on hopes of their return.

Chorus

Fare and batten on pollution of the right, while 'tis thy turn.

Ægisthus

Thou shalt pay, be well assurèd, heavy quittance for thy pride.

Chorus

Crow and strut, with her to watch thee, like a cock, his mate beside!

Clytemnestra

Heed not thou too highly of them—let the cur-pack growl and yell:
I and thou will rule the palace and will order all things well.

[*Exeunt.*

THE HOUSE OF ATREUS

BEING

THE AGAMEMNON, THE LIBATION-BEARERS, AND THE FURIES OF ÆSCHYLUS

THE LIBATION-BEARERS

DRAMATIS PERSONÆ

Orestes	Chorus of Captive Women	Electra
A Nurse	Clytemnestra	Ægisthus
	An Attendant Pylades	

The Scene is the Tomb of Agamemnon at Mycenæ; afterwards, the Palace of Atreus, hard by the Tomb.

Orestes

LORD of the shades and patron of the realm
 That erst my father swayed, list now my prayer,
 Hermes, and save me with thine aiding arm,
Me who from banishment returning stand
On this my country; lo, my foot is set
On this grave-mound, and herald-like, as thou,
Once and again, I bid my father hear.
And these twin locks, from mine head shorn, I bring,
And one to Inachus the river-god,
My young life's nurturer, I dedicate,
And one in sign of mourning unfulfilled
I lay, though late, on this my father's grave.
For O my father, not beside thy corse
Stood I to wail thy death, nor was my hand
Stretched out to bear thee forth to burial.

What sight is yonder? what this woman-throng
Hitherward coming, by their sable garb
Made manifest as mourners? What hath chanced?

THE LIBATION-BEARERS

Doth some new sorrow hap within the home!
Or rightly may I deem that they draw near
Bearing libations, such as soothe the ire
Of dead men angered, to my father's grave?
Nay, such they are indeed; for I descry
Electra, mine own sister, pacing hither,
In moody grief conspicuous. Grant, O Zeus,
Grant me my father's murder to avenge—
Be thou my willing champion!
                              Pylades,
Pass we aside, till rightly I discern
Wherefore these women throng in suppliance.

> [*Exeunt Pylades and Orestes; enter the Chorus, bearing vessels for libation; Electra follows them; they pace slowly towards the tomb of Agamemnon.*

Chorus

Forth from the royal halls by high command
  I bear libations for the dead.
Rings on my smitten breast my smiting hand,
  And all my cheek is rent and red,
Fresh-furrowed by my nails, and all my soul
This many a day doth feed on cries of dole.
  And trailing tatters of my vest,
In looped and windowed raggedness forlorn,
  Hang rent around my breast,
Even as I, by blows of Fate most stern
      Saddened and torn.

  Oracular thro' visions, ghastly clear,
Bearing a blast of wrath from realms below,
And stiffening each rising hair with dread,
      Came out of dreamland Fear,
      And, loud and awful, bade
The shriek ring out at midnight's witching hour,
      And brooded, stern with woe,

Above the inner house, the woman's bower.
And seers inspired did read the dream on oath,
   Chanting aloud, *In realms below*
     The dead are wroth;
Against their slayers yet their ire doth glow.

Therefore to bear this gift of graceless worth—
   O Earth, my nursing mother!—
The woman god-accurs'd doth send me forth
   Lest one crime bring another.
Ill is the very word to speak, for none
     Can ransom or atone
For blood once shed and darkening the plain.
   O hearth of woe and bane,
   O state that low doth lie!
Sunless, accursed of men, the shadows brood
   Above the home of murdered majesty.

Rumour of might, unquestioned, unsubdued,
Pervading ears and soul of lesser men,
   Is silent now and dead.
   Yet rules a viler dread;
   For bliss and power, however won,
As gods, and more than gods, dazzle our mortal ken.

Justice doth mark, with scales that swiftly sway,
   Some that are yet in light;
Others in interspace of day and night,
   Till Fate arouse them, stay;
And some are lapped in night, where all things are undone.

   On the life-giving lap of Earth
     Blood hath flowed forth,
And now, the seed of vengeance, clots the plain—
   Unmelting, uneffaced the stain.
And Atè tarries long, but at the last
     The sinner's heart is cast
Into pervading, waxing pangs of pain.

Lo, when man's force doth ope
The virgin doors, there is nor cure nor hope
  For what is lost,—even so, I deem,
Though in one channel ran Earth's every stream,
  Laving the hand defiled from murder's stain,
    It were vain.

And upon me—ah me!—the gods have laid
  The woe that wrapped round Troy,
What time they led me down from home and kin
    Unto a slave's employ—
  The doom to bow the head
    And watch our master's will
    Work deeds of good and ill—
To see the headlong sway of force and sin,
  And hold restrained the spirit's bitter hate,
  Wailing the monarch's fruitless fate,
Hiding my face within my robe, and fain
Of tears, and chilled with frost of hidden pain.

Electra

Handmaidens, orderers of the palace-halls,
Since at my side ye come, a suppliant train,
Companions of this offering, counsel me
As best befits the time: for I, who pour
Upon the grave these streams funereal,
With what fair word can I invoke my sire?
Shall I aver, *Behold, I bear these gifts
From well-loved wife unto her well-loved lord,*
When 'tis from her, my mother, that they come?
I dare not say it: of all words I fail
Wherewith to consecrate unto my sire
These sacrificial honours on his grave.
Or shall I speak this word, as mortals use—
*Give back, to those who send these coronals,
Full recompense—of ills for acts malign?*

Or shall I pour this draught for Earth to drink,
Sans word or reverence, as my sire was slain,
And homeward pass with unreverted eyes,
Casting the bowl away, as one who flings
The household cleansings to the common road?
Be art and part, O friends, in this my doubt,
Even as ye are in that one common hate
Whereby we live attended: fear ye not
The wrath of any man, nor hide your word
Within your breast: the day of death and doom
Awaits alike the freeman and the slave.
Speak, then, if aught thou know'st to aid us more.

Chorus

Thou biddest; I will speak my soul's thought out,
Revering as a shrine thy father's grave.

Electra

Say then thy say, as thou his tomb reverest.

Chorus

Speak solemn words to them that love, and pour.

Electra

And of his kin whom dare I name as kind?

Chorus

Thyself; and next, whoe'er Ægisthus scorns.

Electra

Then 'tis myself and thou my prayer must name.

Chorus

Whoe'er they be, 'tis thine to know and name them.

Electra

Is there no other we may claim as ours?

Chorus

Think of Orestes, though far-off he be.

Electra

Right well in this too hast thou schooled my thought.

Chorus

Mindfully, next, on those who shed the blood——

Electra

Pray on them what? expound, instruct my doubt.

Chorus

This: *Upon them some god or mortal come*——

Electra

As judge or as avenger? speak thy thought.

Chorus

Pray in set terms, *Who shall the slayer slay.*

Electra

Beseemeth it to ask such boon of heaven?

Chorus

How not, to wreak a wrong upon a foe?

Electra

O mighty Hermes, warder of the shades,
Herald of upper and of under world,
Proclaim and usher down my prayer's appeal
Unto the gods below, that they with eyes
Watchful behold these halls, my sire's of old—
And unto Earth, the mother of all things,
And foster-nurse, and womb that takes their seed.

Lo, I that pour these draughts for men now dead,
Call on my father, who yet holds in ruth
Me and mine own Orestes, Father, speak—
How shall thy children rule thine halls again?
Homeless we are and sold; and she who sold
Is she who bore us; and the price she took
Is he who joined with her to work thy death,
Ægisthus, her new lord. Behold me here
Brought down to slave's estate, and far away
Wanders Orestes, banished from the wealth
That once was thine, the profit of thy care,
Whereon these revel in a shameful joy.
Father, my prayer is said; 'tis thine to hear—
Grant that some fair fate bring Orestes home,
And unto me grant these—a purer soul
Than is my mother's, a more stainless hand.

These be my prayers for us; for thee, O sire,
I cry that one may come to smite thy foes,
And that the slayers may in turn be slain.
Cursed is their prayer, and thus I bar its path,
Praying mine own, a counter-curse on them.
And thou, send up to us the righteous boon
For which we pray; thine aids be heaven and earth,
And justice guide the right to victory.
[*To the Chorus.*
Thus have I prayed, and thus I shed these streams,
And follow ye the wont, and as with flowers
Crown ye with many a tear and cry the dirge
Your lips ring out above the dead man's grave.
[*She pours the libations.*

Chorus

Woe, woe, woe!
Let the teardrop fall, plashing on the ground
Where our lord lies low:
Fall and cleanse away the cursed libation's stain,

　　　　　　Shed on this grave-mound,
　　　Fenced wherein together, gifts of good or bane
　　　　　　From the dead are found.
　　　　　　Lord of Argos, hearken!
　　　　　　Though around thee darken
　　　Mist of death and hell, arise and hear!
　Hearken and awaken to our cry of woe!
　　　　　　Who with might of spear
　　　　　　Shall our home deliver?
　　　Who like Ares bend until it quiver,
　　　　　　Bend the northern bow?
Who with hand upon the hilt himself will thrust with glaive,
　　　　　　Thrust and slay and save?

Electra

Lo! the earth drinks them, to my sire they pass—
Learn ye with me of this thing new and strange.

Chorus

Speak thou; my breast doth palpitate with fear.

Electra

I see upon the tomb a curl new shorn.

Chorus

Shorn from what man or what deep-girded maid?

Electra

That may he guess who will; the sign is plain.

Chorus

Let me learn this of thee; let youth prompt age.

Electra

None is there here but I, to clip such gift.

Chorus

For they who thus should mourn him hate him sore.

Electra

And lo! in truth the hair exceeding like——

Chorus

Like to what locks and whose? instruct me that.

Electra

Like unto those my father's children wear.

Chorus

Then is this lock Orestes' secret gift?

Electra

Most like it is unto the curls he wore.

Chorus

Yet how dared he to come unto his home?

Electra

He hath but sent it, clipt to mourn his sire.

Chorus

It is a sorrow grievous at his death,
That he should live, yet never dare return.

Electra

Yea, and my heart o'erflows with gall of grief,
And I am pierced as with a cleaving dart;
Like to the first drops after drought, my tears
Fall down at will, a bitter bursting tide,
As on this lock I gaze; I cannot deem
That any Argive save Orestes' self
Was ever lord thereof; nor, well I wot,

Hath she, the murd'ress, shorn and laid this lock
To mourn him whom she slew—my mother she,
Bearing no mother's heart, but to her race
A loathing spirit, loathed itself of heaven!
Yet to affirm, as utterly made sure,
That this adornment cometh of the hand
Of mine Orestes, brother of my soul,
I may not venture, yet hope flatters fair!
Ah well-a-day, that this dumb hair had voice
To glad mine ears, as might a messenger,
Bidding me sway no more 'twixt fear and hope,
Clearly commanding, *Cast me hence away,
Clipped was I from some head thou lovest not;*
Or, *I am kin to thee, and here, as thou,
I come to weep and deck our father's grave.*
Aid me, ye gods! for well indeed ye know
How in the gale and counter-gale of doubt,
Like to the seaman's bark, we whirl and stray.
But, if God will our life, how strong shall spring,
From seed how small, the new tree of our home!—
Lo ye, a second sign—these footsteps, look,—
Like to my own, a corresponsive print;
And look, another footmark,—this his own,
And that the foot of one who walked with him.
Mark, how the heel and tendons' print combine,
Measured exact, with mine coincident!
Alas! for doubt and anguish rack my mind.

Orestes (*approaching suddenly*)

Pray thou, in gratitude for prayers fulfilled,
Fair fall the rest of what I ask of heaven.

Electra

Wherefore? what win I from the gods by prayer?

Orestes

This, that thine eyes behold thy heart's desire.

Electra

On whom of mortals know'st thou that I call?

Orestes

I know thy yearning for Orestes deep.

Electra

Say then wherein event hath crowned my prayer?

Orestes

I, I am he; seek not one more akin.

Electra

Some fraud, O stranger, weavest thou for me?

Orestes

Against myself I weave it, if I weave.

Electra

Ah, thou hast mind to mock me in my woe!

Orestes

'Tis at mine own I mock then, mocking thine.

Electra

Speak I with thee then as Orestes' self?

Orestes

My very face thou see'st and know'st me not,
And yet but now, when thou didst see the lock
Shorn for my father's grave, and when thy quest
Was eager on the footprints I had made,
Even I, thy brother, shaped and sized as thou,
Fluttered thy spirit, as at sight of me!
Lay now this ringlet whence 'twas shorn, and judge,
And look upon this robe, thine own hands' work,

The shuttle-prints, the creature wrought thereon—
Refrain thyself, nor prudence lose in joy,
For well I wot, our kin are less than kind.

Electra

O thou that art unto our father's home
Love, grief, and hope, for thee the tears ran down,
For thee, the son, the saviour that should be;
Trust thou thine arm and win thy father's halls!
O aspect sweet of fourfold love to me,
Whom upon thee the heart's constraint bids call
As on my father, and the claim of love
From me unto my mother turns to thee,
For she is very hate; to thee too turns
What of my heart went out to her who died
A ruthless death upon the altar-stone;
And for myself I love thee—thee that wast
A brother leal, sole stay of love to me.
Now by thy side be strength and right, and Zeus
Saviour almighty, stand to aid the twain!

Orestes

Zeus, Zeus! look down on our estate and us,
The orphaned brood of him, our eagle-sire,
Whom to his death a fearful serpent brought,
Enwinding him in coils; and we, bereft
And foodless, sink with famine, all too weak
To bear unto the eyrie, as he bore,
Such quarry as he slew. Lo! I and she,
Electra, stand before thee, fatherless,
And each alike cast out and homeless made.

Electra

And if thou leave to death the brood of him
Whose altar blazed for thee, whose reverence
Was thine, all thine,—whence, in the after years,
Shall any hand like his adorn thy shrine

With sacrifice of flesh? the eaglets slain,
Thou wouldst not have a messenger to bear
Thine omens, once so clear, to mortal men;
So, if this kingly stock be withered all,
None on high festivals will fend thy shrine.
Stoop thou to raise us! strong the race shall show,
Though puny now it seem, and fallen low.

Chorus

O children, saviours of your father's home,
Beware ye of your words, lest one should hear
And bear them, for the tongue hath lust to tell,
Unto our masters—whom God grant to me
In pitchy reek of fun'ral flame to see!

Orestes

Nay, mighty is Apollo's oracle
And shall not fail me, whom it bade to pass
Thro' all this peril; clear the voice rang out
With many warnings, sternly threatening
To my hot heart the wintry chill of pain,
Unless upon the slayers of my sire
I pressed for vengeance: this the god's command—
That I, in ire for home and wealth despoiled,
Should with a craft like theirs the slayers slay:
Else with my very life I should atone
This deed undone, in many a ghastly wise.
For he proclaimed unto the ears of men
That offerings, poured to angry power of death,
Exude again, unless their will be done,
As grim disease on those that poured them forth—
As leprous ulcers mounting on the flesh
And with fell fangs corroding what of old
Wore natural form; and on the brow arise
White poisoned hairs, the crown of this disease.
He spake, moreover, of assailing fiends
Empowered to quit on me my father's blood,

Wreaking their wrath on me, what time in night
Beneath shut lids the spirit's eye sees clear.
The dart that flies in darkness, sped from hell
By spirits of the murdered dead who call
Unto their kin for vengeance, formless fear,
The nighttide's visitant, and madness' curse
Should drive and rack me; and my tortured frame
Should be chased forth from man's community
As with the brazen scorpions of the scourge.
For me and such as me no lustral bowl
Should stand, no spilth of wine be poured to God
For me, and wrath unseen of my dead sire
Should drive me from the shrine; no man should dare
To take me to his hearth, nor dwell with me:
Slow, friendless, cursed of all should be mine end,
And pitiless horror wind me for the grave.
This spake the god—this dare I disobey?
Yea, though I dared, the deed must yet be done;
For to that end diverse desires combine,—
The god's behest, deep grief for him who died,
And last, the grievous blank of wealth despoiled—
All these weigh on me, urge that Argive men,
Minions of valour, who with soul of fire
Did make of fencèd Troy a ruinous heap,
Be not left slaves to two and each a woman!
For he, the man, wears woman's heart; if not,
Soon shall he know, confronted by a man.

> [*Orestes, Electra, and the Chorus gather round the tomb of Agamemnon for the invocation which follows.*

Chorus

Mighty Fates, on you we call!
Bid the will of Zeus ordain
Power to those to whom again
Justice turns with hand and aid!
Grievous was the prayer one made—

Grievous let the answer fall!
Where the mighty doom is set,
Justice claims aloud her debt.
Who in blood hath dipped the steel,
Deep in blood her meed shall feel!
List an immemorial word—
*Whosoe'er shall take the sword
Shall perish by the sword.*

Orestes

Father, unblest in death, O father mine!
    What breath of word or deed
Can I waft on thee from this far confine
    Unto thy lowly bed,—
Waft upon thee, in midst of darkness lying,
    Hope's counter-gleam of fire?
Yet the loud dirge of praise brings grace undying
    Unto each parted sire.

Chorus

O child, the spirit of the dead,
Altho' upon his flesh have fed
  The grim teeth of the flame,
Is quelled not; after many days
The sting of wrath his soul shall raise,
  A vengeance to reclaim!
To the dead rings loud our cry—
Plain the living's treachery—
Swelling, shrilling, urged on high,
  The vengeful dirge, for parents slain,
  Shall strive and shall attain.

Electra

Hear me too, even me, O father, hear!
Not by one child alone these groans, these tears are shed
    Upon thy sepulchre.
Each, each, where thou art lowly laid,

Stands, a suppliant, homeless made:
  Ah, and all is full of ill,
Comfort is there none to say!
Strive and wrestle as we may,
  Still stands doom invincible.

Chorus

Nay, if so he will, the god
  Still our tears to joy can turn.
He can bid a triumph-ode
  Drown the dirge beside this urn;
He to kingly halls can greet
The child restored, the homeward-guided feet.

Orestes

Ah my father! hadst thou lain
  Under Ilion's wall,
By some Lycian spearman slain,
  Thou hadst left in this thine hall
Honour; thou hadst wrought for us
Fame and life most glorious.
  Overseas if thou hadst died,
Heavily had stood thy tomb,
  Heaped on high; but, quenched in pride,
Grief were light unto thy home.

Chorus

Loved and honoured hadst thou lain
  By the dead that nobly fell,
In the underworld again,
  Where are throned the kings of hell
  Full of sway adorable
Thou hadst stood at their right hand—
Thou that wert, in mortal land,
  By Fate's ordinance and law,
King of kings who bear the crown
  And the staff, to which in awe
Mortal men bow down.

Electra

Nay, O father, I were fain
Other fate had fallen on thee.
Ill it were if thou hadst lain
One among the common slain,
Fallen by Scamander's side—
Those who slew thee there should be!
Then, untouched by slavery,
    We had heard as from afar
      Deaths of those who should have died
        'Mid the chance of war.

Chorus

O child, forbear! things all too high thou sayest.
    Easy, but vain, thy cry!
A boon above all gold is that thou prayest,
    An unreached destiny,
As of the blessèd land that far aloof
    Beyond the north wind lies;
Yet doth your double prayer ring loud reproof;
    A double scourge of sighs
Awakes the dead; th' avengers rise, though late;
    Blood stains the guilty pride
Of the accursed who rule on earth, and Fate
    Stands on the children's side.

Electra

That hath sped thro' mine ear, like a shaft from a bow!
Zeus, Zeus! it is thou who dost send from below
A doom on the desperate doer—ere long
On a mother a father shall visit his wrong.

Chorus

Be it mine to upraise thro' the reek of the pyre
The chant of delight, while the funeral fire
    Devoureth the corpse of a man that is slain
    And a woman laid low!

For who bids me conceal it! outrending control,
Blows ever the stern blast of hate thro' my soul,
    And before me a vision of wrath and of bane
        Flits and waves to and fro.

Orestes

Zeus, thou alone to us art parent now.
    Smite with a rending blow
  Upon their heads, and bid the land be well:
Set right where wrong hath stood; and thou give ear,
    O Earth, unto my prayer—
Yea, hear, O mother Earth, and monarchy of hell!

Chorus

Nay, the law is sternly set—
  Blood-drops shed upon the ground
Plead for other bloodshed yet;
  Loud the call of death doth sound,
Calling guilt of olden time,
A Fury, crowning crime with crime.

Electra

Where, where are ye, avenging powers,
    Puissant Furies of the slain?
Behold the relics of the race
Of Atreus, thrust from pride of place!
O Zeus, what home henceforth is ours,
    What refuge to attain?

Chorus

Lo, at your wail my heart throbs, wildly stirred;
    Now am I lorn with sadness,
Darkened in all my soul, to hear your sorrow's word.
  Anon to hope, the seat of strength, I rise,—
  She, thrusting grief away, lifts up mine eyes
    To the new dawn of gladness.

Orestes

Skills it to tell of aught save wrong on wrong,
  Wrought by our mother's deed?
Though now she fawn for pardon, sternly strong
  Standeth our wrath, and will nor hear nor heed;
Her children's soul is wolfish, born from hers,
  And softens not by prayers.

Chorus

  I dealt upon my breast the blow
  That Asian mourning women know;
  Wails from my breast the fun'ral cry,
  The Cissian weeping melody;
Stretched rendingly forth, to tatter and tear,
My clenched hands wander, here and there,
  From head to breast; distraught with blows
    Throb dizzily my brows.

Electra

Aweless in hate, O mother, sternly brave!
    As in a foeman's grave
Thou laid'st in earth a king, but to the bier
    No citizen drew near,—
Thy husband, thine, yet for his obsequies,
    Thou bad'st no wail arise!

Orestes

Alas, the shameful burial thou dost speak!
Yet I the vengeance of his shame will wreak—
    That do the gods command!
    That shall achieve mine hand!
Grant me to thrust her life away, and I
    Will dare to die!

Chorus

List thou the deed! Hewn down and foully torn,
    He to the tomb was borne;

Yea, by her hand, the deed who wrought,
With like dishonour to the grave was brought,
And by her hand she strove, with strong desire,
Thy life to crush, O child, by murder of thy sire:
  Bethink thee, hearing, of the shame, the pain
    Wherewith that sire was slain!

Electra

Yea, such was the doom of my sire; well-a-day,
    I was thrust from his side,—
As a dog from the chamber they thrust me away,
And in place of my laughter rose sobbing and tears,
    As in darkness I lay.
O father, if this word can pass to thine ears,
    To thy soul let it reach and abide!

Chorus

Let it pass, let it pierce, thro' the sense of thine ear,
  To thy soul, where in silence it waiteth the hour!
The past is accomplished; but rouse thee to hear
What the future prepareth; awake and appear,
    Our champion, in wrath and in power!

Orestes

  O father, to thy loved ones come in aid.

Electra

  With tears I call on thee.

Chorus

    Listen and rise to light!
Be thou with us, be thou against the foe!
Swiftly this cry arises—even so
  Pray we, the loyal band, as we have prayed!

Orestes

Let their might meet with mine, and their right with my right.

Electra
O ye gods, it is yours to decree.

Chorus
Ye call unto the dead; I quake to hear.
Fate is ordained of old, and shall fulfil your prayer.

Electra
Alas, the inborn curse that haunts our home,
   Of Atè's bloodstained scourge the tuneless sound!
Alas, the deep insufferable doom,
    The stanchless wound!

Orestes
It shall be stanched, the task is ours,—
   Not by a stranger's, but by kindred hand,
Shall be chased forth the blood-fiend of our land.
   Be this our spoken spell, to call Earth's nether powers!

Chorus
   Lords of a dark eternity,
   To you has come the children's cry,
   Send up from hell, fulfil your aid
     To them who prayed.

Orestes
O father, murdered in unkingly wise,
Fulfil my prayer, grant me thine halls to sway.

Electra
To me, too, grant this boon—dark death to deal
Unto Ægisthus, and to 'scape my doom.

Orestes
So shall the rightful feasts that mortals pay
Be set for thee; else, not for thee shall rise
The scented reek of altars fed with flesh,
But thou shalt lie dishonoured: hear thou me!

Electra

I too, from my full heritage restored,
Will pour the lustral streams, what time I pass
Forth as a bride from these paternal halls,
And honour first, beyond all graves, thy tomb.

Orestes

Earth, send my sire to fend me in the fight!

Electra

Give fair-faced fortune, O Persephone!

Orestes

Bethink thee, father, in the laver slain——

Electra

Bethink thee of the net they handselled for thee!

Orestes

Bonds not of brass ensnared thee, father mine.

Electra

Yea, the ill craft of an enfolding robe.

Orestes

By this our bitter speech arise, O sire!

Electra

Raise thou thine head at love's last, dearest call!

Orestes

Yea, speed forth Right to aid thy kinsmen's cause;
Grip for grip, let them grasp the foe, if thou
Willest in triumph to forget thy fall.

Electra

Hear me, O father, once again hear me.
Lo! at thy tomb, two fledglings of thy brood—
A man-child and a maid; hold them in ruth,
Nor wipe them out, the last of Pelops' line.
For while they live, thou livest from the dead;
Children are memory's voices, and preserve
The dead from wholly dying: as a net
Is ever by the buoyant corks upheld,
Which save the flax-mesh, in the depth submerged.
Listen, this wail of ours doth rise for thee,
And as thou heedest it thyself art saved.

Chorus

In sooth, a blameless prayer ye spake at length—
The tomb's requital for its dirge denied:
Now, for the rest, as thou art fixed to do,
Take fortune by the hand and work thy will.

Orestes

The doom is set; and yet I fain would ask—
Not swerving from the course of my resolve,—
Wherefore she sent these offerings, and why
She softens all too late her cureless deed?
An idle boon it was, to send them here
Unto the dead who recks not of such gifts.
I cannot guess her thought, but well I ween
Such gifts are skilless to atone such crime.
Be blood once spilled, an idle strife he strives
Who seeks with other wealth or wine outpoured
To atone the deed. So stands the word, nor fails.
Yet would I know her thought; speak, if thou knowest.

Chorus

I know it, son; for at her side I stood.
'Twas the night-wandering terror of a dream

That flung her shivering from her couch, and bade her—
Her, the accursed of God—these offerings send.

Orestes

Heard ye the dream, to tell it forth aright?

Chorus

Yea, from herself; her womb a serpent bare.

Orestes

What then the sum and issue of the tale?

Chorus

Even as a swaddled child, she lull'd the thing.

Orestes

What suckling craved the creature, born full-fanged?

Chorus

Yet in her dreams she proffered it the breast.

Orestes

How? did the hateful thing not bite her teat?

Chorus

Yea, and sucked forth a blood-gout in the milk.

Orestes

Not vain this dream—it bodes a man's revenge.

Chorus

Then out of sleep she started with a cry,
And thro' the palace for their mistress' aid
Full many lamps, that erst lay blind with night,
Flared into light; then, even as mourners use,

She sends these offerings, in hope to win
A cure to cleave and sunder sin from doom.

Orestes

Earth and my father's grave, to you I call—
Give this her dream fulfilment, and thro' me.
I read it in each part coincident
With what shall be; for mark, that serpent sprang
From the same womb as I, in swaddling bands
By the same hands was swathed, lipped the same breast,
And sucking forth the same sweet mother's-milk
Infused a clot of blood; and in alarm
She cried upon her wound the cry of pain.
The rede is clear: the thing of dread she nursed,
The death of blood she dies; and I, 'tis I,
In semblance of a serpent, that must slay her.
Thou art my seer, and thus I read the dream.

Chorus

So do; yet ere thou doest, speak to us,
Bidding some act, some, by not acting, aid.

Orestes

Brief my command: I bid my sister pass
In silence to the house, and all I bid
This my design with wariness conceal,
That they who did by craft a chieftain slay
May by like craft and in like noose be ta'en,
Dying the death which Loxias foretold—
Apollo, king and prophet undisproved.
I with this warrior Pylades will come
In likeness of a stranger, full equipt
As travellers come, and at the palace gates
Will stand, as stranger, yet in friendship's bond
Unto this house allied; and each of us
Will speak the tongue that round Parnassus sounds,
Feigning such speech as Phocian voices use.

And what if none of those that tend the gates
Shall welcome us with gladness, since the house
With ills divine is haunted? if this hap,
We at the gate will bide, till, passing by,
Some townsman make conjecture and proclaim,
How? is Ægisthus here, and knowingly
Keeps suppliants aloof, by bolt and bar?
Then shall I win my way; and if I cross
The threshold of the gate, the palace' guard,
And find him throned where once my father sat—
Or if he come anon, and face to face
Confronting, drop his eyes from mine—I swear
He shall not utter, *Who art thou and whence?*
Ere my steel leap, and compassed round with death
Low he shall lie: and thus, full-fed with doom,
The Fury of the house shall drain once more
A deep third draught of rich unmingled blood.
But thou, O sister, look that all within
Be well prepared to give these things event.
And ye—I say 'twere well to bear a tongue
Full of fair silence and of fitting speech
As each beseems the time; and last, do thou,
Hermes the warder-god, keep watch and ward,
And guide to victory my striving sword.
                    [*Exit with Pylades.*

Chorus

Many and marvellous the things of fear
  Earth's breast doth bear;
And the sea's lap with many monsters teems,
And windy levin-bolts and meteor-gleams
  Breed many deadly things—
Unknown and flying forms, with fear upon their wings,
  And in their tread is death;
And rushing whirlwinds, of whose blasting breath
  Man's tongue can tell.
But who can tell aright the fiercer thing,

> The aweless soul, within man's breast inhabiting?
> Who tell, how, passion-fraught and love-distraught,
> The woman's eager, craving thought
> Doth wed mankind to woe and ruin fell?
> Yea, how the loveless love that doth possess
> The woman, even as the lioness,
> Doth rend and wrest apart, with eager strife,
>   The link of wedded life?

Let him be the witness, whose thought is not borne on light wings thro' the air,
But abideth with knowledge, what thing was wrought by Althea's despair;
For she marr'd the life-grace of her son, with ill counsel rekindled the flame
That was quenched as it glowed on the brand, what time from his mother he came,
With the cry of a new-born child; and the brand from the burning she won,
For the Fates had foretold it coeval, in life and in death, with her son.

Yea, and man's hate tells of another, even Scylla of murderous guile,
Who slew for an enemy's sake her father, won o'er by the wile
And the gifts of Cretan Minos, the gauds of the high-wrought gold;
For she clipped from her father's head the lock that should never wax old,
As he breathed in the silence of sleep, and knew not her craft and her crime—
But Hermes, the guard of the dead, doth grasp her, in fulness of time.

And since of the crimes of the cruel I tell, let my singing record
The bitter wedlock and loveless, the curse on these halls outpoured
The crafty device of a woman, whereby did a chieftain fall,
A warrior stern in his wrath, the fear of his enemies all,—

A song of dishonour, untimely! and cold is the hearth that was warm,
And ruled by the cowardly spear, the woman's unwomanly arm.

But the summit and crown of all crimes is that which in Lemnos befel;
A woe and a mourning it is, a shame and a spitting to tell;
And he that in aftertime doth speak of his deadliest thought,
Doth say, *It is like to the deed that of old time in Lemnos was wrought;*
And loathed of men were the doers, and perished, they and their seed,
For the gods brought hate upon them; none loveth the impious deed.

It is well of these tales to tell; for the sword in the grasp of Right
With a cleaving, a piercing blow to the innermost heart doth smite,
And the deed unlawfully done is not trodden down nor forgot,
When the sinner outsteppeth the law and heedeth the high God not;
But Justice hath planted the anvil, and Destiny forgeth the sword
That shall smite in her chosen time; by her is the child restored;
And, darkly devising, the Fiend of the house, world-cursed, will repay
The price of the blood of the slain that was shed in the bygone day.

[*Enter Orestes and Pylades, in guise of travellers.*

Orestes (*knocking at the palace gate*)
What ho! slave, ho! I smite the palace gate
In vain, it seems; what ho, attend within,—
Once more, attend; come forth and ope the halls,
If yet Ægisthus holds them hospitable.

Slave (*from within*)
Anon, anon! [*Opens the door.*
Speak, from what land art thou, and sent from whom?

Orestes
Go, tell to them who rule the palace halls,
Since 'tis to them I come with tidings new—

(Delay not—Night's dark car is speeding on,
And time is now for wayfarers to cast
Anchor in haven, wheresoe'er a house
Doth welcome strangers)—that there now come forth
Some one who holds authority within—
The queen, or, if some man, more seemly were it;
For when man standeth face to face with man,
No stammering modesty confounds their speech,
But each to each doth tell his meaning clear.

                   [*Enter Clytemnestra.*

Clytemnestra

Speak on, O strangers; have ye need of aught?
Here is whate'er beseems a house like this—
Warm bath and bed, tired Nature's soft restorer,
And courteous eyes to greet you; and if aught
Of graver import needeth act as well,
That, as man's charge, I to a man will tell.

Orestes

A Daulian man am I, from Phocis bound,
And as with mine own travel-scrip self-laden
I went toward Argos, parting hitherward
With travelling foot, there did encounter me
One whom I knew not and who knew not me,
But asked my purposed way nor hid his own,
And, as we talked together, told his name—
Strophius of Phocis; then he said, "Good sir,
Since in all case thou art to Argos bound,
Forget not this my message, heed it well,
Tell to his own, *Orestes is no more.*
And—whatsoe'er his kinsfolk shall resolve,
Whether to bear his dust unto his home,
Or lay him here, in death as erst in life
Exiled for aye, a child of banishment—
Bring me their hest, upon thy backward road;
For now in brazen compass of an urn

His ashes lie, their dues of weeping paid."
So much I heard, and so much tell to thee,
Not knowing if I speak unto his kin
Who rule his home; but well, I deem, it were,
Such news should earliest reach a parent's ear.

Clytemnestra

Ah woe is me! thy word our ruin tells;
From roof-tree unto base are we despoiled.—
O thou whom nevermore we wrestle down,
Thou Fury of this home, how oft and oft
Thou dost descry what far aloof is laid,
Yea, from afar dost bend th' unerring bow
And rendest from my wretchedness its friends;
As now Orestes—who, a brief while since,
Safe from the mire of death stood warily,—
Was the home's hope to cure th' exulting wrong;
Now thou ordainest, *Let the ill abide.*

Orestes

To host and hostess thus with fortune blest,
Lief had I come with better news to bear
Unto your greeting and acquaintanceship;
For what goodwill lies deeper than the bond
Of guest and host? and wrong abhorred it were,
As well I deem, if I, who pledged my faith
To one, and greetings from the other had,
Bore not aright the tidings 'twixt the twain.

Clytemnestra

Whate'er thy news, thou shalt not welcome lack,
Meet and deserved, nor scant our grace shall be.
Hadst thou thyself not come, such tale to tell,
Another, sure, had borne it to our ears.
But lo! the hour is here when travelling guests,
Fresh from the daylong labour of the road,
Should win their rightful due. Take him within

                                               [*To the slave.*
To the man-chamber's hospitable rest—
Him and these fellow-farers at his side;
Give them such guest-right as beseems our halls;
I bid thee do as thou shalt answer for it.
And I unto the prince who rules our home
Will tell the tale, and, since we lack not friends,
With them will counsel how this hap to bear.
                                    [*Exit Clytemnestra.*

Chorus

    So be it done—
Sister-servants, when draws nigh
Time for us aloud to cry,
Orestes and his victory?

    O holy earth and holy tomb
Over the grave-pit heaped on high,
Where low doth Agamemnon lie,
    The king of ships, the army's lord!
Now is the hour—give ear and come,
    For now doth Craft her aid afford,
And Hermes, guard of shades in hell,
Stands o'er their strife, to sentinel
    The dooming of the sword.
I wot the stranger worketh woe within—
For lo! I see come forth, suffused with tears,
Orestes' nurse. What ho, Kilissa—thou
Beyond the doors? Where goest thou? Methinks
Some grief unbidden walketh at thy side.
                                  [*Enter Kilissa, a nurse.*

Kilissa

My mistress bids me, with what speed I may,
Call in Ægisthus to the stranger guests,
That he may come, and standing face to face,
A man with men, may thus more clearly learn
This rumour new. Thus speaking, to her slaves

She hid beneath the glance of fictive grief
Laughter for what is wrought—to her desire
Too well; but ill, ill, ill besets the house,
Brought by the tale these guests have told so clear.
And he, God wot, will gladden all his heart
Hearing this rumour. Woe and well-a-day!
The bitter mingled cup of ancient woes,
Hard to be borne, that here in Atreus' house
Befel, was grievous to mine inmost heart,
But never yet did I endure such pain.
All else I bore with set soul patiently;
But now—alack, alack!—Orestes dear,
The day- and night-long travail of my soul!
Whom from his mother's womb, a new-born child,
I clasped and cherished! Many a time and oft
Toilsome and profitless my service was,
When his shrill outcry called me from my couch!
For the young child, before the sense is born,
Hath but a dumb thing's life, must needs be nursed
As its own nature bids. The swaddled thing
Hath nought of speech, whate'er discomfort come—
Hunger or thirst or lower weakling need,—
For the babe's stomach works its own relief.
Which knowing well before, yet oft surprised,
'Twas mine to cleanse the swaddling clothes—poor I
Was nurse to tend and fuller to make white;
Two works in one, two handicrafts I took,
When in mine arms the father laid the boy.
And now he's dead—alack and well-a-day!
Yet must I go to him whose wrongful power
Pollutes this house—fair tidings these to him!

Chorus

Say then with what array she bids him come?

Kilissa

What say'st thou! Speak more clearly for mine ear.

Chorus

Bids she bring henchmen, or to come alone?

Kilissa

She bids him bring a spear-armed body-guard.

Chorus

Nay, tell not that unto our loathèd lord,
But speed to him, put on the mien of joy,
Say, *Come along, fear nought, the news is good:*
A bearer can tell straight a twisted tale.

Kilissa

Does then thy mind in this new tale find joy?

Chorus

What if Zeus bid our ill wind veer to fair?

Kilissa

And how? the home's hope with Orestes dies.

Chorus

Not yet—a seer, though feeble, this might see.

Kilissa

What say'st thou? Know'st thou aught this tale belying?

Chorus

Go, tell the news to him, perform thine hest,—
What the gods will, themselves can well provide.

Kilissa

Well, I will go, herein obeying thee;
And luck fall fair, with favour sent from heaven.

[*Exit.*

Chorus

Zeus, sire of them who on Olympus dwell,
    Hear thou, O hear my prayer!
Grant to my rightful lords to prosper well
    Even as their zeal is fair!
For right, for right goes up aloud my cry—
    Zeus, aid him, stand anigh!

    Into his father's hall he goes
    To smite his father's foes.
Bid him prevail! by thee on throne of triumph set,
Twice, yea and thrice with joy shall he acquit the debt.

Bethink thee, the young steed, the orphan foal
  Of sire beloved by thee, unto the car
  Of doom is harnessed fast.
Guide him aright, plant firm a lasting goal,
Speed thou his pace,—O that no chance may mar
  The homeward course, the last!

And ye who dwell within the inner chamber
  Where shines the storèd joy of gold—
Gods of one heart, O hear ye, and remember;
Up and avenge the blood shed forth of old,
    With sudden rightful blow;
  Then let the old curse die, nor be renewed
    With progeny of blood,—
Once more, and not again, be latter guilt laid low!

O thou who dwell'st in Delphi's mighty cave,
  Grant us to see this home once more restored
    Unto its rightful lord!
Let it look forth, from veils of death, with joyous eye
    Unto the dawning light of liberty;
And Hermes, Maia's child, lend hand to save,
    Willing the right, and guide
Our state with Fortune's breeze adown the favouring tide.

> Whate'er in darkness hidden lies,
>   He utters at his will;
> He at his will throws darkness on our eye,
>   By night and eke by day inscrutable.

>   Then, then shall wealth atone
>   The ills that here were done.
>   Then, then will we unbind,
>   Fling free on wafting wind
> Of joy, the woman's voice that waileth now
> In piercing accents for a chief laid low;
>   And this our song shall be—
>   *Hail to the commonwealth restored!*
>   *Hail to the freedom won to me!*
> *All hail! for doom hath passed from him, my well-loved lord!*

> And thou, O child, when Time and Chance agree,
>   Up to the deed that for thy sire is done!
>   And if she wail unto thee, *Spare, O son*—
> Cry, *Aid, O father*—and achieve the deed,
> The horror of man's tongue, the gods' great need!
>   Hold in thy breast such heart as Perseus had,
>   The bitter woe work forth,
>   Appease the summons of the dead,
>   The wrath of friends on earth;
>   Yea, set within a sign of blood and doom,
> And do to utter death him that pollutes thy home.

[Enter Ægisthus.

Ægisthus

Hither and not unsummoned have I come;
For a new rumour, borne by stranger men
Arriving hither, hath attained mine ears,
Of hap unwished-for, even Orestes' death.
This were new sorrow, a blood-bolter'd load
Laid on the house that doth already bow
Beneath a former wound that festers deep.

Dare I opine these words have truth and life?
Or are they tales, of woman's terror born,
That fly in the void air, and die disproved?
Canst thou tell aught, and prove it to my soul?

Chorus

What we have heard, we heard; go thou within
Thyself to ask the strangers of their tale.
Strengthless are tidings, thro' another heard;
Question is his to whom the tale is brought.

Ægisthus

I too will meet and test the messenger,
Whether himself stood witness of the death,
Or tells it merely from dim rumour learnt:
None shall cheat me, whose soul hath watchful eyes.

[*Exit.*

Chorus

 Zeus, Zeus! what word to me is given?
 What cry or prayer, invoking heaven,
  Shall first by me be utterèd?
 What speech of craft—nor all revealing,
 Nor all too warily concealing—
  Ending my speech, shall aid the deed?
 For lo! in readiness is laid
 The dark emprise, the rending blade;
  Blood-dropping daggers shall achieve
 The dateless doom of Atreus' name,
 Or—kindling torch and joyful flame
  In sign of new-won liberty—
   Once more Orestes shall retrieve
  His father's wealth, and, throned on high,
  Shall hold the city's fealty.
  So mighty is the grasp whereby,
 Heaven-holpen, he shall trip and throw
 Unseconded, a double foe.
   Ho for the victory!

[*A loud cry within.*

Voice of Ægisthus
Help, help, alas!

Chorus
Ho there, ho! how is't within?
Is't done? is't over? Stand we here aloof
While it is wrought, that guiltless we may seem
Of this dark deed; with death is strife fulfilled.
                                         [*Enter a slave.*

Slave
O woe, O woe, my lord is done to death!
Woe, woe, and woe again, Ægisthus gone!
Hasten, fling wide the doors, unloose the bolts
Of the queen's chamber. O for some young strength
To match the need! but aid availeth nought
To him laid low for ever. Help, help, help!
Sure to deaf ears I shout, and call in vain
To slumber ineffectual. What ho!
The queen! how fareth Clytemnestra's self?
Her neck too, hers, is close upon the steel,
And soon shall sink, hewn thro' as justice wills.
                                    [*Enter Clytemnestra.*

Clytemnestra
What ails thee, raising this ado for us?

Slave
I say the dead are come to slay the living.

Clytemnestra
Alack, I read thy riddles all too clear—
We slew by craft and by like craft shall die.
Swift, bring the axe that slew my lord of old;
I'll know anon or death or victory—
So stands the curse, so I confront it here.
                  [*Enter Orestes, his sword dropping with blood.*

Orestes

Thee too I seek: for him what's done will serve.

Clytemnestra

Woe, woe! Ægisthus, spouse and champion, slain!

Orestes

What, lov'st the man? then in his grave lie down,
Be his in death, desert him nevermore!

Clytemnestra

Stay, child, and fear to strike. O son, this breast
Pillowed thine head full oft, while, drowsed with sleep,
Thy toothless mouth drew mother's milk from me.

Orestes

Can I my mother spare? speak, Pylades.

Pylades

Where then would fall the hest Apollo gave
At Delphi, where the solemn compact sworn?
Choose thou the hate of all men, not of gods.

Orestes

Thou dost prevail; I hold thy counsel good.
              [*To Clytemnestra.*
Follow; I will to slay thee at his side.
With him whom in his life thou lovedst more
Than Agamemnon, sleep in death, the meed
For hate where love, and love where hate was due!

Clytemnestra

I nursed thee young; must I forego mine eld?

Orestes

Thou slew'st my father; shalt thou dwell with me?

Clytemnestra
Fate bore a share in these things, O my child!

Orestes
Fate also doth provide this doom for thee.

Clytemnestra
Beware, O child, a parent's dying curse.

Orestes
A parent who did cast me out to ill!

Clytemnestra
Not cast thee out, but to a friendly home.

Orestes
Born free, I was by twofold bargain sold.

Clytemnestra
Where then the price that I received for thee?

Orestes
The price of shame; I taunt thee not more plainly.

Clytemnestra
Nay, but recount thy father's lewdness too.

Orestes
Home-keeping, chide not him who toils without.

Clytemnestra
'Tis hard for wives to live as widows, child.

Orestes
The absent husband toils for them at home.

Clytemnestra

Thou growest fain to slay thy mother, child.

Orestes

Nay, 'tis thyself wilt slay thyself, not I.

Clytemnestra

Beware thy mother's vengeful hounds from hell.

Orestes

How shall I 'scape my father's, sparing thee?

Clytemnestra

Living, I cry as to a tomb, unheard.

Orestes

My father's fate ordains this doom for thee.

Clytemnestra

Ah, me! this snake it was I bore and nursed.

Orestes

Ay, right prophetic was thy visioned fear.
Shameful thy deed was—die the death of shame!
        [*Exit, driving Clytemnestra before him.*

Chorus

Lo, even for these I mourn, a double death:
Yet since Orestes, driven on by doom,
Thus crowns the height of murders manifold,
I say, 'tis well that not in night and death
Should sink the eye and light of this our home.

    There came on Priam's race and name
        A vengeance; though it tarried long,

With heavy doom it came.
Came, too, on Agamemnon's hall
   A lion-pair, twin swordsmen strong.
And last, the heritage doth fall
  To him to whom from Pythian cave
  The god his deepest counsel gave.
Cry out, rejoice! our kingly hall
   Hath 'scaped from ruin—ne'er again
Its ancient wealth be wasted all
   By two usurpers, sin-defiled—
  An evil path of woe and bane!
On him who dealt the dastard blow
   Comes Craft, Revenge's scheming child.
And hand in hand with him doth go,
    Eager for fight,
The child of Zeus, whom men below
  Call Justice, naming her aright.
    And on her foes her breath
    Is as the blast of death;
For her the god who dwells in deep recess
   Beneath Parnassus' brow,
   Summons with loud acclaim
   To rise, though late and lame,
And come with craft that worketh righteousness.

For even o'er powers divine this law is strong—
   Thou shalt not serve the wrong.
To that which ruleth heaven beseems it that we bow.
  Lo, freedom's light hath come!
  Lo, now is rent away
The grim and curbing bit that held us dumb.
  Up to the light, ye halls! this many a day
   Too low on earth ye lay.
  And Time, the great Accomplisher,
  Shall cross the threshold, whensoe'er
  He choose with purging hand to cleanse
  The palace, driving all pollution thence.

And fair the cast of Fortune's die
Before our state's new lords shall lie,
Not as of old, but bringing fairer doom.
   Lo, freedom's light hath come!
   [*The scene opens, disclosing Orestes standing over the corpses of Ægisthus and Clytemnestra; in one hand he holds his sword, in the other the robe in which Agamemnon was entangled and slain.*

Orestes

There lies our country's twofold tyranny,
My father's slayers, spoilers of my home.
Erst were they royal, sitting on the throne,
And loving are they yet,—their common fate
Tells the tale truly, shows their trothplight firm.
They swore to work mine ill-starred father's death,
They swore to die together; 'tis fulfilled.
   O ye who stand, this great doom's witnesses,
Behold this too, the dark device which bound
My sire unhappy to his death,—behold
The mesh which trapped his hands, enwound his feet!
Stand round, unfold it—'tis the trammel-net
That wrapped a chieftain; hold it that he see,
The father—not my sire, but he whose eye
Is judge of all things, the all-seeing Sun!
Let him behold my mother's damnèd deed,
Then let him stand, when need shall be to me,
Witness that justly I have sought and slain
My mother; blameless was Ægisthus' doom—
He died the death law bids adulterers die.
But she who plotted this accursèd thing
To slay her lord, by whom she bare beneath
Her girdle once the burden of her babes,
Beloved erewhile, now turned to hateful foes—
What deem ye of her? or what venomed thing,
Sea-snake or adder, had more power than she
To poison with a touch the flesh unscarred?

So great her daring, such her impious will.
How name her, if I may not speak a curse?
A lion-springe! a laver's swathing cloth,
Wrapping a dead man, twining round his feet—
A net, a trammel, an entangling robe?
Such were the weapon of some strangling thief,
The terror of the road, a cut-purse hound—
With such device full many might he kill,
Full oft exult in heat of villainy.
Ne'er have my house so cursed an indweller—
Heaven send me, rather, childless to be slain!

Chorus

Woe for each desperate deed!
   Woe for the queen, with shame of life bereft!
   And ah, for him who still is left,
Madness, dark blossom of a bloody seed!

Orestes

Did she the deed or not? this robe gives proof,
Imbrued with blood that bathed Ægisthus' sword:
Look, how the spurted stain combines with time
To blur the many dyes that once adorned
Its pattern manifold! I now stand here,
Made glad, made sad with blood, exulting, wailing—
Hear, O thou woven web that slew my sire!
I grieve for deed and death and all my home—
Victor, pollution's damnèd stain for prize.

Chorus

   Alas, that none of mortal men
   Can pass his life untouched by pain!
   Behold, one woe is here—
   Another loometh near.

Orestes

Hark ye and learn—for what the end shall be
For me I know not: breaking from the curb,

My spirit whirls me off, a conquered prey,
Borne as a charioteer by steeds distraught
Far from the course, and madness in my breast
Burneth to chant its song, and leap, and rave—
Hark ye and learn, friends, ere my reason goes!
I say that rightfully I slew my mother,
A thing God-scorned, that foully slew my sire.
And chiefest wizard of the spell that bound me
Unto this deed I name the Pythian seer
Apollo, who foretold that if I slew,
The guilt of murder done should pass from me;
But if I spared, the fate that should be mine
I dare not blazon forth—the bow of speech
Can reach not to the mark, that doom to tell.
And now behold me, how with branch and crown
I pass, a suppliant made meet to go
Unto Earth's midmost shrine, the holy ground
Of Loxias, and that renownèd light
Of ever-burning fire, to 'scape the doom
Of kindred murder: to no other shrine
(So Loxias bade) may I for refuge turn.
Bear witness, Argives, in the aftertime,
How came on me this dread fatality.
Living, I pass a banished wanderer hence,
To leave in death the memory of this cry.

Chorus

Nay, but the deed is well; link not thy lips
To speech ill-starred, nor vent ill-boding words—
Who hast to Argos her full freedom given,
Lopping two serpents' heads with timely blow.

Orestes

Look, look, alas!
Handmaidens, see—what Gorgon shapes throng up,
Dusky their robes and all their hair enwound—
Snakes coiled with snakes—off, off, I must away!

Chorus

Most loyal of all sons unto thy sire,
What visions thus distract thee? Hold, abide;
Great was thy victory, and shalt thou fear?

Orestes

These are no dreams, void shapes of haunting ill,
But clear to sight my mother's hell-hounds come!

Chorus

Nay, the fresh bloodshed still imbrues thine hands,
And thence distraction sinks into thy soul.

Orestes

O king Apollo—see, they swarm and throng—
Black blood of hatred dripping from their eyes!

Chorus

One remedy thou hast; go, touch the shrine
Of Loxias, and rid thee of these woes.

Orestes

Ye can behold them not, but I behold them.
Up and away! I dare abide no more.

[*Exit.*

Chorus

Farewell then as thou mayst,—the god thy friend
Guard thee and aid with chances favouring.

> Behold, the storm of woe divine
> That raves and beats on Atreus' line
>   Its great third blast hath blown.
> First was Thyestes' loathly woe—
> The rueful feast of long ago,
>   On children's flesh, unknown.

And next the kingly chief's despite,
When he who led the Greeks to fight
  Was in the bath hewn down.
And now the offspring of the race
Stands in the third, the saviour's place,
  To save—or to consume?
O whither, ere it be fulfilled,
Ere its fierce blast be hushed and stilled,
  Shall blow the wind of doom?

[*Exeunt.*

THE HOUSE OF ATREUS

BEING

THE AGAMEMNON, THE LIBATION-BEARERS, AND THE FURIES OF ÆSCHYLUS

THE FURIES

DRAMATIS PERSONÆ

The Pythian Priestess	Apollo	Orestes
The Ghost of Clytemnestra		Chorus of Furies
Athena	Attendants of Athena	
	Twelve Athenian Citizens	

The Scene of the Drama is the Temple of Apollo, at Delphi; afterwards, the Temple of Athena, on the Acropolis of Athens, and the adjoining Areopagus.

The Temple at Delphi

The Pythian Priestess

FIRST, in this prayer, of all the gods I name
The prophet-mother Earth; and Themis next,
Second who sat—for so with truth is said—
On this her mother's shrine oracular.
Then by her grace, who unconstrained allowed,
There sat thereon another child of Earth—
Titanian Phœbe. She, in aftertime,
Gave o'er the throne, as birth-gift to a god,
Phœbus, who in his own bears Phœbe's name.
He from the lake and ridge of Delos' isle
Steered to the port of Pallas' Attic shores,
The home of ships; and thence he passed and came
Unto this land and to Parnassus' shrine.
And at his side, with awe revering him,
There went the children of Hephæstus' seed,
The hewers of the sacred way, who tame
The stubborn tract that erst was wilderness.

And all this folk, and Delphos, chieftain-king
Of this their land, with honour gave him home;
And in his breast Zeus set a prophet's soul,
And gave to him this throne, whereon he sits,
Fourth prophet of the shrine, and, Loxias hight,
Gives voice to that which Zeus, his sire, decrees.

Such gods I name in my preluding prayer,
And after them, I call with honour due
On Pallas, wardress of the fane, and Nymphs
Who dwell around the rock Corycian,
Where in the hollow cave, the wild birds' haunt,
Wander the feet of lesser gods; and there,
Right well I know it, Bromian Bacchus dwells,
Since he in godship led his Mænad host,
Devising death for Pentheus, whom they rent
Piecemeal, as hare among the hounds. And last,
I call on Pleistus' springs, Poseidon's might,
And Zeus most high, the great Accomplisher.
Then as a seeress to the sacred chair
I pass and sit; and may the powers divine
Make this mine entrance fruitful in response
Beyond each former advent, triply blest.
And if there stand without, from Hellas bound,
Men seeking oracles, let each pass in
In order of the lot, as use allows;
For the god guides whate'er my tongue proclaims.

[*She goes into the interior of the temple; after a short interval, she returns in great fear.*

Things fell to speak of, fell for eyes to see,
Have sped me forth again from Loxias' shrine,
With strength unstrung, moving erect no more,
But aiding with my hands my failing feet,
Unnerved by fear. A beldame's force is naught—
Is as a child's, when age and fear combine.
For as I pace towards the inmost fane
Bay-filleted by many a suppliant's hand,

Lo, at the central altar I descry
One crouching as for refuge—yea, a man
Abhorred of heaven; and from his hands, wherein
A sword new-drawn he holds, blood reeked and fell:
A wand he bears, the olive's topmost bough,
Twined as of purpose with a deep close tuft
Of whitest wool. This, that I plainly saw,
Plainly I tell. But lo, in front of him,
Crouched on the altar-steps, a grisly band
Of women slumbers—not like women they,
But Gorgons rather; nay, that word is weak,
Nor may I match the Gorgons' shape with theirs!
Such have I seen in painted semblance erst—
Winged Harpies, snatching food from Phineus' board,—
But these are wingless, black, and all their shape
The eye's abomination to behold.
Fell is the breath—let none draw nigh to it—
Wherewith they snort in slumber; from their eyes
Exude the damnèd drops of poisonous ire:
And such their garb as none should dare to bring
To statues of the gods or homes of men.
I wot not of the tribe wherefrom can come
So fell a legion, nor in what land Earth
Could rear, unharmed, such creatures, nor avow
That she had travailed and brought forth death.
But, for the rest, be all these things a care
Unto the mighty Loxias, the lord
Of this our shrine: healer and prophet he,
Discerner he of portents, and the cleanser
Of other homes—behold, his own to cleanse! [*Exit.*

> [*The scene opens, disclosing the interior of the temple: Orestes clings to the central altar; the Furies lie slumbering at a little distance; Apollo and Hermes appear from the innermost shrine.*

THE FURIES

Apollo

Lo, I desert thee never: to the end,
Hard at thy side as now, or sundered far,
I am thy guard, and to thine enemies
Implacably oppose me: look on them,
These greedy fiends, beneath my craft subdued!
See, they are fallen on sleep, these beldames old,
Unto whose grim and wizened maidenhood
Nor god nor man nor beast can e'er draw near.
Yea, evil were they born, for evil's doom,
Evil the dark abyss of Tartarus
Wherein they dwell, and they themselves the hate
Of men on earth, and of Olympian gods.
But thou, flee far and with unfaltering speed;
For they shall hunt thee through the mainland wide
Where'er throughout the tract of travelled earth
Thy foot may roam, and o'er and o'er the seas
And island homes of men. Faint not nor fail,
Too soon and timidly within thy breast
Shepherding thoughts forlorn of this thy toil;
But unto Pallas' city go, and there
Crouch at her shrine, and in thine arms enfold
Her ancient image: there we well shall find
Meet judges for this cause and suasive pleas,
Skilled to contrive for thee deliverance
From all this woe. Be such my pledge to thee,
For by my hest thou didst thy mother slay.

Orestes

O king Apollo, since right well thou know'st
What justice bids, have heed, fulfil the same,—
Thy strength is all-sufficient to achieve.

Apollo

Have thou too heed, nor let thy fear prevail
Above thy will. And do thou guard him, Hermes,

Whose blood is brother unto mine, whose sire
The same high God. Men call thee guide and guard,
Guide therefore thou and guard my suppliant;
For Zeus himself reveres the outlaw's right,
Boon of fair escort, upon man conferred.
              [*Exeunt Apollo, Hermes, and Orestes.*
              The Ghost of Clytemnestra rises.

Ghost of Clytemnestra

Sleep on! awake! what skills your sleep to me—
Me, among all the dead by you dishonoured—
Me from whom never, in the world of death,
Dieth this curse, *'Tis she who smote and slew,*
And shamed and scorned I roam? Awake, and hear
My plaint of dead men's hate intolerable.
Me, sternly slain by them that should have loved,
Me doth no god arouse him to avenge,
Hewn down in blood by matricidal hands.
Mark ye these wounds from which the heart's blood ran,
And by whose hand, bethink ye! for the sense
When shut in sleep hath then the spirit-sight,
But in the day the inward eye is blind.
List, ye who drank so oft with lapping tongue
The wineless draught by me outpoured to soothe
Your vengeful ire! how oft on kindled shrine
I laid the feast of darkness, at the hour
Abhorred of every god but you alone!
Lo, all my service trampled down and scorned!
And he hath baulked your chase, as stag the hounds;
Yea, lightly bounding from the circling toils,
Hath wried his face in scorn, and flieth far.
Awake and hear—for mine own soul I cry—
Awake, ye powers of hell! the wandering ghost
That once was Clytemnestra calls—Arise!
           [*The Furies mutter grimly, as in a dream.*
Mutter and murmur! He hath flown afar—

My kin have gods to guard them, I have none!
                    [The Furies mutter as before.
O drowsed in sleep too deep to heed my pain!
Orestes flies, who me, his mother, slew.
                    [The Furies give a confused cry.
Yelping, and drowsed again? Up and be doing
That which alone is yours, the deed of hell!
                    [The Furies give another cry.
Lo, sleep and toil, the sworn confederates,
Have quelled your dragon-anger, once so fell!

The Furies (*muttering more fiercely and loudly*)
Seize, seize, seize, seize—mark, yonder!

Ghost

In dreams ye chase a prey, and like some hound,
That even in sleep doth ply his woodland toil,
Ye bell and bay. What do ye, sleeping here?
Be not o'ercome with toil, nor, sleep-subdued,
Be heedless of my wrong. Up! thrill your heart
With the just chidings of my tongue,—such words
Are as a spur to purpose firmly held.
Blow forth on him the breath of wrath and blood,
Scorch him with reek of fire that burns in you,
Waste him with new pursuit—swift, hound him down!
                    [Ghost sinks.

First Fury (*awaking*)

Up! rouse another as I rouse thee; up!
Sleep'st thou? Rise up, and spurning sleep away,
See we if false to us this prelude rang.

Chorus of Furies

Alack, alack, O sisters, we have toiled,
  O much and vainly have we toiled and borne!
Vainly! and all we wrought the gods have foiled,
            And turnèd us to scorn!

He hath slipped from the net, whom we chased: he hath
    'scaped us who should be our prey—
O'ermastered by slumber we sank, and our quarry hath
    stolen away!
Thou, child of the high God Zeus, Apollo, hast robbed us
    and wronged;
Thou, a youth, hast downtrodden the right that to god-
    ship more ancient belonged;
Thou hast cherished thy suppliant man; the slayer, the
    God-forsaken,
The bane of a parent, by craft from out of our grasp thou
    hast taken;
A god, thou hast stolen from us, the avengers, a matricide
    son—
And who shall consider thy deed and say, *It is rightfully
    done?*

        The sound of chiding scorn
        Came from the land of dream;
  Deep to mine inmost heart I felt it thrill and burn,
      Thrust as a strong-grasped goad, to urge
        Onward the chariot's team.
      Thrilled, chilled with bitter inward pain
  I stand as one beneath the doomsman's scourge.
  Shame on the younger gods who tread down right,
      Sitting on thrones of might!
  Woe on the altar of earth's central fane!
      Clotted on step and shrine,
Behold, the guilt of blood, the ghastly stain!
  Woe upon thee, Apollo! uncontrolled,
    Unbidden, hast thou, prophet-god, imbrued
      The pure prophetic shrine with wrongful blood!
  For thou too heinous a respect didst hold
Of man, too little heed of powers divine!
    And us the Fates, the ancients of the earth,
      Didst deem as nothing worth.
Scornful to me thou art, yet shalt not fend
  My wrath from him; though unto hell he flee,
      There too are we!

And he, the blood-defiled, should feel and rue,
Though I were not, fiend-wrath that shall not end,
Descending on his head who foully slew.
>   [*Re-enter Apollo from the inner shrine.*

Apollo

Out! I command you. Out from this my home—
Haste, tarry not! Out from the mystic shrine,
Lest thy lot be to take into thy breast
The winged bright dart that from my golden string
Speeds hissing as a snake,—lest, pierced and thrilled
With agony, thou shouldst spew forth again
Black frothy heart's-blood, drawn from mortal men,
Belching the gory clots sucked forth from wounds.
These be no halls where such as you can prowl—
Go where men lay on men the doom of blood,
Heads lopped from necks, eyes from their spheres
       plucked out,
Hacked flesh, the flower of youthful seed crushed out,
Feet hewn away, and hands, and death beneath
The smiting stone, low moans and piteous
Of men impaled—Hark, hear ye for what feast
Ye hanker ever, and the loathing gods
Do spit upon your craving? Lo, your shape
Is all too fitted to your greed; the cave
Where lurks some lion, lapping gore, were home
More meet for you. Avaunt from sacred shrines,
Nor bring pollution by your touch on all
That nears you. Hence! and roam unshepherded—
No god there is to tend such herd as you.

Chorus

O king Apollo, in our turn hear us.
Thou hast not only part in these ill things,
But art chief cause and doer of the same.

Apollo

How? stretch thy speech to tell this, and have done.

Chorus
Thine oracle bade this man slay his mother.

Apollo
I bade him quit his sire's death,—wherefore not?

Chorus
Then didst thou aid and guard red-handed crime.

Apollo
Yea, and I bade him to this temple flee.

Chorus
And yet forsooth dost chide us following him!

Apollo
Ay—not for you it is, to near this fane.

Chorus
Yet is such office ours, imposed by fate.

Apollo
What office? vaunt the thing ye deem so fair.

Chorus
From home to home we chase the matricide.

Apollo
What? to avenge a wife who slays her lord?

Chorus
That is not blood outpoured by kindred hands.

Apollo
How darkly ye dishonour and annul
The troth to which the high accomplishers,

Hera and Zeus, do honour. Yea, and thus
Is Aphrodite to dishonour cast,
The queen of rapture unto mortal men.
Know that above the marriage-bed ordained
For man and woman standeth Right as guard,
Enhancing sanctity of troth-plight sworn;
Therefore, if thou art placable to those
Who have their consort slain, nor will'st to turn
On them the eye of wrath, unjust art thou
In hounding to his doom the man who slew
His mother. Lo, I know thee full of wrath
Against one deed, but all too placable
Unto the other, minishing the crime.
But in this cause shall Pallas guard the right.

Chorus

Deem not my quest shall ever quit that man.

Apollo

Follow then, make thee double toil in vain!

Chorus

Think not by speech mine office to curtail.

Apollo

None hast thou, that I would accept of thee!

Chorus

Yea, high thine honour by the throne of Zeus:
But I, drawn on by scent of mother's blood,
Seek vengeance on this man and hound him down.

Apollo

But I will stand beside him; 'tis for me
To guard my suppliant: gods and men alike

Do dread the curse of such an one betrayed,
And in me Fear and Will say, *Leave him not.*
                              [*Exeunt omnes.*

*The scene changes to Athens. In the foreground, the
    Temple of Athena on the Acropolis; her statue
    stands in the centre; Orestes is seen clinging to it.*

Orestes

Look on me, queen Athena; lo, I come
By Loxias' behest; thou of thy grace
Receive me, driven of avenging powers—
Not now a red-hand slayer unannealed,
But with guilt fading, half effaced, outworn
On many homes and paths of mortal men.
For to the limit of each land, each sea,
I roamed, obedient to Apollo's hest,
And come at last, O Goddess, to thy fane,
And clinging to thine image, bide my doom.
       [*Enter the Chorus of Furies, questing like hounds.*

Chorus

Ho! clear is here the trace of him we seek:
Follow the track of blood, the silent sign!
Like to some hound that hunts a wounded fawn,
We snuff along the scent of dripping gore,
And inwardly we pant, for many a day
Toiling in chase that shall fordo the man;
For o'er and o'er the wide land have I ranged,
And o'er the wide sea, flying without wings,
Swift as a sail I pressed upon his track,
Who now hard by is crouching, well I wot,
For scent of mortal blood allures me here.
    Follow, seek him—round and round
    Scent and snuff and scan the ground,
    Lest unharmed he slip away,
    He who did his mother slay!

THE FURIES

Hist—he is there! See him his arms entwine
Around the image of the maid divine—
    Thus aided, for the deed he wrought
    Unto the judgment wills he to be brought.

It may not be! a mother's blood, poured forth
    Upon the stained earth,
None gathers up: it lies—bear witness, Hell!—
    For aye indelible!
And thou who sheddest it shalt give thine own
    That shedding to atone!
Yea, from thy living limbs I suck it out,
    Red, clotted, gout by gout,—
A draught abhorred of men and gods; but I
    Will drain it, suck thee dry;
Yea, I will waste thee living, nerve and vein;
    Yea, for thy mother slain,
Will drag thee downward, there where thou shalt dree
    The weird of agony!
And thou and whatsoe'er of men hath sinned—
    Hath wronged or God, or friend,
Or parent,—learn ye how to all and each
    The arm of doom can reach!
Sternly requiteth, in the world beneath,
    The judgment-seat of Death;
Yea, Death, beholding every man's endeavour,
    Recordeth it for ever.

Orestes

I, schooled in many miseries, have learnt
How many refuges of cleansing shrines
There be; I know when law alloweth speech
And when imposeth silence. Lo, I stand
Fixed now to speak, for he whose word is wise
Commands the same. Look, how the stain of blood
Is dull upon mine hand and wastes away,
And laved and lost therewith is the deep curse

Of matricide; for while the guilt was new,
'Twas banished from me at Apollo's hearth,
Atoned and purified by death of swine.
Long were my word if I should sum the tale,
How oft since then among my fellow-men
I stood and brought no curse. Time cleanses all—
Time, the coeval of all things that are.

   Now from pure lips, in words of omen fair,
I call Athena, lady of this land,
To come, my champion: so, in aftertime,
She shall not fail of love and service leal,
Not won by war, from me and from my land
And all the folk of Argos, vowed to her.

   Now, be she far away in Libyan land
Where flows from Triton's lake her natal wave,—
Stand she with planted feet, or in some hour
Of rest conceal them, champion of her friends
Where'er she be,—or whether o'er the plain
Phlegræan she look forth, as warrior bold—
I cry to her to come, where'er she be
(And she, as goddess, from afar can hear),
And aid and free me, set among my foes.

Chorus

Thee not Apollo nor Athena's strength
Can save from perishing, a castaway
Amid the Lost, where no delight shall meet
Thy soul—a bloodless prey of nether powers,
A shadow among shadows. Answerest thou
Nothing? dost cast away my words with scorn,
Thou, prey prepared and dedicate to me?
Not as a victim slain upon the shrine,
But living shalt thou see thy flesh my food.
Hear now the binding chant that makes thee mine.

    Weave the weird dance,—behold the hour
      To utter forth the chant of hell,

THE FURIES

    Our sway among mankind to tell,
The guidance of our power.
Of Justice are we ministers,
    And whosoe'er of men may stand
    Lifting a pure unsullied hand,
That man no doom of ours incurs,
    And walks thro' all his mortal path
    Untouched by woe, unharmed by wrath.
But if, as yonder man, he hath
    Blood on the hands he strives to hide,
    We stand avengers at his side,
Decreeing, *Thou hast wronged the dead:*
We are doom's witnesses to thee.
The price of blood his hands have shed,
We wring from him; in life, in death,
    Hard at his side are we!

Night, Mother Night, who brought me forth, a torment
    To living men and dead,
Hear me, O hear! by Leto's stripling son
    I am dishonourèd:
He hath ta'en from me him who cowers in refuge,
    To me made consecrate,—
A rightful victim, him who slew his mother,
    Given o'er to me and Fate.

    Hear the hymn of hell,
      O'er the victim sounding,—
    Chant of frenzy, chant of ill,
      Sense and will confounding!
    Round the soul entwining
      Without lute or lyre—
    Soul in madness pining,
      Wasting as with fire!

Fate, all-pervading Fate, this service spun, commanding
    That I should bide therein:

Whosoe'er of mortals, made perverse and lawless,
    Is stained with blood of kin,
By his side are we, and hunt him ever onward,
    Till to the Silent Land,
The realm of death, he cometh; neither yonder
    In freedom shall he stand.

    Hear the hymn of hell,
      O'er the victim sounding,—
    Chant of frenzy, chant of ill,
      Sense and will confounding!
    Round the soul entwining
      Without lute or lyre—
    Soul in madness pining,
      Wasting as with fire!

When from womb of Night we sprang, on us this
    labour
    Was laid and shall abide.
Gods immortal are ye, yet beware ye touch not
    That which is our pride!
None may come beside us gathered round the blood
    feast—
    For us no garments white
Gleam on a festal day; for us a darker fate is,
    Another darker rite.
That is mine hour when falls an ancient line—
    When in the household's heart
The god of blood doth slay by kindred hands,—
    Then do we bear our part:
On him who slays we sweep with chasing cry:
    Though he be triply strong,
We wear and waste him; blood atones for blood,
    New pain for ancient wrong.

I hold this task—'tis mine, and not another's.
    The very gods on high,

Though they can silence and annul the prayers
    Of those who on us cry,
They may not strive with us who stand apart,
    A race by Zeus abhorred,
Blood-boltered, held unworthy of the council
    And converse of heaven's lord.
Therefore the more I leap upon my prey;
    Upon their head I bound;
My foot is hard; as one that trips a runner
    I cast them to the ground;
Yea, to the depth of doom intolerable;
    And they who erst were great,
And upon earth held high their pride and glory,
    Are brought to low estate.
In underworld they waste and are diminished,
    The while around them fleet
Dark wavings of my robes, and, subtly woven,
    The paces of my feet.

Who falls infatuate, he sees not, neither knows he
    That we are at his side;
So closely round about him, darkly flitting,
    The cloud of guilt doth glide.
Heavily 'tis uttered, how around his hearthstone
    The mirk of hell doth rise.
Stern and fixed the law is; we have hands t' achieve it,
    Cunning to devise.
Queens are we and mindful of our solemn vengeance.
    Not by tear or prayer
Shall a man avert it. In unhonoured darkness,
    Far from gods, we fare,
Lit unto our task with torch of sunless regions,
    And o'er a deadly way—
Deadly to the living as to those who see not
    Life and light of day—
Hunt we and press onward. Who of mortals hearing
    Doth not quake for awe,

Hearing all that Fate thro' hand of God hath given us
    For ordinance and law?
Yea, this right to us, in dark abysm and backward
    Of ages it befel:
None shall wrong mine office, tho' in nether regions
    And sunless dark I dwell.
              [*Enter Athena from above.*

Athena

Far off I heard the clamour of your cry,
As by Scamander's side I set my foot
Asserting right upon the land given o'er
To me by those who o'er Achaia's host
Held sway and leadership: no scanty part
Of all they won by spear and sword, to me
They gave it, land and all that grew thereon,
As chosen heirloom for my Theseus' clan.
Thence summoned, sped I with a tireless foot,—
Hummed on the wind, instead of wings, the fold
Of this mine ægis, by my feet propelled,
As, linked to mettled horses, speeds a car.
And now, beholding here Earth's nether brood,
I fear it nought, yet are mine eyes amazed
With wonder. Who are ye? of all I ask,
And of this stranger to my statue clinging.
But ye—your shape is like no human form,
Like to no goddess whom the gods behold,
Like to no shape which mortal women wear.
Yet to stand by and chide a monstrous form
Is all unjust—from such words Right revolts.

Chorus

O child of Zeus, one word shall tell thee all.
We are the children of eternal Night,
And Furies in the underworld are called.

Athena

I know your lineage now and eke your name.

Chorus
Yea, and eftsoons indeed my rights shalt know.

Athena
Fain would I learn them; speak them clearly forth.

Chorus
We chase from home the murderers of men.

Athena
And where at last can he that slew make pause?

Chorus
Where this is law—*All joy abandon here.*

Athena
Say, do ye bay this man to such a flight?

Chorus
Yea, for of choice he did his mother slay.

Athena
Urged by no fear of other wrath and doom?

Chorus
What spur can rightly goad to matricide?

Athena
Two stand to plead—one only have I heard.

Chorus
He will not swear nor challenge us to oath.

Athena
The form of justice, not its deed, thou willest.

Chorus

Prove thou that word; thou art not scant of skill.

Athena

I say that oaths shall not enforce the wrong.

Chorus

Then test the cause, judge and award the right.

Athena

Will ye to me then this decision trust?

Chorus

Yea, reverencing true child of worthy sire.

Athena (to Orestes)

O man unknown, make thou thy plea in turn.
Speak forth thy land, thy lineage, and thy woes;
Then, if thou canst, avert this bitter blame—
If, as I deem, in confidence of right
Thou sittest hard beside my holy place,
Clasping this statue, as Ixion sat,
A sacred suppliant for Zeus to cleanse,—
To all this answer me in words made plain.

Orestes

O queen Athena, first from thy last words
Will I a great solicitude remove.
Not one blood-guilty am I; no foul stain
Clings to thine image from my clinging hand;
Whereof one potent proof I have to tell.
Lo, the law stands—*The slayer shall not plead,
Till by the hand of him who cleanses blood
A suckling creature's blood besprinkle him.*
Long since have I this expiation done,—
In many a home, slain beasts and running streams

THE FURIES

Have cleansed me. Thus I speak away that fear.
Next, of my lineage quickly thou shalt learn:
An Argive am I, and right well thou know'st
My sire, that Agamemnon who arrayed
The fleet and them that went therein to war—
That chief with whom thy hand combined to crush
To an uncitied heap what once was Troy;
That Agamemnon, when he homeward came,
Was brought unto no honourable death,
Slain by the dark-souled wife who brought me forth
To him,—enwound and slain in wily nets,
Blazoned with blood that in the laver ran.
And I, returning from an exiled youth,
Slew her, my mother—lo, it stands avowed!
With blood for blood avenging my loved sire;
And in this deed doth Loxias bear part,
Decreeing agonies, to goad my will,
Unless by me the guilty found their doom.
Do thou decide if right or wrong were done—
Thy dooming, whatsoe'er it be, contents me.

Athena

Too mighty is this matter, whatsoe'er
Of mortals claims to judge hereof aright.
Yea, me, even me, eternal Right forbids
To judge the issues of blood-guilt, and wrath
That follows swift behind. This too gives pause,
That thou as one with all due rites performed
Dost come, unsinning, pure, unto my shrine.
Whate'er thou art, in this my city's name,
As uncondemned, I take thee to my side.—
Yet have these foes of thine such dues by fate,
I may not banish them: and if they fail,
O'erthrown in judgment of the cause, forthwith
Their anger's poison shall infect the land—
A dropping plague-spot of eternal ill.
Thus stand we with a woe on either hand:

Stay they, or go at my commandment forth,
Perplexity or pain must needs befal.
Yet, as on me Fate hath imposed the cause,
I choose unto me judges that shall be
An ordinance for ever, set to rule
The dues of blood-guilt, upon oath declared.
But ye, call forth your witness and your proof,
Words strong for justice, fortified by oath;
And I, whoe'er are truest in my town,
Them will I choose and bring, and straitly charge,
Look on this cause, discriminating well,
And pledge your oath to utter nought of wrong.
[*Exit Athena.*

Chorus

Now are they all undone, the ancient laws,
    If here the slayer's cause
Prevail; new wrong for ancient right shall be
    If matricide go free.
Henceforth a deed like his by all shall stand,
    Too ready to the hand:
Too oft shall parents in the aftertime
    Rue and lament this crime,—
Taught, not in false imagining, to feel
    Their children's thrusting steel:
No more the wrath that erst on murder fell
    From us, the queens of hell,
Shall fall, no more our watching gaze impend—
    Death shall smite unrestrained.

Henceforth shall one unto another cry,
Lo, they are stricken, lo, they fall and die
Around me! and that other answers him,
O thou that lookest that thy woes should cease,
    Behold, with dark increase
They throng and press upon thee; yea, and dim
    Is all the cure, and every comfort vain!

Let none henceforth cry out, when falls the blow
    Of sudden-smiting woe,
  Cry out, in sad reiterated strain,
O Justice, aid! aid, O ye thrones of hell!
    So though a father or a mother wail
  New-smitten by a son, it shall no more avail,
Since, overthrown by wrong, the fane of Justice fell!

Know that a throne there is that may not pass away,
    And one that sitteth on it—even Fear,
Searching with steadfast eyes man's inner soul:
Wisdom is child of pain, and born with many a tear;
      But who henceforth,
What man of mortal men, what nation upon earth,
  That holdeth nought in awe nor in the light
  Of inner reverence, shall worship Right
      As in the older day?

  Praise not, O man, the life beyond control,
  Nor that which bows unto a tyrant's sway.
    Know that the middle way
Is dearest unto God, and they thereon who wend,
    They shall achieve the end;
  But they who wander or to left or right
    Are sinners in his sight.
    Take to thy heart this one, this soothfast word—
    Of wantonness impiety is sire;
  Only from calm control and sanity unstirred
Cometh true weal, the goal of every man's desire.

  Yea, whatsoe'er befal, hold thou this word of mine:
    Bow down at Justice' shrine,
    Turn thou thine eyes away from earthly lure,
  Nor with a godless foot that altar spurn.
  For as thou dost shall Fate do in return,
    And the great doom is sure.
  Therefore let each adore a parent's trust,

    And each with loyalty revere the guest
        That in his halls doth rest.
For whoso uncompelled doth follow what is just,
        He ne'er shall be unblest;
    Yea, never to the gulf of doom
        That man shall come.

But he whose will is set against the gods,
    Who treads beyond the law with foot impure,
Till o'er the wreck of Right confusion broods,—
    Know that for him, though now he sail secure,
The day of storm shall be; then shall he strive and fail
Down from the shivered yard to furl the sail,
And call on powers, that heed him nought, to save,
    And vainly wrestle with the whirling wave.
        Hot was his heart with pride—
        I shall not fall, he cried.
        But him with watching scorn
        The god beholds, forlorn,
    Tangled in toils of Fate beyond escape,
    Hopeless of haven safe beyond the cape—
Till all his wealth and bliss of bygone day
    Upon the reef of Rightful Doom is hurled,
        And he is rapt away
Unwept, for ever, to the dead forgotten world.
    [*Re-enter Athena, with twelve Athenian citizens.*

Athena

O herald, make proclaim, bid all men come.
Then let the shrill blast of the Tyrrhene trump,
Fulfilled with mortal breath, thro' the wide air
Peal a loud summons, bidding all men heed.
For, till my judges fill this judgment-seat,
Silence behoves,—that this whole city learn
What for all time mine ordinance commands,
And these men, that the cause be judged aright.
    [*Apollo approaches.*

THE FURIES

Chorus

O king Apollo, rule what is thine own,
But in this thing what share pertains to thee?

Apollo

First, as a witness come I, for this man
Is suppliant of mine by sacred right,
Guest of my holy hearth and cleansed by me
Of blood-guilt: then, to set me at his side
And in his cause bear part, as part I bore
Erst in his deed, whereby his mother fell.
Let whoso knoweth now announce the cause.

Athena (to the Chorus)

'Tis I announce the cause—first speech be yours;
For rightfully shall they whose plaint is tried
Tell the tale first and set the matter clear.

Chorus

Though we be many, brief shall be our tale.
(*To Orestes*) Answer thou, setting word to match with word;
And first avow—hast thou thy mother slain?

Orestes

I slew her. I deny no word hereof.

Chorus

Three falls decide the wrestle—this is one.

Orestes

Thou vauntest thee—but o'er no final fall.

Chorus

Yet must thou tell the manner of thy deed.

Orestes
Drawn sword in hand, I gashed her neck. 'Tis told.

Chorus
But by whose word, whose craft, wert thou impelled?

Orestes
By oracles of him who here attests me.

Chorus
The prophet-god bade thee thy mother slay?

Orestes
Yea, and thro' him less ill I fared, till now.

Chorus
If the vote grip thee, thou shalt change that word.

Orestes
Strong is my hope; my buried sire shall aid.

Chorus
Go to now, trust the dead, a matricide!

Orestes
Yea, for in her combined two stains of sin.

Chorus
How? speak this clearly to the judges' mind.

Orestes
Slaying her husband, she did slay my sire.

Chorus
Therefore thou livest; death assoils her deed.

Orestes

Then while she lived why didst thou hunt her not?

Chorus

She was not kin by blood to him she slew.

Orestes

And I, am I by blood my mother's kin?

Chorus

O cursed with murder's guilt, how else wert thou
The burden of her womb? Dost thou forswear
Thy mother's kinship, closest bond of love?

Orestes

It is thine hour, Apollo—speak the law,
Averring if this deed were justly done;
For done it is, and clear and undenied.
But if to thee this murder's cause seem right
Or wrongful, speak—that I to these may tell.

Apollo

To you, Athena's mighty council-court,
Justly for justice will I plead, even I,
The prophet-god, nor cheat you by one word.
For never spake I from my prophet-seat
One word, of man, of woman, or of state,
Save what the Father of Olympian gods
Commanded unto me. I rede you then,
Bethink you of my plea, how strong it stands,
And follow the decree of Zeus, our sire,—
For oaths prevail not over Zeus' command.

Chorus

Go to; thou sayest that from Zeus befel
The oracle that this Orestes bade

With vengeance quit the slaying of his sire,
And hold as nought his mother's right of kin!

Apollo

Yea, for it stands not with a common death,
That he should die, a chieftain and a king
Decked with the sceptre which high heaven confers—
Die, and by female hands, not smitten down
By a far-shooting bow, held stalwartly
By some strong Amazon. Another doom
Was his: O Pallas, hear, and ye who sit
In judgment, to discern this thing aright!—
She with a specious voice of welcome true
Hailed him, returning from the mighty mart
Where war for life gives fame, triumphant home;
Then o'er the laver, as he bathed himself,
She spread from head to foot a covering net,
And in the endless mesh of cunning robes
Enwound and trapped her lord, and smote him down.
Lo, ye have heard what doom this chieftain met,
The majesty of Greece, the fleet's high lord:
Such as I tell it, let it gall your ears,
Who stand as judges to decide this cause.

Chorus

Zeus, as thou sayest, holds a father's death
As first of crimes,—yet he of his own act
Cast into chains his father, Cronos old:
How suits that deed with that which now ye tell?
O ye who judge, I bid ye mark my words!

Apollo

O monsters loathed of all, O scorn of gods,
He that hath bound may loose: a cure there is,
Yea, many a plan that can unbind the chain.
But when the thirsty dust sucks up man's blood

Once shed in death, he shall arise no more.
No chant nor charm for this my Sire hath wrought.
All else there is, he moulds and shifts at will,
Not scant of strength nor breath, whate'er he do.

Chorus

Think yet for what acquittal thou dost plead:
He who hath shed a mother's kindred blood,
Shall he in Argos dwell, where dwelt his sire?
How shall he stand before the city's shrines,
How share the clansmen's holy lustral bowl?

Apollo

This too I answer; mark a soothfast word:
Not the true parent is the woman's womb
That bears the child; she doth but nurse the seed
New-sown: the male is parent; she for him,
As stranger for a stranger, hoards the germ
Of life, unless the god its promise blight.
And proof hereof before you will I set.
Birth may from fathers, without mothers, be:
See at your side a witness of the same,
Athena, daughter of Olympian Zeus,
Never within the darkness of the womb
Fostered nor fashioned, but a bud more bright
Than any goddess in her breast might bear.
And I, O Pallas, howsoe'er I may,
Henceforth will glorify thy town, thy clan,
And for this end have sent my suppliant here
Unto thy shrine; that he from this time forth
Be loyal unto thee for evermore,
O goddess-queen, and thou unto thy side
Mayst win and hold him faithful, and his line,
And that for aye this pledge and troth remain
To children's children of Athenian seed.

Athena

Enough is said; I bid the judges now
With pure intent deliver just award.

Chorus

We too have shot our every shaft of speech,
And now abide to hear the doom of law.

Athena (*to Apollo and Orestes*)

Say, how ordaining shall I 'scape your blame?

Apollo

I spake, ye heard; enough. O stranger men,
Heed well your oath as ye decide the cause.

Athena

O men of Athens, ye who first do judge
The law of bloodshed, hear me now ordain.
Here to all time for Ægeus' Attic host
Shall stand this council-court of judges sworn,
Here the tribunal, set on Ares' Hill
Where camped of old the tented Amazons,
What time in hate of Theseus they assailed
Athens, and set against her citadel
A counterwork of new sky-pointing towers,
And there to Ares held their sacrifice,
Where now the rock hath name, even Ares' Hill.
And hence shall Reverence and her kinsman Fear
Pass to each free man's heart, by day and night
Enjoining, *Thou shalt do no unjust thing,*
So long as law stands as it stood of old
Unmarred by civic change. Look you, the spring
Is pure; but foul it once with influx vile
And muddy clay, and none can drink thereof.
Therefore, O citizens, I bid ye bow
In awe to this command, *Let no man live*

Uncurbed by law nor curbed by tyranny;
Nor banish ye the monarchy of Awe
Beyond the walls; untouched by fear divine,
No man doth justice in the world of men.
Therefore in purity and holy dread
Stand and revere; so shall ye have and hold
A saving bulwark of the state and land,
Such as no man hath ever elsewhere known,
Nor in far Scythia, nor in Pelops' realm.
Thus I ordain it now, a council-court
Pure and unsullied by the lust of gain,
Sacred and swift to vengeance, wakeful ever
To champion men who sleep, the country's guard.
Thus have I spoken, thus to mine own clan
Commended it for ever. Ye who judge,
Arise, take each his vote, mete out the right,
Your oath revering. Lo, my word is said.

> [*The twelve judges come forward, one by one, to the urns of decision; the first votes; as each of the others follows, the Chorus and Apollo speak alternately.*

Chorus

I rede ye well, beware! nor put to shame,
In aught, this grievous company of hell.

Apollo

I too would warn you, fear mine oracles—
From Zeus they are,—nor make them void of fruit.

Chorus

Presumptuous is thy claim blood-guilt to judge,
And false henceforth thine oracles shall be.

Apollo

Failed then the counsels of my sire, when turned
Ixion, first of slayers, to his side?

Chorus

These are but words; but I, if justice fail me,
Will haunt this land in grim and deadly deed.

Apollo

Scorn of the younger and the elder gods
Art thou: 'tis I that shall prevail anon.

Chorus

Thus didst thou too of old in Pheres' halls,
O'erreaching Fate to make a mortal deathless.

Apollo

Was it not well my worshipper to aid,
Then most of all when hardest was the need?

Chorus

I say thou didst annul the lots of life,
Cheating with wine the deities of eld.

Apollo

I say thou shalt anon, thy pleadings foiled,
Spit venom vainly on thine enemies.

Chorus

Since this young god o'errides mine ancient right,
I tarry but to claim your law, not knowing
If wrath of mine shall blast your state or spare.

Athena

Mine is the right to add the final vote,
And I award it to Orestes' cause.
For me no mother bore within her womb,
And, save for wedlock evermore eschewed,
I vouch myself the champion of the man,
Not of the woman, yea, with all my soul,—

THE FURIES

In heart, as birth, a father's child alone.
Thus will I not too heinously regard
A woman's death who did her husband slay,
The guardian of her home; and if the votes
Equal do fall, Orestes shall prevail.
Ye of the judges who are named thereto,
Swiftly shake forth the lots from either urn.
  [*Two judges come forward, one to each urn.*

Orestes

O bright Apollo, what shall be the end?

Chorus

O Night, dark mother mine, dost mark these things?

Orestes

Now shall my doom be life or strangling cords.

Chorus

And mine, lost honour or a wider sway.

Apollo

O stranger judges, sum aright the count
Of votes cast forth, and, parting them, take heed
Ye err not in decision. The default
Of one vote only bringeth ruin deep;
One, cast aright, doth stablish house and home.

Athena

Behold, this man is free from guilt of blood,
For half the votes condemn him, half set free!

Orestes

O Pallas, light and safety of my home,
Thou, thou hast given me back to dwell once more
In that my fatherland, amerced of which
I wandered; now shall Grecian lips say this,

*The man is Argive once again, and dwells
Again within his father's wealthy hall,
By Pallas saved, by Loxias, and by Him,
The great third saviour, Zeus omnipotent—*
Who thus in pity for my father's fate
Doth pluck me from my doom, beholding these,
Confederates of my mother. Lo, I pass
To mine own home, but proffering this vow
Unto thy land and people: *Nevermore,
Thro' all the manifold years of Time to be,
Shall any chieftain of mine Argive land
Bear hitherward his spears, for fight arrayed.*
For we, though lapped in earth we then shall lie,
By thwart adversities will work our will
On them who shall transgress this oath of mine,
Paths of despair and journeyings ill-starred
For them ordaining, till their task they rue.
But if this oath be rightly kept, to them
Will we, the dead, be full of grace, the while
With loyal league they honour Pallas' town.
And now farewell, thou and thy city's folk—
Firm be thine arms' grasp, closing with thy foes,
And, strong to save, bring victory to thy spear.
             [*Exit Orestes, with Apollo.*

Chorus

Woe on you, younger gods! the ancient right
Ye have o'erridden, rent it from my hands.

I am dishonoured of you, thrust to scorn!
             But heavily my wrath
Shall on this land fling forth the drops that blast and
             burn.
   Venom of vengeance, that shall work such scathe
   As I have suffered; where that dew shall fall,
             Shall leafless blight arise,
   Wasting Earth's offspring,—Justice, hear my call!—

THE FURIES

And thorough all the land in deadly wise
Shall scatter venom, to exude again
  In pestilence on men.
What cry avails me now, what deed of blood,
Unto this land what dark despite?
  Alack, alack, forlorn
Are we, a bitter injury have borne!
Alack, O sisters, O dishonoured brood
  Of mother Night!

Athena

Nay, bow ye to my words, chafe not nor moan:
Ye are not worsted nor disgraced; behold,
With balanced vote the cause had issue fair,
Nor in the end did aught dishonour thee.
But thus the will of Zeus shone clearly forth,
And his own prophet-god avouched the same,
Orestes slew: his slaying is atoned.
Therefore I pray you, not upon this land
Shoot forth the dart of vengeance; be appeased,
Nor blast the land with blight, nor loose thereon
Drops of eternal venom, direful darts
Wasting and marring nature's seed of growth.
For I, the queen of Athens' sacred right,
Do pledge to you a holy sanctuary
Deep in the heart of this my land, made just
By your indwelling presence, while ye sit
Hard by your sacred shrines that gleam with oil
Of sacrifice, and by this folk adored.

Chorus

Woe on you, younger gods! the ancient right
Ye have o'erridden, rent it from my hands.

I am dishonoured of you, thrust to scorn!
  But heavily my wrath

Shall on this land fling forth the drops that blast and burn.
    Venom of vengeance, that shall work such scathe
    As I have suffered; where that dew shall fall,
        Shall leafless blight arise,
Wasting Earth's offspring,—Justice, hear my call!—
And thorough all the land in deadly wise
Shall scatter venom, to exude again
        In pestilence of men.
What cry avails me now, what deed of blood,
Unto this land what dark despite?
      Alack, alack, forlorn
  Are we, a bitter injury have borne!
  Alack, O sisters, O dishonoured brood
        Of mother Night!

Athena

Dishonoured are ye not; turn not, I pray,
As goddesses your swelling wrath on men,
Nor make the friendly earth despiteful to them.
I too have Zeus for champion—'tis enough—
I only of all goddesses do know
To ope the chamber where his thunderbolts
Lie stored and sealed; but here is no such need.
Nay, be appeased, nor cast upon the ground
The malice of thy tongue, to blast the world;
Calm thou thy bitter wrath's black inward surge,
For high shall be thine honour, set beside me
For ever in this land, whose fertile lap
Shall pour its teeming first fruits unto you,
Gifts for fair childbirth and for wedlock's crown:
Thus honoured, praise my spoken pledge for aye.

Chorus

I, I dishonoured in this earth to dwell,—
Ancient of days and wisdom! I breathe forth
Poison and breath of frenzied ire. O Earth,

Woe, woe for thee, for me!
From side to side what pains be these that thrill?
Hearken, O mother Night, my wrath, mine agony!
Whom from mine ancient rights the gods have thrust,
    And brought me to the dust—
Woe, woe is me!—with craft invincible.

Athena

Older art thou than I, and I will bear
With this thy fury. Know, although thou be
More wise in ancient wisdom, yet have I
From Zeus no scanted measure of the same,
Wherefore take heed unto this prophecy—
If to another land of alien men
Ye go, too late shall ye feel longing deep
For mine. The rolling tides of time bring round
A day of brighter glory for this town;
And thou, enshrined in honour by the halls
Where dwelt Erechtheus, shalt a worship win
From men and from the train of womankind,
Greater than any tribe elsewhere shall pay.
Cast thou not therefore on this soil of mine
Whetstones that sharpen souls to bloodshedding,
The burning goads of youthful hearts, made hot
With frenzy of the spirit, not of wine.
Nor pluck as 'twere the heart from cocks that strive,
To set it in the breasts of citizens
Of mine, a war-god's spirit, keen for fight,
Made stern against their country and their kin.
The man who grievously doth lust for fame,
War, full, immitigable, let him wage
Against the stranger; but of kindred birds
I hold the challenge hateful. Such the boon
I proffer thee—within this land of lands,
Most loved of gods, with me to show and share
Fair mercy, gratitude and grace as fair.

Chorus

I, I dishonoured in this earth to dwell,—
Ancient of days and wisdom! I breathe forth
Poison and breath of frenzied ire. O Earth,
      Woe, woe for thee, for me!
From side to side what pains be these that thrill?
Hearken, O mother Night, my wrath, mine agony!
Whom from mine ancient rights the gods have thrust,
      And brought me to the dust—
Woe, woe is me!—with craft invincible.

Athena

I will not weary of soft words to thee,
That never mayst thou say, *Behold me spurned,*
An elder by a younger deity,
And from this land rejected and forlorn,
Unhonoured by the men who dwell therein.
But, if Persuasion's grace be sacred to thee,
Soft in the soothing accents of my tongue,
Tarry, I pray thee; yet, if go thou wilt,
Not rightfully wilt thou on this my town
Sway down the scale that beareth wrath and teen
Or wasting plague upon this folk. 'Tis thine,
If so thou wilt, inheritress to be
Of this my land, its utmost grace to win.

Chorus

O queen, what refuge dost thou promise me?

Athena

Refuge untouched by bale: take thou my boon.

Chorus

What, if I take it, shall mine honour be?

Athena

No house shall prosper without grace of thine.

THE FURIES

Chorus

Canst thou achieve and grant such power to me?

Athena

Yea, for my hand shall bless thy worshippers.

Chorus

And wilt thou pledge me this for time eterne?

Athena

Yea: none can bid me pledge beyond my power.

Chorus

Lo, I desist from wrath, appeased by thee.

Athena

Then in the land's heart shalt thou win thee friends.

Chorus

What chant dost bid me raise, to greet the land?

Athena

Such as aspires towards a victory
Unrued by any: chants from breast of earth,
From wave, from sky; and let the wild winds' breath
Pass with soft sunlight o'er the lap of land,—
Strong wax the fruits of earth, fair teem the kine,
Unfailing, for my town's prosperity,
And constant be the growth of mortal seed.
But more and more root out the impious,
For as a gardener fosters what he sows,
So foster I this race, whom righteousness
Doth fend from sorrow. Such the proffered boon.
But I, if wars must be, and their loud clash
And carnage, for my town, will ne'er endure
That aught but victory shall crown her fame.

Chorus

Lo, I accept it; at her very side
    Doth Pallas bid me dwell:
I will not wrong the city of her pride,
Which even Almighty Zeus and Ares hold
    Heaven's earthly citadel,
Loved home of Grecian gods, the young, the old,
    The sanctuary divine,
    The shield of every shrine!
For Athens I say forth a gracious prophecy,—
    The glory of the sunlight and the skies
    Shall bid from earth arise
Warm wavelets of new life and glad prosperity.

Athena

Behold, with gracious heart well pleased
    I for my citizens do grant
    Fulfilment of this covenant:
And here, their wrath at length appeased,
    These mighty deities shall stay,
    For theirs it is by right to sway
    The lot that rules our mortal day,
    And he who hath not inly felt
    Their stern decree, ere long on him,
    Not knowing why and whence, the grim
    Life-crushing blow is dealt.
    The father's sin upon the child
Descends, and sin is silent death,
And leads him on the downward path,
    By stealth beguiled,
    Unto the Furies: though his state
On earth were high, and loud his boast,
    Victim of silent ire and hate
    He dwells among the Lost.

Chorus

To my blessing now give ear.—
Scorching blight nor singèd air
Never blast thine olives fair!
Drouth, that wasteth bud and plant,
Keep to thine own place. Avaunt,
Famine fell, and come not hither
Stealthily to waste and wither!
Let the land, in season due,
Twice her waxing fruits renew;
Teem the kine in double measure;
Rich in new god-given treasure;
Here let men the powers adore
For sudden gifts unhoped before!

Athena

O hearken, warders of the wall
  That guards mine Athens, what a dower
Is unto her ordained and given!
For mighty is the Furies' power,
  And deep-revered in courts of heaven
And realms of hell; and clear to all
  They weave thy doom, mortality!
And some in joy and peace shall sing;
But unto other some they bring
  Sad life and tear-dimmed eye.

Chorus

And far away I ban thee and remove,
  Untimely death of youths too soon brought low!
And to each maid, O gods, when time is come for love,
  Grant ye a warrior's heart, a wedded life to know.
Ye too, O Fates, children of mother Night,
  Whose children too are we, O goddesses
Of just award, of all by sacred right
  Queens, who in time and in eternity

Do rule, a present power for righteousness,
  Honoured beyond all gods, hear ye and grant my cry!

Athena

And I too, I with joy am fain,
Hearing your voice this gift ordain
Unto my land. High thanks be thine,
Persuasion, who with eyes divine
Into my tongue didst look thy strength,
To bend and to appease at length
  Those who would not be comforted.
Zeus, king of parley, doth prevail,
And ye and I will strive nor fail,
  That good may stand in evil's stead,
And lasting bliss for bale.

Chorus

And nevermore these walls within
Shall echo fierce sedition's din,
  Unslaked with blood and crime;
The thirsty dust shall nevermore
Suck up the darkly streaming gore
Of civic broils, shed out in wrath
And vengeance, crying death for death!
But man with man and state with state
Shall vow, *The pledge of common hate
And common friendship, that for man
Hath oft made blessing out of ban,*
  Be ours unto all time.

Athena

Skill they, or not, the path to find
Of favouring speech and presage kind?
Yea, even from these, who, grim and stern,
  Glared anger upon you of old,
O citizens, ye now shall earn
  A recompense right manifold.

Deck them aright, extol them high,
Be loyal to their loyalty,
   And ye shall make your town and land
   Sure, propped on Justice' saving hand,
     And Fame's eternity.

Chorus

Hail ye, all hail! and yet again, all hail,
  O Athens, happy in a weal secured!
O ye who sit by Zeus' right hand, nor fail
  Of wisdom set among you and assured,
Loved of the well-loved Goddess-Maid! the King
Of gods doth reverence you, beneath her guarding
    wing.

Athena

All hail unto each honoured guest!
Whom to the chambers of your rest
'Tis mine to lead, and to provide
The hallowed torch, the guard and guide.
Pass down, the while these altars glow
With sacred fire, to earth below
   And your appointed shrine.
There dwelling, from the land restrain
The force of fate, the breath of bane,
But waft on us the gift and gain
   Of Victory divine!
And ye, the men of Cranaos' seed,
I bid you now with reverence lead
These alien powers that thus are made
Athenian evermore. To you
Fair be their will henceforth, to do
   Whate'er may bless and aid!

Chorus

Hail to you all! hail yet again,
All who love Athens, gods and men,

Adoring her as Pallas' home!
And while ye reverence what ye grant—
My sacred shrine and hidden haunt—
Blameless and blissful be your doom!

Athena

Once more I praise the promise of your vows,
And now I bid the golden torches' glow
Pass down before you to the hidden depth
Of earth, by mine own sacred servants borne,
My loyal guards of statue and of shrine.
Come forth, O flower of Theseus' Attic land,
O glorious band of children and of wives,
And ye, O train of matrons crowned with eld!
Deck you with festal robes of scarlet dye
In honour of this day: O gleaming torch,
Lead onward, that these gracious powers of earth
Henceforth be seen to bless the life of men.

[*Athena leads the procession downwards into the Cave of the Furies, under Areopagus: as they go, the escort of women and children chant aloud.*

Chant

With loyalty we lead you; proudly go,
Night's childless children, to your home below!
(*O citizens, awhile from words forbear!*)
To darkness' deep primeval lair,
Far in Earth's bosom, downward fare,
  Adored with prayer and sacrifice.
(*O citizens, forbear your cries!*)
Pass hitherward, ye powers of Dread,
With all your former wrath allayed,
  Into the heart of this loved land;
With joy unto your temple wend,
The while upon your steps attend
  The flames that fed upon the brand—
(*Now, now ring out your chant, your joy's acclaim!*)

Behind them, as they downward fare,
Let holy hands libations bear,
   And torches' sacred flame.
All-seeing Zeus and Fate come down
To battle fair for Pallas' town!
Ring out your chant, ring out your joy's acclaim!
                        [*Exeunt omnes.*

PROMETHEUS BOUND
OF ÆSCHYLUS

DRAMATIS PERSONÆ

PROMETHEUS	HERMES	OKEANOS
STRENGTH	HEPHÆSTOS	FORCE

Chorus of Ocean Nymphs

SCENE—Skythia, *on the heights of Caucasos. The Euxine seen in the distance.*

Enter HEPHÆSTOS, STRENGTH, *and* FORCE, *leading*
PROMETHEUS *in chains*[1]

Strength

LO! to a plain, earth's boundary remote,
    We now are come,—the tract as Skythian known,
    A desert inaccessible: and now,
Hephæstos, it is thine to do the hests
The Father gave thee, to these lofty crags
To bind this crafty trickster fast in chains
Of adamantine bonds that none can break;
For he, thy choice flower stealing, the bright glory
Of fire that all arts spring from, hath bestowed it
On mortal men. And so for fault like this
He now must pay the Gods due penalty,
That he may learn to bear the sovereign rule
Of Zeus, and cease from his philanthropy.

    Heph. O Strength, and thou, O Force, the hest of Zeus,
As far as touches you, attains its end,
And nothing hinders. Yet my courage fails

---

[1] The scene seems at first an exception to the early conventional rule, which forbade the introduction of a third actor on the Greek stage. But it has been noticed that (1) Force does not speak, and (2) Prometheus does not speak till Strength and Force have retired, and that it is therefore probable that the whole work of nailing is done on a lay figure or effigy of some kind, and that one of the two who had before taken part in the dialogue then speaks behind it in the character of Prometheus. So the same actor must have appeared in succession as Okeanos, Io, and Hermes.

To bind a God of mine own kin by force
To this bare rock where tempests wildly sweep;
And yet I needs must muster courage for it:
'Tis no slight thing the Father's words to scorn.
O thou of Themis [*to* PROMETHEUS] wise in counsel son,
Full deep of purpose, lo! against my will,[2]
I fetter thee against thy will with bonds
Of bronze that none can loose, to this lone height,
Where thou shalt know nor voice nor face of man,
But scorching in the hot blaze of the sun,
Shalt lose thy skin's fair beauty. Thou shalt long
For starry-mantled night to hide day's sheen,
For sun to melt the rime of early dawn;
And evermore the weight of present ill
Shall wear thee down. Unborn as yet is he
Who shall release thee: this the fate thou gain'st
As due reward for thy philanthropy.
For thou, a God not fearing wrath of Gods,
In thy transgression gav'st their power to men;
And therefore on this rock of little ease
Thou still shalt keep thy watch, nor lying down,
Nor knowing sleep, nor ever bending knee;
And many groans and wailings profitless
Thy lips shall utter; for the mind of Zeus
Remains inexorable. Who holds a power
But newly gained[3] is ever stern of mood.
   Strength. Let be! Why linger in this idle pity?
Why dost not hate a God to Gods a foe,
Who gave thy choicest prize to mortal men?
   Heph. Strange is the power of kin and intercourse.[4]

[2] Prometheus (*Forethought*) is the son of Themis (*Right*), the second occupant of the Pythian Oracle (*Eumen.* v. 2). His sympathy with man leads him to impart the gift which raised them out of savage animal life, and for this Zeus, who appears throughout the play as a hard taskmaster, sentences him to fetters. Hephæstos, from whom this fire had been stolen, has a touch of pity for him. Strength, who comes as the servant, not of Hephæstos, but of Zeus himself, acts, as such, with merciless cruelty.

[3] The generalised statement refers to Zeus, as having but recently expelled Cronos from his throne in heaven.

[4] Hephæstos, as the great fire-worker, had taught Prometheus to use the fire which he afterwards bestowed on men.

Strength. I own it; yet to slight the Father's words,
How may that be? Is not that fear the worse?
   Heph. Still art thou ruthless, full of savagery.
   Strength. There is no help in weeping over him:
Spend not thy toil on things that profit not.
   Heph. O handicraft to me intolerable!
   Strength. Why loath'st thou it? Of these thy present griefs
That craft of thine is not one whit the cause.
   Heph. And yet I would some other had that skill.
   Strength. All things bring toil except for Gods to reign;[5]
For none but Zeus can boast of freedom true.
   Heph. Too well I see the proof, and gainsay not.
   Strength. Wilt thou not speed to fix the chains on him,
Lest He, the Father, see thee loitering here?
   Heph. Well, here the handcuffs thou mayst see prepared.
   Strength. In thine hands take him. Then with all thy might
Strike with thine hammer; nail him to the rocks.
   Heph. The work goes on, I ween, and not in vain.
   Strength. Strike harder, rivet, give no whit of ease:
A wondrous knack has he to find resource,
Even where all might seem to baffle him.
   Heph. Lo! this his arm is fixed inextricably.
   Strength. Now rivet thou this other fast, that he
May learn, though sharp, that he than Zeus is duller.
   Heph. No one but he could justly blame my work.
   Strength. Now drive the stern jaw of the adamant wedge
Right through his chest with all the strength thou hast.
   Heph. Ah me! Prometheus, for thy woes I groan.
   Strength. Again, thou'rt loth, and for the foes of Zeus
Thou groanest: take good heed to it lest thou
Ere long with cause thyself commiserate.
   Heph. Thou seest a sight unsightly to our eyes.

---

[5] Perhaps, "All might is ours except o'er Gods to rule."

Strength. I see this man obtaining his deserts:
Nay, cast thy breast-chains round about his ribs.
  Heph. I must needs do it. Spare thine o'ermuch bidding;
Go thou below and rivet both his legs.[6]
  Strength. Nay, I will bid thee, urge thee to thy work.
  Heph. There, it is done, and that with no long toil.
  Strength. Now with thy full power fix the galling fetters:
Thou hast a stern o'erlooker of thy work.
  Heph. Thy tongue but utters words that match thy
            form.[7]
  Strength. Choose thou the melting mood; but chide not
            me
For my self-will and wrath and ruthlessness.
  Heph. Now let us go, his limbs are bound in chains.
  Strength. Here then wax proud, and stealing what
            belongs
To the Gods, to mortals give it. What can they
Avail to rescue thee from these thy woes?
Falsely the Gods have given thee thy name,
Prometheus, Forethought; forethought thou dost need
To free thyself from this rare handiwork.
            [*Exeunt* HEPHÆSTOS, STRENGTH, *and* FORCE,
                    leaving PROMETHEUS *on the rock.*
  Prom.[8] Thou firmament of God, and swift-winged
            winds,
Ye springs of rivers, and of ocean waves
That smile innumerous! Mother of us all,
O Earth, and Sun's all-seeing eye, behold,
I pray, what I, a God, from Gods endure.
      Behold in what foul case
      I for ten thousand years

---

[6] The words indicate that the effigy of Prometheus, now nailed to the rock, was, as being that of a Titan, of colossal size.

[7] The touch is characteristic as showing that here, as in the *Eumenides,* Æschylos relied on the horribleness of the masks, as part of the machinery of his plays.

[8] The silence of Prometheus up to this point was partly, as has been said, consequent on the conventional laws of the Greek drama, but it is also a touch of supreme insight into the heroic temper. In the presence of his torturers, the Titan will not utter even a groan. When they are gone, he appeals to the sympathy of Nature.

   Shall struggle in my woe,
   In these unseemly chains.
  Such doom the new-made Monarch of the Blest
   Hath now devised for me.
  Woe, woe! The present and the oncoming pang
   I wail, as I search out
  The place and hour when end of all these ills
   Shall dawn on me at last.
  What say I? All too clearly I foresee
  The things that come, and nought of pain shall be
  By me unlooked-for; but I needs must bear
  My destiny as best I may, knowing well
  The might resistless of Necessity.
  And neither may I speak of this my fate,
  Nor hold my peace. For I, poor I, through giving
  Great gifts to mortal men, am prisoner made
  In these fast fetters; yea, in fennel stalk[9]
  I snatched the hidden spring of stolen fire,
  Which is to men a teacher of all arts,
  Their chief resource. And now this penalty
  Of that offence I pay, fast riveted
  In chains beneath the open firmament.
    Ha! ha! What now?
  What sound, what odour floats invisibly?[10]
  Is it of God or man, or blending both?
  And has one come to this remotest rock
  To look upon my woes? Or what wills he?
  Behold me bound, a God to evil doomed,

---

[9] The legend is from Hesiod (*Theogon.* v. 567). The fennel, or *narthex,* seems to have been a large umbelliferous plant, with a large stem filled with a sort of pith, which was used when dry as tinder. Stalks were carried as wands (the *thyrsi*) by the men and women who joined in Bacchanalian processions. In modern botany, the name is given to the plant which produces Asafœtida, and the stem of which, from its resinous character, would burn freely, and so connect itself with the Promethean myth. On the other hand, the Narthex Asafœtida is found at present only in Persia, Afghanistan, and the Punjaub.

[10] The ocean nymphs, like other divine ones, would be anointed with ambrosial unguents, and the odour would be wafted before them by the rustling of their wings. This, too, we may think of as part of the "stage effects" of the play.

> The foe of Zeus, and held
> In hatred by all Gods
> Who tread the courts of Zeus:
> And this for my great love,
> Too great, for mortal men.
> Ah me! what rustling sounds
> Hear I of birds not far?
> With the light whirr of wings
> The air re-echoeth:
> All that draws nigh to me is cause of fear.[11]

Enter Chorus of Ocean Nymphs, *with wings, floating in the air*[12]

> *Chor.* Nay, fear thou nought: in love
> All our array of wings
> In eager race hath come
> To this high peak, full hardly gaining o'er
> Our Father's mind and will;
> And the swift-rushing breezes bore me on:
> For lo! the echoing sound of blows on iron
> Pierced to our cave's recess, and put to flight
> My shamefast modesty,
> And I in unshod haste, on wingèd car,
> To thee rushed hitherward.
> *Prom.* Ah me! ah me!
> Offspring of Tethys blest with many a child,
> Daughters of Old Okeanos that rolls
> Round all the earth with never-sleeping stream,
> Behold ye me, and see
> With what chains fettered fast,
> I on the topmost crags of this ravine
> Shall keep my sentry-post unenviable.

---

[11] The words are not those of a vague terror only. The sufferer knows that his tormentor is to come to him before long on wings, and therefore the sound as of the flight of birds is full of terrors.

[12] By the same stage mechanism the Chorus remains in the air till verse 14, page 176, when, at the request of Prometheus, they alight.

Chor. I see it, O Prometheus, and a mist
Of fear and full of tears comes o'er mine eyes,
    Thy frame beholding thus,
    Writhing on these high rocks
    In adamantine ills.
New pilots now o'er high Olympos rule,
    And with new-fashioned laws
    Zeus reigns, down-trampling Right,
And all the ancient powers He sweeps away.
    Prom. Ah! would that 'neath the Earth, 'neath Hades too,
Home of the dead, far down to Tartaros
Unfathomable He in fetters fast
    In wrath had hurled me down:
    So neither had a God
Nor any other mocked at these my woes;
But now, the wretched plaything of the winds,
I suffer ills at which my foes rejoice.
    Chor. Nay, which of all the Gods
Is so hard-hearted as to joy in this?
Who, Zeus excepted, doth not pity thee
    In these thine ills? But He,
    Ruthless, with soul unbent,
Subdues the heavenly host, nor will He cease[13]
Until His heart be satiate with power,
Or some one seize with subtle stratagem
The sovran might that so resistless seemed.
    Prom. Nay, of a truth, though put to evil shame,
    In massive fetters bound,
    The Ruler of the Gods
Shall yet have need of me, yes, e'en of me,
    To tell the counsel new
    That seeks to strip from Him

[13] Here, as throughout the play, the poet puts into the mouth of his *dramatis personæ* words which must have seemed to the devouter Athenians sacrilegious enough to call for an indictment before the Areiopagos. But the final play of the Trilogy came, we may believe, as the *Eumenides* did in its turn, as a reconciliation of the conflicting thoughts that rise in men's minds out of the seeming anomalies of the world.

His sceptre and His might of sovereignty.
    In vain will He with words
    Or suasion's honeyed charms
    Soothe me, nor will I tell
    Through fear of His stern threats,
    Ere He shall set me free
From these my bonds, and make,
    Of His own choice, amends
    For all these outrages.
  Chor. Full rash art thou, and yield'st
In not a jot to bitterest form of woe;
Thou art o'erfree and reckless in thy speech:
    But piercing fear hath stirred
    My inmost soul to strife;
For I fear greatly touching thy distress,
As to what haven of these woes of thine
Thou now must steer: the son of Cronos hath
A stubborn mood and heart inexorable.
  Prom. I know that Zeus is hard,
And keeps the Right supremely to Himself;
    But then, I trow, He'll be
    Full pliant in His will,
    When He is thus crushed down.
    Then, calming down His mood
    Of hard and bitter wrath,
    He'll hasten unto me,
    As I to Him shall haste,
    For friendship and for peace.
  Chor. Hide it not from us, tell us all the tale:
For what offence Zeus, having seized thee thus,
So wantonly and bitterly insults thee:
If the tale hurt thee not, inform thou us.
  Prom. Painful are these things to me e'en to speak:
Painful is silence; everywhere is woe.
For when the high Gods fell on mood of wrath
And hot debate of mutual strife was stirred,
Some wishing to hurl Cronos from his throne,

That Zeus, forsooth, might reign; while others strove,
Eager that Zeus might never rule the Gods:
Then I, full strongly seeking to persuade
The Titans, yea, the sons of Heaven and Earth,
Failed of my purpose. Scorning subtle arts,
With counsels violent, they thought that they
By force would gain full easy mastery.
But then not once or twice my mother Themis
And Earth, one form though bearing many names,[14]
Had prophesied the future, how 'twould run,
That not by strength nor yet by violence,
But guile, should those who prospered gain the day.
And when in my words I this counsel gave,
They deigned not e'en to glance at it at all.
And then of all that offered, it seemed best
To join my mother, and of mine own will,
Not against His will, take my side with Zeus,
And by my counsels, mine, the dark deep pit
Of Tartaros the ancient Cronos holds,
Himself and his allies. Thus profiting
By me, the mighty ruler of the Gods
Repays me with these evil penalties:
For somehow this disease in sovereignty
Inheres, of never trusting to one's friends.[15]
And since ye ask me under what pretence
He thus maltreats me, I will show it you:
For soon as He upon His father's throne
Had sat secure, forthwith to divers Gods
He divers gifts distributed, and His realm
Began to order. But of mortal men

---

[14] The words leave it uncertain whether Themis is identified with Earth, or, as in the *Eumenides* (v. 2), distinguished from her. The Titans as a class, then, children of Okeanos and Chthôn (another name for *Land* or *Earth*), are the kindred rather than the brothers of Prometheus.

[15] The generalising words here, as in v. 12, page 175, appeal to the Athenian hatred of all that was represented by the words *tyrant* and *tyranny*.

He took no heed, but purposed utterly
To crush their race and plant another new;
And, I excepted, none dared cross His will;
But I did dare, and mortal men I freed
From passing on to Hades thunderstricken;
And therefore am I bound beneath these woes,
Dreadful to suffer, pitiable to see:
And I, who in my pity thought of men
More than myself, have not been worthy deemed
To gain like favour, but all ruthlessly
I thus am chained, foul shame this sight to Zeus.

Chor. Iron-hearted must he be and made of rock
Who is not moved, Prometheus, by thy woes:
Fain could I wish I ne'er had seen such things,
And, seeing them, am wounded to the heart.

Prom. Yea, I am piteous for my friends to see.
Chor. Didst thou not go to farther lengths than this?
Prom. I made men cease from contemplating death.[16]
Chor. What medicine didst thou find for that disease?
Prom. Blind hopes I gave to live and dwell with them.
Chor. Great service that thou didst for mortal men!
Prom. And more than that, I gave them fire, yes, I.
Chor. Do short-lived men the flaming fire possess?
Prom. Yea, and full many an art they'll learn from it.
Chor. And is it then on charges such as these
That Zeus maltreats thee, and no respite gives
Of many woes? And has thy pain no end?
Prom. End there is none, except as pleases Him.
Chor. How shall it please? What hope hast thou?
　　　　　Seest not
That thou hast sinned? Yet to say how thou sinned'st

---

[16] The state described is that of men who "through fear of death are all their lifetime subject to bondage." That state, the parent of all superstition, fostered the slavish awe in which Zeus delighted. Prometheus, representing the active intellect of man, bestows new powers, new interests, new hopes, which at last divert them from that fear.

Gives me no pleasure, and is pain to thee.
Well! let us leave these things, and, if we may,
Seek out some means to 'scape from this thy woe.
  Prom. 'Tis a light thing for one who has his foot
Beyond the reach of evil to exhort
And counsel him who suffers. This to me
Was all well known. Yea, willing, willingly
I sinned, nor will deny it. Helping men,
I for myself found trouble: yet I thought not
That I with such dread penalties as these
Should wither here on these high-towering crags,
Lighting on this lone hill and neighbourless.
Wherefore wail not for these my present woes,
But, drawing nigh, my coming fortunes hear,
That ye may learn the whole tale to the end.
Nay, hearken, hearken; show your sympathy
With him who suffers now. 'Tis thus that woe,
Wandering, now falls on this one, now on that.
  Chor. Not to unwilling hearers hast thou uttered,
    Prometheus, thy request,
And now with nimble foot abounding
    My swiftly rushing car,
And the pure æther, path of birds of heaven,
I will draw near this rough and rocky land,
    For much do I desire
To hear this tale, full measure of thy woes.

Enter OKEANOS, *on a car drawn by a winged gryphon*

  Okean. Lo, I come to thee, Prometheus,
    Reaching goal of distant journey,[17]
    Guiding this my winged courser
    By my will, without a bridle;
    And thy sorrows move my pity.

[17] The home of Okeanos was in the far West, at the boundary of the great stream surrounding the whole world, from which he took his name.

Force, in part, I deem, of kindred
Leads me on, nor know I any,
Whom, apart from kin, I honour
More than thee, in fuller measure.
This thou shalt own true and earnest:
I deal not in glozing speeches.
Come then, tell me how to help thee;
Ne'er shalt thou say that one more friendly
Is found than unto thee is Okean.
Prom. Let be. What boots it? Thou then too art come
To gaze upon my sufferings. How didst dare
Leaving the stream that bears thy name, and caves
Hewn in the living rock, this land to visit,
Mother of iron? What then, art thou come
To gaze upon my fall and offer pity?
Behold this sight: see here the friend of Zeus,
Who helped to seat Him in His sovereignty,
With what foul outrage I am crushed by Him!
Okean. I see, Prometheus, and I wish to give thee
My best advice, all subtle though thou be.
Know thou thyself,[18] and fit thy soul to moods
To thee full new. New king the Gods have now;
But if thou utter words thus rough and sharp,
Perchance, though sitting far away on high,
Zeus yet may hear thee, and His present wrath
Seem to thee but as child's play of distress.
Nay, thou poor sufferer, quit the rage thou hast,
And seek a remedy for these thine ills.
A tale thrice told, perchance I seem to speak:
Lo! this, Prometheus, is the punishment
Of thine o'erlofty speech, nor art thou yet
Humbled, nor yieldest to thy miseries,
And fain wouldst add fresh evils unto these.

---

[18] One of the sayings of the Seven Sages, already recognised and quoted as a familiar proverb.

But thou, if thou wilt take me as thy teacher,
Wilt not kick out against the pricks;[19] seeing well
A monarch reigns who gives account to none.
And now I go, and will an effort make,
If I, perchance, may free thee from thy woes;
Be still then, hush thy petulance of speech,
Or knowest thou not, o'erclever as thou art,
That idle tongues must still their forfeit pay?

  Prom. I envy thee, seeing thou art free from blame
Though thou shared'st all, and in my cause wast bold;[20]
Nay, let me be, nor trouble thou thyself;
Thou wilt not, canst not soothe Him; very hard
Is He of soothing. Look to it thyself,
Lest thou some mischief meet with in the way.

  Okean. It is thy wont thy neighbours' minds to school
Far better than thine own. From deeds, not words,
I draw my proof. But do not draw me back
When I am hasting on, for lo! I deem,
I deem that Zeus will grant this boon to me,
That I should free thee from these woes of thine.

  Prom. I thank thee much, yea, ne'er will cease to
        thank;
For thou no whit of zeal dost lack; yet take,
I pray, no trouble for me; all in vain
Thy trouble, nothing helping, e'en if thou
Shouldst care to take the trouble. Nay, be still;
Keep out of harm's way; sufferer though I be,
I would not therefore wish to give my woes
A wider range o'er others. No, not so:
For lo! my mind is wearied with the grief
Of that my kinsman Atlas,[21] who doth stand

---

[19] See note on *Agam.* 1602 in E. H. Plumptre's translation.

[20] In the mythos, Okeanos had given his daughter Hesione in marriage to Prometheus after the theft of fire, and thus had identified himself with his transgression.

[21] In the *Theogony* of Hesiod (v. 509), Prometheus and Atlas appear as the sons of two sisters. As other Titans were thought of as buried under volcanoes, so this one was identified with the mountain which had been seen by travellers to Western Africa, or in the seas beyond it, rising like a column to support the vault of heaven.

In the far West, supporting on his shoulders
The pillars of the earth and heaven, a burden
His arms can ill but hold: I pity too
The giant dweller of Kilikian caves,
Dread portent, with his hundred hands, subdued
By force, the mighty Typhon,[22] who arose
'Gainst all the Gods, with sharp and dreadful jaws
Hissing out slaughter, and from out his eyes
There flashed the terrible brightness as of one
Who would lay low the sovereignty of Zeus.
But the unsleeping dart of Zeus came on him,
Down-swooping thunderbolt that breathes out flame,
Which from his lofty boastings startled him,
For he i' the heart was struck, to ashes burnt,
His strength all thunder-shattered; and he lies
A helpless, powerless carcase, near the strait
Of the great sea, fast pressed beneath the roots
Of ancient Ætna, where on highest peak
Hephæstos sits and smites his iron red-hot,
From whence hereafter streams of fire shall burst,[23]
Devouring with fierce jaws the golden plains
Of fruitful, fair Sikelia. Such the wrath
That Typhon shall belch forth with bursts of storm,
Hot, breathing fire, and unapproachable,

In Herodotos (iv. 174) and all later writers, the name is given to the chain of mountains in Lybia, as being the "pillar of the firmament"; but Humboldt and others identify it with the lonely peak of Teneriffe, as seen by Phœnikian or Hellenic voyagers. Teneriffe, too, like most of the other Titan mountains, was at one time volcanic. Homer (*Odyss.* i. 53) represents him as holding the pillars which separate heaven from earth; Hesiod (*Theogon.* v. 517) as himself standing near the Hesperides (this, too, points to Teneriffe), sustaining the heavens with his head and shoulders.

[22] The volcanic character of the whole of Asia Minor, and the liability to earthquakes which has marked nearly every period of its history, led men to connect it also with the traditions of the Titans, some accordingly placing the home of Typhon in Phrygia, some near Sardis, some, as here, in Kilikia. Hesiod (*Theogon.* v. 820) describes Typhon (or Typhoeus) as a serpent-monster hissing out fire; Pindar (*Pyth.* i. 30, viii. 21) as lying with his head and breast crushed beneath the weight of Ætna, and his feet extending to Cumæ.

[23] The words point probably to an eruption, then fresh in men's memories, which had happened B.C. 476.

Though burnt and charred by thunderbolts of Zeus.
Not inexperienced art thou, nor dost need
My teaching: save thyself, as thou know'st how;
And I will drink my fortune to the dregs,
Till from His wrath the mind of Zeus shall rest.[24]

Okean. Know'st thou not this, Prometheus, even this:
Of wrath's disease wise words the healers are?

Prom. Yea, could one soothe the troubled heart in time,
Nor seek by force to tame the soul's proud flesh.

Okean. But, in due forethought with bold daring blent,
What mischief seest thou lurking? Tell me this.

Prom. Toil bootless, and simplicity full fond.

Okean. Let me, I pray, that sickness suffer, since
'Tis best being wise to have not wisdom's show.

Prom. Nay, but this error shall be deemed as mine.

Okean. Thy word then clearly sends me home at once.

Prom. Yea, lest thy pity for me make a foe. . . .

Okean. What! of that new king on His mighty throne?

Prom. Look to it, lest His heart be vexed with thee.

Okean. Thy fate, Prometheus, teaches me that lesson.

Prom. Away, withdraw! keep thou the mind thou hast.

Okean. Thou urgest me who am in act to haste;
For this my bird four-footed flaps with wings
The clear path of the æther; and full fain
Would he bend knee in his own stall at home. [*Exit.*

Strophe I

Chor. I grieve, Prometheus, for thy dreary fate,
    Shedding from tender eyes
    The dew of plenteous tears;
With streams, as when the watery south wind blows,
    My cheek is wet;
For lo! these things are all unenviable,

---

[24] By some editors this speech from "No, not so," to "thou know'st how," is assigned to Okeanos.

And Zeus, by His own laws His sway maintaining,
Shows to the elder Gods
A mood of haughtiness.

Antistrophe I

And all the country echoeth with the moan,
And poureth many a tear
For that magnific power
Of ancient days far-seen that thou didst share
With those of one blood sprung;
And all the mortal men who hold the plain
Of holy Asia as their land of sojourn,
They grieve in sympathy
For thy woes lamentable.

Strophe II

And they, the maiden band who find their home
On distant Colchian coasts,
Fearless of fight,[25]
Or Skythian horde in earth's remotest clime,
By far Mæotic lake;[26]

Antistrophe II

And warlike glory of Arabia's tribes,[27]
Who nigh to Caucasos
In rock-fort dwell,
An army fearful, with sharp-pointed spear
Raging in war's array.

Strophe III

One other Titan only have I seen,
One other of the Gods,

---

[25] These are, of course, the Amazons, who were believed to have come through Thrakè from the Tauric Chersonesos, and had left traces of their name and habits in the Attic traditions of Theseus.

[26] Beyond the plains of Skythia and the lake Mæotis (the sea of Azov) there would be the great river Okeanos, which was believed to flow round the earth.

[27] Sarmatia has been conjectured instead of Arabia. No Greek author sanctions the extension of the latter name to so remote a region as that north of the Caspian.

ÆSCHYLUS

Thus bound in woes of adamantine strength—
    Atlas, who ever groans
Beneath the burden of a crushing might,
    The outspread vault of heaven.

Antistrophe III

And lo! the ocean billows murmur loud
    In one accord with him;[28]
The sea-depths groan, and Hades' swarthy pit
    Re-echoeth the sound,
And fountains of clear rivers, as they flow,
    Bewail his bitter griefs.

  Prom. Think not it is through pride or stiff self-will
That I am silent. But my heart is worn,
Self-contemplating, as I see myself
Thus outraged. Yet what other hand than mine
Gave these young Gods in fulness all their gifts?
But these I speak not of; for I should tell
To you that know them. But those woes of men,[29]
List ye to them,—how they, before as babes,
By me were roused to reason, taught to think;
And this I say, not finding fault with men,
But showing my good-will in all I gave.
For first, though seeing, all in vain they saw,
And hearing, heard not rightly. But, like forms
Of phantom-dreams, throughout their life's whole length
They muddled all at random; did not know
Houses of brick that catch the sunlight's warmth,
Nor yet the work of carpentry. They dwelt
In hollowed holes, like swarms of tiny ants,

---

[28] The Greek leaves the object of the sympathy undefined, but it seems better to refer it to that which Atlas receives from the waste of waters around, and the dark world beneath, than to the pity shown to Prometheus. This has already been dwelt on in the first stanza, page 181.

[29] The passage that follows has for modern palæontologists the interest of coinciding with their views as to the progress of human society, and the condition of mankind during what has been called the "Stone" period. Comp. Lucretius, v. 955-984.

In sunless depths of caverns; and they had
No certain signs of winter, nor of spring
Flower-laden, nor of summer with her fruits;
But without counsel fared their whole life long,
Until I showed the risings of the stars,
And settings hard to recognise.[30] And I
Found Number for them, chief device of all,
Groupings of letters, Memory's handmaid that,
And mother of the Muses.[31] And I first
Bound in the yoke wild steeds, submissive made
Or to the collar or men's limbs, that so
They might in man's place bear his greatest toils;
And horses trained to love the rein I yoked
To chariots, glory of wealth's pride of state;[32]
Nor was it any one but I that found
Sea-crossing, canvas-wingèd cars of ships:
Such rare designs inventing (wretched me!)
For mortal men, I yet have no device
By which to free myself from this my woe.[33]

   Chor. Foul shame thou sufferest: of thy sense
       bereaved,
Thou errest greatly: and, like leech unskilled,
Thou losest heart when smitten with disease,
And know'st not how to find the remedies
Wherewith to heal thine own soul's sicknesses.

   Prom. Hearing what yet remains, thou'lt wonder
       more,
What arts and what resources I devised:
And this the chief: if any one fell ill,

---

[30] Comp. Mr. Blakesley's note on Herod. ii. 4, as showing that here there was the greater risk of faulty observation.

[31] Another reading gives perhaps a better sense—
      "Memory, handmaid true
    And mother of the Muses."

[32] In Greece, as throughout the East, the ox was used for all agricultural labours, the horse by the noble and the rich, either in war chariots, or stately processions, or in chariot races in the great games.

[33] Compare with this the account of the inventions of Palamedes in Sophocles, *Fragm.* 379.

There was no help for him, nor healing food
Nor unguent, nor yet potion; but for want
Of drugs they wasted, till I showed to them
The blendings of all mild medicaments,[34]
Wherewith they ward the attacks of sickness sore.
I gave them many modes of prophecy;[35]
And I first taught them what dreams needs must prove
True visions, and made known the ominous sounds
Full hard to know; and tokens by the way,
And flights of taloned birds I clearly marked,—
Those on the right propitious to mankind,
And those sinister,—and what form of life
They each maintain, and what their enmities
Each with the other, and their loves and friendships;
And of the inward parts the plumpness smooth.
And with what colour they the Gods would please,
And the streaked comeliness of gall and liver:
And with burnt limbs enwrapt in fat, and chine,
I led men on to art full difficult:
And I gave eyes to omens drawn from fire,
Till then dim-visioned. So far, then, for this.
And 'neath the earth the hidden boons for men,
Bronze, iron, silver, gold, who else could say
That he, ere I did, found them? None, I know,
Unless he fain would babble idle words.
In one short word, then, learn the truth condensed,—
All arts of mortals from Prometheus spring.
Chor. Nay, be not thou to men so overkind,

---

[34] Here we can recognise the knowledge of one who had studied in the schools of Pythagoras, or had at any rate picked up their terminology. A more immediate connexion may perhaps be traced with the influence of Epimenides, who was said to have spent many years in searching out the healing virtues of plants, and to have written books about them.

[35] The lines that follow form almost a manual of the art of divination as then practised. The "ominous sounds" include chance words, strange cries, any unexpected utterance that connected itself with men's fears for the future. The flights of birds were watched by the diviner as he faced the north, and so the region on the right hand was that of the sunrise, light, blessedness; on the left there were darkness and gloom and death.

While thou thyself art in sore evil case;
For I am sanguine that thou too, released
From bonds, shalt be as strong as Zeus Himself.

Prom. It is not thus that Fate's decree is fixed;
But I, long crushed with twice ten thousand woes
And bitter pains, shall then escape my bonds;
Art is far weaker than Necessity.

Chor. Who guides the helm, then, of Necessity?
Prom. Fates triple-formed, Erinyes unforgetting.
Chor. Is Zeus, then, weaker in His might than these?
Prom. Not even He can 'scape the thing decreed.
Chor. What is decreed for Zeus but still to reign?
Prom. Thou mayst no further learn, ask thou no more.
Chor. 'Tis doubtless some dread secret which thou hidest.
Prom. Of other theme make mention, for the time
Is not yet come to utter this, but still
It must be hidden to the uttermost;
For by thus keeping it it is that I
Escape my bondage foul, and these my pains.

STROPHE I

Chor. Ah! ne'er may Zeus the Lord,
    Whose sovran sway rules all,
    His strength in conflict set
    Against my feeble will!
    Nor may I fail to serve
    The Gods with holy feast
    Of whole burnt-offerings,
    Where the stream ever flows
    That bears my father's name,
    The great Okeanos!
    Nor may I sin in speech!
    May this grace more and more
    Sink deep into my soul
    And never fade away!

Antistrophe I

Sweet is it in strong hope
To spend long years of life,
With bright and cheering joy
Our heart's thoughts nourishing
I shudder, seeing thee
Thus vexed and harassed sore
By twice ten thousand woes;
For thou in pride of heart,
Having no fear of Zeus,
In thine own obstinacy,
Dost show for mortal men,
Prometheus, love o'ermuch.

Strophe II

See how that boon, dear friends,
For thee is bootless found.
Say, where is any help?
What aid from mortals comes?
Hast thou not seen this brief and powerless life,
Fleeting as dreams, with which man's purblind race
    Is fast in fetters bound?
    Never shall counsels vain
    Of mortal men break through
    The harmony of Zeus.

Antistrophe II

This lesson have I learnt
Beholding thy sad fate,
Prometheus! Other strains
Come back upon my mind,
When I sang wedding hymns around thy bath,
And at thy bridal bed, when thou didst take
    In wedlock's holy bands
    One of the same sire born,
    Our own Hesione,

Persuading her with gifts
As wife to share thy couch.

Enter Io *in form like a fair woman with a heifer's horns,*[36] *followed by the Spectre of* Argos

Io. What land is this? What people? Whom shall I
Say that I see thus vexed
With bit and curb of rock?
For what offence dost thou
Bear fatal punishment?
Tell me to what far land
I've wandered here in woe.
　　Ah me! ah me!
Again the gadfly stings me miserable.
　Spectre of Argos, thou, the earth-born one—
　　Ah, keep him off, O Earth!
I fear to look upon that herdsman dread,
　Him with ten thousand eyes:
Ah lo! he cometh with his crafty look,
Whom Earth refuses even dead to hold;[37]
　　But coming from beneath,
　　He hunts me miserable,
And drives me famished o'er the sea-beach sand.

Strophe

And still his waxened reed-pipe soundeth clear
　A soft and slumberous strain;
　　O heavens! O ye Gods!

---

[36] So Io was represented, we are told, by Greek sculptors (Herod. ii. 41), as Isis was by those of Egypt. The points of contact between the myth of Io and that of Prometheus, as adopted, or perhaps developed, by Æschylos, are—(1) that from her the destined deliverer of the chained Titan is to come; (2) that both were suffering from the cruelty of Zeus; (3) that the wanderings of Io gave scope for the wild tales of far countries on which the imagination of the Athenians fed greedily. But, as the *Suppliants* may serve to show, the story itself had a strange fascination for him. In the birth of Epaphos, and Io's release from her frenzy, he saw, it may be, a reconciliation of what had seemed hard to reconcile, a solution of the problems of the world, like in kind to that which was shadowed forth in the lost *Prometheus Unbound*.

[37] Argos had been slain by Hermes, and his eyes transferred by Hera to the tail of the peacock, and that bird was henceforth sacred to her.

Whither do these long wanderings lead me on?
For what offence, O son of Cronos, what,
>   Hast thou thus bound me fast
>   In these great miseries?
>   Ah me! ah me!
And why with terror of the gadfly's sting
Dost thou thus vex me, frenzied in my soul?
Burn me with fire, or bury me in earth,
Or to wild sea-beasts give me as a prey:
>   Nay, grudge me not, O King,
>   An answer to my prayers:
Enough my many-wandered wanderings
>   Have exercised my soul,
>   Nor have I power to learn
>   How to avert the woe.
>   (*To Prometheus.*) Hear'st thou the voice of maiden
>   crowned with horns?

Prom. Surely I heard the maid by gadfly driven,
Daughter of Inachos, who warmed the heart
Of Zeus with love, and now through Hera's hate
Is tried, perforce, with wanderings overlong?

Antistrophe

>   *Io.* How is it that thou speak'st my father's name?
>   Tell me, the suffering one,
>   Who art thou, who, poor wretch,
Who thus so truly nam'st me miserable,
>   And tell'st the plague from Heaven,
>   Which with its haunting stings
>   Wears me to death? Ah woe!
And I with famished and unseemly bounds
Rush madly, driven by Hera's jealous craft.
Ah, who of all that suffer, born to woe,
Have trouble like the pain that I endure?
>   But thou, make clear to me
>   What yet for me remains,

What remedy, what healing for my pangs.
　　Show me, if thou dost know:
　　Speak out and tell to me,
　　The maid by wanderings vexed.
　Prom. I will say plainly all thou seek'st to know;
Not in dark tangled riddles, but plain speech,
As it is meet that friends to friends should speak;
Thou seest Prometheus who gave fire to men.
　Io. O thou to men as benefactor known,
Why, poor Prometheus, sufferest thou this pain?
　Prom. I have but now mine own woes ceased to wail.
　Io. Wilt thou not then bestow this boon on me?
　Prom. Say what thou seek'st, for I will tell thee all.
　Io. Tell me, who fettered thee in this ravine?
　Prom. The counsel was of Zeus, the hand Hephæstos'.
　Io. Of what offence dost thou the forfeit pay?
　Prom. Thus much alone am I content to tell.
　Io. Tell me, at least, besides, what end shall come
To my drear wanderings; when the time shall be.
　Prom. Not to know this is better than to know.
　Io. Nay, hide not from me what I have to bear.
　Prom. It is not that I grudge the boon to thee.
　Io. Why then delayest thou to tell the whole?
　Prom. Not from ill will, but loth to vex thy soul.
　Io. Nay, care thou not beyond what pleases me.
　Prom. If thou desire it I must speak. Hear then.
　Chor. Not yet though; grant me share of pleasure too.
Let us first ask the tale of her great woe,
While she unfolds her life's consuming chances;
Her future sufferings let her learn from thee.
　Prom. 'Tis thy work, Io, to grant these their wish,
On other grounds and as thy father's kin;[38]
For to bewail and moan one's evil chance,
Here where one trusts to gain a pitying tear

---

[38] Inachos, the father of Io (identified with the Argive river of the same name), was, like all rivers, a son of Okeanos, and therefore brother to the nymphs who had come to see Prometheus.

From those who hear,—this is not labour lost.
  Io. I know not how to disobey your wish;
So ye shall learn the whole that ye desire
In speech full clear. And yet I blush to tell
The storm that came from God, and brought the loss
Of maiden face, what way it seized on me.
For nightly visions coming evermore
Into my virgin bower, sought to woo me
With glozing words. "O virgin greatly blest,
Why art thou still a virgin when thou might'st
Attain to highest wedlock? For with dart
Of passion for thee Zeus doth glow, and fain
Would make thee His. And thou, O child, spurn not
The bed of Zeus, but go to Lerna's field,
Where feed thy father's flocks and herds,
That so the eye of Zeus may find repose
From this His craving." With such visions I
Was haunted every evening, till I dared
To tell my father all these dreams of night,
And he to Pytho and Dodona sent
Full many to consult the Gods, that he
Might learn what deeds and words would please
        Heaven's lords.
And they came bringing speech of oracles
Shot with dark sayings, dim and hard to know.
At last a clear word came to Inachos
Charging him plainly, and commanding him
To thrust me from my country and my home,
To stray at large[39] to utmost bounds of earth;
And, should he gainsay, that the fiery bolt
Of Zeus should come and sweep away his race.
And he, by Loxias' oracles induced,
Thrust me, against his will, against mine too,
And drove me from my home; but spite of all,

---

[39] The words used have an almost technical meaning as applied to animals that were consecrated to the service of a God, and set free to wander where they liked. The fate of Io, as at once devoted to Zeus and animalised in form, was thus shadowed forth in the very language of the Oracle.

The curb of Zeus constrained him this to do.
And then forthwith my face and mind were changed;
And hornèd, as ye see me, stung to the quick
By biting gadfly, I with maddened leap
Rushed to Kerchneia's fair and limpid stream,
And fount of Lerna.[40] And a giant herdsman,
Argos, full rough of temper, followed me,
With many an eye beholding, on my track:
And him a sudden and unlooked-for doom
Deprived of life. And I, by gadfly stung,
By scourge from Heaven am driven from land to land.
What has been done thou hearest. And if thou
Canst tell what yet remains of woe, declare it;
Nor in thy pity soothe me with false words;
For hollow words, I deem, are worst of ills.
 Chor. Away, away, let be:
  Ne'er thought I that such tales
Would ever, ever come unto mine ears;
Nor that such terrors, woes and outrages,
  Hard to look on, hard to bear,
Would chill my soul with sharp goad, double-edged.
  Ah fate! Ah fate!
I shudder, seeing Io's fortune strange.
 Prom. Thou art too quick in groaning, full of fear:
Wait thou awhile until thou hear the rest.
 Chor. Speak thou and tell. Unto the sick 'tis sweet
Clearly to know what yet remains of pain.
 Prom. Your former wish ye gained full easily.
Your first desire was to learn of her
The tale she tells of her own sufferings;
Now therefore hear the woes that yet remain
For this poor maid to bear at Hera's hands.
And thou, O child of Inachos! take heed
To these my words, that thou mayst hear the goal
Of all thy wanderings. First then, turning hence

[40] Lerna was the lake near the mouth of the Inachos, close to the sea. Kerchneia may perhaps be identified with the Kenchreæ, the haven of Korinth in later geographies.

Towards the sunrise, tread the untilled plains,
And thou shalt reach the Skythian nomads, those[41]
Who on smooth-rolling waggons dwell aloft
In wicker houses, with far-darting bows
Duly equipped. Approach thou not to these,
But trending round the coasts on which the surf
Beats with loud murmurs,[42] traverse thou that clime.
On the left hand there dwell the Chalybes,[43]
Who work in iron. Of these do thou beware,
For fierce are they and most inhospitable;
And thou wilt reach the river fierce and strong,
True to its name.[44] This seek not thou to cross,
For it is hard to ford, until thou come
To Caucasos itself, of all high hills
The highest, where a river pours its strength
From the high peaks themselves. And thou must cross
Those summits near the stars, must onward go
Towards the south, where thou shalt find the host
Of the Amâzons, hating men, whose home
Shall one day be around Thermôdon's bank,
By Themiskyra,[45] where the ravenous jaws
Of Salmydessos ope upon the sea,
Treacherous to sailors, stepdame stern to ships.[46]
And they with right good-will shall be thy guides;

[41] The wicker huts used by Skythian or Thrakian nomads (the Calmucks of modern geographers) are described by Herodotos (iv. 46) and are still in use.

[42] Sc., the N.E. boundary of the Euxine, where spurs of the Caucasos ridge approach the sea.

[43] The Chalybes are placed by geographers to the south of Colchis. The description of the text indicates a locality farther to the north.

[44] Probably the Araxes, which the Greeks would connect with a word conveying the idea of a torrent dashing on the rocks. The description seems to imply a river flowing into the Euxine from the Caucasos, and the condition is fulfilled by the Hypanis or *Kouban*.

[45] When the Amazons appear in contact with Greek history, they are found in Thrace. But they had come from the coast of Pontos, and near the mouth of the Thermodon (*Thermeh*). The words of Prometheus point to yet earlier migrations from the East.

[46] Here, as in Soph. *Antig.* (970), the name Salmydessos represents the rock-bound, havenless coast from the promontory of Thynias to the entrance of the Bosporos, which had given to the Black Sea its earlier name of Axenos, the "inhospitable."

And thou, hard by a broad pool's narrow gates,
Wilt pass to the Kimmerian isthmus. Leaving
This boldly, thou must cross Mæotic channel;[47]
And there shall be great fame 'mong mortal men
Of this thy journey, and the Bosporos[48]
Shall take its name from thee. And Europe's plain
Then quitting, thou shalt gain the Asian coast.
Doth not the all-ruling monarch of the Gods
Seem all ways cruel? For, although a God,
He, seeking to embrace this mortal maid,
Imposed these wanderings on her. Thou hast found,
O maiden! bitter suitor for thy hand;
For great as are the ills thou now hast heard,
Know that as yet not e'en the prelude's known.

Io. Ah woe! woe! woe!

Prom. Again thou groan'st and criest. What wilt do
When thou shalt learn the evils yet to come?

Chor. What! are there troubles still to come for her?

Prom. Yea, stormy sea of woe most lamentable.

Io. What gain is it to live? Why cast I not
Myself at once from this high precipice,
And, dashed to earth, be free from all my woes?
Far better were it once for all to die
Than all one's days to suffer pain and grief.

Prom. My struggles then full hardly thou wouldst bear,
For whom there is no destiny of death;
For that might bring a respite from my woes:
But now there is no limit to my pangs
Till Zeus be hurled out from His sovereignty.

Io. What! shall Zeus e'er be hurled from His high state?

Prom. Thou wouldst rejoice, I trow, to see that fall.

Io. How should I not, when Zeus so foully wrongs me?

Prom. That this is so thou now mayst hear from me.

---

[47] The track is here in some confusion. From the Amazons south of the Caucasos, Io is to find her way to the Tauric Chersonese (the Crimea) and the Kimmerian Bosporos, which flows into the sea of Azov, and so to return to Asia.

[48] Here, as in a hundred other instances, a false etymology has become the parent of a myth. The name Bosporos is probably Asiatic, not Greek, and has an entirely different signification.

Io. Who then shall rob Him of His sceptred sway?
Prom. Himself shall do it by His own rash plans.
Io. But how? Tell this, unless it bringeth harm.
Prom. He shall wed one for whom one day He'll grieve.
Io. Heaven-born or mortal? Tell, if tell thou mayst.
Prom. Why ask'st thou who? I may not tell thee that.
Io. Shall His bride hurl Him from His throne of might?
Prom. Yea; she shall bear child mightier than his sire.
Io. Has He no way to turn aside that doom?
Prom. No, none; unless I from my bonds be loosed.[49]
Io. Who then shall loose thee 'gainst the will of Zeus?
Prom. It must be one of thy posterity.
Io. What, shall a child of mine free thee from ills?
Prom. Yea, the third generation after ten.[50]
Io. No more thine oracles are clear to me.
Prom. Nay, seek not thou thine own drear fate to know.
Io. Do not, a boon presenting, then withdraw it.
Prom. Of two alternatives, I'll give thee choice.
Io. Tell me of what, then give me leave to choose.
Prom. I give it then. Choose, or that I should tell
Thy woes to come, or who shall set me free.
Chor. Of these be willing one request to grant
To her, and one to me; nor scorn my words:
Tell her what yet of wanderings she must bear,
And me who shall release thee. This I crave.
Prom. Since ye are eager, I will not refuse
To utter fully all that ye desire.
Thee, Io, first I'll tell thy wanderings wild,
Thou, write it in the tablets of thy mind.
When thou shalt cross the straits, of continents

---

[49] The lines refer to the story that Zeus loved Thetis, the daughter of Nereus, and followed her to Caucasos, but abstained from marriage with her because Prometheus warned him that the child born of that union should overthrow his father. Here the future is used of what was still contingent only. In the lost play of the Trilogy the myth was possibly brought to its conclusion and connected with the release of Prometheus.

[50] Heracles, whose genealogy was traced through Alcmena, Perseus, Danae, Danaos, and seven other names, to Epaphos and Io.

The boundary,[51] take thou the onward path
On to the fiery-hued and sun-tracked East.
[And first of all, to frozen Northern blasts
Thou'lt come, and there beware the rushing whirl,
Lest it should come upon thee suddenly,
And sweep thee onward with the cloud-rack wild;][52]
Crossing the sea-surf till thou come at last
Unto Kisthene's Gorgoneian plains,
Where dwell the grey-haired virgin Phorkides,[53]
Three, swan-shaped, with one eye between them all
And but one tooth; whom nor the sun beholds
With radiant beams, nor yet the moon by night:
And near them are their wingèd sisters three,
The Gorgons, serpent-tressed, and hating men,
Whom mortal wight may not behold and live.
Such is one ill I bid thee guard against;
Now hear another monstrous sight: Beware
The sharp-beaked hounds of Zeus that never bark,[54]
The Gryphons, and the one-eyed mounted host
Of Arimaspians, who around the stream
That flows o'er gold, the ford of Pluto, dwell:[55]
Draw not thou nigh to them. But distant land
Thou shalt approach, the swarthy tribes who dwell

[51] Probably the Kimmerian Bosporos. The Tanais or Phasis has, however, been conjectured.
[52] The history of the passage in brackets is curious enough to call for a note. It is not in any extant MS., but it is found in a passage quoted by Galen as from the *Prometheus Bound,* and is inserted here by Mr. Paley.
[53] Kisthene belongs to the geography of legend, lying somewhere on the shore of the great ocean-river in Lybia or Æthiopia, at the end of the world, a great mountain in the far West, beyond the Hesperides, the dwelling-place, as here, of the Gorgons, the daughters of Phorkys. Those first named are the Graiæ.
[54] Here, like the "wingèd hound" of verse 1043, page 203, for the eagles that are the messengers of Zeus.
[55] We are carried back again from the fabled West to the fabled East. The Arimaspians, with one eye, and the Grypes or Gryphons (the griffins of mediæval heraldry), quadrupeds with the wings and beaks of eagles, were placed by most writers (Herod. iv. 13, 27) in the north of Europe, in or beyond the *terra incognita* of Skythia. The mention of the "ford of Pluto" and Æthiopia, however, may possibly imply (if we identify it, as Mr. Paley does, with the Tartessos of Spain, or Bœtis—*Guadalquivir*) that Æschylos followed another legend which placed them in the West. There is possibly a *paronomasia* between Pluto, the God of Hades, and Plutos, the ideal God of riches.

By the sun's fountain,[56] Æthiopia's stream:
By its banks wend thy way until thou come
To that great fall where from the Bybline hills
The Neilos pours its pure and holy flood;
And it shall guide thee to Neilotic land,
Three-angled, where, O Io, 'tis decreed
For thee and for thy progeny to found
A far-off colony. And if of this
Aught seem to thee as stammering speech obscure,
Ask yet again and learn it thoroughly:
Far more of leisure have I than I like.
  Chor. If thou hast aught to add, aught left untold
Of her sore-wasting wanderings, speak it out;
But if thou hast said all, then grant to us
The boon we asked. Thou dost not, sure, forget it.
  Prom. The whole course of her journeying she hath heard,
And that she know she hath not heard in vain
I will tell out what troubles she hath borne
Before she came here, giving her sure proof
Of these my words. The greater bulk of things
I will pass o'er, and to the very goal
Of all thy wanderings go. For when thou cam'st
To the Molossian plains, and by the grove[57]
Of lofty-ridged Dodona, and the shrine
Oracular of Zeus Thesprotian,
And the strange portent of the talking oaks,
By which full clearly, not in riddle dark,
Thou wast addressed as noble spouse of Zeus,—
If aught of pleasure such things give to thee,—
Thence strung to frenzy, thou didst rush along
The sea-coast's path to Rhea's mighty gulf,[58]
In backward way from whence thou now art vexed,

---

[56] The name was applied by later writers (Quintus Curtius, iv. 7, 22; Lucretius, vi. 848) to the fountain in the temple of Jupiter Ammon in the great Oasis. The "river Æthiops" may be purely imaginary, but it may also suggest the possibility of some vague knowledge of the Niger, or more probably of the Nile itself in the upper regions of its course. The "Bybline hills" carry the name Byblos, which we only read of as belonging to a town in the Delta, to the Second Cataract.
[57] Comp. Sophocles, *Trachin.* v. 1168.   [58] The Adriatic or Ionian Gulf.

And for all time to come that reach of sea,
Know well, from thee Ionian shall be called,
To all men record of thy journeyings.
These then are tokens to thee that my mind
Sees somewhat more than that is manifest.
What follows (*to the Chorus*) I will speak to you and her
In common, on the track of former words
Returning once again. A city stands,
Canôbos, at its country's furthest bound,
Hard by the mouth and silt-bank of the Nile;
There Zeus shall give thee back thy mind again,[59]
With hand that works no terror touching thee,—
Touch only—and thou then shalt bear a child
Of Zeus begotten, Epaphos, "Touch-born,"
Swarthy of hue, whose lot shall be to reap
The whole plain watered by the broad-streamed Neilos:
And in the generation fifth from him
A household numbering fifty shall return
Against their will to Argos, in their flight
From wedlock with their cousins.[60] And they too
(Kites but a little space behind the doves),
With eager hopes pursuing marriage rites,
Beyond pursuit shall come; and God shall grudge
To give up their sweet bodies. And the land
Pelasgian[61] shall receive them, when by stroke
Of woman's murderous hand these men shall lie
Smitten to death by daring deed of night:
For every bride shall take her husband's life,
And dip in blood the sharp two-edgèd sword

[59] In the *Suppliants*, Zeus is said to have soothed her, and restored her to her human consciousness by his "divine breathings." The thought underlying the legend may be taken either as a distortion of some primitive tradition, or as one of the "unconscious prophecies" of heathenism. The deliverer is not to be born after the common manner of men, and is to have a divine as well as a human parentage.

[60] See the argument of the *Suppliants*, who, as the daughters of Danaos, descended from Epaphos, are here referred to. The passage is noticeable as showing that the theme of that tragedy was already present to the poet's thoughts.

[61] Argos. So, in the *Suppliants*, Pelasgos is the mythical king of the Apian land who receives them.

(So to my foes may Kypris show herself!).[62]
Yet one of that fair band shall love persuade
Her husband not to slaughter, and her will
Shall lose its edge; and she shall make her choice
Rather as weak than murderous to be known.
And she at Argos shall a royal seed
Bring forth (long speech 'twould take to tell this clear)
Famed for his arrows, who shall set me free[63]
From these my woes. Such was the oracle
Mine ancient mother Themis, Titan-born,
Gave to me; but the manner and the means,—
That needs a lengthy tale to tell the whole,
And thou canst nothing gain by learning it.

Io. Eleleu! Oh, Eleleu![64]
The throbbing pain inflames me, and the mood
  Of frenzy-smitten rage;
  The gadfly's pointed sting,
  Not forged with fire, attacks,
And my heart beats against my breast with fear.
  Mine eyes whirl round and round:
  Out of my course I'm borne
By the wild spirit of fierce agony,
  And cannot curb my lips,
And turbid speech at random dashes on
Upon the waves of dread calamity.

Strophe I

Chor. Wise, very wise was he
Who first in thought conceived this maxim sage,
  And spread it with his speech,[65]—
 That the best wedlock is with equals found,

---

[62] Hypermnæstra, who spared Lynceus, and by him became the mother of Abas and a line of Argive kings.

[63] Heracles, who came to Caucasos, and with his arrows slew the eagle that devoured Prometheus.

[64] The word is simply an interjection of pain, but one so characteristic that I have thought it better to reproduce it than to give any English equivalent.

[65] The maxim, "Marry with a woman thine equal," was ascribed to Pittacos.

And that a craftsman, born to work with hands,
  Should not desire to wed
Or with the soft luxurious heirs of wealth,
Or with the race that boast their lineage high.

Antistrophe I

  Oh ne'er, oh ne'er, dread Fates,
May ye behold me as the bride of Zeus,
  The partner of His couch,
Nor may I wed with any heaven-born spouse!
For I shrink back, beholding Io's lot
  Of loveless maidenhood,
Consumed and smitten low exceedingly
By the wild wanderings from great Hera sent!

Strophe II

To me, when wedlock is on equal terms,
  It gives no cause to fear:
Ne'er may the love of any of the Gods,
  The strong Gods, look on me
  With glance I cannot 'scape!

Antistrophe II

That fate is war that none can war against,
  Source of resourceless ill;
Nor know I what might then become of me:
  I see not how to 'scape
  The counsel deep of Zeus.
  Prom. Yea, of a truth shall Zeus, though stiff of will,
Be brought full low. Such bed of wedlock now
Is He preparing, one to cast Him forth
In darkness from His sovereignty and throne.
And then the curse His father Cronos spake
Shall have its dread completion, even that
He uttered when he left his ancient throne;

And from these troubles no one of the Gods
But me can clearly show the way to 'scape.
I know the time and manner: therefore now
Let Him sit fearless, in His peals on high
Putting His trust, and shaking in His hands
His darts fire-breathing. Nought shall they avail
To hinder Him from falling shamefully
A fall intolerable. Such a combatant
He arms against Himself, a marvel dread,
Who shall a fire discover mightier far
Than the red levin, and a sound more dread
Than roaring of the thunder, and shall shiver
That plague sea-born that causeth earth to quake,
The trident, weapon of Poseidon's strength:
And stumbling on this evil, He shall learn
How far apart a king's lot from a slave's.
   Chor. What thou dost wish thou mutterest against Zeus.
   Prom. Things that shall be, and things I wish, I speak.
   Chor. And must we look for one to master Zeus?
   Prom. Yea, troubles harder far than these are His.
   Chor. Art not afraid to vent such words as these?
   Prom. What can I fear whose fate is not to die?
   Chor. But He may send on thee worse pain than this.
   Prom. So let Him do: nought finds me unprepared.
   Chor. Wisdom is theirs who Adrasteia worship.[66]
   Prom. Worship then, praise and flatter Him that rules;
My care for Zeus is nought, and less than nought:
Let Him act, let Him rule this little while,
E'en as He will; for long He shall not rule
Over the Gods. But lo! I see at hand
The courier of the Gods, the minister
Of our new sovereign. Doubtless he has come
To bring me tidings of some new device.

[66] The Euhemerism of later scholiasts derived the name from a king Adrastos, who was said to have been the first to build a temple to Nemesis, and so the power thus worshipped was called after his name. A better etymology leads us to see in it the idea of the "inevitable" law of retribution working unseen by men, and independently even of the arbitrary will of the Gods, and bringing destruction upon the proud and haughty.

Enter HERMES

Herm. Thee do I speak to,—thee, the teacher wise,
The bitterly o'erbitter, who 'gainst Gods
Hast sinned in giving gifts to short-lived men—
I speak to thee, the filcher of bright fire.
The Father bids thee say what marriage thou
Dost vaunt, and who shall hurl Him from His might;
And this too not in dark mysterious speech,
But tell each point out clearly. Give me not,
Prometheus, task of double journey. Zeus,
Thou seest, is not with such words appeased.

Prom. Stately of utterance, full of haughtiness
Thy speech, as fits a messenger of Gods.
Ye yet are young in your new rule, and think
To dwell in painless towers. Have I not
Seen two great rulers driven forth from thence?[67]
And now the third, who reigneth, I shall see
In basest, quickest fall. Seem I to thee
To shrink and quail before these new-made Gods?
Far, very far from that am I. But thou,
Track once again the path by which thou camest;
Thou shalt learn nought of what thou askest me.

Herm. It was by such self-will as this before
That thou didst bring these sufferings on thyself.

Prom. I for my part, be sure, would never change
My evil state for that thy bondslave's lot.

Herm. To be the bondslave of this rock, I trow,
Is better than to be Zeus' trusty herald!

Prom. So it is meet the insulter to insult.

Herm. Thou waxest proud, 'twould seem, of this thy doom.

Prom. Wax proud! God grant that I may see my foes
Thus waxing proud, and thee among the rest!

Herm. Dost blame me then for thy calamities?

Prom. In one short sentence—all the Gods I hate,

[67] Comp. *Agam.* 162–6.

Who my good turns with evil turns repay.
Herm. Thy words prove thee with no slight madness plagued.
Prom. If to hate foes be madness, mad I am.
Herm. Not one could bear thee wert thou prosperous.
Prom. Ah me!
Herm. That word is all unknown to Zeus.
Prom. Time waxing old can many a lesson teach.
Herm. Yet thou at least hast not true wisdom learnt.
Prom. I had not else addressed a slave like thee.
Herm. Thou wilt say nought the Father asks, 'twould seem.
Prom. Fine debt I owe Him, favour to repay.
Herm. Me as a boy thou scornest then, forsooth.
Prom. And art thou not a boy, and sillier far,
If that thou thinkest to learn aught from me?
There is no torture nor device by which
Zeus can impel me to disclose these things
Before these bonds that outrage me be loosed.
Let then the blazing levin-flash be hurled;
With white-winged snow-storm and with earth-born thunders
Let Him disturb and trouble all that is;
Nought of these things shall force me to declare
Whose hand shall drive Him from His sovereignty.
Herm. See if thou findest any help in this.
Prom. Long since all this I've seen, and formed my plans.
Herm. O fool, take heart, take heart at last in time,
To form right thoughts for these thy present woes.
Prom. Like one who soothes a wave, thy speech in vain
Vexes my soul. But deem not thou that I,
Fearing the will of Zeus, shall e'er become
As womanised in mind, or shall entreat
Him whom I greatly loathe, with upturned hand,
In woman's fashion, from these bonds of mine
To set me free. Far, far am I from that.
Herm. It seems that I, saying much, shall speak in vain;
For thou in nought by prayers art pacified,
Or softened in thy heart, but like a colt
Fresh harnessed, thou dost champ thy bit, and strive,

And fight against the reins. Yet thou art stiff
In weak device; for self-will, by itself,
In one who is not wise, is less than nought.
Look to it, if thou disobey my words,
How great a storm and triple wave of ills,[68]
Not to be 'scaped, shall come on thee; for first,
With thunder and the levin's blazing flash
The Father this ravine of rocks shall crush,
And shall thy carcase hide, and stern embrace
Of stony arms shall keep thee in thy place.
And having traversed space of time full long,
Thou shalt come back to light, and then his hound,
The wingèd hound of Zeus, the ravening eagle,
Shall greedily make banquet of thy flesh,
Coming all day an uninvited guest,
And glut himself upon thy liver dark.
And of that anguish look not for the end,
Before some God shall come to bear thy woes,
And will to pass to Hades' sunless realm,
And the dark cloudy depths of Tartaros.[69]
Wherefore take heed. No feignèd boast is this,
But spoken all too truly; for the lips
Of Zeus know not to speak in lying speech,
But will perform each single word. And thou,
Search well, be wise, nor think that self-willed pride
Shall ever better prove than counsel good.

Chor. To us doth Hermes seem to utter words
Not out of season; for he bids thee quit
Thy self-willed pride and seek for counsel good.
Hearken thou to him. To the wise of soul
It is foul shame to sin persistently.

---

[68] Either a mere epithet of intensity, as in our "thrice blest," or rising from the supposed fact that every third wave was larger and more impetuous than the others, like the *fluctus decumanus* of the Latins, or from the sequence of three great waves which some have noted as a common phenomenon in storms.

[69] Here again we have a strange shadowing forth of the mystery of Atonement, and what we have learnt to call "vicarious" satisfaction. In the later legend, Cheiron, suffering from the agony of his wounds, resigns his immortality, and submits to die in place of the ever-living death to which Prometheus was doomed.

Prom. To me who knew it all
He hath this message borne;
And that a foe from foes
Should suffer is not strange.
Therefore on me be hurled
The sharp-edged wreath of fire;
And let heaven's vault be stirred
With thunder and the blasts
Of fiercest winds; and earth
From its foundations strong,
E'en to its deepest roots,
Let storm-wind make to rock;
And let the ocean wave,
With wild and foaming surge,
Be heaped up to the paths
Where move the stars of heaven;
And to dark Tartaros
Let Him my carcase hurl,
With mighty blasts of force:
Yet me He shall not slay.

Herm. Such words and thoughts from one
Brain-stricken one may hear.
What space divides his state
From frenzy? What repose
Hath he from maddened rage?
But ye who pitying stand
And share his bitter griefs,
Quickly from hence depart,
Lest the relentless roar
Of thunder stun your soul.

Chor. With other words attempt
To counsel and persuade,
And I will hear: for now
Thou hast this word thrust in
That we may never bear.
How dost thou bid me train
My soul to baseness vile?

With him I will endure
Whatever is decreed.
Traitors I've learned to hate,
Nor is there any plague
That more than this I loathe.
  Herm. Nay then, remember ye
What now I say, nor blame
Your fortune: never say
That Zeus hath cast you down
To evil not foreseen.
Not so; ye cast yourselves:
For now with open eyes,
Not taken unawares,
In Atè's endless net
Ye shall entangled be
By folly of your own.

  [*A pause, and then flashes of lightning and
    peals of thunder*[70]

  Prom. Yea, now in very deed,
No more in word alone,
The earth shakes to and fro,
And the loud thunder's voice
Bellows hard by, and blaze
The flashing levin-fires;
And tempests whirl the dust,
And gusts of all wild winds
On one another leap,
In wild conflicting blasts,
And sky with sea is blent:
Such is the storm from Zeus
That comes as working fear,

---

[70] It is noticeable that both Æschylos and Sophocles have left us tragedies which end in a thunderstorm as an element of effect. But the contrast between the *Prometheus* and the *Œdipus at Colonos* as to the impression left in the one case of serene reconciliation, and in the other of violent antagonism, is hardly less striking than the resemblance in the outward phenomena which are common to the two.

In terrors manifest.
O Mother venerable!
O Æther! rolling round
The common light of all,
Seest thou what wrongs I bear?

ŒDIPUS THE KING
AND
ANTIGONE
OF
SOPHOCLES

TRANSLATED BY
E. H. PLUMPTRE

INTRODUCTORY NOTE

SOPHOCLES, the most perfectly balanced among the three great masters of Greek tragedy, was born in Colonus, near Athens, about 495 B.C. His father was a man of wealth, and the poet received the best education of the time, being especially distinguished in music. He began his career as a dramatist at the age of twenty-seven, when he gained a victory over Æschylus; and from that time till his death in 405 B.C. he retained the foremost place as a writer of tragedy. Like a true Greek, he played his part in public affairs, both in peace and in war, and served his country as a diplomat and as a general. He was profoundly admired by his contemporaries for character as well as genius, and after his death was honored as a hero with annual sacrifices. His son, Iophon, and his grandson, Sophocles, both gained distinction as tragic poets.

Besides lyrics, elegies, and epigrams, Sophocles is said to have composed upward of one hundred and twenty plays, one hundred of which are known by name, but only seven have come down to us entire. These are the "Trachiniæ," dealing with the death of Heracles; "Ajax," "Philoctetes," "Electra," "Œdipus Rex," "Œdipus at Colonus," and Antigone."

The development of tragedy by Æschylus was continued by Sophocles, who introduced a third actor and, later, a fourth; reduced still further the importance of the chorus, and elaborated the costumes of the players. He did not, like Æschylus, write trilogies which carried one story through three plays, but made each work complete in itself. The art of clear and full characterization was carried to a pitch of perfection by him, the figures in the plays of Æschylus being in comparison rather drawings in outline, while those of Euripides are frequently direct transcripts from real life, without the idealization given by Sophocles. With his restraint, his balance, his clearness of vision, his aptness in the fitting of means to ends, and the beauty of his style, he stands as the most perfect example in literature of the characteristic excellences of the Greek artist. In the two dramas here given will be found illustrations of these qualities at their highest.

ŒDIPUS THE KING
OF SOPHOCLES

DRAMATIS PERSONÆ

Œdipus, *King of* Thebes
Creon, *brother of* Jocasta
Teiresias, *a soothsayer*
Priest *of* Zeus
Messenger *from* Corinth
Shepherd
Second Messenger
Jocasta, *wife of* Œdipus

Chorus of Priests and Suppliants

Scene—Thebes. *In the background, the palace of* Œdipus; *in front, the altar of* Zeus, *Priests and Boys round it in the attitude of suppliants.*

Enter Œdipus

Œdipus

WHY sit ye here, my children, brood last reared
Of Cadmus famed of old, in solemn state,
Uplifting in your hands the suppliants' boughs?
And all the city reeks with incense smoke,
And all re-echoes with your wailing hymns;
And I, my children, counting it unmeet
To hear report from others, I have come
Myself, whom all name Œdipus the Great.—
Do thou, then, agèd Sire, since thine the right
To speak for these, tell clearly why ye stand
Awe-stricken, or adoring; speak to me
As willing helper. Dull and cold this heart
To see you prostrate thus, and feel no ruth.
   Priest. Yes, Œdipus, thou ruler of my land,
Thou seest us how we sit, as suppliants, bowed
Around thine altars; some as yet unfledged
To wing their flight, and some weighed down with age.
Priest, I, of Zeus, and these the chosen youth:
And in the open spaces of the town

The people sit and wail, with wreath in hand,
By the twin shrine of Pallas, or the grove
Oracular that bears Ismenus' name.
For this our city, as thine eyes may see,
Is sorely tempest-tossed, nor lifts its head
From out the surging sea of blood-flecked waves,
All smitten in the fruitful blooms of earth,
All smitten in the herds that graze the fields,
Yea, and in timeless births of woman's fruit;
And still the God sends forth his darts of fire,
And lays us low. The plague, abhorred and feared,
Makes desolate the home where Cadmus dwelt,
And Hades dark grows rich in sighs and groans.
It is not that we count thee as a God,
Equalled with them in power, that we sit here,
These little ones and I, as suppliants prone;
But, judging thee, in all life's shifting scenes,
Chiefest of men, yea, and of chiefest skill,
To soothe the powers of Heaven. For thou it was
That freed'st this city, named of Cadmus old,
From the sad tribute which of yore we paid
To that stern songstress, all untaught of us,
And all unprompted; but at God's behest,
Men think and say, thou guidest all our life.
And now, O Œdipus, most honoured lord,
We pray thee, we, thy suppliants, find for us
Some succour, whether floating voice of God,
Or speech of man brings knowledge to thy soul;
For still I see, with those whom life has trained
To long-tried skill, the issues of their thoughts
Live and are mighty. Come, then, noblest one,
Come, save our city; look on us, and fear.
As yet this land, for all thy former zeal,
Calls thee its saviour: do not give us cause
So to remember this thy reign, as men
Who, having risen, then fall low again;
But save us, save our city. Omens good

Were then with thee; thou didst thy work, and now
Be equal to thyself! If thou wilt rule,
As thou dost rule, this land wherein we dwell,
'Twere better far to reign o'er living men
Than o'er a realm dispeopled. Naught avails,
Or tower or ship, when crew and guards are gone.
 Œdip. O children, wailing loud, ye tell me not
Of woes unknown; too well I know them all,
Your sorrows and your wants. For one and all
Are stricken, yet no sorrow like to mine
Weighs on you. Each his own sad burden bears,
His own and not another's. But my heart
Mourns for the people's sorrow and mine own;
And, lo! ye have not come to break my sleep,
But found me weeping, weeping bitter tears,
And treading weary paths in wandering thought;
And that one way of healing which I found,
That have I acted on. Menœkeus' son,
Creon, my kinsman, have I sent to seek
The Pythian home of Phœbus, there to learn
The words or deeds wherewith to save the state;
And even now I measure o'er the time
And wonder how he fares, for, lo! he stays,
I know not why, beyond the appointed day;
But when he comes I should be base indeed,
Failing to do whate'er the God declares.
 Priest. Well hast thou spoken! Tidings come e'en now
Of Creon seen approaching.
 Œdip.   Grant, O King
Apollo, that he come with omen good,
Bright with the cheer of one that bringeth life.
 Priest. If one may guess, 'tis well. He had not come
His head all wreathed with boughs of laurel else.
 Œdip. Soon we shall know. Our voice can reach him
   now.
Say, prince, our well-beloved, Menœkeus' son,
What sacred answer bring'st thou from the God?

Enter CREON

Creon. A right good answer! That our evil plight,
If all goes well, may end in highest good.
  Œdip. What means this speech? Nor full of eager hope,
Nor trembling panic, list I to thy words.
  Creon. I for my part am ready, these being by,
To tell thee all, or go within the gates.
  Œdip. Speak out to all. I sorrow more for them
Than for the woe which touches me alone.
  Creon. Well, then, I speak the things the God declared.
Phœbus, our king, he bids us chase away
(The words were plain) the infection of our land,
Nor cherish guilt which still remains unhealed.
  Œdip. But with what rites? And what the deed itself?
  Creon. Drive into exile, blood for blood repay.
That guilt of blood is blasting all the state.
  Œdip. But whose fate is it that thou hintest at?
  Creon. Once, O my king, ere thou didst raise our state,
Our sovereign Laius ruled o'er all the land.
  Œdip. This know I well, though him I never saw.
  Creon. Well, then, the God commands us, he being dead,
To take revenge on those who shed his blood.
  Œdip. Yes; but where are they? How to track the course
Of guilt all shrouded in the doubtful past?
  Creon. In this our land, so said he, those who seek
Shall find; unsought, we lose it utterly.
  Œdip. Was it at home, or in the field, or else
In some strange land that Laius met his doom?
  Creon. He went, so spake he, pilgrim-wise afar,
And nevermore came back as forth he went.
  Œdip. Was there no courier, none who shared his road,
From whom, inquiring, one might learn the truth?
  Creon. Dead are they all, save one who fled for fear,
And he had naught to tell but this: . . .
  Œdip. [*interrupting*] And what was that? One fact might
      teach us much,

Had we but one small starting-point of hope.
  Creon. He used to tell that robbers fell on him,
Not man for man, but with outnumbering force.
  Œdip. Yet sure no robber would have dared this deed,
Unless some bribe had tempted him from hence.
  Creon. So men might think; but Laius at his death
Found none to help, or 'venge him in his woe.
  Œdip. What hindered you, when thus your sovereignty
Had fallen low, from searching out the truth?
  Creon. The Sphinx, with her dark riddle, bade us look
At nearer facts, and leave the dim obscure.
  Œdip. Well, be it mine to track them to their source.
Right well hath Phœbus, and right well hast thou,
Shown for the dead your care, and ye shall find,
As is most meet, in me a helper true,
Aiding at once my country and the God.
Not for the sake of friends, or near or far,
But for mine own, will I dispel this curse;
For he that slew him, whosoe'er he be,
Will wish, perchance, with such a blow to smite
Me also. Helping him, I help myself.
And now, my children, rise with utmost speed
From off these steps, and raise your suppliant boughs;
And let another call my people here,
The race of Cadmus, and make known that I
Will do my taskwork to the uttermost:
So, as God wills, we prosper, or we fail.
  Priest. Rise, then, my children, 'twas for this we came,
For these good tidings which those lips have brought,
And Phœbus, he who sent these oracles,
Pray that he come to heal, and save from woe.

             [*Exeunt* CREON *and* Priest.

Strophe I

  Chorus. O voice of Zeus sweet-toned, with what intent
Cam'st thou from Pytho, where the red gold shines,
        To Thebes, of high estate?

Fainting for fear, I quiver in suspense
(Hear us, O healer! God of Delos, hear!),
In brooding dread, what doom, of present growth,
Or as the months roll on, thy hand will work;
Tell me, O Voice divine, thou child of golden hope!

Antistrophe I

Thee first, Zeus-born Athene, thee I call;
And next thy sister, Goddess of our land,
Our Artemis, who in the market sits
In queenly pride, upon her orbèd throne;
And Phœbus, the fair darter! O ye Three,
Shine on us, and deliver us from ill!
If e'er before, when waves or storms of woe
    Rushed on our state, ye drove away
    The fiery tide of ill,
    Come also now!

Strophe II

Yea, come, ye Gods, for sorrows numberless
    Press on my soul;
And all the host is smitten, and our thoughts
    Lack weapons to resist.
For increase fails of all the fruits of earth,
And women faint in childbirth's wailing pangs,
And one by one, as flit the swift-winged birds,
So, flitting to the shore of Hades dark,
    Fleeter than lightning's flash,
    Thou seest them passing on.

Antistrophe II

Yea, numberless are they who perish thus,
    And on the soil, plague-breeding, lie
Infants unpitied, cast out ruthlessly;
And wives and mothers, gray with hoary age,
Some here, some there, by every altar mourn,
    With woe and sorrow crushed,
    And chant their wailing plaint.

Clear thrills the sense their solemn litany,
And the low anthem sung in unison.
Hear, then, thou golden daughter of great Zeus,
And send us help, bright-faced as is the morn.

Strophe III

And Ares the destroyer drive away!
Who now, though hushed the din of brazen shield,
With battle-cry wars on me fierce and hot.
>Bid him go back in flight,
>Retreat from this our land,
>Or to the ocean bed,
>Where Amphitrite sleeps,
>Or to that homeless sea
>Which sweeps the Thracian shore.
>If waning night spares aught
>That doth the day assail:
>Do thou, then, Sire almighty,
>Wielding the lightning's strength,
>Blast him with thy hot thunder.

Antistrophe III

And thou, Lyceian king, the wolf's dread foe,
>Fain would I see thy darts
>From out thy golden bow
>Go forth invincible,
>Helping and bringing aid;
>And with them, winged with fire,
>The rays of Artemis,
>With which, on Lycian hills,
>She moveth on her course.
>And last I call on thee,
>Thou of the golden crown,
>Guardian of this our land,
>Bacchus, all purple-flushed,
>With clamour loud and long,
>Wandering with Mænads wild;

I call on thee to come,
Flashing with blazing torch,
Against the God whom all the Gods disown.

Œdip. Thou prayest, and for thy prayers, if thou wilt hear
My words, and treat the dire disease with skill,
Thou shalt find help and respite from thy pain,—
My words, which I, a stranger to report,
A stranger to the deed, will now declare:
For I myself should fail to track it far,
Unless some footprints guided me aright.
But now, since here I stand, the latest come,
A citizen to citizens, I speak
To all the sons of Cadmus. Lives there one
Who knows of Laius, son of Labdacus,
The hand that slew him; him I bid to tell
His tale to me; and should it chance he shrinks,
Fearing the charge against himself to bring,
Still let him speak; no heavier doom is his
Than to depart uninjured from the land;
Or, if there be that knows an alien arm
As guilty, let him hold his peace no more;
I will secure his gain and thanks beside.
But if ye hold your peace, if one through fear
Shall stifle words his bosom friend may drop,
What then I purpose let him hear from me:
That man I banish, whosoe'er he be,
From out the land whose power and throne are mine;
And none may give him shelter, none speak to him,
Nor join with him in prayer and sacrifice,
Nor pour for him the stream that cleanses guilt;
But all shall thrust him from their homes, abhorred,
Our curse and our pollution, as the word
Prophetic of the Pythian God has shown:
Such as I am, I stand before you here,
A helper to the God and to the dead.
And for the man who did the guilty deed,
Whether alone he lurks, or leagued with more,

I pray that he may waste his life away,
For vile deeds vilely dying; and for me,
If in my house, I knowing it, he dwells,
May every curse I speak on my head fall.
And this I charge you do, for mine own sake,
And for the God's, and for the land that pines,
Barren and god-deserted. Wrong 'twould be,
E'en if no voice from heaven had urged us on,
That ye should leave the stain of guilt uncleansed,
Your noblest chief, your king himself, being slain.
Yea, rather, seek and find. And since I reign,
Wielding the might his hand did wield before,
Filling his couch, and calling his wife mine,
Yea, and our children too, but for the fate
That fell on his, had grown up owned by both;
But so it is. On his head fell the doom;
And therefore will I strive my best for him,
As for my father, and will go all lengths
To seek and find the murderer, him who slew
The son of Labdacus, and Polydore,
And earlier Cadmus, and Agenor old;
And for all those who hearken not, I pray
The Gods to give them neither fruit of earth,
Nor seed of woman, but consume their lives
With this dire plague, or evil worse than this.
And you, the rest, the men from Cadmus sprung,
To whom these words approve themselves as good,
May righteousness befriend you, and the Gods,
In full accord, dwell with you evermore.

Chorus. Since thou hast bound me by a curse, O king,
I needs must speak. I neither slew the man,
Nor know who slew. To say who did the deed
Belongs to him who sent this oracle.

Œdip. Right well thou speak'st, but man's best strength must fail
To force the Gods to do the things they will not.

Chorus. And may I speak a second time my thoughts?

Œdip. If 'twere a third, shrink not from speaking out.
Chorus. One man I know, a prince, whose insight deep
Sees clear as princely Phœbus, and from him,
Teiresias, one might learn, O king, the truth.
Œdip. That, too, is done. No loiterer I in this,
For I have sent, on Creon's hint, two bands
To summon him, and wonder that he comes not.
Chorus. Old rumours are there also, dark and dumb.
Œdip. And what are they? I weigh the slightest word.
Chorus. 'Twas said he died by some chance traveller's hand.
Œdip. I, too, heard that. But none knows who was by.
Chorus. If yet his soul is capable of awe,
Hearing thy curses, he will shrink from them.
Œdip. Words fright not him who, doing, knows no fear.
Chorus. Well, here is one who'll put him to the proof.
For, lo! they bring the seer inspired of God;
Chosen of all men, vessel of the truth.

Enter TEIRESIAS, *blind, and guided by a boy*

Œdip. Teiresias! thou whose mind embraceth all,
Told or untold, the things of heaven or earth;
Thou knowest, although thou seest not, what a pest
Dwells on us, and we find in thee, O prince,
Our one deliverer, yea, our only help.
For Phœbus (if, perchance, thou hast not heard)
Sent back this word to us, who sent to ask,
That this one way was open to escape
From the fell plague; if those who Laius slew,
We in our turn, discovering, should slay,
Or drive them forth as exiles from the land.
Thou, therefore, grudge not either sign from birds,
Or any other path of prophecy;
But save the city, save thyself, save me;
Lift off the guilt that death has left behind;
On thee we hang. To use our means, our power,
In doing good, is noblest service owned.

Teir. Ah me! ah me! how sad is wisdom's gift,
When no good issue waiteth on the wise!
Right well I knew this, but in evil hour
Forgot, alas! or else I had not come.
 Œdip. What means this? How despondingly thou com'st!
 Teir. Let me go home; for thus thy fate shalt thou,
And I mine own, bear easiest, if thou yield.
 Œdip. No loyal words thou speak'st, nor true to Thebes
Who reared thee, holding back this oracle.
 Teir. It is because I see thy lips speak words
Ill-timed, ill-omened, that I guard my speech.
 Œdip. Now, by the Gods, unless thy reason fails,
Refuse us not, who all implore thy help.
 Teir. Yes. Reason fails you all; but ne'er will I
So speak my sorrows as to unveil thine.
 Œdip. What mean'st thou, then? Thou know'st and wilt not tell,
But giv'st to ruin both the state and us?
 Teir. I will not pain myself nor thee. Why, then,
All vainly urge it? Thou shalt never know.
 Œdip. Oh, basest of the base! (for thou wouldst stir
A heart of stone;) and wilt thou never tell,
But still abide relentless and unmoved?
 Teir. My mood thou blamest, but thou dost not know
That which dwells with thee while thou chidest me.
 Œdip. And who would not feel anger, as he hears
The words which bring dishonour to the state?
 Teir. Well! come they will, though I should hold my peace.
 Œdip. If come they must, thy duty is to speak.
 Teir. I speak no more. So, if thou wilt, rage on,
With every mood of wrath most desperate.
 Œdip. Yes; I will not refrain, so fierce my wrath,
From speaking all my thought. I think that thou
Didst plot the deed, and do it, though the blow
Thy hands, it may be, dealt not. Hadst thou seen,
I would have said it was thy deed alone.

Teir. And it has come to this? I charge thee, hold
To thy late edict, and from this day forth
Speak not to me, nor yet to these, for thou,
Thou art the accursèd plague-spot of the land.
　Œdip. Art thou so shameless as to vent such words,
And thinkest to escape thy righteous doom?
　Teir. I have escaped. The strength of truth is mine.
　Œdip. Who prompted thee? This comes not from thine art.
　Teir. Thou art the man. 'Twas thou who mad'st me speak.
　Œdip. What say'st thou? Tell it yet again, that I
May know more clearly.
　Teir. 　　　　　When I spoke before,
Didst thou not know? Or dost thou challenge me?
　Œdip. I could not say I knew it. Speak again.
　Teir. I say that thou stand'st there a murderer.
　Œdip. Thou shalt not twice revile, and go unharmed.
　Teir. And shall I tell thee more to stir thy rage?
　Œdip. Say what thou pleasest. All in vain 'tis said.
　Teir. I say that thou, in vilest intercourse
With those thou lovest best, dost blindly live,
Nor seest the evil thou hast made thine own.
　Œdip. And dost thou think to say these things and live?
　Teir. Of that I doubt not, if truth holds her own.
　Œdip. Truth is for all but thee, but thou hast none,
Blind in thine ears, thy reason, and thine eyes.
　Teir. How wretched thou, thus hurling this reproach!
Such, all too soon, the world will hurl at thee.
　Œdip. Thou livest wrapt in one continual night,
And canst not hurt or me, or any man
Who sees the light.
　Teir. 　　　　Fate's firm decree stands fixed:
Thou diest not by me. Apollo's might
Suffices. His the task to bring thee low.
　Œdip. Are these devices Creon's or thine own?
　Teir. It is not Creon harms thee, but thyself.

Œdip. O wealth, and sovereignty, and noblest skill
Surpassing skill in life that men admire,
How great the envy dogging all your steps!
If for the sake of kingship, which the state
Hath given, unasked for, freely in mine hands,
Creon the faithful, found mine earliest friend,
Now seeks with masked attack to drive me forth,
And hires this wizard, plotter of foul schemes,
A vagrant mountebank, whose sight is clear
For pay alone, but in his art stone-blind.
Is it not so? When wast thou known a seer?
Why, when the monster with her song was here,
Didst thou not give our countrymen thy help?
And yet the riddle lay above the ken
Of common men, and called for prophet's skill.
And this thou show'dst thou hadst not, nor by bird,
Nor any God made known; but then I came,
I, Œdipus, who nothing knew, and slew her,
With mine own counsel winning, all untaught
By flight of birds. And now thou wouldst expel me,
And think'st to take thy stand by Creon's throne.
But, as I think, both thou and he that plans
With thee, will to your cost attack my fame;
And but that thou stand'st there all old and weak,
Thou shouldst be taught what kind of plans are thine.

Chorus. Far as we dare to measure, both his words
And thine, O Œdipus, in wrath are said.
Not such as these we need, but this to see,
How best to do the bidding of the God.

Teir. King though thou be, I claim an equal right
To make reply. Here I call no man lord:
For I am not thy slave, but Loxias'.
Nor shall I stand on Creon's patronage;
And this I say, since thou hast dared revile
My blindness, that thou seest, yet dost not see
Thy evil plight, nor where thou liv'st, nor yet
With whom thou dwellest. Know'st thou even this,

Whence thou art sprung? All ignorant thou sinn'st
Against thine own, the living and the dead.
And soon a curse from mother and from sire
With fearful foot shall chase thee forth from us,
Now seeing all things clear, then all things dark.
And will not then each shore repeat thy wail,
And will not old Kithæron echoing ring
When thou discern'st the marriage, fatal port,
To which thy prosp'rous voyage brought thy bark?
And other ills, in countless multitude,
Thou seest not yet, on thee and on thy seed
Shall fall alike. Vent forth thy wrath then loud,
On Creon and on me. There lives not man
Who wastes his life more wretchedly than thou.

Œdip. This can be borne no longer! Out with thee!
A curse light on thee! Wilt thou not depart?
Wilt thou not turn and wend thy backward way?

Teir. I had not come hadst thou not called me here.

Œdip. I knew not thou wouldst speak so foolishly;
Else I had hardly fetched thee to my house.

Teir. We then, for thee (so deemest thou), are fools,
But, for thy parents, who begot thee, wise. [*Turns to go.*

Œdip. [*starting forward*] What? Stay thy foot. What
    mortal gave me birth?

Teir. This day shall give thy birth, and work thy doom.

Œdip. What riddles dark and dim thou lov'st to speak.

Teir. Yes. But thy skill excels in solving such.

Œdip. Scoff as thou wilt, in this thou'lt find me strong.

Teir. And yet success in this has worked thy fall.

Œdip. I little care, if I have saved the state.

Teir. Well, then, I go. Do thou, boy, lead me on!

Œdip. Let him lead on. So hateful art thou near,
Thou canst not pain me more when thou art gone.

Teir. I go, then, having said the things I came
To say. No fear of thee compels me. Thine
Is not the power to hurt me. And I say,
This man whom thou art seeking out with threats,

As murderer of Laius, he is here,
In show an alien sojourner, but in truth
A home-born Theban. No delight to him
Will that discovery bring. Blind, having seen,
Poor, having rolled in wealth,—he, with a staff
Feeling his way, to other lands shall go!
And by his sons shall he be known at once
Father and brother, and of her who bore him
Husband and son, sharing his father's bed,
His father's murd'rer. Go thou, then, within,
And brood o'er this, and, if thou find'st me fail,
Say that my skill in prophecy is gone.

[*Exeunt* ŒDIPUS *and* TEIRESIAS.

STROPHE I

Chorus. Who was it that the rock oracular
    Of Delphi spake of, working
With bloody hand his nameless deed of shame?
    Time is it now for him,
    Swifter than fastest steed,
    To bend his course in flight.
    For, in full armour clad,
    Upon him darts, with fire
And lightning flash, the radiant Son of Zeus.
And with him come in train the dreaded ones,
The Destinies that may not be appeased.

ANTISTROPHE I

For from Parnassus' heights, enwreathed with snow,
    Gleaming, but now there shone
The oracle that bade us, one and all,
    Track the unnamed, unknown one.
For, lo! he wanders through the forest wild,
    In caves and over rocks,
    As strays the mountain bull,
In dreary loneliness with dreary tread,
    Seeking in vain to shun

The words prophetic of the central shrine;
Yet they around him hover, full of life.

Strophe II

Dread things, yea, dread, the augur skilled has stirred
That leave the question open, aye or no!
    And which to say I know not,
But hover still in hopes, and fail to scan
    Things present or to come.
For neither now nor in the former years
    Learnt I what cause of strife
    Set the Labdacid race
At variance with the house of Polybus.
    Nor can I test the tale,
And take my stand against the well-earned fame
    Of Œdipus, my lord,
As champion of the house of Labdacus,
    For deaths that none may trace!

Antistrophe II

For Zeus and King Apollo, they are wise,
    And know the hearts of men:
But that a prophet passeth me in skill,
    This is no judgment true;
And one man may another's wisdom pass,
    By wisdom higher still.
I, for my part, before the word is clear,
Will ne'er assent to those that speak in blame.
'Tis clear, the Maiden-monster with her wings
Came on him, and he proved by sharpest test
That he was wise, by all the land beloved,
    And, from my heart at least,
    The charge of baseness comes not.

Enter Creon

Creon. I come, my friends, as having learnt but now
Our ruler, Œdipus, accuses me

With dreadful words I cannot bear to hear.
For if, in these calamities of ours,
He thinks he suffers wrongly at my hands,
In word or deed, aught tending to his hurt,
I set no value on a life prolonged,
If this reproach hangs on me; for its harm
Affects not slightly, but is direst shame,
If through the land my name as villain rings,
By thee and by thy friends a villain called.

Chorus. But this reproach, it may be, came from wrath
All hasty, rather than from judgment calm.

Creon. And who informed him that the seer, seduced
By my false counsel, spoke his lying words?

Chorus. The words were said, but on what grounds I know
    not.

Creon. And was it with calm eyes and judgment clear,
The charge was brought against my name and fame?

Chorus. I cannot say. To what our rulers do
I close my eyes. But here he comes himself.

Enter ŒDIPUS

Œdip. Ho, there! is't thou? And does thy boldness soar
So shameless as to come beneath my roof,
When thou, 'tis clear, hast done the deed of blood,
And now wilt rob me of my sovereignty?
Is it, by all the Gods, that thou hast seen
Or cowardice or folly in my soul,
That thou hast laid thy plans? Or thoughtest thou
That I should neither see thy sinuous wiles,
Nor, knowing, ward them off? This scheme of thine,
Is it not wild, backed nor by force nor friends,
To seek the power which calls for force or wealth?

Creon. Do as thou pleasest. But for words of scorn
Hear like words back, and as thou hearest, judge.

Œdip. Cunning of speech art thou! But I am slow
To learn of thee, whom I have found my foe.

Creon. Hear this, then, first, that thus I have to speak. . . .

Œdip. But this, then, say not, that thou art not vile.
Creon. If that thou thinkest self-willed pride avails,
Apart from judgment, know thou art not wise.
Œdip. If that thou thinkest, injuring thy friend,
To do it unchastised, thou art not wise.
Creon. In this, I grant, thou speakest right; but tell,
What form of suffering hast thou to endure?
Œdip. Didst thou, or didst thou not, thy counsel give
Some one to send to fetch this reverend seer?
Creon. And even now by that advice I hold!
Œdip. How long a time has passed since Laius
    chanced . . .   [*Pauses.*
Creon. Chanced to do what? I understand not yet.
Œdip. Since he was smitten with the deadly blow?
Creon. The years would measure out a long, long tale.
Œdip. And was this seer then practising his art?
Creon. Full wise as now, and equal in repute.
Œdip. Did he at that time say a word of me?
Creon. No word, while I, at any rate, was by.
Œdip. And yet ye held your quest upon the dead?
Creon. Of course we held it, but we nothing heard.
Œdip. How was it he, the wise one, spoke not then?
Creon. I know not, and, not knowing, hold my peace.
Œdip. One thing thou know'st, and, meaning well, wouldst
    speak!
Creon. And what is that? for if I know, I'll speak.
Œdip. Why, unless thou wert in the secret, then
He spake not of me as the murderer.
Creon. If he says this, thou know'st it. I of thee
Desire to learn, as thou hast learnt of me.
Œdip. Learn then; no guilt of blood shall rest on me.
Creon. Well, then,—my sister? dost thou own her wife?
Œdip. I will not meet this question with denial.
Creon. And sharest thou an equal rule with her?
Œdip. Her every wish by me is brought to act.
Creon. And am not I coequal with you twain?
Œdip. Yes; and just here thou show'st thyself false friend.

Creon. Not so, if thou wouldst reason with thyself,
As I must reason. First reflect on this:
Supposest thou that one would rather choose
To reign with fears than sleeping calmest sleep,
His power being equal? I, for one, prize less
The name of king than deeds of kingly power;
And so would all who learn in wisdom's school.
Now without fear I have what I desire,
At thy hand given. Did I rule, myself,
I might do much unwillingly. Why, then,
Should sovereignty exert a softer charm
Than power and might unchequered by a care?
I am not yet so cheated by myself
As to desire aught else but honest gain.
Now all goes well, now every one salutes,
Now they who seek thy favour court my smiles,
For on this hinge does all their fortune turn.
Why, then, should I leave this to hunt for that?
My mind, retaining reason, ne'er could act
The villain's part. I was not born to love
Such thoughts myself, nor bear with those that do.
And as a proof of this, go thou thyself,
And ask at Pytho whether I brought back,
In very deed, the oracles I heard.
And if thou find me plotting with the seer,
In common concert, not by one decree,
But two, thine own and mine, proclaim my death.
But charge me not with crime on shadowy proof;
For neither is it just, in random thought,
The bad to count as good, nor good as bad;
For to thrust out a friend of noble heart,
Is like the parting with the life we love.
And this in time thou'lt know, for time alone
Makes manifest the righteous. Of the vile
Thou mayst detect the vileness in a day.
 Chorus. To one who fears to fall, he speaketh well;
O king, swift counsels are not always safe.

Œdip. But when a man is swift in wily schemes,
Swift must I be to baffle plot with plot;
And if I stand and wait, he wins the day,
And all my life is found one great mistake.

Creon. What seek'st thou, then? to drive me from the land?
Œdip. Not so. I seek not banishment, but death.
Creon. When thou show'st first what grudge I bear to thee?
Œdip. And say'st thou this defying, yielding not?
Creon. I see thy judgment fails.
Œdip.   I hold mine own.
Creon. Mine has an equal claim.
Œdip.   Thou villain born!
Creon. And if thy mind is darkened . . . ?
Œdip.   Still obey!
Creon. Not to a tyrant ruler.
Œdip.   O my country!
Creon. I, too, can claim that country. 'Tis not thine!
Chorus. Cease, O my princes! In good time I see
Jocasta coming hither from the house;
And it were well with her to hush this strife.

Enter JOCASTA

Joc. Why, O ye wretched ones, this strife of tongues
Raise ye in your unwisdom, nor are shamed,
Our country suffering, private griefs to stir?
Come thou within. And thou, O Creon, go,
Nor bring a trifling sore to mischief great!

Creon. My sister! Œdipus, thy husband, claims
The right to wrong me, giving choice of ills,
Or to be exiled from my home, or die.

Œdip. 'Tis even so, for I have found him, wife,
Against my life his evil wiles devising.

Creon. May I ne'er prosper, but accursèd die,
If I have done the things he says I did!

Joc. Oh, by the Gods, believe him, Œdipus!
Respect his oath, which calls the Gods to hear;
And reverence me, and these who stand by thee.
  Chorus. Hearken, my king! be calmer, I implore!
  Œdip. What! wilt thou that I yield?
  Chorus. Respect is due
To one not weak before, who now is strong
In this his oath.
  Œdip. And know'st thou what thou ask'st?
  Chorus. I know right well.
  Œdip. Say on, then, what thou wilt.
  Chorus. Hurl not to shame, on grounds of mere mistrust,
The friend on whom his own curse still must hang.
  Œdip. Know, then, that, seeking this, thou seek'st, in truth,
To work my death, or else my banishment.
  Chorus. Nay, by the sun, chief God of all the Gods!
May I, too, die, of God and man accursed,
If I wish aught like this! But on my soul,
Our wasting land dwells heavily; ills on ills
Still coming, and your strife embittering all.
  Œdip. Let him depart, then, even though I die,
Or from my country wander forth in shame:
Thy face, not his, I view with pitying eye;
For him, where'er he be, is naught but hate.
  Creon. Thou'rt loath to yield, 'twould seem, and wilt be vexed
When this thy wrath is over: moods like thine
Are fitly to themselves most hard to bear.
  Œdip. Wilt thou not go, and leave me?
  Creon. I will go,
By thee misjudged, but known as just by these.   [*Exit.*
  Chorus. Why, lady, art thou slow to lead him in?
  Joc. I fain would learn how this sad chance arose.
  Chorus. Blind hasty speech there was, and wrong will sting.
  Joc. From both of them?
  Chorus. Yea, both.

Joc. And what said each?
Chorus. Enough for me, our land laid low in grief,
It seems, to leave the quarrel where it stopped.
Œdip. Seest thou, with all thy purposes of good,
Thy shifting and thy soothing, what thou dost?
Chorus. My chief, not once alone I spoke,
    And wild and erring should I be,
    Were I to turn from thee aside,
    Who, when my country rocked in storm,
    Righted her course, and, if thou couldst,
    Wouldst send her speeding now.
Joc. Tell me, my king, what cause of fell debate
Has bred this discord, and provoked thy soul.
Œdip. Thee will I tell, for thee I honour more
Than these. The cause was Creon and his plots.
Joc. Say, then, if clearly thou canst tell the strife.
Œdip. He says that I am Laius' murderer.
Joc. Of his own knowledge, or by some one taught?
Œdip. Yon scoundrel seer suborning. For himself,
He takes good care to free his lips from blame.
Joc. Leave now thyself, and all thy thoughts of this,
And list to me, and learn how little skill
In arts prophetic mortal man may claim;
And of this truth I'll give thee proof full clear.
There came to Laius once an oracle
(I say not that it came from Phœbus' self,
But from his servants) that his fate was fixed
By his son's hand to fall—his own and mine:
And him, so rumour runs, a robber band
Of aliens slew, where meet the three great roads.
Nor did three days succeed the infant's birth,
Before, by other hands, he cast him forth,
Maiming his ankles, on a lonely hill.
Here, then, Apollo failed to make the boy
His father's murderer; nor did Laius die
By his son's hand. So fared the oracles;
Therefore regard them not. Whate'er the God

Desires to search he will himself declare.
  Œdip. [*trembling*] O what a fearful boding! thoughts dis-
     turbed
Thrill through my soul, my queen, at this thy tale.
  Joc. What means this shuddering, this averted glance?
  Œdip. I thought I heard thee say that Laius died,
Slain in a skirmish where the three roads meet?
  Joc. So was it said, and still the rumours hold.
  Œdip. Where was the spot in which this matter passed?
  Joc. They call the country Phocis, and the roads
From Delphi and from Daulia there converge.
  Œdip. And time? what interval has passed since then?
  Joc. But just before thou camest to possess
And rule this land the tidings were proclaimed.
  Œdip. Great Zeus! what fate hast thou decreed for me?
  Joc. What thought is this, my Œdipus, of thine?
  Œdip. Ask me not yet, but tell of Laius' frame,
His build, his features, and his years of life.
  Joc. Tall was he, and the white hairs snowed his head,
And in his face not much unlike to thee.
  Œdip. Woe, woe is me! so seems it I have plunged
All blindly into curses terrible.
  Joc. What sayest thou? I shudder as I see thee.
  Œdip. Desponding fear comes o'er me, lest the seer
Has seen indeed. But one thing more I'll ask.
  Joc. I fear to speak, yet what thou ask'st I'll tell.
  Œdip. Went he in humble guise, or with a troop
Of spearmen, as becomes a man that rules?
  Joc. Five were they altogether, and of them
One was a herald, and one chariot had he.
  Œdip. Woe! woe! 'tis all too clear. And who was he
That told these tidings to thee, O my queen?
  Joc. A servant who alone escaped with life.
  Œdip. And does he chance to dwell among us now?
  Joc. Not so; for from the time when he returned,
And found thee bearing sway, and Laius dead,
He, at my hand, a suppliant, implored

This boon, to send him to the distant fields
To feed his flocks, where never glance of his
Might Thebes behold. And so I sent him forth;
For though a slave he might have claimed yet more.
   Œdip. And could we fetch him quickly back again?
Joc. That may well be. But why dost thou wish this?
Œdip. I fear, O queen, that words best left unsaid
Have passed these lips, and therefore wish to see him.
   Joc. Well, he shall come. But some small claim have I,
O king, to learn what touches thee with woe.
   Œdip. Thou shalt not fail to learn it, now that I
Have such forebodings reached. To whom should I
More than to thee tell all the passing chance?
I had a father, Polybus of Corinth,
And Merope of Doris was my mother,
And I was held in honour by the rest
Who dwelt there, till this accident befel,
Worthy of wonder, of the heat unworthy
It roused within me. Thus it chanced: A man
At supper, in his cups, with wine o'ertaken,
Reviles me as a spurious changeling boy;
And I, sore vexèd, hardly for that day
Restrained myself. And when the morrow came
I went and charged my father and my mother
With what I thus had heard. They heaped reproach
On him who stirred the matter, and I soothed
My soul with what they told me; yet it teased,
Still vexing more and more; and so I went,
Unknown to them, to Pytho, and the God
Sent me forth shamed, unanswered in my quest;
And more he added, dread and dire and dark,
How that the doom of incest lay on me,
Most foul, unnatural; and that I should be
Father of children men would loathe to look on,
And murderer of the father that begot me.
And, hearing this, I cast my wistful looks
To where the stars hang over Corinth's towers,

And fled where nevermore mine eyes might see
The shame of those dire oracles fulfilled;
And as I went I reached the spot where he,
The king, thou tell'st me, met the fatal blow.
And now, O lady, I will tell thee all.
Wending my steps that way where three roads meet,
There met me first a herald, and a man
Like him thou told'st of, riding on his car,
Drawn by young colts. With rough and hasty words
They drove me from the road,—the driver first,
And that old man himself; and then in rage
I struck the driver, who had turned me back.
And when the old man saw it, watching me
As by the chariot side I stood, he struck
My forehead with a double-pointed goad.
But we were more than quits, for in a trice
With this right hand I struck him with my staff,
And he rolled backward from his chariot's seat.
And then I slew them all. And if it chance
That Laius and this stranger are akin,
What man more wretched than this man who speaks,
What man more harassed by the vexing Gods?
He whom none now, or alien, or of Thebes,
May welcome to their house, or speak to him,
But thrust him forth an exile. And 'twas I,
None other, who against myself proclaimed
These curses. And the bed of him that died
I with my hands, by which he fell, defile.
Am I not vile by nature, all unclean?
If I must flee, yet still in flight my doom
Is nevermore to see the friends I love,
Nor tread my country's soil; or else to bear
The guilt of incest, and my father slay,
Yea, Polybus, who reared me from the womb.
Would not a man say right who said that here
Some cruel God was pressing hard on me?
Not that, not that, at least, thou Presence, pure

And awful, of the Gods. May I ne'er look
On such a day as that, but far away
Depart unseen from all the haunts of men
Before such great pollution comes on me.

   Chorus. Us, too, O king, these things perplex, yet still,
Till thou hast asked the man who then was by,
Have hope.

   Œdip. And this indeed is all my hope,
Waiting until that shepherd-slave appear.

   Joc. And when he comes, what meanest thou to ask?

   Œdip. I'll tell thee. Should he now repeat the tale
Thou told'st to me, it frees me from this guilt.

   Joc. What special word was that thou heard'st from me?

   Œdip. Thou said'st he told that robbers slew his lord,
And should he give their number as the same
Now as before, it was not I who slew him,
For one man could not be the same as many.
But if he speak of one man, all alone,
Then, all too plain, the deed cleaves fast to me.

   Joc. But know, the thing was said, and clearly said,
And now he cannot from his word draw back.
Not I alone, but the whole city, heard it;
And should he now retract his former tale,
Not then, my husband, will he rightly show
The death of Laius, who, as Loxias told,
By my son's hand should die; and yet, poor boy,
He killed him not, but perished long ago.
So I for one, both now and evermore,
Will count all oracles as things of naught.

   Œdip. Thou reasonest well. Yet send a messenger
To fetch that peasant. Be not slack in this.

   Joc. I will make haste to send. But go thou in;
I would do nothing that displeaseth thee.   [*Exeunt.*

Strophe I

   Chorus. O that my fate were fixed
To live in holy purity of speech,

Pure in all deeds whose laws stand firm and high,
    In heaven's clear æther born,
Of whom Olympus only is the sire,
    Whom man's frail flesh begat not,
Nor ever shall forgetfulness o'erwhelm;
In them our God is great and grows not old.

Antistrophe I

But pride begets the mood of tyrant power;
Pride filled with many thoughts, yet filled in vain,
    Untimely, ill-advised,
    Scaling the topmost height,
    Falls down the steep abyss,
Down to the pit, where step that profiteth
    It seeks in vain to take.
I cannot ask the Gods to stop midway
The conflict sore that works our country's good;
I cannot cease to call on God for aid.

Strophe II

But if there be who walketh haughtily,
    In action or in speech,
Whom righteousness herself has ceased to awe,
Who counts the temples of the Gods profane,
    An evil fate be his,
Fit meed for all his boastfulness of heart;
Unless in time to come he gain his gains
All justly, and draws back from godless deeds,
Nor lays rash hand upon the holy things,
    By man inviolable.
If such deeds prosper who will henceforth pray
To guard his soul from passion's fiery darts?
If such as these are held in high repute,
What profit is there of my choral strain?

Antistrophe II

No longer will I go in pilgrim guise,
To yon all holy place, Earth's central shrine,

　　　　　Nor unto Abæ's temple,
　　　　　Nor to far-famed Olympia,
　　Unless these pointings of a hand divine
　　In sight of all men stand out clear and true.
　　But, O thou sovereign ruler! if that name,
　　O Zeus, belongs to thee, who reign'st o'er all,
　　Let not this trespass hide itself from thee,
　　　　　Or thine undying sway;
　　　　　For now they set at naught
　　　　　The oracles, half dead,
　　　　　That Laius heard of old,
　　And king Apollo's wonted worship flags,
　　　　　And all to wreck is gone
　　　　　The homage due to God.

　　　　Enter JOCASTA, *followed by an* Attendant

　　Joc. Princes of this our land, across my soul
There comes the thought to go from shrine to shrine
Of all the Gods, these garlands in my hand,
And waving incense; for our Œdipus
Vexes his soul too wildly with his woes,
And speaks not as a man should speak who scans
The present by the experience of the past,
But hangs on every breath that tells of fear.
And since I find that my advice avails not,
To thee, Lyceian King, Apollo, first
I come,—for thou art nearest,—suppliant
With these devotions, trusting thou wilt work
Some way of healing for us, free from guilt;
For now we shudder, all of us, seeing him,
The good ship's pilot, panic-struck and lost.

　　　　　　Enter Messenger

　　Mess. May I inquire of you, O strangers, where
To find the house of Œdipus the king,
And, above all, where he is, if ye know?

Chorus. This is the house, and he, good sir, within,
And this his wife, and mother of his children.
  Mess. Good fortune be with her and all her kin,
Being, as she is, his true and honoured wife.
  Joc. Like fortune be with thee, my friend. Thy speech,
So kind, deserves no less. But tell me why
Thou comest, what thou hast to ask or tell.
  Mess. Good news to thee, and to thy husband, lady.
  Joc. What is it, then? and who has sent thee here?
  Mess. I come from Corinth, and the news I'll tell
May give thee joy. Why not? Yet thou mayst grieve.
  Joc. What is the news that has this twofold power?
  Mess. The citizens that on the Isthmus dwell
Will make him sovereign. So the rumour ran.
  Joc. What then? Is agèd Polybus no more?
  Mess. E'en so. Death holds him in the stately tomb.
  Joc. What say'st thou? Polybus, thy king, is dead?
  Mess. If I speak false, I have no wish to live!
  Joc. Go, maiden, at thy topmost speed, and tell
Thy master this. Now, oracles of Gods,
Where are ye now? Long since my Œdipus
Fled, fearing lest his hand should slay the man;
And now he dies by fate, and not by him.

Enter ŒDIPUS

  Œdip. Mine own Jocasta, why, O dearest one,
Why hast thou sent to fetch me from the house?
  Joc. List this man's tale, and when thou hearest, see
The woeful plight of those dread oracles.
  Œdip. Who, then, is this, and what has he to tell?
  Joc. He comes from Corinth, and he brings thee word
That Polybus, thy father, lives no more.
  Œdip. What say'st thou, friend? Tell me thy tale thyself.
  Mess. If I must needs report the story clear,
Know well that he has gone the way of death.
  Œdip. Was it by plot, or chance of natural death?
  Mess. An old man's frame a little stroke lays low!

Œdip. He suffered, then, it seems, from some disease?
Mess. E'en so, and many a weary month he passed.
Œdip. Ha! ha! Why now, my queen, should we regard
The Pythian hearth oracular, or birds
In mid-air crying? By their auguries,
I was to slay my father. And he dies,
And the grave hides him; and I find myself
Handling no sword; unless for love of me
He pined away, and so I caused his death.
So Polybus is gone, and with him lie,
In Hades whelmed, those worthless oracles.
Joc. Did I not tell thee this long time ago?
Œdip. Thou didst, but I was led away by fears.
Joc. Dismiss them, then, for ever from thy thoughts!
Œdip. And yet that "incest"; must I not fear that?
Joc. Why should we fear, when chance rules everything,
And foresight of the future there is none;
'Tis best to live at random, as one can.
But thou, fear not that marriage with thy mother:
Such things men oft have dreams of; but who cares
The least about them lives the happiest.
Œdip. Right well thou speakest all things, save that she
Still lives that bore me, and I can but fear,
Seeing that she lives, although thou speakest well.
Joc. And yet thy father's grave's a spot of light.
Œdip. 'Tis so: yet while she liveth there is fear.
Mess. Who is this woman about whom ye fear?
Œdip. 'Tis Merope, old sir, who lived with Polybus.
Mess. And what leads you to think of her with fear?
Œdip. A fearful oracle, my friend, from God.
Mess. Canst tell it; or must others ask in vain?
Œdip. Most readily; for Loxias said of old
The doom of incest lay on me, and I
With mine own hands should spill my father's blood.
And therefore Corinth long ago I left,
And journeyed far, right prosperously I own;—
And yet 'tis sweet to see a parent's face.

Mess. And did this fear thy steps to exile lead?
Œdip. I did not wish to take my father's life.
Mess. Why, then, O king, did I who came with good
Not free thee from this fear that haunts thy soul?
Œdip. For this, I own, I owe thee worthy thanks.
Mess. For this, *I* own, I chiefly came to thee;
That I on thy return may prosper well.
Œdip. But I return not while a parent lives.
Mess. 'Tis clear, my son, thou know'st not what thou dost.
Œdip. What is't? By all the Gods, old man, speak out.
Mess. If 'tis for them thou fearest to return . . .
Œdip. I fear lest Phœbus prove himself too true.
Mess. Is it lest thou shouldst stain thy soul through them?
Œdip. This selfsame fear, old man, for ever haunts me.
Mess. And know'st thou not there is no cause for fear?
Œdip. Is there no cause if I was born their son?
Mess. None is there. Polybus is naught to thee.
Œdip. What say'st thou? Did not Polybus beget me?
Mess. No more than he thou speak'st to; just as much.
Œdip. How could a father's claim become as naught?
Mess. Well, neither he begat thee nor did I.
Œdip. Why, then, did he acknowledge me as his?
Mess. He at my hands received thee as a gift.
Œdip. And could he love another's child so much?
Mess. Yes; for his former childlessness wrought on him.
Œdip. And gav'st thou me as buying or as finding?
Mess. I found thee in Kithæron's shrub-grown hollow.
Œdip. And for what cause didst travel thitherwards?
Mess. I had the charge to tend the mountain flocks.
Œdip. Wast thou a shepherd born, or seeking hire?
Mess. At any rate, my son, I saved thee then.
Œdip. What evil plight, then, didst thou find me in?
Mess. The sinews of thy feet would tell that tale.
Œdip. Ah, me! why speak'st thou of that ancient wrong?
Mess. I freed thee when thy insteps both were pierced.
Œdip. A foul disgrace I had in swaddling clothes.

Mess. Thus from this chance there came the name thou bearest.

Œdip. [*starting*] Who gave the name, my father or my mother;
In heaven's name tell me?

Mess. This I do not know;
Who gave thee to me better knows than I.

Œdip. Didst thou, then, take me from another's hand,
Not finding me thyself?

Mess. Not I, indeed;
Another shepherd made a gift of thee.

Œdip. Who was he? know'st thou where to find him out?

Mess. They called him one of those that Laius owned.

Œdip. Mean'st thou the former sovereign of this land?

Mess. E'en so. He fed the flocks of him thou nam'st.

Œdip. And is he living still that I might see him?

Mess. You, his own countrymen, should know that best.

Œdip. Is there of you who stand and listen here
One who has known the shepherd that he tells of,
Or seeing him upon the hills or here?
If so, declare it; 'tis full time to speak!

Chorus. I think that this is he whom from the hills
But now thou soughtest. But Jocasta here
Could tell thee this with surer word than I.

Œdip. Knowest thou, my queen, the man whom late we sent
To fetch; and him of whom this stranger speaks?

Joc. [*with forced calmness*] Whom did he speak of? Care not thou for it,
But wish his words may be but idle tales.

Œdip. I cannot fail, once getting on the scent,
To track at last the secret of my birth.

Joc. Ah, by the Gods, if that thou valuest life
Inquire no further. Let my woe suffice.

Œdip. Take heart; though I should turn out thrice a slave,
Born of a thrice vile mother, thou art still
Free from all stain.

Joc.   Yet, I implore thee, pause!
Yield to my counsels, do not do this deed.
  Œdip. I may not yield, and fail to search it out.
  Joc. And yet good counsels give I, for thy good.
  Œdip. This "for my good" has been my life's long plague.
  Joc. Who thou art, hapless, mayst thou never know!
  Œdip. Will some one bring that shepherd to me here?
Leave her to glory in her high descent.
  Joc. Woe! woe! ill-fated one! my last word this,
This only, and no more for evermore.   [*Rushes out.*
  Chorus. Why has thy queen, O Œdipus, gone forth
In her wild sorrow rushing. Much I fear
Lest from such silence evil deeds burst out.
  Œdip. Burst out what will, I seek to know my birth,
Low though it be, and she perhaps is shamed
(For, like a woman, she is proud of heart)
At thoughts of my low birth; but I, who count
Myself the child of Fortune, fear no shame.
My mother she, and she has prospered me.
And so the months that span my life have made me
Both high and low; but whatsoe'er I be,
Such as I am I am, and needs must on
To fathom all the secret of my birth.

Strophe

  Chorus. If the seer's gift be mine,
      Or skill in counsel wise,
Thou, O Kithæron, when the morrow comes,
      Our full-moon festival,
      Shalt fail not to resound
The voice that greets thee, fellow-citizen,
      Parent and nurse of Œdipus;
And we will on thee weave our choral dance,
As bringing to our princes glad good news.
Hail, hail! O Phœbus, smile on this our prayer.

Antistrophe

Who was it, child, that bore thee?
Blest daughter of the ever-living Ones,
Or meeting in the ties of love with Pan,
    Who wanders o'er the hills,
Or with thee, Loxias, for to thee are dear
All the high lawns where roam the pasturing flocks;
Or was it he who rules Kyllene's height;
    Or did the Bacchic God,
    Upon the mountain's peak,
Receive thee as the gift of some fair nymph
    Of Helicon's fair band,
With whom he sports and wantons evermore?

Œdip. If I must needs conjecture, who as yet
Ne'er met the man, I think I see the shepherd,
Whom this long while we sought for. With the years
His age fits well. And now I see, besides,
My servants bring him. Thou perchance canst say
From former knowledge yet more certainly.

Chorus. I know him well, O king! For this man stood,
If any, known as Laius' faithful slave.

Enter Shepherd

Œdip. Thee first I ask, Corinthian stranger, say,
Is this the man?

Mess.   The very man thou seek'st.

Œdip. Ho, there, old man. Come hither, look on me,
And tell me all. Did Laius own thee once?

Shep. Not as a slave from market, but home-reared.

Œdip. What was thy work, or what thy mode of life?

Shep. Near all my life I followed with the flock.

Œdip. And in what regions didst thou chiefly dwell?

Shep. Now 'twas Kithæron, now on neighbouring fields.

Œdip. Know'st thou this man? Didst ever see him
    there?

Shep. What did he do? Of what man speakest thou?

Œdip. This man now present. Did ye ever meet?
Shep. My memory fails when taxed thus suddenly.
Mess. No wonder that, my lord. But I'll remind him
Right well of things forgotten. Well I know
He'll call to mind when on Kithæron's fields,
He with a double flock, and I with one,
I was his neighbour during three half years,
From springtide on to autumn; and in winter
I drove my flocks to mine own fold, and he
To those of Laius. [*To* SHEPHERD] Is this false or true?
  Shep. Thou tell'st the truth, although long years have passed.
Mess. Come, then, say on. Rememberest thou a boy
Thou gav'st me once, that I might rear him up
As mine own child?
  Shep.   Why askest thou of this?
Mess. Here stands he, fellow! that same tiny boy!
Shep. A curse befall thee! Wilt not hold thy tongue?
Œdip. Rebuke him not, old man; thy words need more
The language of reproaches than do his.
  Shep. Say, good my lord, what fault have I committed?
Œdip. This, that thou tell'st not of the child he asks for.
Shep. Yes, for he speaks in blindness, wasting breath.
Œdip. Thou wilt not speak for favour, but a blow . . .

                                  [*Strikes him.*
Shep. By all the Gods, hurt not my feeble age.
Œdip. Will no one bind his hands behind his back?
Shep. O man most wretched! what, then, wilt thou learn?
Œdip. Gav'st thou this man the boy of whom he asks?
Shep. I gave him. Would that day had been my last!
Œdip. That doom will soon be thine if thou speak'st wrong.
Shep. Nay, much more shall I perish if I speak.
Œdip. This fellow, as it seems, would tire us out.
Shep. Not so. I said long since I gave it him.
Œdip. Whence came it? Was the child thine own or not?

Shep. Mine own 'twas not, but some one gave it me.
Œdip. Which of our people, or beneath what roof?
Shep. Oh, by the Gods, my master, ask no more!
Œdip. Thou diest if I question this again.
Shep. Some one it was in Laius' household born.
Œdip. Was it a slave, or some one born to him?
Shep. Ah, me! I stand upon the very brink
Where most I dread to speak.
    Œdip.   And I to hear:
And yet I needs must hear it, come what may.
    Shep. The boy was said to be his son; but she,
Thy queen within, could tell thee best the truth.
    Œdip. What! was it she who gave it?
    Shep.   Yea, O king!
    Œdip. And to what end?
    Shep.   To make away with it.
    Œdip. And dared a mother . . . ?
    Shep.   Evil doom she feared.
    Œdip. What doom?
    Shep.   'Twas said that he his sire should kill.
    Œdip. Why, then, didst thou to this old man resign him?
    Shep. I pitied him, O master, and I thought
That he would bear him to another land,
Whence he himself had come. But him he saved
For direst evil. For if thou be he
Whom this man speaks of, thou art born to ill.
    Œdip. Woe! woe! woe! woe! all cometh clear at last.
O light, may I ne'er look on thee again,
Who now am seen owing my birth to those
To whom I ought not, and with whom I ought not
In wedlock living, whom I ought not slaying.   [*Exit.*

Strophe I

    Chorus. Ah, race of mortal men,
        How as a thing of naught
        I count ye, though ye live;
        For who is there of men

That more of blessing knows
Than just a little while
In a vain show to stand,
And, having stood, to fall?
With thee before mine eyes,
Thy destiny, e'en thine,
Ill-fated Œdipus,
I can count no man blest.

Antistrophe I

For thou, with wondrous skill,
Taking thine aim, didst hit
Success, in all things prosperous;
And didst, O Zeus! destroy
The Virgin with her talons bent,
And sayings wild and dark;
And against many deaths
A tower and strong defence
Didst for my country rise;
And therefore dost thou bear the name of king,
With highest glory crowned,
Ruling in mighty Thebes.

Strophe II

And now, who lives than thou more miserable?
Who equals thee in wild woes manifold,
In shifting turns of life?
Ah, noble one, our Œdipus!
For whom the selfsame port
Sufficed for sire and son,
In wedlock's haven met:
Ah how, ah how, thou wretched one, so long
Could that incestuous bed
Receive thee, and be dumb?

Antistrophe II

Time, who sees all things, he hath found thee out,
Against thy will, and long ago condemned

>   The wedlock none may wed,
>   Begetter and begotten
>   In strange confusion joined.
>   Ah, child of Laius! ah!
>   Would that I ne'er had looked upon thy face!
>   For I mourn sore exceedingly,
>   From lips with wailing full.
>   In simplest truth, by thee I rose from death,
>   By thee I close mine eyes in deadly sleep.

Enter Second Messenger

Sec. Mess. Ye chieftains, honoured most in this our land,
For all the deeds ye hear of, all ye see,
How great a wailing will ye raise, if still
Ye truly love the house of Labdacus;
For sure I think that neither Ister's stream
Nor Phasis' floods could purify this house,
Such horrors does it hold. But all too soon,
Will we or will we not, they'll come to light.
Self-chosen sorrows ever pain men most.
  Chorus. The ills we knew before lacked nothing meet
For plaint and moaning. Now, what add'st thou more?
  Sec. Mess. Quickest for me to speak, and thee to learn;
Our godlike queen Jocasta—she is dead.
  Chorus. Ah, crushed with many sorrows! How and why?
  Sec. Mess. Herself she slew. The worst of all that passed
I must pass o'er, for none were there to see.
Yet, far as memory suffers me to speak,
That sorrow-stricken woman's end I'll tell;
How, yielding to her passion, on she passed
Within the porch, made straightway for the couch,
Her bridal bed, with both hands tore her hair,
And as she entered, dashing through the doors,
Calls on her Laius, dead long years ago,
Remembering all that birth of long ago,
Which brought him death, and left to her who bore,
With his own son a hateful motherhood.

And o'er her bed she wailed, where she had borne
Spouse to her spouse, and children to her child;
And how she perished after this I know not;
For Œdipus struck in with woeful cry,
And we no longer looked upon her fate,
But gazed on him as to and fro he rushed,
For so he comes, and asks us for a sword,
Wherewith to smite the wife that wife was none,
The bosom stained by those accursèd births,
Himself, his children—so, as thus he raves,
Some spirit shows her to him (none of us
Who stood hard by had done so): with a shout
Most terrible, as some one led him on,
Through the two gates he leapt, and from the hasp
He slid the hollow bolt, and falls within;
And there we saw his wife had hung herself,
By twisted cords suspended. When her form
He saw, poor wretch! with one wild, fearful cry,
The twisted rope he loosens, and she fell,
Ill-starred one, on the ground. Then came a sight
Most fearful. Tearing from her robe the clasps,
All chased with gold, with which she decked herself,
He with them struck the pupils of his eyes,
Such words as these exclaiming: "They should see
No more the ills he suffered or had done;
But in the dark should look, in time to come,
On those they ought not, not know whom they would."
With such like wails, not once or twice alone,
Raising the lids, he tore his eyes, and they,
All bleeding, stained his cheek, nor ceased to pour
Thick clots of gore, but still the purple shower
Fell fast and full, a very rain of blood.
Such were the ills that fell on both of them,
Not on one only, wife and husband both.
His former fortune, which he held of old,
Was rightly honoured; but for this day's doom
Wailing and woe, and death and shame, all forms

That man can name of evil, none have failed.
  Chorus. And hath the wretched man a pause of ill?
  Sec. Mess. He calls to us to ope the gates, and show
To all in Thebes his father's murderer,
His mother's . . . Foul and fearful were the words
He spoke. I dare not speak them. Then he said
That he would cast himself adrift, nor stay
At home accursèd, as himself had cursed.
Some stay he surely needs, or guiding hand,
For greater is the ill than he can bear,
And this he soon will show thee, for the bolts
Of the two gates are opening, and thou'lt see
A sight to touch e'en hatred's self with pity.

The doors of the Palace are thrown open, and ŒDIPUS *is seen within*
  Chorus. Oh, fearful, piteous sight!
    Most fearful of all woes
I hitherto have known! What madness strange
    Has come on thee, thou wretched one?
    What power with one fell swoop,
    Ills heaping upon ills,
    Each greater than the last,
    Has marked thee for its prey?
Woe! woe! thou doomed one, wishing much to ask,
And much to learn, and much to gaze into,
    I cannot look on thee,
    So horrible the sight!
  Œdip. Ah, woe! ah, woe! ah, woe!
    Woe for my misery!
Where am I wand'ring in my utter woe?
    Where floats my voice in air?
    Dread power, where leadest thou?
  Chorus. To doom of dread nor sight nor speech may bear.
  Œdip. O cloud of darkest guilt
That onwards sweeps with dread ineffable,

Resistless, borne along by evil blast,
    Woe, woe, and woe again!
How through my soul there darts the sting of pain,
    The memory of my crimes.
  Chorus. And who can wonder that in such dire woes
Thou mournest doubly, bearing twofold ills?
  Œdip. Ah, friend,
Thou only keepest by me, faithful found,
    Nor dost the blind one slight.
    Woe, woe,
For thou escap'st me not, I know thee well;
Though all is dark, I still can hear thy voice.
  Chorus. O man of fearful deeds, how couldst thou bear
Thine eyes to outrage? What power stirred thee to it?
  Œdip. Apollo! oh, my friends, the God, Apollo!
Who worketh all my woes—yes, all my woes.
No human hand but mine has done this deed.
    What need for me to see,
When nothing's left that's sweet to look upon?
  Chorus. Too truly dost thou speak the thing that is.
  Œdip. Yea, what remains to see,
    Or what to love, or hear,
    With any touch of joy?
Lead me away, my friends, with utmost speed,
Lead me away, the foul polluted one,
    Of all men most accursed,
    Most hateful to the Gods.
  Chorus. Ah, wretched one, alike in soul and doom,
Would that my eyes had never known thy face!
  Œdip. Ill fate be his who loosed the fetters sharp,
    That ate into my flesh,
    And freed me from the doom of death,
    And saved me—thankless boon!
    Ah! had I died but then,
Nor to my friends nor me had been such woe.
  Chorus. That I, too, vainly wish!

Œdip. Yes; then I had not been
    My father's murderer:
Nor had men pointed to me as the man
    Wedded with her who bore him.
But now all god-deserted, born in sins,
In incest joined with her who gave me birth;
Yea, if there be an evil worse than all,
    It falls on Œdipus!
    Chorus. I may not call thy acts or counsels good,
For better wert thou dead than living blind.
    Œdip. Persuade me not, nor counsel give to show
That what I did was not the best to do.
I know not how, on entering Hades dark,
To look for my own father or my mother,
Crimes worse than deadly done against them both.
And though my children's face was sweet to see
With their growth growing, yet these eyes no more
That sight shall see, nor citadel, nor tower,
Nor sacred shrines of Gods whence I, who stood
Most honoured one in Thebes, myself have banished,
Commanding all to thrust the godless forth,
Him whom the Gods do show accursed, the stock
Of Laius old. And could I dare to look,
Such dire pollution fixing on myself,
And meet them face to face? Not so, not so.
Yea, if I could but stop the stream of sound,
And dam mine ears against it, I would do it,
Closing each wretched sense that I might live
Both blind, and hearing nothing. Sweet 'twould be
To keep the soul beyond the reach of ills.
Why, O Kithæron, didst thou shelter me,
Nor kill me out of hand? I had not shown,
In that case, all men whence I drew my birth.
O Polybus, and Corinth, and the home
I thought was mine, how strange a growth ye reared,
All fair outside, all rotten at the core;

For vile I stand, descended from the vile.
Ye threefold roads and thickets half concealed,
The hedge, the narrow pass where three ways meet,
Which at my hands did drink my father's blood,
Remember ye what deeds I did in you;
What, hither come, I did?—the marriage rites
That gave me birth, and then, commingling all,
In horrible confusion, showed in one
A father, brother, son, all kindreds mixed,
Mother, and wife, and daughter, hateful names,
All foulest deeds that men have ever done.
But, since, where deeds are evil, speech is wrong,
With utmost speed, by all the Gods, or hide,
Or take my life, or cast me in the sea,
Where nevermore your eyes may look on me.
Come, scorn ye not to touch my misery,
But hearken; fear ye not; no soul but I
Can bear the burden of my countless ills.

Chorus. The man for what thou need'st is come in time,
Creon, to counsel and to act, for now
He in thy place is left our only guide.

Œdip. Ah, me! what language shall I hold to him,
What trust at his hands claim? In all the past
I showed myself to him most vile and base.

Enter CREON

Creon. I have not come, O Œdipus, to scorn,
Nor to reproach thee for thy former crimes;
But ye, if ye have lost your sense of shame
For mortal men, yet reverence the light
Of him, our King, the Sun-God, source of life,
Nor sight so foul expose unveiled to view,
Which neither earth, nor shower from heaven, nor light,
Can see and welcome. But with utmost speed
Convey him in; for nearest kin alone
Can meetly see and hear their kindred's ills.

Œdip. Oh, by the Gods! since thou, beyond my hopes,
Dost come all noble unto me all base,
In one thing hearken. For thy good I ask.
  Creon. And what request seek'st thou so wistfully?
  Œdip. Cast me with all thy speed from out this land,
Where nevermore a man may look on me!
  Creon. Be sure I would have done so, but I wished
To learn what now the God will bid us do.
  Œdip. The oracle was surely clear enough
That I, the parricide, the pest, should die.
  Creon. So ran the words. But in our present need
'Tis better to learn surely what to do.
  Œdip. And will ye ask for one so vile as I?
  Creon. Yea, now thou, too, wouldst trust the voice of God.
  Œdip. And this I charge thee, yea, and supplicate,
For her within, provide what tomb thou wilt,
For for thine own most meetly thou wilt care;
But never let this city of my fathers
Be sentenced to receive me as its guest;
But suffer me on yon lone hills to dwell,
Where stands Kithæron, chosen as my tomb
While still I lived, by mother and by sire,
That I may die by those who sought to kill.
And yet this much I know, that no disease,
Nor aught else could have killed me; ne'er from death
Had I been saved but for this destined doom.
But for our fate, whatever comes may come:
And for my boys, O Creon, lay no charge
Of them upon me. They are grown, nor need,
Where'er they be, feel lack of means to live.
But for my two poor girls, all desolate,
To whom their table never brought a meal
Without my presence, but whate'er I touched
They still partook of with me; these I care for.
Yea, let me touch them with my hands, and weep
To them my sorrows. Grant it, O my prince,
    O born of noble nature!

Could I but touch them with my hands, I feel
Still I should have them mine, as when I saw.

Enter ANTIGONE *and* ISMENE

What say I? What is this?
Do I not hear, ye Gods, their dear, loved tones,
Broken with sobs, and Creon, pitying me,
Hath sent the dearest of my children to me?
  Is it not so?
Creon. It is so. I am he who gives thee this,
Knowing the joy thou hadst in them of old.
Œdip. Good luck have thou! And may the powers on high
Guard thy path better than they guarded mine!
Where are ye, O my children? Come, oh, come
To these your brother's hands, which but now tore
Your father's eyes, that once were bright to see,
Who, O my children, blind and knowing naught,
Became your father—how, I may not tell.
I weep for you, though sight is mine no more,
Picturing in mind the sad and dreary life
Which waits you in the world in years to come;
For to what friendly gatherings will ye go,
Or festive joys, from whence, for stately show
Once yours, ye shall not home return in tears?
And when ye come to marriageable age,
Who is there, O my children, rash enough
To make his own the shame that then will fall
On those who bore me, and on you as well?
What evil fails us here? Your father killed
His father, and was wed in incest foul
With her who bore him, and ye owe your birth
To her who gave him his. Such shame as this
Will men lay on you, and who then will dare
To make you his in marriage? None, not one,
My children! but ye needs must waste away,
Unwedded, childless. Thou, Menœkeus' son,
Since thou alone art left a father to them

(For we, their parents, perish utterly),
Suffer them not to wander husbandless,
Nor let thy kindred beg their daily bread;
But look on them with pity, seeing them
At their age, but for thee, deprived of all.
O noble soul, I pray thee, touch my hand
In token of consent. And ye, my girls,
Had ye the minds to hearken I would fain
Give ye much counsel. As it is, pray for me
To live where'er is meet; and for yourselves
A brighter life than his ye call your sire.

Creon. Enough of tears and words. Go thou within.
Œdip. I needs must yield, however hard it be.
Creon. In their right season all things prosper best.
Œdip. Know'st thou my wish?
Creon. Speak and I then shall hear.
Œdip. That thou shouldst send me far away from home.
Creon. Thou askest what the Gods alone can give.
Œdip. And yet I go most hated of the Gods.
Creon. And therefore it may chance thou gain'st thy wish.
Œdip. And dost thou promise, then, to grant it me?
Creon. I am not wont to utter idle words.
Œdip. Lead me, then, hence.
Creon. Go thou, but leave the girls.
Œdip. Ah, take them not from me!
Creon. Thou must not think
To have thy way in all things all thy life.
Thou hadst it once, yet went it ill with thee.

Chorus. Ye men of Thebes, behold this Œdipus,
Who knew the famous riddle and was noblest,
Who envied no one's fortune and success.
And, lo! in what a sea of direst woe
He now is plunged. From hence the lesson draw,
To reckon no man happy till ye see
The closing day; until he pass the bourn
Which severs life from death, unscathed by woe.

ANTIGONE
OF SOPHOCLES

DRAMATIS PERSONÆ

CREON, *King of* Thebes
HÆMON, *son of* CREON
TEIRESIAS, *a seer*
Guard
First Messenger
Second Messenger
EURYDICE, *wife of* CREON
ANTIGONE } *daughters of* ŒDIPUS
ISMENE
Chorus of Theban Elders

SCENE—Thebes, *in front of the Palace.*

Enter ANTIGONE *and* ISMENE

Antigone

ISMENE, mine own sister, dearest one;
  Is there, of all the ills of Œdipus,
  One left that Zeus will fail to bring on us,
While still we live? for nothing is there sad
Or full of woe, or base, or fraught with shame,
But I have seen it in thy woes and mine.
And now, what new decree is this they tell,
Our ruler has enjoined on all the state?
Know'st thou? hast heard? or is it hid from thee,
The doom of foes that comes upon thy friends?
  Ism. No tidings of our friends, Antigone,
Painful or pleasant since that hour have come
When we, two sisters, lost our brothers twain,
In one day dying by each other's hand.
And since in this last night the Argive host
Has left the field, I nothing further know,
Nor brightening fortune, nor increasing gloom.
  Antig. That knew I well, and therefore sent for thee
Beyond the gates, that thou mayst hear alone.
  Ism. What meanest thou? It is but all too clear
Thou broodest darkly o'er some tale of woe.

Antig. And does not Creon treat our brothers twain
One with the rites of burial, one with shame?
Eteocles, so say they, he interred
Fitly, with wonted rites, as one held meet
To pass with honour to the gloom below.
But for the corpse of Polynices, slain
So piteously, they say, he has proclaimed
To all the citizens, that none should give
His body burial, or bewail his fate,
But leave it still unsepulchred, unwept,
A prize full rich for birds that scent afar
Their sweet repast. So Creon bids, they say,
Creon the good, commanding thee and me,
Yes, me, I say, and now is coming here,
To make it clear to those who knew it not,
And counts the matter not a trivial thing;
But whoso does the things that he forbids,
For him, there waits within the city's walls
The death of stoning. Thus, then, stands thy case;
And quickly thou wilt show, if thou art born
Of noble nature, or degenerate liv'st,
Base child of honoured parents.

Ism.   How could I,
O daring in thy mood, in this our plight,
Or doing or undoing, aught avail?

Antig. Wilt thou with me share risk and toil? Look to it.

Ism. What risk is this? What purpose fills thy mind?

Antig. Wilt thou with me go forth to help the dead?

Ism. And dost thou mean to give him sepulture,
When all have been forbidden?

Antig.   He is still
My brother; yes, and thine, though thou, it seems,
Wouldst fain he were not. I desert him not.

Ism. O daring one, when Creon bids thee not!

Antig. What right has he to keep me from mine own?

Ism. Ah me! remember, sister, how our sire
Perished, with hate o'erwhelmed and infamy,

From evils that he brought upon himself,
And with his own hand robbed himself of sight,
And how his wife and mother, both in one,
With twist and cordage, cast away her life;
And thirdly, how our brothers in one day
In suicidal conflict wrought the doom,
Each of the other. And we twain are left;
And think, how much more wretchedly than all
We twain shall perish, if, against the law,
We brave our sovereign's edict and his power.
For this we need remember, we were born
Women; as such, not made to strive with men.
And next, that they who reign surpass in strength,
And we must bow to this, and worse than this.
I, then, entreating those that dwell below,
To judge me leniently, as forced to yield,
Will hearken to our rulers. Overzeal
In act or word but little wisdom shows.

Antig. I would not ask thee. No! if thou shouldst wish
To do it, and wouldst gladly join with me.
Do what thou wilt, I go to bury him;
And good it were, this having done, to die.
Loved I shall be with him whom I have loved,
Guilty of holiest crime. More time have I
In which to win the favour of the dead,
Than that of those who live; for I shall rest
For ever there. But thou, if thus thou please,
Count as dishonoured what the Gods approve.

Ism. I do them no dishonour, but I find
Myself too weak to war against the state.

Antig. Make what excuse thou wilt, I go to rear
A grave above the brother whom I love.

Ism. Ah, wretched me! how much I fear for thee.

Antig. Fear not for me. Thine own fate guide aright.

Ism. At any rate, disclose this deed to none;
Keep it close hidden. I will hide it too.

Antig. Speak out! I bid thee. Silent, thou wilt be

More hateful to me than if thou shouldst tell
My deed to all men.
 Ism.   Fiery is thy mood,
Although thy deeds might chill the very blood.
 Antig. I know I please the souls I seek to please.
 Ism. If thou canst do it; but thy passion craves
For things impossible.
 Antig.   I'll cease to strive
When strength shall fail me.
 Ism.   Even from the first,
It is not meet to seek what may not be.
 Antig. If thou speak thus, my hatred wilt thou gain,
And rightly wilt be hated of the dead.
Leave me and my ill counsel to endure
This dreadful doom. I shall not suffer aught
So evil as a death dishonourable.
 Ism. Go, then, if so thou wilt. Of this be sure,
Wild as thou art, thy friends must love thee still. [*Exeunt.*

Enter Chorus

Strophe I

 Chor. Ray of the glorious sun,
Brightest of all that ever shone on Thebes,
  Thebes with her seven high gates,
  Thou didst appear that day,
  Eye of the golden dawn,
  O'er Dirke's streams advancing,
  Driving with quickened curb,
  In haste of headlong flight,
The warrior who, in panoply of proof,
From Argos came, with shield as white as snow;
  Who came to this our land,
  Roused by the strife of tongues
  That Polynices stirred;
  Shrieking his shrill sharp cry,
  The eagle hovered round,

With snow-white wing bedecked,
Begirt with myriad arms,
And flowing horsehair crests.

Antistrophe I

He stood above our towers,
Circling, with blood-stained spears,
The portals of our gates;
He went, before he filled
His jaws with blood of men,
Before Hephæstus with his pitchy flame
Had seized our crown of towers.
So loud the battle din that Ares loves,
Was raised around his rear,
A conflict hard and stiff,
E'en for his dragon foe.
For breath of haughty speech
Zeus hateth evermore exceedingly;
And seeing them advance,
Exulting in the clang of golden arms,
With brandished fire he hurls them headlong down,
In act, upon the topmost battlement
Rushing, with eager step,
To shout out, "Victory!"

Strophe II

Crashing to earth he fell,
Who came, with madman's haste,
Drunken, but not with wine,
And swept o'er us with blasts,
The whirlwind blasts of hate.
Thus on one side they fare,
And mighty Ares, bounding in his strength,
Dashing now here, now there,
Elsewhere brought other fate.
For seven chief warriors at the seven gates met,
Equals with equals matched,

To Zeus, the Lord of War,
Left tribute, arms of bronze;
All but the hateful ones
Who, from one father and one mother sprung,
Stood wielding, hand to hand,
Their doubly pointed spears;
They had their doom of death,
In common, shared by both.

Antistrophe II

But now, since Victory, of mightiest name,
Hath come to Thebes, of many chariots proud,
Joying and giving joy,
After these wars just past,
Learn ye forgetfulness,
And all night long, with dance and voice of hymns,
Let us go round to all the shrines of Gods,
While Bacchus, making Thebes resound with shouts,
Begins the strain of joy;
But, lo! the sovereign of this land of ours,
Creon, Menœkeus' son,
He, whom strange change and chances from the God
Have nobly raised to power,
Comes to us, steering on some new device;
For, lo! he hath convened,
By herald's loud command,
This council of the elders of our land.

Enter Creon

Creon. My friends, for what concerns our commonwealth,
The Gods who vexed it with the billowing storms
Have righted it again; but I have sent,
By special summons, calling you to come
Apart from all the others. This, in part,
As knowing ye did all along uphold
The might of Laius' throne, in part again,
Because when Œdipus our country ruled,

And, when he perished, then towards his sons
Ye still were faithful in your steadfast mind.
And since they fell, as by a double death,
Both on the selfsame day with murderous blow,
Smiting and being smitten, now I hold
Their thrones and all their power of sov'reignty
By nearness of my kindred to the dead.
And hard it is to learn what each man is,
In heart and mind and judgment, till one gains
Experience in the exercise of power.
For me, whoe'er is called to guide a state,
And does not catch at counsels wise and good,
But holds his peace through any fear of man,
I deem him basest of all men that are,
Of all that ever have been; and whoe'er
As worthier than his country counts his friend,
I utterly despise him. I myself,
Zeus be my witness, who beholdeth all,
Will not keep silence, seeing danger come,
Instead of safety, to my subjects true.
Nor could I take as friend my country's foe;
For this I know, that there our safety lies,
And sailing in her while she holds her course,
We gather friends around us. By these rules
And such as these will I maintain the state.
And now I come, with edicts close allied
To these in spirit, for my subjects all,
Concerning those two sons of Œdipus.
Eteocles, who died in deeds of might
Illustrious, fighting for our fatherland,
To honour him with sepulture, all rites
Duly performed that to the noblest dead
Of right belong. Not so his brother; him
I speak of, Polynices, who, returned
From exile, sought with fire and sword to waste
His father's city and the shrines of Gods,
Yea, sought to glut his rage with blood of men,

And lead them captives to the bondslave's doom;
Him I decree that none should dare entomb,
That none should utter wail or loud lament,
But leave his corpse unburied, by the dogs
And vultures mangled, foul to look upon.
Such is my purpose. Ne'er, if I can help,
Shall the vile share the honours of the just;
But whoso shows himself my country's friend,
Living or dead, from me shall honour gain.

Chor. This is thy pleasure, O Menœkeus' son,
For him who hated, him who loved our state;
And thou hast power to make what laws thou wilt,
Both for the dead and all of us who live.

Creon. Be ye, then, guardians of the things I speak.
Chor. Commit this task to one of younger years.
Creon. The watchmen are appointed for the corpse.
Chor. What duty, then, enjoin'st thou on another?
Creon. Not to consent with those that disobey.
Chor. None are so foolish as to seek for death.
Creon. And that shall be his doom; but love of gain
Hath oft with false hopes lured men to their death.

Enter Guard

Guard. I will not say, O king, that I am come
Panting with speed and plying nimble feet,
For I had many halting-points of thought,
Backwards and forwards turning, round and round;
For now my mind would give me sage advice:
"Poor wretch, and wilt thou go and bear the blame?"
Or—"Dost thou tarry now? Shall Creon know
These things from others? How wilt thou escape?"
Resolving thus, I came in haste, yet slow,
And thus a short way finds itself prolonged,
But, last of all, to come to thee prevailed.
And though I tell of naught, thou shalt hear all;
For this one hope I cling to steadfastly,
That I shall suffer nothing but my fate.

ANTIGONE

Creon. What is it, then, that causes such dismay?
Guard. First, for mine own share in it, this I say,
I did not do it, do not know who did,
Nor should I rightly come to ill for it.
Creon. Thou tak'st good aim and fencest up thy tale
All round and round. 'Twould seem thou hast some news.
Guard. Yea, news of fear engenders long delay.
Creon. Tell thou thy tale, and then depart in peace.
Guard. And speak I will. The corpse . . . Some one has been
But now and buried it, a little dust
O'er the skin scattering, with the wonted rites.
Creon. What say'st thou? Who has dared this deed of guilt?
Guard. I know not. Neither was there stroke of spade,
Nor earth cast up by mattock. All the soil
Was dry and hard, no track of chariot wheel;
But he who did it went and left no sign.
But when the first day's watchman showed it us,
The sight caused wonder and sore grief to all,
For he had disappeared. No tomb, indeed,
Was over him, but dust all lightly strown,
As by some hand that shunned defiling guilt;
And no work was there of a beast of prey
Or dog devouring. Evil words arose
Among us, guard to guard imputing blame,
Which might have come to blows, for none was there
To check its course, and each to each appeared
The man whose hand had done it. As for proof,
That there was none, and so he 'scaped our ken.
And we were ready in our hands to take
Bars of hot iron, and to walk through fire,
And call the Gods to witness none of us
Had done the deed, nor knew who counselled it,
Nor who had wrought it. Then at last, when naught
Was gained by all our searching, some one says
What made us bend our gaze upon the ground

In fear and trembling; for we neither saw
How to oppose it, nor, accepting it,
How we might prosper in it. And his speech
Was this, that all our tale should go to thee,
Not hushed up anywise. This gained the day;
And me, ill-starred, the lot condemns to win
This precious prize. So here I come to thee
Against my will; and surely do I trow
Thou dost not wish to see me. Still 'tis true
That no man loves the messenger of ill.

   Chor. For me, my prince, my mind some time has thought
That this perchance has some divine intent.

   Creon. Cease thou, before thou fillest me with wrath,
Lest thou be found a dastard and a fool.
For what thou say'st is most intolerable,
That for this corpse the providence of Gods
Has any care. What! have they buried him,
As to their patron paying honours high,
Who came to waste their columned shrines with fire,
To desecrate their offerings and their lands,
And all their wonted customs? Dost thou see
The Gods approving men of evil deeds?
It is not so; but men of rebel mood,
Lifting their head in secret long ago,
Have stirred this thing against me. Never yet
Had they their neck beneath the yoke, content
To own me as their ruler. They, I know,
Have bribed these men to let the deed be done.
No thing in use by man, for power of ill,
Can equal money. This lays cities low,
This drives men forth from quiet dwelling-place,
This warps and changes minds of worthiest stamp,
To turn to deeds of baseness, teaching men
All shifts of cunning, and to know the guilt
Of every impious deed. But they who, hired,
Have wrought this crime, have laboured to their cost,
Or soon or late to pay the penalty.

But if Zeus still claims any awe from me,
Know this, and with an oath I tell it thee,
Unless ye find the very man whose hand
Has wrought this burial, and before mine eyes
Present him captive, death shall not suffice,
Till first, impaled still living, ye shall show
The story of this outrage, that henceforth,
Knowing what gain is lawful, ye may grasp
At that, and learn it is not meet to love
Gain from all quarters. By base profit won,
You will see more destroyed than prospering.

 Guard. May I, then, speak? Or shall I turn and go?
 Creon. Dost thou not see how vexing are thy words?
 Guard. Is it thine ears they trouble, or thy soul?
 Creon. Why dost thou gauge my trouble where it is?
 Guard. The doer grieves thy heart, but I thine ears.
 Creon. Pshaw! what a babbler, born to prate, art thou.
 Guard. And therefore not the man to do this deed.
 Creon. Yes, that too; selling e'en thy soul for pay.
 Guard.   Ah me!
How fearful 'tis, in thinking, false to think.
 Creon. Prate about thinking; but unless ye show
To me the doers, ye shall say ere long
That evil gains still work their punishment. [*Exit.*
 Guard. God send we find him! Should we find him not,
As well may be, for this must chance decide,
You will not see me coming here again;
For now, being safe beyond all hope of mine,
Beyond all thought, I owe the Gods much thanks. [*Exit.*

Strophe I

 Chor. Many the forms of life,
 Fearful and strange to see,
 But man supreme stands out,
 For strangeness and for fear.
 He, with the wintry gales,
 O'er the foam-crested sea,

'Mid billows surging round,
Tracketh his way across:
Earth, of all Gods, from ancient days, the first,
Mightiest and undecayed,
He, with his circling plough,
Wears ever year by year.

Antistrophe I

The thoughtless tribe of birds,
The beasts that roam the fields,
The finny brood of ocean's depths,
He takes them all in nets of knotted mesh,
Man, wonderful in skill.
And by his arts he holds in sway
The wild beasts on the mountain's height;
And brings the neck-encircling yoke
On horse with shaggy mane,
Or bull that walks untamed upon the hills.

Strophe II

And speech, and thought as swift as wind,
And tempered mood for higher life of states,
These he has learnt, and how to flee
The stormy sleet of frost unkind,
The tempest thunderbolts of Zeus.
So all-preparing, unprepared
He meeteth naught the coming days may bring;
Only from Hades, still
He fails to find a refuge at the last,
Though skill of art may teach him to escape
From depths of fell disease incurable.

Antistrophe II

So, gifted with a wondrous might,
Above all fancy's dreams, with skill to plan,
Now unto evil, now to good,

He wends his way. Now holding fast the laws,
    His country's sacred rights,
That rest upon the oath of Gods on high,
    High in the state he stands.
An outlaw and an exile he who loves
    The thing that is not good,
    In wilful pride of soul:
Ne'er may he sit beside my hearth,
Ne'er may my thoughts be like to his,
Who worketh deeds like this.

Enter Guards, *bringing in* ANTIGONE

As to this portent which the Gods have sent,
I stand in doubt. Can I, who know her, say
That this is not the maid Antigone?
O wretched one of wretched father born,
What means this? Surely 'tis not that they bring
Thee as a rebel 'gainst the king's decree,
And taken in the folly of thine act?
    Guard. Yes! She it was by whom the deed was done.
We found her burying. Where is Creon, pray?
    Chor. Forth from his palace comes he just in time.

Enter CREON

    Creon. What chance is this with which my coming fits?
    Guard. Men, O my king, should pledge themselves to
        naught;
For cool reflection makes their purpose void.
I hardly thought to venture here again,
Cowed by thy threats, which then fell thick on me;
But since no joy is like the sweet delight
Which comes beyond, above, against our hopes,
I come, although I swore the contrary,
Bringing this maiden, whom in act we found
Decking the grave. No need for lots was now;
The prize was mine, no other claimed a share.
And now, O king, take her, and as thou wilt,

Judge and convict her. I can claim a right
To wash my hands of all this troublous coil.
   Creon. How and where was it that ye seized and brought
      her?
   Guard. She was in act of burying. Now thou knowest
All that I have to tell.
   Creon.   And dost thou know
And rightly weigh the tale thou tellest me?
   Guard. I saw her burying that selfsame corpse
Thou bad'st us not to bury. Speak I clear?
   Creon. How was she seen, detected, prisoner made?
   Guard. The matter passed as follows: When we came,
With all those dreadful threats of thine upon us,
Sweeping away the dust which, lightly spread,
Covered the corpse, and laying stript and bare
The tainted carcase, on the hill we sat
To windward, shunning the infected air,
Each stirring up his fellow with strong words,
If any shirked his duty. This went on
Some time, until the glowing orb of day
Stood in mid-heaven, and the scorching heat
Fell on us. Then a sudden whirlwind rose,
A scourge from heaven, raising squalls on earth,
And filled the plain, the leafage stripping bare
Of all the forest, and the air's vast space
Was thick and troubled, and we closed our eyes
Until the plague the Gods had sent was past;
And when it ceased, a weary time being gone,
The girl was seen, and with a bitter cry,
Shrill as a bird's, she wails, when it beholds
Its nest all emptied of its infant brood;
So she, when she beholds the corpse all stript,
Groaned loud with many moanings. And she called
Fierce curses down on those who did the deed,
And in her hand she brings some sandlike dust,
And from a well-chased ewer, all of bronze,
She pours the three libations o'er the dead.

And we, beholding, started up forthwith,
And ran her down, in nothing terrified.
And then we charged her with the former deed,
As well as this. And nothing she denied.
But this to me both bitter is and sweet,
For to escape one's self from ill is sweet,
But to bring friends to trouble, this is hard
And bitter. Yet my nature bids me count
Above all these things safety for myself.
    Creon [*to* Antigone]. And thou, then, bending to the
        ground thy head,
Confessest thou, or dost deny the deed?
    Antig. I own I did it. I will not deny.
    Creon [*to* Guard]. Go thou thy way, where'er thy will may
        choose,
Freed from a weighty charge.   [*Exit* Guard.
[*To* Antigone]   And now for thee,
Say in few words, not lengthening out thy speech,
Didst thou not know the edicts which forbade
The things thou ownest?
    Antig.   Right well I knew them all.
How could I not? Full clear and plain were they.
    Creon. Didst thou, then, dare to disobey these laws?
    Antig. Yes, for it was not Zeus who gave them forth,
Nor Justice, dwelling with the Gods below,
Who traced these laws for all the sons of men;
Nor did I deem thy edicts strong enough,
Coming from mortal man, to set at naught
The unwritten laws of God that know not change.
They are not of to-day nor yesterday,
But live for ever, nor can man assign
When first they sprang to being. Not through fear
Of any man's resolve was I prepared
Before the Gods to bear the penalty
Of sinning against these. That I should die
I knew (how should I not?), though thy decree
Had never spoken. And, before my time

If I should die, I reckon this a gain;
For whoso lives, as I, in many woes,
How can it be but death shall bring him gain?
And so for me to bear this doom of thine
Has nothing painful. But, if I had left
My mother's son unburied on his death,
I should have given them pain. But as things are,
Pain I feel none. And should I seem to thee
To have done a foolish deed, 'tis simply this,—
I bear the charge of folly from a fool.

   Chor. The maiden's stubborn will, of stubborn sire
The offspring shows itself. She knows not yet
To yield to evils.

   Creon.   Know, then, minds too stiff
Most often stumble, and the rigid steel
Baked in the furnace, made exceeding hard,
Thou seest most often split and broken lie;
And I have known the steeds of fiery mood
With a small curb subdued. It is not meet
That one who lives in bondage to his neighbours
Should boast too loudly. Wanton outrage then
She learnt when first these laws of mine she crossed,
But, having done it, this is yet again
A second outrage over it to boast,
And laugh at having done it. Surely, then,
She is the man, not I, if all unscathed
Such deeds of might are hers. But be she child
Of mine own sister, nearest kin of all
That Zeus o'erlooks within our palace court,
She and her sister shall not 'scape their doom
Most foul and shameful; for I charge her, too,
With having planned this deed of sepulture.
Go ye and call her. 'Twas but now within
I saw her raving, losing self-command.
And still the mind of those who in the dark
Plan deeds of evil is the first to fail,
And so convicts itself of secret guilt.

But most I hate when one found out in guilt
Will seek to gloze and brave it to the end.
  Antig. And dost thou seek aught else beyond my death?
  Creon. Naught else for me. That gaining, I gain all.
  Antig. Wilt thou delay? Of all thy words not one
Pleases me now, nor aye is like to please,
And so all mine must grate upon thine ears.
And yet how could I higher glory gain
Than giving my true brother all the rites
Of solemn burial? These who hear would say
It pleases them, did not their fear of thee
Close up their lips. This power has sovereignty,
That it can do and say whate'er it will.
  Creon. Of all the race of Cadmus thou alone
Look'st thus upon the deed.
  Antig.   They see it too
As I do, but in fear of thee they keep
Their tongue between their teeth.
  Creon.   And dost thou feel
No shame to plan thy schemes apart from these?
  Antig. There is no baseness in the act which shows
Our reverence for our kindred.
  Creon.   Was he not
Thy brother also, who against him fought?
  Antig. He was my brother, of one mother born,
And of the selfsame father.
  Creon.   Why, then, pay
Thine impious honours to the carcase there?
  Antig. The dead below will not accept thy words.
  Creon. Yes, if thou equal honours pay to him,
And that most impious monster.
  Antig.   'Twas no slave
That perished, but my brother.
  Creon.   Yes, in act
To waste this land, while *he* in its defence
Stood fighting bravely.
  Antig.   Not the less does death

Crave equal rites for all.
Creon. But not that good
And evil share alike?
Antig. And yet who knows
If in that world these things are counted good?
Creon. Our foe, I tell thee, ne'er becomes our friend,
Not even when he dies.
Antig. My bent is fixed,
I tell thee, not for hatred, but for love.
Creon. Go, then, below. And if thou must have love,
Love those thou find'st there. While I live, at least,
A woman shall not rule.

Enter ISMENE

Chor. And, lo! Ismene at the gate
Comes shedding tears of sisterly regard,
And o'er her brow a gathering cloud
Mars the deep roseate blush,
Bedewing her fair cheek.
Creon [*to* ISMENE]. And thou who, creeping as a viper creeps,
Didst drain my life in secret, and I knew not
That I was rearing two accursèd ones,
Subverters of my throne: come, tell me, then,
Dost thou confess thou took'st thy part in it?
Or wilt thou swear thou didst not know of it?
Ism. I did the deed. Since she will have it so,
I share the guilt; I bear an equal blame.
Antig. This, Justice will not suffer, since, in truth,
Thou wouldst have none of it. And I, for one,
Shared it not with thee.
Ism. I am not ashamed
To count myself companion in thy woes.
Antig. Whose was the deed, Death knows, and those below.
I do not love a friend who loves in words.
Ism. Do not, my sister, put me to such shame

As not to let me share thy death with thee,
And with thee pay due reverence to the dead.
   Antig. Share not my death, nor make thine own this deed
Thou hadst no hand in. Let my death suffice.
   Ism. And what to me is life, bereaved of thee?
   Antig. Ask Creon there. To him thy tender care
Is given so largely.
   Ism.   Why wilt thou torture me,
In nothing bettered by it?
   Antig.   Yes—at thee,
E'en while I laugh, I laugh with pain of heart.
   Ism. But now, at least, how may I profit thee?
   Antig. Save thou thyself. I grudge not thy escape.
   Ism. Ah, woe is me! and must I miss thy fate?
   Antig. Thou mad'st thy choice to live, and I to die.
   Ism. 'Tis not through want of any words of mine.
   Antig. To these thou seemest, doubtless, to be wise;
I to those others.
   Ism.   Yet our fault is one.
   Antig. Take courage. Thou wilt live. My soul long since
Has given itself to Death, that to the dead
I might bring help.
   Creon.   Of these two maidens here,
The one, I say, hath lost her mind but now,
The other ever since her life began.
   Ism. Yea, O my king. No mind that ever lived
Stands firm in evil days, but still it goes,
Beside itself, astray.
   Creon.   So then did thine
When thou didst choose thy evil deeds to do,
With those already evil.
   Ism.   How could I,
Alone, apart from her, endure to live?
   Creon. Speak not of her. She stands no longer here.
   Ism. And wilt thou slay thy son's betrothèd bride?

Creon. Full many a field there is which he may plough.
Ism. But none like that prepared for him and her.
Creon. Wives that are vile, I love not for my son.
Antig. Ah, dearest Hæmon, how thy father shames thee!
Creon. Thou art too vexing, thou, and these thy words,
On marriage ever harping.
   Ism.   Wilt thou rob
Thine own dear son of her whom he has loved?
   Creon. 'Tis Death who breaks the marriage contract off.
   Ism. Her doom is fixed, it seems, then. She must die.
   Creon. So thou dost think, and I. No more delay,
Ye slaves. Our women henceforth must be kept
As women—suffered not to roam abroad;
For even boldest natures shrink in fear
When they behold the end of life draw nigh.
                [*Exeunt* Guards *with* ANTIGONE *and* ISMENE.

STROPHE I

Chor. Blessed are those whose life has known no woe!
      For unto those whose house
The Gods have shaken, nothing fails of curse
        Or woe, that creepeth on,
          To generations far,
As when a wave, where Thracian blasts blow strong
        On that tempestuous shore,
Up surges from the depths beneath the sea,
        And from the deep abyss
        Rolls the black wind-vexed sand,
And every jutting peak that drives it back
        Re-echoes with the roar.

ANTISTROPHE I

      I see the ancient doom
That fell upon the seed of Labdacus,
        Who perished long ago,
          Still falling, woes on woes;
That generation cannot rescue this;

Some God still urges on,
And will not be appeased.
So now there rose a gleam
Over the last weak shoots
That sprang from out the race of Œdipus;
And thus the blood-stained sword
Of those that reign below
Cuts off relentlessly
Madness of speech, and fury of the soul.

Strophe II

Thy power, O Zeus, what haughtiness of man
    Could ever hold in check?
Which neither sleep, that maketh all things old,
Nor the long months of Gods that wax not faint,
    Can for a moment seize.
    But still as Lord supreme,
    Through time that grows not old,
Thou dwellest in thy sheen of radiancy
    On far Olympus' height.
Through all the future and the coming years,
    As through all time that's past,
    One law holds ever good,
That nothing comes to life of man on earth,
    Unscathed throughout by woe.

Antistrophe II

To many, hope may come, in wanderings wild,
    A solace and a joy;
To many, shows of fickle-hearted love;
    But still it creepeth on,
    On him who knows it not,
    Until he brings his foot
    Within the scorching flame.
    Wisely from one of old
    The far-famed saying came
That evil ever seems to be as good

                To those whose thoughts of heart
                    God leadeth unto woe,
And without woe, but shortest time he spends.
And here comes Hæmon, youngest of thy sons.
            Comes he bewailing sore
The fate of her who should have been his wife,
            His bride Antigone,
Sore grieving at the failure of his joys?

              Enter HÆMON

    Creon. Soon we shall know much more than seers can tell.
Surely thou dost not come, my son, to rage
Against thy father, hearing his decree,
Fixing her doom who should have been thy bride;
Or are we still, whate'er we do, beloved?
    Hæm. My father, I am thine. Do thou direct
With thy wise counsels, I will follow them.
No marriage weighs one moment in the scales
With me, while thou art prospering in thy reign.
    Creon. This thought, my son, should dwell within thy breast,
That all things stand below a father's will:
For this men pray that they may rear and keep
Obedient offspring by their hearths and homes,
That they may both requite their father's foes,
And pay with him like honours to his friend.
But he who reareth sons that profit not,
What could one say of him but this, that he
Breeds his own sorrow, laughter to his foes?
Lose not thy reason, then, my son, o'ercome
By pleasure, for a woman's sake, but know,
A cold embrace is that to have at home
A worthless wife, the partner of thy bed.
What ulcerous sore is worse than one we love
Who proves all worthless? No! with loathing scorn,
As hateful to thee, let her go and wed
A spouse in Hades. Taken in the act

I found her, her alone of all the state,
Rebellious. And I will not make myself
False to the state. She dies. So let her call
On Zeus, the lord of kindred. If I rear
Of mine own stock things foul and orderless,
I shall have work enough with those without.
For he who in the life of home is good
Will still be seen as just in things of state;
While he who breaks or goes beyond the laws,
Or thinks to bid the powers that be obey,
He must not hope to gather praise from me.
No! we must follow whom the state appoints
In things or just and lowly, or, may be,
The opposite of these. Of such a man
I should be sure that he would govern well,
And know well to be governed, and would stand,
In war's wild storm, on his appointed post,
A just and good defender. Anarchy
Is our worst evil, brings our commonwealth
To utter ruin, lays whole houses low,
In battle strife hurls men in shameful flight;
But they who walk uprightly, these shall find
Obedience saves most men. Sure help should come
To what our rulers order; least of all
Ought we to bow before a woman's sway.
Far better, if it must be so, to fall
By a man's hand, than thus to bear reproach,
By woman conquered.
 Chor.   Unto us, O king,
Unless our years have robbed us of our wit,
Thou seemest to say wisely what thou say'st.
 Hæm. The Gods, my father, have bestowed on man
His reason, noblest of all earthly gifts;
Nor dare I say nor prove that what thou speak'st
Is aught but right. And yet another's thoughts
May have some reason. I am wont to watch
What each man says or does, or blames in thee

(For dread thy face to one of low estate),
In words thou wouldst not much rejoice to hear.
But I can hear the things in darkness said,
How the whole city wails this maiden's fate,
As one "who of all women worthiest praise,
For noblest deed must die the foulest death.
She who, her brother fallen in the fray,
Would neither leave unburied, nor expose
To carrion dogs, or any bird of prey,
May she not claim the meed of golden crown?"
Such is the whisper that in secret runs
All darkling. And for me, my father, naught
Is dearer than thy welfare. What can be
A nobler form of honour for the son
Than a sire's glory, or for sire than son's?
I pray thee, then, wear not one mood alone,
That what thou say'st is right, and naught but that;
For he who thinks that he alone is wise,
His mind and speech above what others boast,
Such men when searched are mostly empty found.
But for a man to learn, though he be wise,
Yea, to learn much, and know the time to yield,
Brings no disgrace. When winter floods the streams,
Thou seest the trees that bend before the storm,
Save their last twigs, while those that will not yield
Perish with root and branch. And when one hauls
Too tight the mainsail sheet, and will not slack,
He has to end his voyage with deck o'erturned.
Do thou, then, yield. Permit thyself to change.
Young though I be, if any prudent thought
Be with me, I at least will dare assert
The higher worth of one who, come what will,
Is full of knowledge. If that may not be
(For nature is not wont to take that bent),
'Tis good to learn from those who counsel well.

Chor. My king! 'tis fit that thou shouldst learn from him,
If he speaks words in season; and, in turn,

That thou [*to* Hæmon] shouldst learn of him, for both speak
    well.
  Creon. Shall we at our age stoop to learn from him,
Such as he is, our lesson?
  Hæm.   'Twere not wrong.
And if I be but young, not age but deeds
Thou shouldst regard.
  Creon.   Fine deeds, I trow, to pay
Such honour to the lawless.
  Hæm.   'Tis not I
Would bid you waste your honour on the base.
  Creon. And has she not been seized with that disease?
  Hæm. The men of Thebes with one accord say, No.
  Creon. And will my subjects tell me how to rule?
  Hæm. Dost thou not see that these words fall from thee
As from some beardless boy?
  Creon.   And who, then, else
But me should rule this land?
  Hæm.   That is no state
Which hangs on one man's will.
  Creon.   The state, I pray,
Is it not reckoned his who governs it?
  Hæm. Brave rule! Alone, and o'er an empty land!
  Creon. Here, as it seems, is one who still will fight,
A woman's friend.
  Hæm.   If thou a woman be,
For all my care I lavish upon thee.
  Creon. Basest of base, who with thy father still
Wilt hold debate!
  Hæm.   For, lo! I see thee still
Guilty of wrong.
  Creon.   And am I guilty, then,
Claiming due reverence for my sovereignty?
  Hæm. Thou show'st no reverence, trampling on the laws
The Gods hold sacred.
  Creon.   O thou sin-stained soul,
A woman's victim.

Hæm. Yet thou wilt not find
In me the slave of baseness.
Creon. All thy speech
Still hangs on her.
Hæm. Yes, and on thee, myself,
And the great Gods below.
Creon. Of this be sure,
Thou shalt not wed her in the land of life.
Hæm. She, then, must die, and in her death will slay
Another than herself.
Creon. And dost thou dare
To come thus threatening?
Hæm. Is it, then, a threat
To speak to erring judgment?
Creon. To thy cost
Thou shalt learn wisdom, having none thyself.
Hæm. If thou wert not my father, I would say
Thou wert not wise.
Creon. Thou woman's slave, I say,
Prate on no longer.
Hæm. Dost thou wish to speak,
And, speaking, wilt not listen? Is it so?
Creon. No, by Olympus! Thou shalt not go free
To flout me with reproaches. Lead her out
Whom my soul hates, that she may die forthwith
Before mine eyes, and near her bridegroom here.
Hæm. No! Think it not! Near me she shall not die,
And thou shalt never see my face alive,
So mad art thou with all that would be friends. [*Exit.*
Chor. The man has gone, O king, in hasty mood.
A mind distressed in youth is hard to bear.
Creon. Let him do what he will, and bear himself
Too high for mortal state, he shall not free
Those maidens from their doom!
Chor. And dost thou mean
To slay them both?
Creon. Not her who touched it not.

ANTIGONE

Chor. There thou say'st well: and with what kind of death
Mean'st thou to kill her?
 Creon.   Where the desert path
Is loneliest, there, alive, in rocky cave
Will I immure her, just so much of food
Before her set as may appease the Gods,
And save the city from the guilt of blood;
And there, invoking Hades, whom alone
Of all the Gods she worships, she, perchance,
Shall gain escape from death, or else shall know
That all her worship is but labour lost.   [*Exit.*

STROPHE

Chor. O Love, in every battle victor owned;
Love, now assailing wealth and lordly state,
  Now on a girl's soft cheek,
  Slumbering the livelong night;
  Now wandering o'er the sea,
  And now in shepherd's folds;
The Undying Ones have no escape from thee,
Nor men whose lives are measured as a day;
  And who has thee is mad.

ANTISTROPHE

Thou makest vile the purpose of the just,
  To his own fatal harm;
Thou stirrest up this fierce and deadly strife,
  Of men of nearest kin;
The glowing eyes of bride beloved and fair
  Reign, crowned with victory,
And dwell on high among the powers that rule,
  Equal with holiest laws;
For Aphrodite, she whom none subdues,
  Sports in her might divine.
  I, even I, am borne
  Beyond the bounds of right;

I look on this, and cannot stay
        The fountain of my tears.
   For, lo! I see her, see Antigone
        Wind her sad, lonely way
To that dread chamber where is room for all.
   Antig. Yes! O ye men of this my fatherland,
        Ye see me on my way,
Life's last long journey, gazing on the sun,
His last rays watching, now and nevermore;
Alone he leads me, who has room for all,
        Hades, the Lord of Death,
        To Acheron's dark shore,
With neither part nor lot in marriage rites,
No marriage hymn resounding in my ears,
But Acheron shall claim me as his bride.
   Chor. And hast thou not all honour, worthiest praise,
Who goest to the home that hides the dead,
Not smitten by the sickness that decays,
        Nor by the sword's sharp edge,
But of thine own free will, in fullest life,
        To Hades tak'st thy way?
   Antig. I heard of old her pitiable end,
Where Sipylus rears high its lofty crag,
The Phrygian daughter of a stranger land,
        Whom Tantalus begot;
        Whom growth of rugged rock,
        Clinging as ivy clings,
        Subdued, and made its own:
        And now, so runs the tale,
        There, as she melts in shower,
        The snow abideth aye,
And still bedews yon cliffs that lie below
        Those brows that ever weep.
With fate like hers doth Fortune bring me low.
   Chor. Godlike in nature, godlike, too, in birth,
        Was she of whom thou tell'st,
And we are mortals, born of mortal seed.

And, lo! for one who liveth but to die,
To gain like doom with those of heavenly race
    Is great and strange to hear.
  Antig. Ye mock me, then. Alas! Why wait ye not?
By all our fathers' Gods, I ask of you,
Why wait ye not till I have passed away,
    But flout me while I live?
O city that I love, O men that dwell,
    That city's wealthiest lords,
    O Dirke, fairest fount,
O grove of Thebes, that boasts her chariot host,
I take you all to witness, look and see,
    How, with no friends to weep,
    By what stern laws condemned,
I go to that strong dungeon of the tomb,
    For burial new and strange.
    Oh, miserable me!
Whom neither mortal men nor spirits own,
Nor those that live, nor those that fall asleep.
  Chor. Forward and forward still to farthest verge
    Of daring hast thou gone,
And now, O child, thou fallest heavily
    Where Right erects her throne;
Surely thou payest to the uttermost
    Thy father's debt of guilt.
  Antig. Ah! thou hast touched the quick of all my grief,
The thrice-told tale of all my father's woe,
    The fate which dogs us all,
The race of Labdacus of ancient fame.
    Woe for the curses dire
    Of that defilèd bed,
    With foulest incest stained,
Whence I myself have sprung, most miserable.
    And now, I go to them,
    To sojourn in the grave,
    Bound by a curse, unwed;
    Ah, brother, thou didst find

Thy marriage fraught with ill,
And in thy death hast smitten down my life.
   Chor. Acts reverent and devout
      May claim devotion's name,
But power, in one who cares to keep his power,
      May never be defied;
      And thee thy stubborn mood,
      Self-chosen, layeth low.
   Antig. Unwept, without a friend,
      Unwed, and whelmed in woe,
I journey on the road that open lies.
No more shall it be mine (O misery!)
To look upon the holy eye of day,
      And yet, of all my friends,
      Not one bewails my fate,
      No kindly tear is shed.

         Enter CREON

   Creon. And know ye not, if men can vantage gain
By songs and wailings at the hour of death,
That they will never stop? Lead, lead her on,
And, as I said, without delay immure
In yon cavernous tomb, and then depart.
Leave her, or lone and desolate to die,
Or, living, in the tomb to find her home.
Our hands are clean in all that touches her;
But she no more shall sojourn here with us.
   Antig. [*turning towards the cavern*] O tomb, my bridal
      chamber, vaulted home,
Guarded right well for ever, where I go
To join mine own, of whom, of all that die,
As most in number Persephassa owns;
And I, of all the last and lowest, wend
My way below, life's little span unfilled.
And yet I go, and feed myself with hopes
That I shall meet them, by my father loved,
Dear to my mother, well-beloved of thee,

Thou dearest brother: I, with these my hands,
Washed each dear corpse, arrayed you, poured the stream,
In rites of burial. And in care for thee,
Thy body, Polynices, honouring,
I gain this recompense. And yet 'twas well;
I had not done it had I come to be
A mother with her children,—had not dared,
Though 'twere a husband dead that mouldered there,
Against my country's will to bear this toil.
And dost thou ask what law constrained me thus?
I answer, had I lost a husband dear,
I might have had another; other sons
By other spouse, if one were lost to me;
But when my father and my mother sleep
In Hades, then no brother more can come.
And therefore, giving thee the foremost place,
I seemed in Creon's eyes, O brother dear,
To sin in boldest daring. So himself,
He leads me, having taken me by force,
Cut off from marriage bed and marriage feast,
Untasting wife's true joy, or mother's bliss,
With infant at her breast, but all forlorn,
Bereaved of friends, in utter misery,
Alive, I tread the chambers of the dead.
What law of Heaven have I transgressed against?
What use for me, ill-starred one, still to look
To any God for succour, or to call
On any friend for aid? For holiest deed
I bear this charge of rank unholiness.
If acts like these the Gods on high approve,
We, taught by suffering, own that we have sinned;
But if they sin [*looking at* CREON], I pray they suffer not
Worse evils than the wrongs they do to me.
  Chor. Still do the same wild blasts
     Vex her poor storm-tossed soul.
  Creon. Therefore shall these her guards
     Weep sore for this delay.

Antig. Ah me! this word of thine
   Tells of death drawing nigh.
Creon. I cannot bid thee hope
   That other fate is thine.
Antig. O citadel of Thebes, my native land,
   Ye Gods of old renown,
   I go, and linger not.
Behold me, O ye senators of Thebes,
The last, lone scion of the kingly race,
What things I suffer, and from whom they come,
Revering still where reverence most is due.

              [Guards *lead* ANTIGONE *away.*

STROPHE I

Chor. So Danaë's form endured of old,
   In brazen palace hid,
   To lose the light of heaven,
And in her tomblike chamber was enclosed,
And yet high honour came to her, O child,
And on her flowed the golden shower of Zeus.
But great and dread the might of Destiny:
     Nor tempest-storm, nor war,
     Nor tower, nor dark-hulled ships
     That sweep the sea, escape.

ANTISTROPHE I

   Bitter and sharp in mood,
   The son of Dryas, king
   Of yon Edonian tribes,
   By Dionysus' hands,
   Was shut in prison cave,
And so his frenzy wild and soul o'erbold
   Waste slowly evermore.
And he was taught that he, with ribald tongue
In that wild frenzy, had attacked the Gods.
For fain had he the Mænad throng brought low,

And that bright flashing fire,
And roused the wrath of Muses sweet in song.

Strophe II

And by Kyanean waters' double sea
Are shores of Bosphorus, and Thracian isle,
As Salmydessus known, inhospitable,
Where Ares, God of all the region round,
    Saw the accursèd wound
That smote with blindness Phineus' twin-born sons
    By a fierce stepdame's hand,—
Dark wound, upon the dark-doomed eyeballs struck,
    Not with the stroke of sword,
But blood-stained hands, on point of spindle sharp.

Antistrophe II

And they in misery, miserable fate
    Lamenting, waste away,
Born of a mother wedded to a curse.
    And she who claimed descent
    From men of ancient fame,
    The old Erechtheid race,
Daughter of Boreas, in far distant caves
    Amid her father's woods,
    Was reared, a child of Gods,
Swift moving as the steed, o'er lofty crag,
    And yet, my child, on her
    Bore down the Destinies,
    Whose years are infinite.

Enter TEIRESIAS, *guided by a boy*

Teir. Princes of Thebes, we come as travellers joined,
One seeing for both, for still the blind must use
A guide's assistance to direct his steps.
  Creon. And what new thing, Teiresias, brings thee here?
  Teir. That I will tell thee, and do thou obey

The seer who speaks.
 Creon.   Of old I was not wont
To differ from thy judgment.
 Teir.   Therefore, well
And safely dost thou steer our good ship's course.
 Creon. I, from experience, bear my witness still
Of good derived from thee.
 Teir.   Bethink thee, then,
Thou walkest now upon a razor's edge.
 Creon. What means this? Lo! I shudder at thy speech.
 Teir. Soon shalt thou know, as I unfold the signs
Of my dread art. For sitting, as of old,
Upon my ancient seat of augury,
Where every bird has access, lo! I hear
Strange cry of wingèd creatures, shouting shrill,
In clamour sharp and savage, and I knew
That they were tearing each the other's breast
With bloody talons, for their whirring wings
Made that quite clear; and straightway I, in fear,
Made trial of the sacrifice that lay
On fiery altar. But the living flame
Shone not from out the offering; then there oozed
Upon the ashes, trickling from the bones,
A moisture, and it bubbled, and it spat,
And, lo! the gall was scattered to the air,
And forth from out the fat that wrapped them round,
The thigh joints fell. Such omens of decay
From strange mysterious rites I learnt from him,
This boy, who now stands here, for he is still
A guide to me, as I to others am.
And all this evil falls upon the state,
From out thy counsels; for our altars all,
Our sacred hearths, are full of food for dogs
And birds unclean, the flesh of that poor wretch
Who fell, the son of Œdipus. And so
The Gods no longer hear our solemn prayers,
Nor own the flame that burns the sacrifice;

Nor do the birds give cry of omen good,
But feed on carrion of a human corpse.
Think thou on this, my son: to err, indeed,
Is common unto all, but having erred,
He is no longer reckless or unblest,
Who, having fallen into evil, seeks
For healing, nor continues still unmoved.
Self-will must bear the guilt of stubbornness:
Yield to the dead, and outrage not a corpse.
What gain is it a fallen foe to slay?
Good counsel give I, planning good for thee;
And of all joys the sweetest is to learn
From one who speaketh well, should that bring gain.

Creon. Old man, as archers aiming at their mark,
So ye shoot forth your venomed darts at me;
I know your augur's skill, and by your arts
Long since am tricked and sold. Yes, gain your gains,
Get precious bronze from Sardis, Indian gold,
That corpse ye shall not hide in any tomb.
Not though the eagles, birds of Zeus, should bear
Their carrion morsels to their master's throne,
Not even fearing this pollution dire,
Will I consent to burial. Well I know
That man is powerless to pollute the Gods.
But many fall, Teiresias, dotard old,
A shameful fall, who gloze their shameful words,
For lucre's sake, with surface show of good.

Teir. Ah, me! Does no man know, does none consider . . .

Creon. Consider what? What trite poor saw is this?

Teir. How far good counsel heaped-up wealth excels?

Creon. By just so far methinks the greatest hurt
Is sheer unwisdom.

Teir. Thou, at least, hast grown
From head to foot all full of that disease.

Creon. Loath am I with a prophet evil words
To bandy to and fro.

Teir.   And yet thou dost so,
Saying that I utter speech that is not true.
   Creon. The race of seers is ever fond of gold.
   Teir. And that of tyrants loves the gain that comes
Of filthy lucre.
   Creon.   Art thou ignorant, then,
That what thou say'st, thou speak'st of those that rule?
   Teir. I know it. 'Twas from me thou hadst the state,
By me preserved.
   Creon.   Wise art thou as a seer,
But too much given to wrong and injury.
   Teir. Thou wilt provoke me in my wrath to speak
Of things best left unspoken.
   Creon.   Speak them out!
Only take heed thou speak them not for gain.
   Teir. And dost thou, then, already judge me thus?
   Creon. Know that my judgment is not bought and sold.
   Teir. Know, then, and know it well, that thou shalt see
Not many winding circuits of the sun,
Before thou giv'st a quittance for the dead,
A corpse by thee begotten; for that thou
Hast trampled to the ground what stood on high,
And foully placed within a charnel-house
A living soul. And now thou keep'st from them,
The Gods below, the corpse of one unblest,
Unwept, unhallowed. Neither part nor lot
Hast thou in them, nor have the Gods who rule
The worlds above, but at thy hands they meet
This outrage. And for this they wait for thee,
The sure though slow avengers of the grave,
The dread Erinyes of the Gods above,
In these same evils to be snared and caught.
Search well if I say this as one who sells
His soul for money. Yet a little while,
And in thy house men's wailing, women's cry,
Shall make it plain. And every city stirs
Itself in arms against thee, owning those

Whose limbs the dogs have buried, or fierce wolves,
Or wingèd birds have brought the accursèd taint
To city's altar-hearth. Doom like to this,
Sure darting as an arrow to its mark,
I launch at thee (for thou dost grieve me sore),
An archer aiming at the very heart,
And thou shalt not escape its fiery sting.
And now, O boy, lead thou me home again,
And let him vent his spleen on younger men,
And learn to keep his tongue more orderly,
With better thoughts than this his present mood.

[*Exit.*

Chor. The man has gone, O king, predicting woe,
And well we know, since first our raven hair
Was mixed with gray, that never yet his words
Were uttered to our state and failed of truth.

Creon. I know it too, 'tis that that troubles me.
To yield is hard, but, holding out, to smite
One's soul with sorrow, this is harder still.

Chor. Much need is there, O Creon, at this hour,
Of wisest counsel.

Creon. What, then, should I do?
Tell me and I will hearken.

Chor. Go thou first,
Release the maiden from her cavern tomb,
And give a grave to him who lies exposed.

Creon. Is this thy counsel? Dost thou bid me yield?

Chor. Without delay, O king, for, lo! they come,
The God's swift-footed ministers of ill,
And in an instant lay the wicked low.

Creon. Ah, me! 'tis hard; and yet I bend my will
To do thy bidding. With necessity
We must not fight at such o'erwhelming odds.

Chor. Go, then, and act! Commit it not to others.

Creon. E'en as I am I'll go. Come, come, my men,
Present or absent, come, and in your hands
Bring axes. Come to yonder eminence,

And I, since now my judgment leans that way,
Who myself bound her, now myself will loose.
Too much I fear lest it should wisest prove
To end my life, maintaining ancient laws.   [*Exit.*

Strophe I

Chor. O thou of many names,
    Of that Cadmeian maid
    The glory and the joy,
    Child of loud-thundering Zeus,
Who watchest over fair Italia,
And reign'st o'er all the bays that open wide,
Which Deo claims on fair Eleusis' coast:
    Bacchus, who dwell'st in Thebes,
The mother city of thy Bacchant train,
Among Ismenus' stream that glideth on,
    And with the dragon's brood;

Antistrophe I

Thee, o'er the double peak of yonder height,
    The flashing blaze beholds,
    Where nymphs of Corycus
    Go forth in Bacchic dance,
    And by Castalia's stream;
And thee the ivied slopes of Nysa's hills,
    And vine-clad promontory,
While words of more than mortal melody
    Shout out the well-known name,
    Send forth, the guardian lord
    Of all the streets of Thebes.

Strophe II

    Above all cities thou,
With her, thy mother, whom the thunder slew,
    Dost look on it with love;
And now, since all the city bendeth low

Beneath the sullen plague,
Come thou with cleansing tread
O'er the Parnassian slopes,
Or o'er the moaning straits.

Antistrophe II

O thou, who lead'st the band
Of stars still breathing fire,
Lord of the hymns that echo in the night,
Offspring of highest Zeus,
Appear, we pray thee, with thy Naxian train,
Of Thyian maidens, frenzied, passionate,
Who all night long, in maddening chorus, sing
Thy praise, their lord, Iacchus.

Enter Messenger

Mess. Ye men of Cadmus and Amphion's house,
I know no life of mortal man which I
Would either praise or blame. It is but chance
That raiseth up, and chance that bringeth low,
The man who lives in good or evil plight,
And none foretells a man's appointed lot.
For Creon, in my judgment, men might watch
With envy and with wonder, having saved
This land of Cadmus from the bands of foes;
And, having ruled with fullest sovereignty,
He lived and prospered, joyous in a race
Of goodly offspring. Now, all this is gone;
For when men lose the joys that sweeten life,
I cannot count this living, rather deem
As of a breathing corpse. His heaped-up stores
Of wealth are large; so be it, and he lives
With all a sovereign's state, and yet, if joy
Be absent, all the rest I count as naught,
And would not weigh them against pleasure's charm,
More than a vapour's shadow.

Chor.   What is this?
What new disaster tell'st thou of our chiefs?
  Mess. Dead are they, and the living cause their death.
  Chor. Who slays, and who is slaughtered? Tell thy tale.
  Mess. Hæmon is dead. His own hand sheds his blood.
  Chor. Was it a father's hand that struck the blow,
Or his own arm?
  Mess.   He by himself alone,
Yet in his wrath he charged his father with it.
  Chor. O prophet! true, most true, those words of thine.
  Mess. Since thus it stands, we may as well debate
Of other things in council.
  Chor.   Lo! there comes
The wife of Creon, sad Eurydice.
She from the house is come, or hearing speech
About her son, or else by chance.

Enter EURYDICE

  Euryd.   My friends,
I on my way without, as suppliant bound
To pay my vows at Pallas' shrine, have heard
Your words, and so I chanced to slip the bolt
Of the half-opened door, when, lo! a sound
Falls on my ears of evil near at hand,
And terror-struck I fell in deadly swoon
Back in my handmaids' arms; yet tell it me,
Tell the tale once again, for I shall hear,
By long experience disciplined to grief.
  Mess. Dear lady, I will tell thee: I was by,
And will not leave one word of truth untold.
Why should we smooth and gloze, when all **too soon**
We should be found as liars? Truth is still
The best and wisest. Lo! I went with him,
Thy husband, in attendance, to the height
Of yonder plain, where still all ruthlessly
The corpse of Polynices tombless lay,

Mangled by dogs. And, having prayed to her,
The Goddess of all pathways, and to Pluto,
To look with favour on them, him they washed
With holy water; and what yet was left
We burnt in branches freshly cut, and heaped
A high raised grave from out the soil around,
And then we entered on the stone-paved home,
Death's marriage chamber for the ill-starred maid.
And some one hears, while standing yet afar,
Shrill voice of wailing near the bridal bower,
By funeral rites unhallowed, and he comes
And tells my master, Creon. On his ears,
Advancing nearer, falls a shriek confused
Of bitter sorrow, and with grieving loud,
He utters one sad cry: "Me miserable!
And am I, then, a prophet? Do I wend
This day the dreariest way of all my life?
My son's voice greets me. Go, my servants, go,
Quickly draw near, and standing by the tomb,
Search ye and see; and where the joinèd stones
Still leave an opening, look ye in, and say
If I hear Hæmon's voice, or if my soul
Is cheated by the Gods." And then we searched,
As he, our master, in his frenzy, bade us;
And, in the furthest corner of the vault,
We saw her hanging by a twisted cord
Of linen threads entwined, and him we found
Clasping her form in passionate embrace,
And mourning o'er the doom that robbed him of her,
His father's deed, and that his marriage bed,
So full of sorrow. When he saw him there,
Groaning again in bitterness of heart,
He goes to him, and calls in wailing voice,
"Ah! wretched me! what dost thou! Hast thou lost
Thy reason? In what evil sinkest thou?
Come forth, my child, on bended knee I ask thee."

And then the boy, with fierce, wild gleaming eyes,
Glared at him, spat upon his face, and draws,
Still answering naught, the sharp two-edgèd sword.
Missing his aim (his father from the blow
Turning aside), in anger with himself,
The poor ill-doomed one, even as he was,
Fell on his sword, and drove it through his breast,
Full half its length, and clasping, yet alive,
The maiden's arm, still soft, he there breathes out
In broken gasps, upon her fair white cheek,
A rain of blood. And so at last they lie,
Dead bridegroom with dead bride, and he has gained
His marriage rites in Hades' darksome home,
And left to all men witness terrible,
That man's worst ill is stubbornness of heart.

[*Exit* EURYDICE.

Chor. What dost thou make of this? She turns again,
And not one word, or good or ill, will speak.

Mess. I, too, am full of wonder. Yet with hopes
I feed myself, she will not think it meet,
Hearing her son's woes, openly to wail
Before her subjects, but beneath her roof
Will think it best to bear her private griefs.
Too trained a judgment has she so to err.

Chor. I know not. To my mind, or silence hard,
Or vain wild cries, are signs of bitter woe.

Mess. Soon we shall know, within the house advancing,
If, in the passion of her heart, she hides
A secret purpose. Truly dost thou speak;
There is a terror in that silence hard.

Chor. [*seeing* CREON *approaching with the corpse of* HÆMON *in his arms*]
And, lo! the king himself comes on,
And in his hands he bears a record clear,
No woe (if I may speak) by others caused,
Himself the great offender.

Enter CREON, *bearing* HÆMON's *body*

Creon. Woe! for the sins of souls of evil mood,
    Strong, mighty to destroy;
O ye who look on those of kindred race,
    The slayers and the slain,
Woe for mine own rash plans that prosper not;
Woe for thee, son; but new in life's career,
    And by a new fate dying.
        Woe! woe!
    Thou diest, thou art gone,
Not by thine evil counsel, but by mine.
    Chor. Ah me! Too late thou seem'st to see the right.
    Creon.   Ah me!
I learn the grievous lesson. On my head,
God, pressing sore, hath smitten me and vexed,
In ways most rough and terrible (ah me!),
Shattering the joy, and trampling underfoot.
Woe! woe! We toil for that which profits not.

Enter Second Messenger

    Sec. Mess. My master! thou, as one who hast full store,
One source of sorrow bearest in thine arms,
And others in thy house, too soon, it seems,
Thou need'st must come and see.
    Creon.   And what remains
Worse evil than the evils that we bear?
    Sec. Mess. Thy wife is dead. Thy dead son's mother true,
Ill-starred one, smitten with a deadly blow,
But some few moments since.
    Creon.   O agony!
Thou house of Death, that none may purify,
    Why dost thou thus destroy me?
O thou who comest, bringing in thy train
    Woes horrible to tell,
Thou tramplest on a man already slain.
What say'st thou? What new tidings bring'st to me?

　　　　　　　Ah me! ah me!
Is it that over all the slaughter wrought
My own wife's death has come to crown it all?
　　Chor. It is but all too clear! No longer now
Does yon recess conceal her.
　　　　　　　　[*The gates open and show the dead body of*
　　　　　　　　　Eurydice.
Creon.　　　　　　　　Woe is me!
This second stroke I gaze on, miserable,
What fate, yea, what still lies in wait for me?
Here in my arms I bear what was my son;
And there, O misery! look upon the dead.
Ah, wretched mother! ah, my son! my son!
　　Sec. Mess. Sore wounded, she around the altar clung,
And closed her darkening eyelids, and bewailed
The honoured bed of Megareus, who died
Long since, and then again that corpse thou hast;
And last of all she cried a bitter cry
Against thy deeds, the murderer of thy son.
　　Creon. Woe! woe! alas!
I shudder in my fear: Will no one strike
A deadly blow with sharp two-edgèd sword?
　　　　　Fearful my fate, alas!
And with a fearful woe full sore beset.
　　Sec. Mess. She in her death charged thee with being the
　　　　cause
Of all their sorrows, his and hers alike.
　　Creon. And in what way struck she the murderous blow?
　　Sec. Mess. With her own hand below her heart she stabbed,
Hearing her son's most pitiable fate.
　　Creon. Ah me! The fault is mine. On no one else,
Of all that live, the fearful guilt can come;
I, even I, did slay thee, wretched one,
I; yes, I say it clearly. Come, ye guards,
Lead me forth quickly; lead me out of sight,
More crushed to nothing than the dead unborn.

Chor. Thou counsellest gain, if gain there be in ills,
For present evils then are easiest borne
When shortest lived.
 Creon.   Oh, come thou, then, come thou,
Last of my sorrows, that shall bring to me
Best boon, my life's last day. Come, then, oh, come,
That nevermore I look upon the light.
 Chor. These things are in the future. What is near,
That we must do. O'er what is yet to come
They watch, to whom that work of right belongs.
 Creon. I did but pray for what I most desire.
 Chor. Pray thou for nothing more. For mortal man
There is no issue from a doom decreed.
 Creon [*looking at the two corpses*] Lead me, then, forth,
   vain shadow that I am,
Who slew thee, O my son, unwittingly,
And thee, too—(O my sorrow)—and I know not
Which way to look. All near at hand is turned
Aside to evil; and upon my head
There falls a doom far worse than I can bear.
 Chor. Man's highest blessedness
   In wisdom chiefly stands;
And in the things that touch upon the Gods,
   'Tis best in word or deed
   To shun unholy pride;
Great words of boasting bring great punishments;
   And so to gray-haired age
   Comes wisdom at the last.

HIPPOLYTUS
AND
THE BACCHÆ
OF
EURIPIDES

TRANSLATED BY
GILBERT MURRAY

INTRODUCTORY NOTE

EURIPIDES, the youngest of the trio of great Greek tragedians, was born at Salamis in 480 B.C., on the day when the Greeks won their momentous naval victory there over the fleet of the Persians. The precise social status of his parents is not clear, but he received a good education, was early distinguished as an athlete, and showed talent in painting and oratory. He was a fellow student of Pericles, and his dramas show the influence of the philosophical ideas of Anaxagoras and of Socrates, with whom he was personally intimate. Like Socrates, he was accused of impiety, and this, along with domestic infelicity, has been supposed to afford a motive for his withdrawal from Athens, first to Magnesia and later to the court of Archelaus in Macedonia, where he died in 406 B.C.

The first tragedy of Euripides was produced when he was about twenty-five, and he was several times a victor in the tragic contests. In spite of the antagonisms which he aroused and the criticisms which were hurled upon him in, for example, the comedies of Aristophanes, he attained a very great popularity; and Plutarch tells that those Athenians who were taken captive in the disastrous Sicilian expedition of 413 B.C. were offered freedom by their captors if they could recite from the works of Euripides. Of the hundred and twenty dramas ascribed to Euripides, there have come down to us complete eighteen tragedies and one satyric drama, "Cyclops," besides numerous fragments.

The works of Euripides are generally regarded as showing the beginning of the decline of Greek tragedy. The idea of Fate, hitherto dominant in the plays of his predecessors, tends to be degraded by him into mere chance; the characters lose much of their ideal quality; and even gods and heroes are represented as moved by the petty motives of ordinary humanity. The chorus is often quite detached from the action; the poetry is florid; and the action is frequently tinged with sensationalism. In spite of all this, Euripides remains a great poet; and his picturesqueness and tendencies to what are now called realism and romanticism, while marking his inferiority to the chaste classicism of Sophocles, bring him more easily within the sympathetic interest of the modern reader.

HIPPOLYTUS
OF EURIPIDES

DRAMATIS PERSONÆ

The Goddess Aphrodite
Theseus, *King of Athens and Trozên*
Phædra, *daughter of Minos, King of Crete, wife to Theseus*
Hippolytus, *bastard son of Theseus and the Amazon Hippolyte*
The Nurse of Phædra
A Henchman of Hippolytus
The Goddess Artemis
An Old Huntsman
A Chorus of Huntsmen

Attendants on the Three Royal Persons
A Chorus of Trozenian Women, with their Leader

"*The scene is laid in Trozên. The play was first acted when Epameinon was Archon, Olympiad 87, year 4 (B.C. 429). Euripides was first, Iophon second, Ion third.*"

Aphrodite

GREAT among men, and not unnamed am I,
The Cyprian, in God's inmost halls on high.
And wheresoe'er from Pontus to the far
Red West men dwell, and see the glad Day-star,
And worship Me, the pious heart I bless,
And wreck that life that lives in stubbornness.
For that there is, even in a great God's mind,
That hungereth for the praise of humankind.
  So runs my word; and soon the very deed
Shall follow. For this Prince of Theseus' seed,
Hippolytus, child of that dead Amazon,
And reared by saintly Pittheus in his own
Strait ways, hath dared, alone of all Trozên,
To hold me least of spirits and most mean,
And spurns my spell and seeks no woman's kiss.
But great Apollo's sister, Artemis,
He holds of all most high, gives love and praise,
And through the wild dark woods for ever strays,
He and the Maid together, with swift hounds

To slay all angry beasts from out these bounds,
To more than mortal friendship consecrate!
    I grudge it not. No grudge know I, nor hate;
Yet, seeing he hath offended, I this day
Shall smite Hippolytus. Long since my way
Was opened, nor needs now much labour more.
    For once from Pittheus' castle to the shore
Of Athens came Hippolytus overseas
Seeking the vision of the Mysteries.
And Phædra there, his father's Queen high-born,
Saw him, and as she saw, her heart was torn
With great love, by the working of my will.
And for his sake, long since, on Pallas' hill,
Deep in the rock, that Love no more might roam,
She built a shrine, and named it *Love-at-home:*
And the rock held it, but its face alway
Seeks Trozên o'er the seas. Then came the day
When Theseus, for the blood of kinsmen shed,
Spake doom of exile on himself, and fled,
Phædra beside him, even to this Trozên.
And here that grievous and amazèd Queen,
Wounded and wondering, with ne'er a word,
Wastes slowly; and her secret none hath heard
Nor dreamed.
            But never thus this love shall end!
To Theseus' ear some whisper will I send,
And all be bare! And that proud Prince, my foe,
His sire shall slay with curses. Even so
Endeth that boon the great Lord of the Main
To Theseus gave, the Three Prayers not in vain.
    And she, not in dishonour, yet shall die.
I would not rate this woman's pain so high
As not to pay mine haters in full fee
That vengeance that shall make all well with me.

    But soft, here comes he, striding from the chase,
Our Prince Hippolytus!—I will go my ways.—

And hunters at his heels: and a loud throng
Glorying Artemis with praise and song!
Little he knows that Hell's gates opened are,
And this his last look on the great Day-star!

> [APHRODITE *withdraws, unseen by* HIPPOLYTUS *and a band of huntsmen, who enter from the left, singing. They pass the Statue of* APHRODITE *without notice.*

Hippolytus

Follow, O follow me,
  Singing on your ways
Her in whose hand are we,
Her whose own flock we be,
The Zeus-Child, the Heavenly;
  To Artemis be praise!

Huntsmen

Hail to thee, Maiden blest,
Proudest and holiest:
God's Daughter, great in bliss,
Leto-born, Artemis!
Hail to thee, Maiden, far
Fairest of all that are,
  Yea, and most high thine home,
Child of the Father's hall;
Hear, O most virginal,
Hear, O most fair of all,
  In high God's golden dome.

> [*The huntsmen have gathered about the altar of* ARTEMIS. HIPPOLYTUS *now advances from them, and approaches the Statue with a wreath in his hand.*

Hippolytus

To thee this wreathèd garland, from a green
And virgin meadow bear I, O my Queen,

Where never shepherd leads his grazing ewes
Nor scythe has touched. Only the river dews
Gleam, and the spring bee sings, and in the glade
Hath Solitude her mystic garden made.
　No evil hand may cull it: only he
Whose heart hath known the heart of Purity,
Unlearned of man, and true whate'er befall.
Take therefore from pure hands this coronal,
O mistress loved, thy golden hair to twine.
For, sole of living men, this grace is mine,
To dwell with thee, and speak, and hear replies
Of voice divine, though none may see thine eyes.
　Oh, keep me to the end in this same road!
　　　　　[*An* Old Huntsman, *who has stood apart from
　　　　　　the rest, here comes up to* Hippolytus.

Huntsman

My Prince—for "Master" name I none but God—
Gave I good counsel, wouldst thou welcome it?

Hippolytus

Right gladly, friend; else were I poor of wit.

Huntsman

Knowest thou one law, that through the world has won?

Hippolytus

What wouldst thou? And how runs thy law? Say on.

Huntsman

It hates that Pride that speaks not all men fair!

Hippolytus

And rightly. Pride breeds hatred everywhere.

Huntsman

And good words love, and grace in all men's sight?

Hippolytus
Aye, and much gain withal, for trouble slight.

Huntsman
How deem'st thou of the Gods? Are they the same?

Hippolytus
Surely: we are but fashioned on their frame.

Huntsman
Why then wilt thou be proud, and worship not . . .

Hippolytus
Whom? If the name be speakable, speak out!

Huntsman
She stands here at thy gate: the Cyprian Queen!

Hippolytus
I greet her from afar: my life is clean.

Huntsman
Clean? Nay, proud, proud; a mark for all to scan!

Hippolytus
Each mind hath its own bent, for God or man.

Huntsman
God grant thee happiness . . . and wiser thought!

Hippolytus
These Spirits that reign in darkness like me not.

Huntsman
What the Gods ask, O Son, that man must pay!

Hippolytus (*turning from him to the others*)

On, huntsmen, to the castle! Make your way
Straight to the feast room; 'tis a merry thing
After the chase, a board of banqueting.
And see the steeds be groomed, and in array
The chariot dight. I drive them forth to-day.
> [*He pauses, and makes a slight gesture of reverence to the Statue on the left. Then to the* OLD HUNTSMAN.

That for thy Cyprian, friend, and naught beside!
> [HIPPOLYTUS *follows the huntsmen, who stream off by the central door in the Castle. The* OLD HUNTSMAN *remains.*

Huntsman (*approaching the Statue and kneeling*)

O Cyprian—for a young man in his pride
I will not follow!—here before thee, meek,
In that one language that a slave may speak,
I pray thee: Oh, if some wild heart in froth
Of youth surges against thee, be not wroth
For ever! Nay, be far and hear not then:
Gods should be gentler and more wise than men!
> [*He rises and follows the others into the Castle.*

The Orchestra is empty for a moment, then there enter from right and left several Trozenian women, young and old. Their number eventually amounts to fifteen.

Chorus

There riseth a rock-born river,
   Of Ocean's tribe, men say;
The crags of it gleam and quiver,
   And pitchers dip in the spray:
A woman was there with raiment white
To bathe and spread in the warm sunlight,
   And she told a tale to me there by the river,
     The tale of the Queen and her evil day:

How, ailing beyond allayment,
   Within she hath bowed her head,
And with shadow of silken raiment
   The bright brown hair bespread.
For three long days she hath lain forlorn,
Her lips untainted of flesh or corn,
   For that secret sorrow beyond allayment
      That steers to the far sad shore of the dead.

Some Women

Is this some Spirit, O child of man?
Doth Hecat hold thee perchance, or Pan?
Doth she of the Mountains work her ban,
   Or the dread Corybantes bind thee?

Others

Nay, is it sin that upon thee lies,
Sin of forgotten sacrifice,
In thine own Dictynna's sea-wild eyes?
   Who in Limna here can find thee;
For the Deep's dry floor is her easy way,
And she moves in the salt wet whirl of the spray.

Other Women

Or doth the Lord of Erechtheus' race,
Thy Theseus, watch for a fairer face,
For secret arms in a silent place,
   Far from thy love or chiding?

Others

Or hath there landed, amid the loud
Hum of Piræus' sailor-crowd,
Some Cretan venturer, weary-browed,
   Who bears to the Queen some tiding;
Some far home-grief, that hath bowed her low,
And chained her soul to a bed of woe?

An Older Woman

Nay—know ye not?—this burden hath alway lain
On the devious being of woman; yea, burdens twain,
The burden of Wild Will and the burden of Pain.
Through my heart once that wind of terror sped;
    But I, in fear confessèd,
Cried from the dark to Her in heavenly bliss,
The Helper of Pain, the Bow-Maid Artemis:
Whose feet I praise for ever, where they tread
    Far off among the blessèd!

The Leader

But see, the Queen's grey nurse at the door,
Sad-eyed and sterner, methinks, than of yore,
    With the Queen. Doth she lead her hither,
To the wind and sun?—Ah, fain would I know
What strange betiding hath blanched that brow,
    And made that young life wither.

    [*The* NURSE *comes out from the central door, followed by* PHÆDRA, *who is supported by two handmaids. They make ready a couch for* PHÆDRA *to lie upon.*

Nurse

O sick and sore are the days of men!
What wouldst thou? What shall I change again?
Here is the Sun for thee; here is the sky;
And thy weary pillows wind-swept lie,
    By the castle door.
But the cloud of thy brow is dark, I ween;
And soon thou wilt back to thy bower within:
So swift to change is the path of thy feet,
And near things hateful, and far things sweet;
    So was it before!

Oh, pain were better than tending pain!
For that were single, and this is twain,

With grief of heart and labour of limb.
Yet all man's life is but ailing and dim,
  And rest upon earth comes never.
But if any far-off state there be,
Dearer than life to mortality;
The hand of the Dark hath hold thereof,
And mist is under and mist above.
And so we are sick of life, and cling
On earth to this nameless and shining thing.
For other life is a fountain sealed,
And the deeps below are unrevealed,
  And we drift on legends for ever!

[PHÆDRA *during this has been laid on her couch;
she speaks to the handmaids.*

Phædra

Yes; lift me: not my head so low.
  There, hold my arms.—Fair arms they seem!—
My poor limbs scarce obey me now!
Take off that hood that weighs my brow,
  And let my long hair stream.

Nurse

Nay, toss not, Child, so feveredly.
  The sickness best will win relief
By quiet rest and constancy.
  All men have grief.

Phædra (*not noticing her*)

Oh for a deep and dewy spring,
  With runlets cold to draw and drink!
And a great meadow blossoming,
Long-grassed, and poplars in a ring,
  To rest me by the brink!

Nurse

Nay, Child! Shall strangers hear this tone
So wild, and thoughts so fever-flown?

Phædra

Oh, take me to the Mountain! Oh,
Past the great pines and through the wood,
Up where the lean hounds softly go,
  A-whine for wild things' blood,
And madly flies the dappled roe.
O God, to shout and speed them there,
An arrow by my chestnut hair
Drawn tight, and one keen glimmering spear—
    Ah! if I could!

Nurse

What wouldst thou with them—fancies all!—
Thy hunting and thy fountain brink?
What wouldst thou? By the city wall
Canst hear our own brook plash and fall
  Downhill, if thou wouldst drink.

Phædra

O Mistress of the Sea-lorn Mere
  Where horse-hoofs beat the sand and sing,
O Artemis, that I were there
To tame Enetian steeds and steer
    Swift chariots in the ring!

Nurse

Nay, mountainward but now thy hands
  Yearned out, with craving for the chase;
And now toward the unseaswept sands
  Thou roamest, where the coursers pace!
  O wild young steed, what prophet knows
The power that holds thy curb, and throws
  Thy swift heart from its race?
        [*At these words* PHÆDRA *gradually recovers herself
          and pays attention.*

Phædra

What have I said? Woe's me. And where
  Gone straying from my wholesome mind?
What? Did I fall in some god's snare?
  —Nurse, veil my head again, and blind
Mine eyes.—There is a tear behind
That lash.—Oh, I am sick with shame!
  Aye, but it hath a sting,
To come to reason; yet the name
  Of madness is an awful thing.—
Could I but die in one swift flame
  Unthinking, unknowing!

Nurse

I veil thy face, Child.—Would that so
  Mine own were veiled for evermore,
  So sore I love thee! . . . Though the lore
Of long life mocks me, and I know
How love should be a lightsome thing
  Not rooted in the deep o' the heart;
  With gentle ties, to twine apart
If need so call, or closer cling.—
Why do I love thee so? O fool,
  O fool, the heart that bleeds for twain,
  And builds, men tell us, walls of pain,
To walk by love's unswerving rule,
The same for ever, stern and true!
  For "Thorough" is no word of peace:
  'Tis "Naught-too-much" makes trouble cease.
And many a wise man bows thereto.

  [*The* LEADER OF THE CHORUS *here approaches the*
    NURSE.

Leader

Nurse of our Queen, thou watcher old and true,
We see her great affliction, but no clue

Have we to learn the sickness. Wouldst thou tell
The name and sort thereof, 'twould like us well.

Nurse

Small leechcraft have I, and she tells no man.

Leader

Thou know'st no cause? Nor when the unrest began?

Nurse

It all comes to the same. She will not speak.

Leader (*turning and looking at* PHÆDRA)

How she is changed and wasted! And how weak!

Nurse

'Tis the third day she hath fasted utterly.

Leader

What, is she mad? Or doth she seek to die?

Nurse

I know not. But to death it sure must lead.

Leader

'Tis strange that Theseus takes hereof no heed.

Nurse

She hides her wound, and vows it is not so.

Leader

Can he not look into her face and know?

Nurse

Nay, he is on a journey these last days.

Leader

Canst thou not force her, then? Or think of ways
To trap the secret of the sick heart's pain?

Nurse

Have I not tried all ways, and all in vain?
Yet will I cease not now, and thou shalt tell
If in her grief I serve my mistress well!
    [*She goes across to where* PHÆDRA *lies; and
    presently, while speaking, kneels by her.*
Dear daughter mine, all that before was said
Let both of us forget; and thou instead
Be kindlier, and unlock that prisoned brow.
And I, who followed then the wrong road, now
Will leave it and be wiser. If thou fear
Some secret sickness, there be women here
To give thee comfort.   [PHÆDRA *shakes her head.*
    No; not secret? Then
Is it a sickness meet for aid of men?
Speak, that a leech may tend thee.
      Silent still?
Nay, Child, what profits silence? If 'tis ill
This that I counsel, make me see the wrong:
If well, then yield to me.
    Nay, Child, I long
For one kind word, one look!
    [PHÆDRA *lies motionless. The* NURSE *rises.*
      Oh, woe is me!
Women, we labour here all fruitlessly,
All as far off as ever from her heart!
She ever scorned me, and now hears no part
Of all my prayers!   [*Turning to* PHÆDRA *again.*
    Nay, hear thou shalt, and be,
Is so thou will, more wild than the wild sea;
But know, thou art thy little ones' betrayer!
If thou die now, shall child of thine be heir

To Theseus' castle? Nay, not thine, I ween,
But hers! That barbèd Amazonian Queen
Hath left a child to bend thy children low,
A bastard royal-hearted—sayst not so?—
Hippolytus . . .

Phædra

Ah!
[*She starts up, sitting, and throws the veil off.*

Nurse

That stings thee?

Phædra

Nurse, most sore
Thou hast hurt me! In God's name, speak that name no
 more.

Nurse

Thou seest? Thy mind is clear; but with thy mind
Thou wilt not save thy children, nor be kind
To thine own life.

Phædra

My children? Nay, most dear
I love them.—Far, far other grief is here.

Nurse (*after a pause, wondering*)
Thy hand is clean, O Child, from stain of blood?

Phædra
My hand is clean; but is my heart, O God?

Nurse
Some enemy's spell hath made thy spirit dim?

Phædra
He hates me not that slays me, nor I him.

Nurse
Theseus, the King, hath wronged thee in man's wise?

Phædra
Ah, could but I stand guiltless in his eyes!

Nurse
O speak! What is this death-fraught mystery?

Phædra
Nay, leave me to my wrong. I wrong not thee.

Nurse (suddenly throwing herself in supplication at Phædra's *feet)*
Not wrong me, whom thou wouldst all desolate leave!

Phædra (rising and trying to move away)
What wouldst thou? Force me? Clinging to my sleeve?

Nurse
Yea, to thy knees; and weep; and let not go!

Phædra
Woe to thee, Woman, if thou learn it, woe!

Nurse
I know no bitterer woe than losing thee.

Phædra
I am lost! Yet the deed shall honour me.

Nurse
Why hide what honours thee? 'Tis all I claim!

Phædra
Why, so I build up honour out of shame!

Nurse

Then speak, and higher still thy fame shall stand.

Phædra

Go, in God's name!—Nay, leave me; loose my hand!

Nurse

Never, until thou grant me what I pray.

Phædra (yielding, after a pause)

So be it. I dare not tear that hand away.

Nurse (rising and releasing PHÆDRA)

Tell all thou wilt, Daughter. I speak no more.

Phædra (after a long pause)

Mother, poor Mother, that didst love so sore!

Nurse

What mean'st thou, Child? The Wild Bull of the Tide?

Phædra

And thou, sad sister, Dionysus' bride!

Nurse

Child! wouldst thou shame the house where thou wast born?

Phædra

And I the third, sinking most all-forlorn!

Nurse (to herself)

I am all lost and feared. What will she say?

Phædra

From there my grief comes, not from yesterday.

Nurse

I come no nearer to thy parable.

Phædra

Oh, would that thou couldst tell what I must tell!

Nurse

I am no seer in things I wot not of.

Phædra (again hesitating)

What is it that they mean, who say men . . . love?

Nurse

A thing most sweet, my Child, yet dolorous.

Phædra

Only the half, belike, hath fallen on us!

Nurse (starting)

On thee? Love?—Oh, what sayst thou? What man's son?

Phædra

What man's? There was a Queen, an Amazon . . .

Nurse

Hippolytus, sayst thou?

Phædra (again wrapping her face in the veil)

                          Nay, 'twas thou, not I!
[PHÆDRA *sinks back on the couch and covers her face again. The* NURSE *starts violently from her and walks up and down.*

Nurse

O God! what wilt thou say, Child? Wouldst thou try
To kill me?—Oh, 'tis more than I can bear;

Women, I will no more of it, this glare
Of hated day, this shining of the sky.
I will fling down my body, and let it lie
Till life be gone!
      Women, God rest with you,
My works are over! For the pure and true
Are forced to evil, against their own heart's vow,
And love it!

   [*She suddenly sees the Statue of* Cypris, *and
    stands with her eyes riveted upon it.*

   Ah, Cyprian! No god art thou,
But more than god, and greater, that hath thrust
Me and my queen and all our house to dust!

   [*She throws herself on the ground close to the
    Statue.*

Chorus

Some Women

O Women, have ye heard? Nay, dare ye hear
 The desolate cry of the young Queen's misery?

A Woman

My Queen, I love thee dear,
 Yet liefer were I dead than framed like thee.

Others

Woe, woe to me for this thy bitter bane,
Surely the food man feeds upon is pain!

Others

How wilt thou bear thee through this livelong day,
 Lost, and thine evil naked to the light?
Strange things are close upon us—who shall say
 How strange?—save one thing that is plain to sight,
The stroke of the Cyprian and the fall thereof
On thee, thou child of the Isle of fearful Love!

[PHÆDRA *during this has risen from the couch and comes forward collectedly. As she speaks the* NURSE *gradually rouses herself, and listens more calmly.*

Phædra

O Women, dwellers in this portal-seat
Of Pelops' land, gazing towards my Crete,
How oft, in other days than these, have I
Through night's long hours thought of man's misery,
And how this life is wrecked! And, to mine eyes,
Not in man's knowledge, not in wisdom, lies
The lack that makes for sorrow. Nay, we scan
And know the right—for wit hath many a man—
But will not to the last end strive and serve.
For some grow too soon weary, and some swerve
To other paths, setting before the Right
The diverse far-off image of Delight;
And many are delights beneath the sun!
Long hours of converse; and to sit alone
Musing—a deadly happiness!—and Shame:
Though two things there be hidden in one name,
And Shame can be slow poison if it will!

  This is the truth I saw then, and see still;
Nor is there any magic that can stain
That white truth for me, or make me blind again.
Come, I will show thee how my spirit hath moved.
When the first stab came, and I knew I loved,
I cast about how best to face mine ill.
And the first thought that came, was to be still
And hide my sickness.—For no trust there is
In man's tongue, that so well admonishes
And counsels and betrays, and waxes fat
With griefs of its own gathering!—After that
I would my madness bravely bear, and try
To conquer by mine own heart's purity.

  My third mind, when these two availed me naught
To quell love, was to die—

[*Motion of protest among the Women.*
                              —the best, best thought—
—Gainsay me not—of all that man can say!
I would not have mine honour hidden away;
Why should I have my shame before men's eyes
Kept living? And I knew, in deadly wise,
Shame was the deed and shame the suffering;
And I a woman, too, to face the thing,
Despised of all!
                    Oh, utterly accurst
Be she of women, whoso dared the first
To cast her honour out to a strange man!
'Twas in some great house, surely, that began
This plague upon us; then the baser kind,
When the good led towards evil, followed blind
And joyous! Cursed be they whose lips are clean
And wise and seemly, but their hearts within
Rank with bad daring! How can they, O Thou
That walkest on the waves, great Cyprian, how
Smile in their husbands' faces, and not fall,
Not cower before the Darkness that knows all,
Aye, dread the dead still chambers, lest one day
The stones find voice, and all be finished!
                                              Nay,
Friends, 'tis for this I die; lest I stand there
Having shamed my husband and the babes I bare.
In ancient Athens they shall some day dwell,
My babes, free men, free-spoken, honourable,
And when one asks their mother, proud of me!
For, oh, it cows a man, though bold he be,
To know a mother's or a father's sin.

'Tis written, one way is there, one, to win
This life's race, could man keep it from his birth,
A true clean spirit. And through all this earth
To every false man, that hour comes apace
When Time holds up a mirror to his face,
And girl-like, marvelling, there he stares to see
How foul his heart! Be it not so with me!

Leader of the Chorus

Ah, God, how sweet is virtue, and how wise,
And honour its due meed in all men's eyes!

Nurse (who has now risen and recovered herself)

Mistress, a sharp swift terror struck me low
A moment since, hearing of this thy woe.
But now—I was a coward! And men say
Our second thought the wiser is alway.
   This is no monstrous thing; no grief too dire
To meet with quiet thinking. In her ire
A most strong goddess hath swept down on thee.
Thou lovest. Is that so strange? Many there be
Beside thee! . . . And because thou lovest, wilt fall
And die! And must all lovers die, then? All
That are or shall be? A blithe law for them!
Nay, when in might she swoops, no strength can stem
Cypris; and if man yields him, she is sweet;
But is he proud and stubborn? From his feet
She lifts him, and—how think you?—flings to scorn!
   She ranges with the stars of eve and morn,
She wanders in the heaving of the sea,
And all life lives from her.—Aye, this is she
That sows Love's seed and brings Love's fruit to birth;
And great Love's brethren are all we on earth!
   Nay, they who con grey books of ancient days
Or dwell among the Muses, tell—and praise—
How Zeus himself once yearned for Semelê;
How maiden Eôs in her radiancy
Swept Kephalos to heaven away, away,
For sore love's sake. And there they dwell, men say,
And fear not, fret not; for a thing too stern
Hath met and crushed them!
                          And must thou, then, turn
And struggle? Sprang there from thy father's blood
Thy little soul all lonely? Or the god
That rules thee, is he other than our gods?

Nay, yield thee to men's ways, and kiss their rods!
How many, deem'st thou, of men good and wise,
Know their own home's blot, and avert their eyes?
How many fathers, when a son has strayed
And toiled beneath the Cyprian, bring him aid,
Not chiding? And man's wisdom e'er hath been
To keep what is not good to see, unseen!

A straight and perfect life is not for man;
Nay, in a shut house, let him, if he can,
'Mid sheltered rooms, make all lines true. But here,
Out in the wide sea fallen, and full of fear,
Hopest thou so easily to swim to land?

Canst thou but set thine ill days on one hand
And more good days on the other, verily,
O child of woman, life is well with thee!

[*She pauses, and then draws nearer to* PHÆDRA.
Nay, dear my daughter, cease thine evil mind,
Cease thy fierce pride! For pride it is, and blind,
To seek to outpass gods!—Love on and dare:
A god hath willed it! And, since pain is there,
Make the pain sleep! Songs are there to bring calm,
And magic words. And I shall find the balm,
Be sure, to heal thee. Else in sore dismay
Were men, could not we women find our way!

Leader of the Chorus

Help is there, Queen, in all this woman says,
To ease thy suffering. But 'tis thee I praise;
Albeit that praise is harder to thine ear
Than all her chiding was, and bitterer!

Phædra

Oh, this it is hath flung to dogs and birds
Men's lives and homes and cities—fair false words!
Oh, why speak things to please our ears? We crave
Not that. 'Tis honour, honour, we must save!

Nurse

Why prate so proud? 'Tis no words, brave nor base,
Thou cravest; 'tis a man's arms!
                    [PHÆDRA *moves indignantly.*
                            Up and face
The truth of what thou art, and name it straight!
Were not thy life thrown open here for Fate
To beat on; hadst thou been a woman pure
Or wise or strong; never had I for lure
Of joy nor heartache led thee on to this!
But when a whole life one great battle is,
To win or lose—no man can blame me then.

Phædra

Shame on thee! Lock those lips, and ne'er again
Let word nor thought so foul have harbour there!

Nurse

Foul, if thou wilt: but better than the fair
For thee and me. And better, too, the deed
Behind them, if it save thee in thy need,
Than that word Honour thou wilt die to win!

Phædra

Nay, in God's name,—such wisdom and such sin
Are all about thy lips!—urge me no more.
For all the soul within me is wrought o'er
By Love; and if thou speak and speak, I may
Be spent, and drift where now I shrink away.

Nurse

Well, if thou wilt!—'Twere best never to err,
But, having erred, to take a counsellor
Is second.—Mark me now. I have within
Love-philtres, to make peace where storm hath been,

That, with no shame, no scathe of mind, shall save
Thy life from anguish; wilt but thou be brave!
                    [*To herself, reflecting.*
Ah, but from him, the well-beloved, some sign
We need, or word, or raiment's hem, to twine
Amid the charm, and one spell knit from twain.

Phædra

Is it a potion or a salve? Be plain.

Nurse

Who knows? Seek to be helped, Child, not to know.

Phædra

Why art thou ever subtle? I dread thee, so.

Nurse

Thou wouldst dread everything!—What dost thou dread?

Phædra

Lest to his ear some word be whisperèd.

Nurse

Let be, Child! I will make all well with thee!
—Only do thou, O Cyprian of the Sea,
Be with me! And mine own heart, come what may,
Shall know what ear to seek, what word to say!
    [*The* Nurse, *having spoken these last words in prayer apart to the Statue of* Cypris, *turns back and goes into the house.* Phædra *sits pensive again on her couch till towards the end of the following Song, when she rises and bends close to the door.*

Chorus

Erôs, Erôs, who blindest, tear by tear,
   Men's eyes with hunger; thou swift Foe, that pliest
Deep in our hearts joy like an edgèd spear;

Come not to me with Evil haunting near,
Wrath on the wind, nor jarring of the clear
  Wing's music as thou fliest!
There is no shaft that burneth, not in fire,
Not in wild stars, far off and flinging fear,
As in thine hands the shaft of All Desire,
  Erôs, Child of the Highest!

In vain, in vain, by old Alpheüs' shore
  The blood of many bulls doth stain the river,
And all Greece bows on Phœbus' Pythian floor;
Yet bring we to the Master of Man no store,
The Key-bearer, who standeth at the door
  Close-barred, where hideth ever
The heart of the shrine. Yea, though he sack man's life
Like a sacked city, and moveth evermore
Girt with calamity and strange ways of strife,
  Him have we worshipped never!

There roamed a Steed in Œchalia's wild,
  A Maid without yoke, without Master,
And Love she knew not, that far King's child;
But he came, he came, with a song in the night,
With fire, with blood; and she strove in flight,
A Torrent Spirit, a Mænad white,
  Faster and vainly faster,
Sealed unto Heracles by the Cyprian's Might.
  Alas, thou Bride of Disaster!

O Mouth of Dirce, O god-built wall,
  That Dirce's wells run under,
Ye know the Cyprian's fleet footfall!
Ye saw the heavens around her flare,
When she lulled to her sleep that Mother fair
Of Twy-born Bacchus, and decked her there
  The Bride of the bladed Thunder.

For her breath is on all that hath life, and she floats in the air,
  Bee-like, death-like, a wonder.
  [*During the last lines* PHÆDRA *has approached the door and is listening.*

Phædra

Silence, ye Women! Something is amiss.

Leader

How? In the house?—Phædra, what fear is this?

Phædra

Let me but listen! There are voices. Hark!

Leader

I hold my peace: yet is thy presage dark.

Phædra

  Oh, misery!
O God, that such a thing should fall on me!

Leader

  What sound, what word,
O Woman, Friend, makes that sharp terror start
Out at thy lips? What ominous cry half-heard
  Hath leapt upon thine heart?

Phædra

I am undone!—Bend to the door and hark,
  Hark what a tone sounds there, and sinks away!

Leader

Thou art beside the bars. 'Tis thine to mark
  The castle's floating message. Say, oh, say
    What thing hath come to thee?

Phædra (*calmly*)
  Why, what thing should it be?

The son of that proud Amazon speaks again
In bitter wrath: speaks to my handmaiden!

Leader

I hear a noise of voices, nothing clear.
  For thee the din hath words, as through barred locks
  Floating, at thy heart it knocks.

Phædra

"Pander of Sin," it says.—Now canst thou hear?—
And there: "Betrayer of a master's bed."

Leader

  Ah me, betrayed! Betrayed!
Sweet Princess, thou art ill bested,
Thy secret brought to light, and ruin near,
    By her thou heldest dear,
By her that should have loved thee and obeyed!

Phædra

Aye, I am slain. She thought to help my fall
With love instead of honour, and wrecked all.

Leader

  Where wilt thou turn thee, where?
And what help seek, O wounded to despair?

Phædra

I know not, save one thing, to die right soon.
For such as me God keeps no other boon.
  [*The door in the centre bursts open, and* HIPPOLYTUS
  comes forth, closely followed by the NURSE.
  PHÆDRA *cowers aside.*

Hippolytus

O Mother Earth, O Sun that makest clean,
What poison have I heard, what speechless sin!

Nurse

Hush, O my Prince, lest others mark, and guess . . .

Hippolytus

I have heard horrors! Shall I hold my peace?

Nurse

Yea, by this fair right arm, Son, by thy pledge . .

Hippolytus

Down with that hand! Touch not my garment's edge!

Nurse

Oh, by thy knees, be silent or I die!

Hippolytus

Why, when thy speech was all so guiltless? Why?

Nurse

It is not meet, fair Son, for every ear!

Hippolytus

Good words can bravely forth, and have no fear.

Nurse

Thine oath, thine oath! I took thine oath before!

Hippolytus

'Twas but my tongue, 'twas not my soul that swore.

Nurse

O Son, what wilt thou? Wilt thou slay thy kin?

Hippolytus

I own no kindred with the spawn of sin!

[*He flings her from him.*

Nurse

Nay, spare me! Man was born to err; oh, spare!

Hippolytus

O God, why hast Thou made this gleaming snare,
Woman, to dog us on the happy earth?
Was it Thy will to make Man, why his birth
Through Love and Woman? Could we not have rolled
Our store of prayer and offering, royal gold,
Silver and weight of bronze before Thy feet,
And bought of God new child-souls, as were meet
For each man's sacrifice, and dwelt in homes
Free, where nor Love nor Woman goes and comes?
  How, is that daughter not a bane confessed,
Whom her own sire sends forth—(he knows her best!)—
And, will some man but take her, pays a dower!
And he, poor fool, takes home the poison-flower;
Laughs to hang jewels on the deadly thing
He joys in; labours for her robe-wearing,
Till wealth and peace are dead. He smarts the less
In whose high seat is set a Nothingness,
A woman naught availing. Worst of all
The wise deep-thoughted! Never in my hall
May she sit throned who thinks and waits and sighs!
For Cypris breeds most evil in the wise,
And least in her whose heart has naught within;
For puny wit can work but puny sin.
  Why do we let their handmaids pass the gate?
Wild beasts were best, voiceless and fanged, to wait
About their rooms, that they might speak with none,
Nor ever hear one answering human tone!
But now dark women in still chambers lay
Plans that creep out into the light of day
On handmaids' lips—   [*Turning to the* NURSE.
         As thine accursèd head
Braved the high honour of my Father's bed,

And came to traffic. . . . Our white torrent's spray
Shall drench mine ears to wash those words away!
And couldst thou dream that *I* . . . ? I feel impure
Still at the very hearing! Know for sure,
Woman, naught but mine honour saves ye both.
Hadst thou not trapped me with that guileful oath,
No power had held me secret till the King
Knew all! But now, while he is journeying,
I too will go my ways and make no sound.
And when he comes again, I shall be found
Beside him, silent, watching with what grace
Thou and thy mistress greet him face to face!
Then shall I have the taste of it, and know
What woman's guile is.—Woe upon you, woe!
How can I too much hate you, while the ill
Ye work upon the world grows deadlier still?
Too much? Make woman pure, and wild Love tame,
Or let me cry for ever on their shame!

[*He goes off in fury to the left.* PHÆDRA *still cowering in her place begins to sob.*

Phædra

Sad, sad and evil-starred
    Is Woman's state.
  What shelter now is left or guard?
What spell to loose the iron knot of fate?
    And this thing, O my God,
O thou sweet Sunlight, is but my desert!
I cannot fly before the avenging rod
    Falls, cannot hide my hurt.
What help, O ye who love me, can come near,
    What god or man appear,
To aid a thing so evil and so lost?
Lost, for this anguish presses, soon or late,
To that swift river that no life hath crossed.
No woman ever lived so desolate!

Leader of the Chorus

Ah me, the time for deeds is gone; the boast
Proved vain that spake thine handmaid; and all lost!

[*At these words* PHÆDRA *suddenly remembers the* NURSE, *who is cowering silently where* HIP-POLYTUS *had thrown her from him. She turns upon her.*

Phædra

O wicked, wicked, wicked! Murderess heart
To them that loved thee! Hast thou played thy part?
Am I enough trod down?
                       May Zeus, my sire,
Blast and uproot thee! Stab thee dead with fire!
Said I not—knew I not thine heart?—to name
To no one soul this that is now my shame?
And thou couldst not be silent! So no more
I die in honour. But enough; a store
Of new words must be spoke and new things thought.
This man's whole being to one blade is wrought
Of rage against me. Even now he speeds
To abase me to the King with thy misdeeds;
Tell Pittheus; fill the land with talk of sin!
  Cursèd be thou, and whoso else leaps in
To bring bad aid to friends that want it not.

[*The* NURSE *has raised herself, and faces* PHÆDRA, *downcast but calm.*

Nurse

Mistress, thou blamest me; and all thy lot
So bitter sore is, and the sting so wild,
I bear with all. Yet, if I would, my Child,
I have mine answer, couldst thou hearken aught.
  I nursed thee, and I love thee; and I sought
Only some balm to heal thy deep despair,

And found—not what I sought for. Else I were
Wise, and thy friend, and good, had all sped right.
So fares it with us all in the world's sight.

Phædra

First stab me to the heart, then humour me
With words! 'Tis fair; 'tis all as it should be!

Nurse

We talk too long, Child. I did ill; but, oh,
There is a way to save thee, even so!

Phædra

A way? No more ways! One way hast thou trod
Already, foul and false and loathed of God!
Begone out of my sight; and ponder how
Thine own life stands! I need no helpers now.
   [*She turns from the* Nurse, *who creeps abashed
                                   away into the Castle.*
Only do ye, high Daughters of Trozên,
Let all ye hear be as it had not been;
Know naught, and speak of naught! 'Tis my last prayer.

Leader

By God's pure daughter, Artemis, I swear,
No word will I of these thy griefs reveal!

Phædra

'Tis well. But now, yea, even while I reel
And falter, one poor hope, as hope now is,
I clutch at in this coil of miseries;
To save some honour for my children's sake;
Yea, for myself some fragment, though things break
In ruin around me. Nay, I will not shame
The old proud Cretan castle whence I came,
I will not cower before King Theseus' eyes,
Abased, for want of one life's sacrifice!

Leader

What wilt thou? Some dire deed beyond recall?

Phædra (musing)

Die; but how die?

Leader

Let not such wild words fall!

Phædra (turning upon her)

Give thou not such light counsel! Let me be
To sate the Cyprian that is murdering me!
To-day shall be her day; and, all strife past,
Her bitter Love shall quell me at the last.
   Yet, dying, shall I die another's bane!
He shall not stand so proud where I have lain
Bent in the dust! Oh, he shall stoop to share
The life I live in, and learn mercy there!
                [*She goes off wildly into the Castle.*

Chorus

Could I take me to some cavern for mine hiding,
   In the hill-tops where the Sun scarce hath trod;
Or a cloud make the home of mine abiding,
   As a bird among the bird-droves of God!
     Could I wing me to my rest amid the roar
       Of the deep Adriatic on the shore,
Where the waters of Eridanus are clear,
   And Phaëthon's sad sisters by his grave
Weep into the river, and each tear
   Gleams, a drop of amber, in the wave;

To the strand of the Daughters of the Sunset,
   The Apple-tree, the singing and the gold;
Where the mariner must stay him from his onset,
   And the red wave is tranquil as of old;

Yea, beyond that Pillar of the End
  That Atlas guardeth, would I wend;
Where a voice of living waters never ceaseth
  In God's quiet garden by the sea,
And Earth, the ancient life-giver, increaseth
  Joy among the meadows, like a tree.

O shallop of Crete, whose milk-white wing
  Through the swell and the storm-beating,
    Bore us thy Prince's daughter,
Was it well she came from a joyous home
To a far King's bridal across the foam?
    What joy hath her bridal brought her?
Sure some spell upon either hand
Flew with thee from the Cretan strand,
  Seeking Athena's tower divine;
And there, where Munychus fronts the brine,
Crept by the shore-flung cables' line,
  The curse from the Cretan water!

And, for that dark spell that about her clings,
Sick desires of forbidden things
    The soul of her rend and sever;
The bitter tide of calamity
Hath risen above her lips; and she,
    Where bends she her last endeavour?
She will hie her alone to her bridal room,
And a rope swing slow in the rafters' gloom;
And a fair white neck shall creep to the noose,
A-shudder with dread, yet firm to choose
The one strait way for fame, and lose
    The Love and the pain for ever.

[*The Voice of the* Nurse *is heard from within,
    crying, at first inarticulately, then clearly.*

Voice

Help ho! The Queen! Help, whoso hearkeneth!
Help! Theseus' spouse caught in a noose of death!

A Woman

God, is it so soon finished? That bright head
Swinging beneath the rafters! Phædra dead!

Voice

O haste! This knot about her throat is made
So fast! Will no one bring me a swift blade?

A Woman

Say, friends, what think ye? Should we haste within,
And from her own hand's knotting loose the Queen?

Another

Nay, are there not men there? 'Tis an ill road
In life, to finger at another's load.

Voice

Let it lie straight! Alas! the cold white thing
That guards his empty castle for the King!

A Woman

Ah! "Let it lie straight!" Heard ye what she said?
No need for helpers now; the Queen is dead!

> [*The Women, intent upon the voices from the Castle, have not noticed the approach of* THESEUS. *He enters from the left; his dress and the garland on his head show that he has returned from some oracle or special abode of a God. He stands for a moment perplexed.*

Theseus

Ho, Women, and what means this loud acclaim
Within the house? The vassals' outcry came
To smite mine ears far off. It were more meet
To fling out wide the castle gates, and greet
With joy a herald from God's Presence!

[*The confusion and horror of the Women's faces
gradually affects him. A dirge-cry comes from
the Castle.*

How?
Not Pittheus? Hath Time struck that hoary brow?
Old is he, old, I know. But sore it were,
Returning thus, to find his empty chair!
[*The Women hesitate; then the Leader comes
forward.*

Leader

O Theseus, not on any old man's head
This stroke falls. Young and tender is the dead.

Theseus

Ye Gods! One of my children torn from me?

Leader

Thy motherless children live, most grievously.

Theseus

How sayst thou? What? My wife? . . .
                        Say how she died.

Leader

In a high death-knot that her own hands tied.

Theseus

A fit of the old cold anguish—tell me all—
That held her? Or did some fresh thing befall?

Leader

We know no more. But now arrived we be,
Theseus, to mourn for thy calamity.
            [THESEUS *stays for a moment silent, and puts his
            hand on his brow. He notices the wreath.*

Theseus

What? And all garlanded I come to her
With flowers, most evil-starred God's-messenger!
   Ho, varlets, loose the portal bars; undo
The bolts; and let me see the bitter view
Of her whose death hath brought me to mine own.
   [*The great central door of the Castle is thrown
   open wide, and the body of* PHÆDRA *is seen lying
   on a bier, surrounded by a group of Handmaids,
   wailing.*

The Handmaids

Ah me, what thou hast suffered and hast done:
   A deed to wrap this roof in flame!
Why was thine hand so strong, thine heart so bold?
Wherefore, O dead in anger, dead in shame,
   The long, long wrestling ere thy breath was cold?
         O ill-starred Wife,
What brought this blackness over all thy life?
   [*A throng of Men and Women has gradually collected.*

Theseus

      Ah me, this is the last
—Hear, O my countrymen!—and bitterest
Of Theseus' labours! Fortune all unblest,
How hath thine heavy heel across me passed!
Is it the stain of sins done long ago,
      Some fell God still remembereth,
That must so dim and fret my life with death?
I cannot win to shore; and the waves flow
Above mine eyes, to be surmounted not.
      Ah wife, sweet wife, what name
      Can fit thine heavy lot?
Gone like a wild bird, like a blowing flame,
In one swift gust, where all things are forgot!
         Alas! this misery!

Sure 'tis some stroke of God's great anger rolled
    From age to age on me,
For some dire sin wrought by dim kings of old.

Leader

Sire, this great grief hath come to many an one,
A true wife lost. Thou art not all alone.

Theseus

    Deep, deep beneath the Earth,
    Dark may my dwelling be,
And Night my heart's one comrade, in the dearth,
O Love, of thy most sweet society.
This is my death, O Phædra, more than thine.
       [*He turns suddenly on the Attendants.*
Speak who speak can! What was it? What malign
Swift stroke, O heart discounselled, leapt on thee?
       [*He bends over* PHÆDRA; *then, as no one speaks,*
                       looks fiercely up.
What, will ye speak? Or are they dumb as death,
This herd of thralls, my high house harboureth?
       [*There is no answer. He bends again over*
                       PHÆDRA.
Ah me, why shouldst thou die?
A wide and royal grief I here behold,
Not to be borne in peace, not to be told.
    As a lost man am I,
My children motherless and my house undone,
    Since thou art vanished quite,
Purest of hearts that e'er the wandering Sun
Touched, or the star-eyed splendour of the Night.
       [*He throws himself beside the body.*

Chorus

Unhappy one, O most unhappy one;
  With what strange evil is this castle vexed!

HIPPOLYTUS

Mine eyes are molten with the tears that run
  For thee and thine; but what thing follows next?
    I tremble when I think thereon!

> [*They have noticed that there is a tablet with writing fastened to the dead woman's wrist.* THESEUS *also sees it.*

Theseus

Ha, what is this that hangs from her dear hand?
A tablet! It would make me understand
Some dying wish, some charge about her bed
And children. 'Twas the last prayer, ere her head
Was bowed for ever.   [*Taking the tablet.*
              Fear not, my lost bride,
No woman born shall lie at Theseus' side,
Nor rule in Theseus' house!
              A seal! Ah, see
How her gold signet here looks up at me,
Trustfully. Let me tear this thread away,
And read what tale the tablet seeks to say.

> [*He proceeds to undo and read the tablet. The Chorus breaks into horrified groups.*

Some Women

  Woe, woe! God brings to birth
A new grief here, close on the other's tread!
  My life hath lost its worth.
May all go now with what is finishèd!
The castle of my King is overthrown,
A house no more, a house vanished and gone!

Other Women

O God, if it may be in any way,
Let not this house be wrecked! Help us who pray!

I know not what is here: some unseen thing
That shows the Bird of Evil on the wing.
> [THESEUS *has read the tablet and breaks out in uncontrollable emotion.*

Theseus

Oh, horror piled on horror!—Here is writ . . .
Nay, who could bear it, who could speak of it?

Leader

What, O my King? If I may hear it, speak!

Theseus

Doth not the tablet cry aloud, yea, shriek,
Things not to be forgotten?—Oh, to fly
And hide mine head! No more a man am I.
Ah, God, what ghastly music echoes here!

Leader

How wild thy voice! Some terrible thing is near.

Theseus

No; my lips' gates will hold it back no more;
  This deadly word,
That struggles on the brink and will not o'er,
  Yet will not stay unheard.
> [*He raises his hand, to make proclamation to all present.*

  Ho, hearken all this land!
> [*The people gather expectantly about him.*

Hippolytus by violence hath laid hand
On this my wife, forgetting God's great eye.
> [*Murmurs of amazement and horror;* THESEUS, *apparently calm, raises both arms to heaven.*

Therefore, O thou my Father, hear my cry,
Poseidon! Thou didst grant me for mine own
Three prayers; for one of these, slay now my son,

Hippolytus; let him not outlive this day,
If true thy promise was! Lo, thus I pray.

Leader

Oh, call that wild prayer back! O King, take heed!
I know that thou wilt live to rue this deed.

Theseus

It may not be.—And more, I cast him out
From all my realms. He shall be held about
By two great dooms. Or by Poseidon's breath
He shall fall swiftly to the house of Death;
Or wandering, outcast, o'er strange land and sea,
Shall live and drain the cup of misery.

Leader

Ah, see! here comes he at the point of need.
Shake off that evil mood, O King: have heed
For all thine house and folk.—Great Theseus, hear!
  [THESEUS *stands silent in fierce gloom.* HIPPO-
    LYTUS *comes in from the right.*

Hippolytus

Father, I heard thy cry, and sped in fear
To help thee.—But I see not yet the cause
That racked thee so.—Say, Father, what it was.
  [*The murmurs in the crowd, the silent gloom of
   his Father, and the horror of the Chorus-
   women gradually work on* HIPPOLYTUS *and
   bewilder him. He catches sight of the bier.*
Ah, what is that! Nay, Father, not the Queen
Dead!   [*Murmurs in the crowd.*
 'Tis most strange. 'Tis passing strange, I ween.
'Twas here I left her. Scarce an hour hath run
Since here she stood and looked on this same sun.
What is it with her? Wherefore did she die?
  [THESEUS *remains silent. The murmurs increase.*

Father, to thee I speak. Oh, tell me, why,
Why art thou silent? What doth silence know
Of skill to stem the bitter flood of woe?
And human hearts in sorrow crave the more
For knowledge, though the knowledge grieve them sore.
It is not love, to veil thy sorrows in
From one most near to thee, and more than kin.

Theseus (to himself)
Fond race of men, so striving and so blind,
Ten thousand arts and wisdoms can ye find,
Desiring all and all imagining:
But ne'er have reached nor understood one thing,
To make a true heart there where no heart is!

Hippolytus
That were indeed beyond man's mysteries,
To make a false heart true against his will.
But why this subtle talk? It likes me ill,
Father; thy speech runs wild beneath this blow.

Theseus (as before)
O would that God had given us here below
Some test of love, some sifting of the soul,
To tell the false and true! Or through the whole
Of men two voices ran, one true and right,
The other as chance willed it; that we might
Convict the liar by the true man's tone,
And not live duped for ever, every one!

*Hippolytus (misunderstanding him; then guessing at
something of the truth)*
What? Hath some friend proved false?

Or in thine ear
Whispered some slander? Stand I tainted here,
Though utterly innocent?   [*Murmurs from the crowd.*
Yea, dazed am I;
'Tis thy words daze me, falling all awry,
Away from reason, by fell fancies vexed!

Theseus

O heart of man, what height wilt venture next?
What end comes to thy daring and thy crime?
For if with each man's life 'twill higher climb,
And every age break out in blood and lies
Beyond its fathers, must not God devise
Some new world far from ours, to hold therein
Such brood of all unfaithfulness and sin?

   Look, all, upon this man, my son, his life
Sprung forth from mine! He hath defiled my wife;
And standeth here convicted by the dead,
A most black villain!

           [HIPPOLYTUS *falls back with a cry and covers his face with his robe.*

           Nay, hide not thine head!
Pollution, is it? Thee it will not stain.
Look up, and face thy Father's eyes again!
   Thou friend of Gods, of all mankind elect;
Thou the pure heart, by thoughts of ill unflecked!
I care not for thy boasts. I am not mad,
To deem that Gods love best the base and bad.

   Now is thy day! Now vaunt thee; thou so pure,
No flesh of life may pass thy lips! Now lure
Fools after thee; call Orpheus King and Lord;
Make ecstasies and wonders! Thumb thine hoard
Of ancient scrolls and ghostly mysteries—
Now thou art caught and known!

           Shun men like these,
I charge ye all! With solemn words they chase
Their prey, and in their hearts plot foul disgrace.

   My wife is dead.—"Ha, so that saves thee now"?
That is what grips thee worst, thou caitiff, thou!
What oaths, what subtle words, shall stronger be
Than this dead hand, to clear the guilt from thee?

   "She hated thee," thou sayest; "the bastard born
Is ever sore and bitter as a thorn

To the true brood."—A sorry bargainer
In the ills and goods of life thou makest her,
If all her best-beloved she cast away
To wreak blind hate on thee!—What, wilt thou say,
"Through every woman's nature one blind strand
Of passion winds, that men scarce understand"?—
Are we so different? Know I not the fire
And perilous flood of a young man's desire,
Desperate as any woman, and as blind,
When Cypris stings? Save that the man behind
Has all men's strength to aid him. Nay, 'twas thou . . .
   But what avail to wrangle with thee now,
When the dead speaks for all to understand,
A perfect witness!
                 Hie thee from this land
To exile with all speed. Come nevermore
To god-built Athens, not to the utmost shore
Of any realm where Theseus' arm is strong!
What? Shall I bow my head beneath this wrong,
And cower to thee? Not Isthmian Sinis so
Will bear men witness that I laid him low,
Nor Skiron's rocks, that share the salt sea's prey,
Grant that my hand hath weight vile things to slay!

Leader

Alas! whom shall I call of mortal men
Happy? The highest are cast down again.

Hippolytus

Father, the hot strained fury of thy heart
Is terrible. Yet, albeit so swift thou art
Of speech, if all this matter were laid bare,
Speech were not then so swift; nay, nor so fair. . . .
                 [*Murmurs again in the crowd.*
I have no skill before a crowd to tell
My thoughts. 'Twere best with few, that know me well.—

Nay, that is natural; tongues that sound but rude
In wise men's ears, speak to the multitude
With music.
           None the less, since there is come
This stroke upon me, I must not be dumb,
But speak perforce. . . . And there will I begin
Where thou beganst, as though to strip my sin
Naked, and I not speak a word!
                     Dost see
This sunlight and this earth? I swear to thee
There dwelleth not in these one man—deny
All that thou wilt!—more pure of sin than I.

  Two things I know on earth: God's worship first;
Next, to win friends about me, few, that thirst
To hold them clean of all unrighteousness.
Our rule doth curse the tempters, and no less
Who yieldeth to the tempters.—How, thou sayst,
"Dupes that I jest at"? Nay; I make a jest
Of no man. I am honest to the end,
Near or far off, with him I call my friend.
And most in that one thing, where now thy mesh
Would grip me, stainless quite! No woman's flesh
Hath e'er this body touched. Of all such deed
Naught wot I, save what things a man may read
In pictures or hear spoke; nor am I fain,
Being virgin-souled, to read or hear again.

  My life of innocence moves thee not; so be it.
Show then what hath seduced me; let me see it.
Was that poor flesh so passing fair, beyond
All women's loveliness?
                    Was I some fond
False plotter, that I schemed to win through her
Thy castle's heirdom? Fond indeed I were!
Nay, a stark madman! "But a crown," thou sayst,
"Usurped, is sweet." Nay, rather most unblest
To all wise-hearted; sweet to fools and them

Whose eyes are blinded by the diadem.
In contests of all valour fain would I
Lead Hellas; but in rank and majesty
Not lead, but be at ease, with good men near
To love me, free to work and not to fear.
That brings more joy than any crown or throne.

> [*He sees from the demeanour of* THESEUS *and of
> the crowd that his words are not winning them,
> but rather making them bitterer than before. It
> comes to his lips to speak the whole truth.*

I have said my say; save one thing . . . one alone.
 O had I here some witness in my need,
As I was witness! Could she hear me plead,
Face me and face the sunlight; well I know,
Our deeds would search us out for thee, and show
Who lies!
            But now, I swear—so hear me both,
The Earth beneath and Zeus who Guards the Oath—
I never touched this woman that was thine!
No words could win me to it, nor incline
My heart to dream it. May God strike me down,
Nameless and fameless, without home or town,
An outcast and a wanderer of the world;
May my dead bones rest never, but be hurled
From sea to land, from land to angry sea,
If evil is my heart and false to thee!

> [*He waits a moment; but sees that his Father is
> unmoved. The truth again comes to his lips.*

If 'twas some fear that made her cast away
Her life . . . I know not. More I must not say.
Right hath she done when in her was no right;
And Right I follow to mine own despite!

Leader

It is enough! God's name is witness large,
And thy great oath, to assoil thee of this charge.

Theseus

Is not the man a juggler and a mage,
Cool wits and one right oath—what more?—to assuage
Sin and the wrath of injured fatherhood!

Hippolytus

Am I so cool? Nay, Father, 'tis thy mood
That makes me marvel! By my faith, wert thou
The son, and I the sire; and deemed I now
In very truth thou hadst my wife assailed,
I had not exiled thee, nor stood and railed,
But lifted once mine arm, and struck thee dead!

Theseus

Thou gentle judge! Thou shalt not so be sped
To simple death, nor by thine own decree.
Swift death is bliss to men in misery.
Far off, friendless for ever, thou shalt drain
Amid strange cities the last dregs of pain!

Hippolytus

Wilt verily cast me now beyond thy pale,
Not wait for Time, the lifter of the veil?

Theseus

Aye, if I could, past Pontus, and the red
Atlantic marge! So do I hate thine head.

Hippolytus

Wilt weigh nor oath nor faith nor prophet's word
To prove me? Drive me from thy sight unheard?

Theseus

This tablet here, that needs no prophet's lot
To speak from, tells me all. I ponder not
Thy fowls that fly above us! Let them fly.

Hippolytus

O ye great Gods, wherefore unlock not I
My lips, ere yet ye have slain me utterly,
Ye whom I love most? No. It may not be!
The one heart that I need I ne'er should gain
To trust me. I should break mine oath in vain.

Theseus

Death! but he chokes me with his saintly tone!—
Up, get thee from this land! Begone! Begone!

Hippolytus

Where shall I turn me? Think! To what friend's door
Betake me, banished on a charge so sore?

Theseus

Whoso delights to welcome to his hall
Vile ravishers . . . to guard his hearth withal!

Hippolytus

Thou seek'st my heart, my tears? Aye, let it be
Thus! I am vile to all men, and to thee!

Theseus

There was a time for tears and thought; the time
Ere thou didst up and gird thee to thy crime.

Hippolytus

Ye stones, will ye not speak? Ye castle walls!
Bear witness if I be so vile, so false!

Theseus

Aye, fly to voiceless witnesses! Yet here
A dumb deed speaks against thee, and speaks clear!

Hippolytus

Alas!
Would I could stand and watch this thing, and see
My face, and weep for very pity of me!

Theseus

Full of thyself, as ever! Not a thought
For them that gave thee birth; nay, they are naught!

Hippolytus

O my wronged Mother! O my birth of shame!
May none I love e'er bear a bastard's name!

Theseus (*in a sudden blaze of rage*)

Up, thralls, and drag him from my presence! What?
'Tis but a foreign felon! Heard ye not?
> [*The thralls still hesitate in spite of his fury.*

Hippolytus

They touch me at their peril! Thine own hand
Lift, if thou canst, to drive me from the land.

Theseus

That will I straight, unless my will be done!
> [HIPPOLYTUS *comes close to him and kneels.*

Nay! Not for thee my pity! Get thee gone!
> [HIPPOLYTUS *rises, makes a sign of submission,
> and slowly moves away.* THESEUS, *as soon as
> he sees him going, turns rapidly and enters
> the Castle. The door is closed again.* HIPPOLYTUS *has stopped for a moment before the
> Statue of* ARTEMIS, *and, as* THESEUS *departs,
> breaks out in prayer.*

Hippolytus

So; it is done! O dark and miserable!
I see it all, but see not how to tell

The tale.—O thou belovèd, Leto's Maid,
Chase-comrade, fellow-rester in the glade,
Lo, I am driven with a caitiff's brand
Forth from great Athens! Fare ye well, O land
And city of old Erechtheus! Thou, Trozên,
What riches of glad youth mine eyes have seen
In thy broad plain! Farewell! This is the end;
The last word, the last look!
                              Come, every friend
And fellow of my youth that still may stay,
Give me god-speed and cheer me on my way.
Ne'er shall ye see a man more pure of spot
Than me, though mine own Father loves me not!

> [HIPPOLYTUS *goes away to the right, followed by many Huntsmen and other young men. The rest of the crowd has by this time dispersed, except the Women of the Chorus and some Men of the Chorus of Huntsmen.*

Chorus

Men

Surely the thought of the Gods hath balm in it alway, to win me
  Far from my griefs; and a thought, deep in the dark of my mind,
Clings to a great Understanding. Yet all the spirit within me
  Faints, when I watch men's deeds matched with the guerdon they find.

> For Good comes in Evil's traces,
> And the Evil the Good replaces;
> And Life, 'mid the changing faces,
>   Wandereth weak and blind.

Women

What wilt thou grant me, O God? Lo, this is the prayer of my travail—
  Some well-being; and chance not very bitter thereby;

A Spirit uncrippled by pain; and a mind not deep to unravel
 Truth unseen, nor yet dark with the brand of a lie.
        With a veering mood to borrow
        Its light from every morrow,
        Fair friends and no deep sorrow,
          Well could man live and die!

        Men

    Yet my spirit is no more clean,
      And the weft of my hope is torn,
    For the deed of wrong that mine eyes have seen,
      The lie and the rage and the scorn;
    A Star among men, yea, a Star
      That in Hellas was bright,
    By a Father's wrath driven far
      To the wilds and the night.
Oh, alas for the sands of the shore!
    Alas for the brakes of the hill,
Where the wolves shall fear thee no more,
    And thy cry to Dictynna is still!

        Women

No more in the yoke of thy car
    Shall the colts of Enetia fleet;
Nor Limna's echoes quiver afar
    To the clatter of galloping feet.
The sleepless music of old,
    That leaped in the lyre,
Ceaseth now, and is cold,
    In the halls of thy sire.
The bowers are discrowned and unladen
    Where Artemis lay on the lea;
And the love-dream of many a maiden
    Lost, in the losing of thee.

        A Maiden

    And I, even I,
      For thy fall, O Friend,

           Amid tears and tears,
         Endure to the end
           Of the empty years,
     Of a life run dry.
           In vain didst thou bear him,
             Thou Mother forlorn!
           Ye Gods that did snare him,
     Lo, I cast in your faces
             My hate and my scorn!
     Ye love-linkèd Graces,
         (Alas for the day!)
             Was he naught, then, to you,
     That ye cast him away,
             The stainless and true,
     From the old happy places?

Leader

Look yonder! 'Tis the Prince's man, I ween,
Speeding toward this gate, most dark of mien.
                    [A Henchman *enters in haste.*

Henchman

Ye women, whither shall I go to seek
King Theseus? Is he in this dwelling? Speak!

Leader

Lo, where he cometh through the castle gate!
                 [Theseus *comes out from the Castle.*

Henchman

O King, I bear thee tidings of dire weight
To thee, aye, and to every man, I ween,
From Athens to the marches of Trozên.

Theseus

What? Some new stroke hath touched, unknown to me,
The sister cities of my sovranty?

Henchman

Hippolytus is . . . Nay, not dead; but stark
Outstretched, a hair's-breadth this side of the dark.

Theseus (as though unmoved)

How slain? Was there some other man, whose wife
He had like mine defiled, that sought his life?

Henchman

His own wild team destroyed him, and the dire
Curse of thy lips.
    The boon of thy great Sire
Is granted thee, O King, and thy son slain.

Theseus

Ye Gods! And thou, Poseidon! Not in vain
I called thee Father; thou hast heard my prayer!
 How did he die? Speak on. How closed the snare
Of Heaven to slay the shamer of my blood?

Henchman

'Twas by the bank of beating sea we stood,
We thralls, and decked the steeds, and combed each
   mane;
Weeping; for word had come that ne'er again
The foot of our Hippolytus should roam
This land, but waste in exile by thy doom.
 So stood we till he came, and in his tone
No music now save sorrow's, like our own,
And in his train a concourse without end
Of many a chase-fellow and many a friend.
At last he brushed his sobs away, and spake:
"Why this fond loitering? I would not break
My Father's law.—Ho, there! My coursers four
And chariot, quick! This land is mine no more."

Thereat, be sure, each man of us made speed.
Swifter than speech we brought them up, each steed
Well dight and shining, at our Prince's side.
He grasped the reins upon the rail: one stride
And there he stood, a perfect charioteer,
Each foot in its own station set. Then clear
His voice rose, and his arms to heaven were spread:
"O Zeus, if I be false, strike thou me dead!
But, dead or living, let my Father see
One day, how falsely he hath hated me!"
   Even as he spake, he lifted up the goad
And smote; and the steeds sprang. And down the road
We henchmen followed, hard beside the rein,
Each hand, to speed him, toward the Argive plain
And Epidaurus.
              So we made our way
Up toward the desert region, where the bay
Curls to a promontory near the verge
Of our Trozên, facing the southward surge
Of Saron's gulf. Just there an angry sound,
Slow-swelling, like God's thunder underground,
Broke on us, and we trembled. And the steeds
Pricked their ears skyward, and threw back their heads.
And wonder came on all men, and affright,
Whence rose that awful voice. And swift our sight
Turned seaward, down the salt and roaring sand.
   And there, above the horizon, seemed to stand
A wave unearthly, crested in the sky;
Till Skiron's Cape first vanished from mine eye,
Then sank the Isthmus hidden, then the rock
Of Epidaurus. Then it broke, one shock
And roar of gasping sea and spray flung far,
And shoreward swept, where stood the Prince's car.
   Three lines of wave together raced, and, full
In the white crest of them, a wild Sea-Bull
Flung to the shore, a fell and marvellous Thing.
The whole land held his voice, and answering

Roared in each echo. And all we, gazing there,
Gazed seeing not; 'twas more than eyes could bear.
   Then straight upon the team wild terror fell.
Howbeit, the Prince, cool-eyed and knowing well
Each changing mood a horse has, gripped the reins
Hard in both hands; then as an oarsman strains
Up from his bench, so strained he on the thong,
Back in the chariot swinging. But the young
Wild steeds bit hard the curb, and fled afar;
Nor rein nor guiding hand nor morticed car
Stayed them at all. For when he veered them round,
And aimed their flying feet to grassy ground,
In front uprose that Thing, and turned again
The four great coursers, terror-mad. But when
Their blind rage drove them toward the rocky places,
Silent, and ever nearer to the traces,
It followed, rockward, till one wheel-edge grazed.
   The chariot tript and flew, and all was mazed
In turmoil. Up went wheel-box with a din,
Where the rock jagged, and nave and axle-pin.
And there—the long reins round him—there was he
Dragging, entangled irretrievably.
A dear head battering at the chariot side,
Sharp rocks, and ripped flesh, and a voice that cried:
"Stay, stay, O ye who fattened at my stalls,
Dash me not into nothing!—O thou false
Curse of my Father!—Help! Help, whoso can,
An innocent, innocent and stainless man!"
   Many there were that laboured then, I wot,
To bear him succour, but could reach him not,
Till—who knows how?—at last the tangled rein
Unclasped him, and he fell, some little vein
Of life still pulsing in him.
                              All beside,
The steeds, the hornèd Horror of the Tide,
Had vanished—who knows where?—in that wild land.
   O King, I am a bondsman of thine hand;

Yet love nor fear nor duty me shall win
To say thine innocent son hath died in sin.
All women born may hang themselves, for me,
And swing their dying words from every tree
On Ida! For I know that he was true!

Leader

O God, so cometh new disaster, new
Despair! And no escape from what must be!

Theseus

Hate of the man thus stricken lifted me
At first to joy at hearing of thy tale;
But now, some shame before the Gods, some pale
Pity for mine own blood, hath o'er me come.
I laugh not, neither weep, at this fell doom.

Henchman

How then? Behoves it bear him here, or how
Best do thy pleasure?—Speak, Lord. Yet if thou
Wilt mark at all my word, thou wilt not be
Fierce-hearted to thy child in misery.

Theseus

Aye, bring him hither. Let me see the face
Of him who durst deny my deep disgrace
And his own sin; yea, speak with him, and prove
His clear guilt by God's judgments from above.

> [*The* Henchman *departs to fetch* Hippolytus; Theseus *sits waiting in stern gloom, while the* Chorus *sing. At the close of their song a Divine Figure is seen approaching on a cloud in the air and the voice of* Artemis *speaks.*

Chorus

Thou comest to bend the pride
 Of the hearts of God and man,

Cypris; and by thy side,
 In earth-encircling span,
He of the changing plumes,
 The Wing that the world illumes,
As over the leagues of land flies he,
Over the salt and sounding sea.

For mad is the heart of Love,
 And gold the gleam of his wing;
And all to the spell thereof
 Bend, when he makes his spring;
All life that is wild and young
 In mountain and wave and stream,
All that of earth is sprung,
 Or breathes in the red sunbeam;
Yea, and Mankind. O'er all a royal throne,
Cyprian, Cyprian, is thine alone!

A Voice from the Cloud

O thou that rulest in Ægeus' Hall,
I charge thee, hearken!
                    Yea, it is I,
Artemis, Virgin of God most High.
Thou bitter King, art thou glad withal
 For thy murdered son?
For thine ear bent low to a lying Queen,
For thine heart so swift amid things unseen?
Lo, all may see what end thou hast won!
Go, sink thine head in the waste abyss;
Or aloft to another world than this,
 Birdwise with wings,
 Fly far to thine hiding,
Far over this blood that clots and clings;
For in righteous men and in holy things
 No rest is thine nor abiding!
        [*The cloud has become stationary in the air.*

Hear, Theseus, all the story of thy grief!
Verily, I bring but anguish, not relief;
Yet, 'twas for this I came, to show how high
And clean was thy son's heart, that he may die
Honoured of men; aye, and to tell no less
The frenzy, or in some sort the nobleness,
Of thy dead wife. One Spirit there is, whom we
That know the joy of white virginity,
Most hate in heaven. She sent her fire to run
In Phædra's veins, so that she loved thy son.
Yet strove she long with love, and in the stress
Fell not, till by her Nurse's craftiness
Betrayed, who stole, with oaths of secrecy,
To entreat thy son. And he, most righteously,
Nor did her will, nor, when thy railing scorn
Beat on him, broke the oath that he had sworn,
For God's sake. And thy Phædra, panic-eyed,
Wrote a false writ, and slew thy son, and died,
Lying; but thou wast nimble to believe!

[THESEUS, *at first bewildered, then dumbfounded,
now utters a deep groan.*

It stings thee, Theseus?—Nay, hear on, and grieve
Yet sorer. Wottest thou three prayers were thine
Of sure fulfilment, from thy Sire divine?
Hast thou no foes about thee, then, that one—
Thou vile King!—must be turned against thy son?
The deed was thine. Thy Sea-born Sire but heard
The call of prayer, and bowed him to his word.
But thou in his eyes and in mine art found
Evil, who wouldst not think, nor probe, nor sound
The deeps of prophet's lore, nor day by day
Leave Time to search; but, swifter than man may,
Let loose the curse to slay thine innocent son!

Theseus

O Goddess, let me die!

Artemis

       Nay; thou hast done
A heavy wrong; yet even beyond this ill
Abides for thee forgiveness. 'Twas the will
Of Cypris that these evil things should be,
Sating her wrath. And this immutably
Hath Zeus ordained in heaven: no God may thwart
A God's fixed will; we grieve but stand apart.
Else, but for fear of the Great Father's blame,
Never had I to such extreme of shame
Bowed me, be sure, as here to stand and see
Slain him I loved best of mortality!
 Thy fault, O King, its ignorance sunders wide
From very wickedness; and she who died
By death the more disarmed thee, making dumb
The voice of question. And the storm has come
Most bitterly of all on thee! Yet I
Have mine own sorrow, too. When good men die,
There is no joy in heaven, albeit our ire
On child and house of the evil falls like fire.
   [*A throng is seen approaching;* HIPPOLYTUS *enters,*
       supported by his attendants.

Chorus

 Lo, it is he! The bright young head
   Yet upright there!
Ah, the torn flesh and the blood-stained hair;
   Alas for the kindred's trouble!
It falls as fire from a God's hand sped,
   Two deaths, and mourning double.

Hippolytus

 Ah, pain, pain, pain!
O unrighteous curse! O unrighteous sire!
No hope.—My head is stabbed with fire,
And a leaping spasm about my brain.

Stay, let me rest. I can no more.
O fell, fell steeds that my own hand fed,
Have ye maimed me and slain, that loved me of yore?
—Soft there, ye thralls! No trembling hands
As ye lift me, now!—Who is that that stands
At the right?—Now firm, and with measured tread,
Lift one accursèd and stricken sore
      By a father's sinning.

Thou, Zeus, dost see me? Yea, it is I;
The proud and pure, the server of God,
The white and shining in sanctity!
To a visible death, to an open sod,
      I walk my ways;
And all the labour of saintly days
      Lost, lost, without meaning!

    Ah God, it crawls,
      This agony, over me!
    Let be, ye thralls!
      Come, Death, and cover me;
    Come, O thou Healer blest!

    But a little more,
      And my soul is clear,
    And the anguish o'er!
      Oh, a spear, a spear!
    To rend my soul to its rest!

Oh, strange, false Curse! Was there some blood-stained
      head,
Some father of my line, unpunishèd,
      Whose guilt lived in his kin,
And passed, and slept, till after this long day
It lights . . . oh, why on me? Me, far away
      And innocent of sin?

HIPPOLYTUS

        O words that cannot save!
    When will this breathing end in that last deep
Pain that is painlessness? 'Tis sleep I crave.
        When wilt thou bring me sleep,
Thou dark and midnight magic of the grave!

Artemis

Sore-stricken man, bethink thee in this stress,
Thou dost but die for thine own nobleness.

Hippolytus

Ah!
O breath of heavenly fragrance! Though my pain
Burns, I can feel thee and find rest again.
The Goddess Artemis is with me here.

Artemis

With thee and loving thee, poor sufferer!

Hippolytus

Dost see me, Mistress, nearing my last sleep?

Artemis

Aye, and would weep for thee, if Gods could weep.

Hippolytus

Who now shall hunt with thee or hold thy quiver?

Artemis

He dies; but my love cleaves to him for ever.

Hippolytus

Who guide thy chariot, keep thy shrine-flowers fresh?

Artemis

The accursèd Cyprian caught him in her mesh!

Hippolytus
The Cyprian? Now I see it!—Aye, 'twas she.

Artemis
She missed her worship, loathed thy chastity!

Hippolytus
Three lives by her one hand! 'Tis all clear now.

Artemis
Yea, three; thy father and his Queen and thou.

Hippolytus
My father; yea, he too is pitiable!

Artemis
A plotting Goddess tripped him, and he fell.

Hippolytus
Father, where art thou? . . . Oh, thou sufferest sore!

Theseus
Even unto death, Child. There is joy no more.

Hippolytus
I pity thee in this coil; aye, more than me.

Theseus
Would I could lie there dead instead of thee!

Hippolytus
Oh, bitter bounty of Poseidon's love!

Theseus
Would God my lips had never breathed thereof!

Hippolytus (*gently*)
Nay, thine own rage had slain me then, some wise!

Theseus
A lying spirit had made blind mine eyes!

Hippolytus
Ah me!
Would that a mortal's curse could reach to God!

Artemis
Let be! For not, though deep beneath the sod
Thou liest, not unrequited nor unsung
Shall this fell stroke, from Cypris' rancour sprung,
Quell thee, mine own, the saintly and the true!
  My hand shall win its vengeance, through and through
Piercing with flawless shaft what heart soe'er
Of all men living is most dear to Her.
Yea, and to thee, for this sore travail's sake,
Honours most high in Trozên will I make;
For yokeless maids before their bridal night
Shall shear for thee their tresses; and a rite
Of honouring tears be thine in ceaseless store;
And virgins' thoughts in music evermore
Turn toward thee, and praise thee in the song
Of Phædra's far-famed love and thy great wrong.
  O seed of ancient Ægeus, bend thee now
And clasp thy son. Aye, hold and fear not thou!
Not knowingly hast thou slain him; and man's way,
When Gods send error, needs must fall astray.
  And thou, Hippolytus, shrink not from the King,
Thy father. Thou wast born to bear this thing.
  Farewell! I may not watch man's fleeting breath,
Nor stain mine eyes with the effluence of death.
And sure that Terror now is very near.
        [*The cloud slowly rises and floats away.*

Hippolytus

Farewell, farewell, most Blessèd! Lift thee clear
Of soiling men! Thou wilt not grieve in heaven
For my long love! . . . Father, thou art forgiven.
It was Her will. I am not wroth with thee. . . .
I have obeyed Her all my days! . . .
                              Ah me,
The dark is drawing down upon mine eyes;
It hath me! . . . Father! . . . Hold me! Help me rise!

Theseus (*supporting him in his arms*)

Ah, woe! How dost thou torture me, my son!

Hippolytus

I see the Great Gates opening. I am gone.

Theseus

Gone? And my hand red-reeking from this thing!

Hippolytus

Nay, nay; thou art assoiled of manslaying.

Theseus

Thou leav'st me clear of murder? Sayst thou so?

Hippolytus

Yea, by the Virgin of the Stainless Bow!

Theseus

Dear Son! Ah, now I see thy nobleness!

Hippolytus

Pray that a true-born child may fill my place.

Theseus

Ah me, thy righteous and god-fearing heart!

Hippolytus

Farewell;
A long farewell, dear Father, ere we part!
    [THESEUS *bends down and embraces him passionately.*

Theseus

Not yet!—O hope and bear while thou hast breath!

Hippolytus

Lo, I have borne my burden. This is death. . . .
Quick, Father; lay the mantle on my face.
    [THESEUS *covers his face with a mantle and rises.*

Theseus

Ye bounds of Pallas and of Pelops' race,
What greatness have ye lost!
                    Woe, woe is me!
Thou Cyprian, long shall I remember thee!

Chorus

  On all this folk, both low and high,
  A grief hath fallen beyond men's fears.
  There cometh a throbbing of many tears,
    A sound as of waters falling.
      For when great men die,
  A mighty name and a bitter cry
    Rise up from a nation calling.
                [*They move into the Castle, carrying
                        the body of* HIPPOLYTUS.

THE BACCHÆ
OF EURIPIDES

DRAMATIS PERSONÆ

DIONYSUS, THE GOD; *son of Zeus and of the Theban princess Semelê*
CADMUS, *formerly King of Thebes, father of Semelê*
PENTHEUS, *King of Thebes, grandson of Cadmus*
AGÂVÊ, *daughter of Cadmus, mother of Pentheus*
TEIRESIAS, *an aged Theban prophet*
A SOLDIER OF PENTHEUS' GUARD
TWO MESSENGERS
A CHORUS OF INSPIRED DAMSELS, *following Dionysus from the East*

"*The play was first produced after the death of Euripides by his son, who bore the same name, together with the 'Iphigenia in Aulis' and the 'Alcmæon,' probably in the year* 405 B.C."

The background represents the front of the Castle of PENTHEUS, *King of Thebes. At one side is visible the sacred Tomb of Semelê, a little enclosure overgrown with wild vines, with a cleft in the rocky floor of it from which there issues at times steam or smoke. The God* DIONYSUS *is discovered alone.*

Dionysus

BEHOLD, God's Son is come unto this land
Of Thebes, even I, Dionysus, whom the brand
Of heaven's hot splendour lit to life, when she
Who bore me, Cadmus' daughter Semelê,
Died here. So, changed in shape from God to man,
I walk again by Dircê's streams and scan
Ismenus' shore. There by the castle side
I see her place, the Tomb of the Lightning's Bride,
The wreck of smouldering chambers, and the great
Faint wreaths of fire undying—as the hate
Dies not, that Hera held for Semelê.

  Aye, Cadmus hath done well; in purity
He keeps this place apart, inviolate,
His daughter's sanctuary; and I have set
My green and clustered vines to robe it round.

Far now behind me lies the golden ground
Of Lydian and of Phrygian; far away
The wide hot plains where Persian sunbeams play,
The Bactrian war-holds, and the storm-oppressed
Clime of the Mede, and Araby the Blest,
And Asia all, that by the salt sea lies
In proud embattled cities, motley-wise
Of Hellene and Barbarian interwrought;
And now I come to Hellas—having taught
All the world else my dances and my rite
Of mysteries, to show me in men's sight
Manifest God.
          And first of Hellene lands
I cry this Thebes to waken; set her hands
To clasp my wand, mine ivied javelin,
And round her shoulders hang my wild fawn-skin.
For they have scorned me whom it least beseemed,
Semelê's sisters; mocked my birth, nor deemed
That Dionysus sprang from Dian seed.
My mother sinned, said they; and in her need,
With Cadmus plotting, cloaked her human shame
With the dread name of Zeus; for that the flame
From heaven consumed her, seeing she lied to God.
  Thus must they vaunt; and therefore hath my rod
On them first fallen, and stung them forth wild-eyed
From empty chambers; the bare mountain side
Is made their home, and all their hearts are flame.
Yea, I have bound upon the necks of them
The harness of my rites. And with them all
The seed of womankind from hut and hall
Of Thebes, hath this my magic goaded out.
And there, with the old King's daughters, in a rout
Confused, they make their dwelling-place between
The roofless rocks and shadowy pine-trees green.
Thus shall this Thebes, how sore soe'er it smart,
Learn and forget not, till she crave her part
In mine adoring; thus must I speak clear

To save my mother's fame, and crown me here
As true God, born by Semelê to Zeus.

   Now Cadmus yieldeth up his throne and use
Of royal honour to his daughter's son
Pentheus; who on my body hath begun
A war with God. He thrusteth me away
From due drink-offering, and, when men pray,
My name entreats not. Therefore on his own
Head and his people's shall my power be shown.
Then to another land, when all things here
Are well, must I fare onward, making clear
My godhead's might. But should this Theban town
Essay with wrath and battle to drag down
My maids, lo, in their path myself shall be,
And maniac armies battled after me!
For this I veil my godhead with the wan
Form of the things that die, and walk as Man.

   O Brood of Tmolus o'er the wide world flown,
O Lydian band, my chosen and mine own,
Damsels uplifted o'er the orient deep
To wander where I wander, and to sleep
Where I sleep; up, and wake the old sweet sound,
The clang that I and mystic Rhea found,
The Timbrel of the Mountain! Gather all
Thebes to your song round Pentheus' royal hall.
I seek my new-made worshippers, to guide
Their dances up Kithæron's pine-clad side.

        [*As he departs, there comes stealing in from the left a band of fifteen Eastern Women, the light of the sunrise streaming upon their long white robes and ivy-bound hair. They wear fawn-skins over the robes, and carry some of them timbrels, some pipes and other instruments. Many bear the thyrsus, or sacred Wand, made of reed ringed with ivy. They enter stealthily till they see that the place is empty, and then begin their mystic song of worship.*

Chorus

A Maiden

From Asia, from the dayspring that uprises,
  To Bromios ever glorying we came.
We laboured for our Lord in many guises;
We toilèd, but the toil is as the prize is;
  Thou Mystery, we hail thee by thy name!

Another

Who lingers in the road? Who espies us?
  He shall hide him in his house nor be bold.
Let the heart keep silence that defies us;
For I sing this day to Dionysus
  The song that is appointed from of old.

All the Maidens

Oh, blessèd he in all wise,
  Who hath drunk the Living Fountain,
    Whose life no folly staineth,
    And his soul is near to God;
Whose sins are lifted, pall-wise,
  As he worships on the Mountain,
    And where Cybelê ordaineth,
    Our Mother, he has trod:

    His head with ivy laden
      And his thyrsus tossing high,
      For our God he lifts his cry:
    "Up, O Bacchæ, wife and maiden,
      Come, O ye Bacchæ, come;
    Oh, bring the Joy-bestower,
    God-seed of God the Sower,

>   Bring Bromios in his power
>   From Phrygia's mountain dome;
>   To street and town and tower,
>   Oh, bring ye Bromios home!"

Whom erst in anguish lying
  For an unborn life's desire,
    As a dead thing in the Thunder
    His mother cast to earth;
For her heart was dying, dying,
  In the white heart of the fire;
    Till Zeus, the Lord of Wonder,
    Devised new lairs of birth;

>   Yea, his own flesh tore to hide him,
>   And with clasps of bitter gold
>   Did a secret son enfold,
>   And the Queen knew not beside him;
>   Till the perfect hour was there;
>   Then a hornèd God was found,
>   And a God with serpents crowned;
>   And for that are serpents wound
>   In the wands his maidens bear,
>   And the songs of serpents sound
>   In the mazes of their hair.

Some Maidens

All hail, O Thebes, thou nurse of Semelê!
  With Semelê's wild ivy crown thy towers;
Oh, burst in bloom of wreathing bryony,
    Berries and leaves and flowers;
    Uplift the dark divine wand,
    The oak-wand and the pine-wand,
And don thy fawn-skin, fringed in purity
    With fleecy white, like ours.

Oh, cleanse thee in the wands' waving pride!
  Yea, all men shall dance with us and pray,
When Bromios his companies shall guide

Hillward, ever hillward, where they stay,
  The flock of the Believing,
  The maids from loom and weaving
By the magic of his breath borne away.

Others

Hail thou, O Nurse of Zeus, O Caverned Haunt
  Where fierce arms clanged to guard God's cradle rare,
For thee of old some crested Corybant
    First woke in Cretan air
    The wild orb of our orgies,
    Our Timbrel; and thy gorges
Rang with this strain; and blended Phrygian chant
    And sweet keen pipes were there.

But the Timbrel, the Timbrel was another's,
    And away to Mother Rhea it must wend;
And to our holy singing from the Mother's
    The mad Satyrs carried it, to blend
    In the dancing and the cheer
    Of our third and perfect Year;
    And it serves Dionysus in the end!

A Maiden

O glad, glad on the mountains
    To swoon in the race outworn,
        When the holy fawn-skin clings,
        And all else sweeps away,
To the joy of the red quick fountains,
    The blood of the hill-goat torn,
        The glory of wild-beast ravenings,
        Where the hilltops catch the day;
To the Phrygian, Lydian, mountains!
    'Tis Bromios leads the way.

Another Maiden

Then streams the earth with milk, yea, streams
    With wine and nectar of the bee,

And through the air dim perfume steams
  Of Syrian frankincense; and he,
Our leader, from his thyrsus spray
  A torchlight tosses high and higher,
  A torchlight like a beacon-fire,
To waken all that faint and stray;
  And sets them leaping as he sings,
  His tresses rippling to the sky,
  And deep beneath the Mænad cry
    His proud voice rings:
      "Come, O ye Bacchæ, come!"

All the Maidens

Hither, O fragrant of Tmolus the Golden,
  Come with the voice of timbrel and drum;
Let the cry of your joyance uplift and embolden
  The God of the joy-cry; O Bacchanals, come!
With pealing of pipes and with Phrygian clamour,
  On, where the vision of holiness thrills,
And the music climbs and the maddening glamour,
  With the wild White Maids, to the hills, to the hills!
Oh, then, like a colt as he runs by a river,
  A colt by his dam, when the heart of him sings,
With the keen limbs drawn and the fleet foot aquiver,
    Away the Bacchanal springs!

Enter TEIRESIAS. *He is an old man and blind, leaning upon a staff and moving with slow stateliness, though wearing the Ivy and the Bacchic fawn-skin.*

Teiresias

Ho, there, who keeps the gate?—Go, summon me
Cadmus, Agênor's son, who crossed the sea
From Sidon and upreared this Theban hold.
Go, whosoe'er thou art. See he be told
Teiresias seeketh him. Himself will gauge
Mine errand, and the compact, age with age,
I vowed with him, grey hair with snow-white hair,

To deck the new God's thyrsus, and to wear
His fawn-skin, and with ivy crown our brows.

Enter Cadmus *from the Castle. He is even older than*
Teiresias, *and wears the same attire.*

Cadmus

True friend! I knew that voice of thine, that flows
Like mellow wisdom from a fountain wise.
And, lo, I come prepared, in all the guise
And harness of this God. Are we not told
His is the soul of that dead life of old
That sprang from mine own daughter? Surely then
Must thou and I with all the strength of men
Exalt Him.   Where then shall I stand, where tread
The dance and toss this bowed and hoary head?
O friend, in thee is wisdom; guide my grey
And eld-worn steps, eld-worn Teiresias.—Nay;
I am not weak.
   [*At the first movement of worship his manner
   begins to change; a mysterious strength and
   exaltation enter into him.*
                Surely this arm could smite
The wild earth with its thyrsus, day and night,
And faint not! Sweetly and forgetfully
The dim years fall from off me!

Teiresias

                    As with thee,
With me 'tis likewise. Light am I and young,
And will essay the dancing and the song.

Cadmus

Quick, then, our chariots to the mountain road.

Teiresias

Nay; to take steeds were to mistrust the God.

Cadmus

So be it. Mine old arms shall guide thee there.

Teiresias

The God Himself shall guide! Have thou no care.

Cadmus

And in all Thebes shall no man dance but we?

Teiresias

Aye, Thebes is blinded. Thou and I can see.

Cadmus

'Tis weary waiting; hold my hand, friend; so.

Teiresias

Lo, there is mine. So linkèd let us go.

Cadmus

Shall things of dust the Gods' dark ways despise?

Teiresias

Or prove our wit on Heaven's high mysteries?
Not thou and I! That heritage sublime
Our sires have left us, wisdom old as time,
No word of man, how deep soe'er his thought
And won of subtlest toil, may bring to naught.
  Aye, men will rail that I forgot my years,
To dance and wreathe with ivy these white hairs;
What recks it? seeing the God no line hath told
To mark what man shall dance, or young or old;
But craves His honours from mortality
All, no man marked apart; and great shall be!

Cadmus (after looking away towards the Mountain)

Teiresias, since this light thou canst not read,

I must be seer for thee. Here comes in speed
Pentheus, Echîon's son, whom I have raised
To rule my people in my stead.—Amazed
He seems. Stand close, and mark what we shall hear.
> [*The two stand back, partially concealed, while there enters in hot haste* PENTHEUS, *followed by a bodyguard. He is speaking to the* SOLDIER *in command.*

Pentheus

Scarce had I crossed our borders, when mine ear
Was caught by this strange rumour, that our own
Wives, our own sisters, from their hearths are flown
To wild and secret rites; and cluster there
High on the shadowy hills, with dance and prayer
To adore this new-made God, this Dionyse,
Whate'er he be!—And in their companies
Deep wine-jars stand, and ever and anon
Away into the loneliness now one
Steals forth, and now a second, maid or dame,
Where love lies waiting, not of God! The flame,
They say, of Bacchios wraps them. Bacchios! Nay,
'Tis more to Aphrodite that they pray.

  Howbeit, all that I have found, my men
Hold bound and shackled in our dungeon den;
The rest, I will go hunt them! Aye, and snare
My birds with nets of iron, to quell their prayer
And mountain song and rites of rascaldom!

  They tell me, too, there is a stranger come,
A man of charm and spell, from Lydian seas,
A head all gold and cloudy fragrancies,
A wine-red cheek, and eyes that hold the light
Of the very Cyprian. Day and livelong night
He haunts amid the damsels, o'er each lip
Dangling his cup of joyance!—Let me grip
Him once, but once, within these walls, right swift
That wand shall cease its music, and that drift

Of tossing curls lie still—when my rude sword
Falls between neck and trunk! 'Tis all his word,
This tale of Dionysus; how that same
Babe that was blasted by the lightning flame
With his dead mother, for that mother's lie,
Was reconceived, born perfect from the thigh
Of Zeus, and now is God! What call ye these?
Dreams? Gibes of the unknown wanderer? Blasphemies
That crave the very gibbet?
                        Stay! God wot,
Here is another marvel! See I not
In motley fawn-skins robed the vision-seer
Teiresias? And my mother's father here—
O depth of scorn!—adoring with the wand
Of Bacchios?—Father!—Nay, mine eyes are fond;
It is not your white heads so fancy-flown!
It cannot be! Cast off that ivy crown,
O mine own mother's sire! Set free that hand
That cowers about its staff.
                        'Tis thou hast planned
This work, Teiresias! 'Tis thou must set
Another altar and another yet
Amongst us, watch new birds, and win more hire
Of gold, interpreting new signs of fire!
But for thy silver hairs, I tell thee true,
Thou now wert sitting chained amid thy crew
Of raving damsels, for this evil dream
Thou hast brought us, of new Gods! When once the gleam
Of grapes hath lit a Woman's Festival,
In all their prayers is no more health at all!

Leader of the Chorus

(*the words are not heard by* Pentheus)

Injurious King, hast thou no fear of God,
Nor Cadmus, sower of the Giants' Sod,
Life-spring to great Echîon and to thee?

Teiresias

Good words, my son, come easily, when he
That speaks is wise, and speaks but for the right.
Else come they never! Swift are thine, and bright
As though with thought, yet have no thought at all.
  Lo, this new God, whom thou dost flout withal,
I cannot speak the greatness wherewith He
In Hellas shall be great! Two spirits there be,
Young Prince, that in man's world are first of worth.
Dêmêtêr one is named; she is the Earth—
Call her which name thou wilt!—who feeds man's frame
With sustenance of things dry. And that which came
Her work to perfect, second, is the Power
From Semelê born. He found the liquid shower
Hid in the grape. He rests man's spirit dim
From grieving, when the vine exalteth him.
He giveth sleep to sink the fretful day
In cool forgetting. Is there any way
With man's sore heart, save only to forget?
  Yea, being God, the blood of Him is set
Before the Gods in sacrifice, that we
For His sake may be blest.—And so, to thee,
That fable shames Him, how this God was knit
Into God's flesh? Nay, learn the truth of it,
Cleared from the false.—When from that deadly light
Zeus saved the babe, and up to Olympus' height
Raised Him, and Hera's wrath would cast Him thence,
Then Zeus devised Him a divine defence.
A fragment of the world-encircling fire
He rent apart, and wrought to His desire
Of shape and hue, in the image of the child,
And gave to Hera's rage. And so, beguiled
By change and passing time, this tale was born,
How the babe-god was hidden in the torn
Flesh of His sire. He hath no shame thereby.
  A prophet is He likewise. Prophecy

Cleaves to all frenzy, but beyond all else
To frenzy of prayer. Then in us verily dwells
The God Himself, and speaks the thing to be.
Yea, and of Ares' realm a part hath He.
When mortal armies, mailèd and arrayed,
Have in strange fear, or ever blade met blade,
Fled maddened, 'tis this God hath palsied them.
Aye, over Delphi's rock-built diadem
Thou yet shalt see Him leaping with His train
Of fire across the twin-peaked mountain-plain,
Flaming the darkness with His mystic wand,
And great in Hellas.—List and understand,
King Pentheus! Dream not thou that force is power;
Nor, if thou hast a thought, and that thought sour
And sick, oh, dream not thought is wisdom!—Up,
Receive this God to Thebes; pour forth the cup
Of sacrifice, and pray, and wreathe thy brow.

   Thou fearest for the damsels? Think thee now;
How toucheth this the part of Dionyse
To hold maids pure perforce? In them it lies,
And their own hearts; and in the wildest rite
Cometh no stain to her whose heart is white.

   Nay, mark me! Thou hast thy joy, when the Gate
Stands thronged, and Pentheus' name is lifted great
And high by Thebes in clamour; shall not He
Rejoice in His due meed of majesty?

   Howbeit, this Cadmus whom thou scorn'st and I
Will wear His crown, and tread His dances! Aye,
Our hairs are white, yet shall that dance be trod!
I will not lift mine arm to war with God
For thee nor all thy words. Madness most fell
Is on thee, madness wrought by some dread spell,
But not by spell nor leechcraft to be cured!

Chorus

Grey prophet, worthy of Phœbus is thy word,
And wise in honouring Bromios, our great God.

Cadmus

My son, right well Teiresias points thy road.
Oh, make thine habitation here with us,
Not lonely, against men's uses. Hazardous
Is this quick birdlike beating of thy thought
Where no thought dwells.—Grant that this God be naught,
Yet let that Naught be Somewhat in thy mouth;
Lie boldly, and say He is! So north and south
Shall marvel, how there sprang a thing divine
From Semelê's flesh, and honour all our line.
[*Drawing nearer to* PENTHEUS.
Is there not blood before thine eyes even now?
Our lost Actæon's blood, whom long ago
His own red hounds through yonder forest dim
Tore unto death, because he vaunted him
Against most holy Artemis? Oh, beware,
And let me wreathe thy temples. Make thy prayer
With us, and walk thee humbly in God's sight.
[*He makes as if to set the wreath on* PENTHEUS' *head.*

Pentheus

Down with that hand! Aroint thee to thy rite,
Nor smear on me thy foul contagion!
[*Turning upon* TEIRESIAS.
This
Thy folly's head and prompter shall not miss
The justice that he needs!—Go, half my guard,
Forth to the rock-seat where he dwells in ward
O'er birds and wonders; rend the stone with crow
And trident; make one wreck of high and low,
And toss his bands to all the winds of air!
Ha, have I found the way to sting thee, there?
The rest, forth through the town! And seek amain
This girl-faced stranger, that hath wrought such bane
To all Thebes, preying on our maids and wives.
Seek till ye find; and lead him here in gyves,

Till he be judged and stoned, and weep in blood
The day he troubled Pentheus with his God!
> [*The guards set forth in two bodies;* PENTHEUS
> *goes into the Castle*,

Teiresias

Hard heart, how little dost thou know what seed
Thou sowest! Blind before, and now indeed
Most mad!—Come, Cadmus, let us go our way,
And pray for this our persecutor, pray
For this poor city, that the righteous God
Move not in anger.—Take thine ivy rod
And help my steps, as I help thine. 'Twere ill
If two old men should fall by the roadway. Still,
Come what come may, our service shall be done
To Bacchios, the All-Father's mystic son.

  O Pentheus, named of sorrow! Shall he claim
From all thy house fulfilment of his name,
Old Cadmus?—Nay, I speak not from mine art,
But as I see—blind words and a blind heart!
> [*The two Old Men go off towards the Mountain.*

Chorus

Some Maidens

Thou Immaculate on high;
Thou Recording Purity;
Thou that stoopest, Golden Wing,
Earthward, manward, pitying,
Hearest thou this angry King?
Hearest thou the rage and scorn
  'Gainst the Lord of Many Voices,
Him of mortal mother born,
  Him in whom man's heart rejoices,
Girt with garlands and with glee,
First in Heaven's sovranty?
  For His kingdom, it is there,
  In the dancing and the prayer,

In the music and the laughter,
  In the vanishing of care,
And of all before and after;
In the Gods' high banquet, when
  Gleams the grape-flood, flashed to Heaven;
Yea, and in the feasts of men
Comes His crownèd slumber; then
  Pain is dead and hate forgiven!

Others

Loose thy lips from out the rein;
Lift thy wisdom to disdain;
Whatso law thou canst not see,
Scorning; so the end shall be
Uttermost calamity!
'Tis the life of quiet breath,
  'Tis the simple and the true,
Storm nor earthquake shattereth,
  Nor shall aught the house undo
Where they dwell. For, far away,
Hidden from the eyes of day,
  Watchers are there in the skies,
  That can see man's life, and prize
Deeds well done by things of clay.
But the world's Wise are not wise,
Claiming more than mortal may.
Life is such a little thing;
  Lo, their present is departed,
And the dreams to which they cling
Come not. Mad imagining
  Theirs, I ween, and empty-hearted!

Divers Maidens

Where is the home for me?
O Cyprus, set in the sea,
Aphrodite's home In the soft sea-foam,
  Would I could wend to thee;

Where the wings of the Loves are furled,
And faint the heart of the world.

    Aye, unto Paphos' isle,
    Where the rainless meadows smile
With riches rolled From the hundredfold
    Mouths of the far-off Nile,
Streaming beneath the waves
To the roots of the seaward caves.

    But a better land is there
    Where Olympus cleaves the air,
The high still dell Where the Muses dwell,
    Fairest of all things fair!
O there is Grace, and there is the Heart's Desire,
And peace to adore thee, thou Spirit of Guiding Fire!

    A God of Heaven is He,
    And born in majesty;
Yet hath He mirth In the joy of the Earth,
    And He loveth constantly
Her who brings increase,
The Feeder of Children, Peace.

    No grudge hath He of the great;
    No scorn of the mean estate;
But to all that liveth His wine he giveth,
    Griefless, immaculate;
Only on them that spurn
Joy, may His anger burn.

    Love thou the Day and the Night;
    Be glad of the Dark and the Light;
And avert thine eyes From the lore of the wise,
    That have honour in proud men's sight.
The simple nameless herd of Humanity
Hath deeds and faith that are truth enough for me!

[*As the Chorus ceases, a party of the guards return, leading in the midst of them* DIONYSUS, *bound. The* SOLDIER *in command stands forth, as* PENTHEUS, *hearing the tramp of feet, comes out from the Castle.*]

Soldier

Our quest is finished, and thy prey, O King,
Caught; for the chase was swift, and this wild thing
Most tame; yet never flinched, nor thought to flee,
But held both hands out unresistingly—
No change, no blanching of the wine-red cheek.
He waited while we came, and bade us wreak
All thy decree; yea, laughed, and made my hest
Easy, till I for very shame confessed
And said: "O stranger, not of mine own will
I bind thee, but his bidding to fulfil
Who sent me."
           And those prisoned Maids withal
Whom thou didst seize and bind within the wall
Of thy great dungeon, they are fled, O King,
Free in the woods, a-dance and glorying
To Bromios. Of their own impulse fell
To earth, men say, fetter and manacle,
And bars slid back untouched of mortal hand.
Yea, full of many wonders to thy land
Is this man come. . . . Howbeit, it lies with thee!

Pentheus

Ye are mad!—Unhand him. Howso swift he be,
My toils are round him and he shall not fly.
      [*The guards loose the arms of* DIONYSUS; PENTHEUS *studies him for a while in silence, then speaks jeeringly.* DIONYSUS *remains gentle and unafraid.*]

Marry, a fair shape for a woman's eye,
Sir stranger! And thou seek'st no more, I ween!

Long curls, withal! That shows thou ne'er hast been
A wrestler!—down both cheeks so softly tossed
And winsome! And a white skin! It hath cost
Thee pains to please thy damsels with this white
And red of cheeks that never face the light!

[DIONYSUS *is silent.*

Speak, sirrah; tell me first thy name and race.

Dionysus

No glory is therein, nor yet disgrace.
Thou hast heard of Tmolus, the bright hill of flowers?

Pentheus

Surely, the ridge that winds by Sardis' towers.

Dionysus

Thence am I; Lydia was my fatherland.

Pentheus

And whence these revelations, that thy band
Spreadeth in Hellas?

Dionysus

Their intent and use
Dionysus oped to me, the Child of Zeus.

Pentheus (*brutally*)

Is there a Zeus there, that can still beget
Young Gods?

Dionysus

Nay, only He whose seal was set
Here in thy Thebes on Semelê.

Pentheus

What way
Descended He upon thee? In full day
Or vision of night?

Dionysus

                Most clear He stood, and scanned
My soul, and gave His emblems to mine hand.

Pentheus

What like be they, these emblems?

Dionysus

                        That may none
Reveal, nor know, save His Elect alone.

Pentheus

And what good bring they to the worshipper?

Dionysus

Good beyond price, but not for thee to hear.

Pentheus

Thou trickster! Thou wouldst prick me on the more
To seek them out!

Dionysus

            His mysteries abhor
The touch of sin-lovers.

Pentheus

                And so thine eyes
Saw this God plain; what guise had He?

Dionysus

                        What guise
It liked Him. 'Twas not I ordained His shape.

Pentheus

Aye, deftly turned again. An idle jape,
And nothing answered!

Dionysus

                Wise words being brought
To blinded eyes will seem as things of naught.

Pentheus

And comest thou first to Thebes, to have thy God
Established?

Dionysus

          Nay; all Barbary hath trod
His dance ere this.

Pentheus

             A low blind folk, I ween,
Beside our Hellenes!

Dionysus

            Higher and more keen
In this thing, though their ways are not thy way.

Pentheus

How is thy worship held, by night or day?

Dionysus

Most oft by night; 'tis a majestic thing,
The darkness.

Pentheus

          Ha! with women worshipping?
'Tis craft and rottenness!

Dionysus

            By day no less,
Whoso will seek may find unholiness.

Pentheus

Enough! Thy doom is fixed, for false pretence
Corrupting Thebes.

Dionysus
              Not mine; but thine, for dense
Blindness of heart, and for blaspheming God!

Pentheus
A ready knave it is, and brazen-browed,
This mystery-priest!

Dionysus
             Come, say what it shall be,
My doom; what dire thing wilt thou do to me?

Pentheus
First, shear that delicate curl that dangles there.
    [*He beckons to the soldiers, who approach* Dionysus.

Dionysus
I have vowed it to my God; 'tis holy hair.
                  [*The soldiers cut off the tress.*

Pentheus
Next, yield me up thy staff!

Dionysus
                  Raise thine own hand
To take it. This is Dionysus' wand.
                  [Pentheus *takes the staff.*

Pentheus
Last, I will hold thee prisoned here.

Dionysus
               My Lord
God will unloose me, when I speak the word.

Pentheus
He may, if e'er again amid His bands
Of saints He hears thy voice!

Dionysus

        Even now He stands
Close here, and sees all that I suffer.

Pentheus

          What?
Where is He? For mine eyes discern Him not.

Dionysus

Where I am! 'Tis thine own impurity
That veils Him from thee.

Pentheus

        The dog jeers at me!
At me and Thebes! Bind him!
     [*The soldiers begin to bind him.*

Dionysus

        I charge ye, bind
Me not! I having vision and ye blind!

Pentheus

And I, with better right, say bind the more!
         [*The soldiers obey.*

Dionysus

Thou knowest not what end thou seekest, nor
What deed thou doest, nor what man thou art!

Pentheus (*mocking*)

Agâvê's son, and on the father's part
Echîon's, hight Pentheus!

Dionysus

      So let it be,
A name fore-written to calamity!

Pentheus

Away, and tie him where the steeds are tied;
Aye, let him lie in the manger!—There abide
And stare into the darkness!—And this rout
Of womankind that clusters thee about,
Thy ministers of worship, are my slaves!
It may be I will sell them o'er the waves,
Hither and thither; else they shall be set
To labour at my distaffs, and forget
Their timbrel and their songs of dawning day!

Dionysus

I go; for that which may not be, I may
Not suffer! Yet for this thy sin, lo, He
Whom thou deniest cometh after thee
For recompense. Yea, in thy wrong to us,
Thou hast cast Him into thy prison-house!

[Dionysus, *without his wand, his hair shorn, and his arms tightly bound, is led off by the guards to his dungeon.* Pentheus *returns into the Palace.*

Chorus
Some Maidens

Acheloüs' roaming daughter,
Holy Dircê, virgin water,
Bathed He not of old in thee,
The Babe of God, the Mystery?
When from out the fire immortal
  To Himself His God did take Him,
  To His own flesh, and bespake Him:
"Enter now life's second portal,
Motherless Mystery; lo, I break
Mine own body for thy sake,
  Thou of the Twofold Door, and seal thee
Mine, O Bromios,"—thus he spake—
  "And to this thy land reveal thee."

All

Still my prayer toward thee quivers,
  Dircê, still to thee I hie me;
Why, O Blessèd among Rivers,
  Wilt thou fly me and deny me?
    By His own joy I vow,
    By the grape upon the bough,
Thou shalt seek Him in the midnight, thou shalt love
    Him, even now!

Other Maidens

Dark and of the dark impassioned
Is this Pentheus' blood; yea, fashioned
Of the Dragon, and his birth
From Echîon, child of Earth.
He is no man, but a wonder;
  Did the Earth-Child not beget him,
  As a red Giant, to set him
Against God, against the Thunder?
He will bind me for his prize,
Me, the Bride of Dionyse;
  And my priest, my friend, is taken
Even now, and buried lies;
  In the dark he lies forsaken!

All

Lo, we race with death, we perish,
  Dionysus, here before thee!
Dost thou mark us not, nor cherish,
  Who implore thee, and adore thee?
    Hither down Olympus' side,
    Come, O Holy One defied,
Be thy golden wand uplifted o'er the tyrant in his
    pride!

A maiden

Oh, where art thou? In thine own
Nysa, thou our help alone?
O'er fierce beasts in orient lands
    Doth thy thronging thyrsus wave,
    By the high Corycian Cave,
Or where stern Olympus stands;
In the elm woods and the oaken,
    There where Orpheus harped of old,
  And the trees awoke and knew him,
  And the wild things gathered to him,
As he sang amid the broken
    Glens his music manifold?
Blessèd Land of Piërie,
Dionysus loveth thee;
  He will come to thee with dancing,
Come with joy and mystery;
With the Mænads at His hest
Winding, winding to the West;
    Cross the flood of swiftly glancing
Axios in majesty;
Cross the Lydias, the giver
  Of good gifts and waving green;
Cross that Father-Stream of story,
Through a land of steeds and glory
Rolling, bravest, fairest River
  E'er of mortals seen!

A Voice Within

Io! Io!
Awake, ye damsels; hear my cry,
  Calling my Chosen; hearken ye!

A Maiden

Who speaketh? Oh, what echoes thus?

Another

A Voice, a Voice, that calleth us!

The Voice

Be of good cheer! Lo, it is I,
    The Child of Zeus and Semelê.

A Maiden

O Master, Master, it is Thou!

Another

O Holy Voice, be with us now!

The Voice

Spirit of the Chained Earthquake,
Hear my word; awake, awake!
    [*An Earthquake suddenly shakes the pillars of*
                                               the Castle.

A Maiden

Ha! what is coming? Shall the hall
Of Pentheus racked in ruin fall?

Leader

Our God is in the house! Ye maids adore Him!

Chorus
                  We adore Him all!

The Voice

Unveil the Lightning's eye; arouse
The fire that sleeps, against this house!
        [*Fire leaps upon the Tomb of Semelê.*

A Maiden

Ah, saw ye, marked ye there the flame
    From Semelê's enhallowed sod

Awakened? Yea, the Death that came
Ablaze from Heaven of old, the same
Hot splendour of the shaft of God?

Leader

Oh, cast ye, cast ye to the earth! The Lord
Cometh against this house! Oh, cast ye down,
Ye trembling damsels; He, our own adored,
God's Child hath come, and all is overthrown!

[*The Maidens cast themselves upon the ground, their eyes earthward.* DIONYSUS, *alone and unbound, enters from the Castle.*

Dionysus

Ye Damsels of the Morning Hills, why lie ye thus dismayed?
Ye marked Him, then, our Master, and the mighty hand He laid
On tower and rock, shaking the house of Pentheus?— But arise,
And cast the trembling from your flesh, and lift untroubled eyes.

Leader

O Light in Darkness, is it thou? O Priest, is this thy face?
My heart leaps out to greet thee from the deep of loneliness.

Dionysus

Fell ye so quick despairing, when beneath the Gate I passed?
Should the gates of Pentheus quell me, or his darkness make me fast?

Leader

Oh, what was left if thou wert gone? What could I but despair?

How hast thou 'scaped the man of sin? Who freed thee
    from the snare?

Dionysus

I had no pain nor peril; 'twas mine own hand set me free.

Leader

Thine arms were gyvèd!

Dionysus

              Nay, no gyve, no touch, was laid on me!
'Twas there I mocked him, in his gyves, and gave him
    dreams for food.
For when he laid me down, behold, before the stall there
    stood
A Bull of Offering. And this King, he bit his lips, and
    straight
Fell on and bound it, hoof and limb, with gasping wrath
    and sweat.
And I sat watching!—Then a Voice; and lo, our Lord
    was come,
And the house shook, and a great flame stood o'er His
    mother's tomb.
And Pentheus hied this way and that, and called his thralls
    amain
For water, lest his roof-tree burn; and all toiled, all in vain;
Then deemed a-sudden I was gone; and left his fire, and
    sped
Back to the prison portals, and his lifted sword shone red.
But there, methinks, the God had wrought—I speak but as
    I guess—
Some dream-shape in mine image; for he smote at empti-
    ness,
Stabbed in the air, and strove in wrath, as though 'twere me
    he slew.
Then 'mid his dreams God smote him yet again! He over-
    threw

All that high house. And there in wreck for evermore it
    lies,
That the day of this my bondage may be sore in Pentheus'
    eyes!
  And now his sword is fallen, and he lies outworn and
    wan
Who dared to rise against his God in wrath, being but man.
And I uprose and left him, and in all peace took my path
Force to my Chosen, recking light of Pentheus and his
    wrath.
  But soft, methinks a footstep sounds even now within the
    hall;
'Tis he; how think ye he will stand, and what words speak
    withal?
I will endure him gently, though he come in fury hot.
For still are the ways of Wisdom, and her temper trem
    bleth not!

Enter PENTHEUS *in fury*

Pentheus

It is too much! This Eastern knave hath slipped
His prison, whom I held but now, hard gripped
In bondage.—Ha! 'Tis he!—What, sirrah, how
Show'st thou before my portals?

[*He advances furiously upon him.*

Dionysus

                    Softly, thou!
And set a quiet carriage to thy rage.

Pentheus

How comest thou here? How didst thou break thy cage?
Speak!

Dionysus

    Said I not, or didst thou mark not me,
There was One living that should set me free?

Pentheus

Who? Ever wilder are these tales of thine.

Dionysus

He who first made for man the clustered vine.

Pentheus

I scorn Him and His vines.

Dionysus

          For Dionyse
'Tis well; for in thy scorn His glory lies.

Pentheus (*to his guard*)

Go swift to all the towers, and bar withal
Each gate!

Dionysus

          What, cannot God o'erleap a wall?

Pentheus

Oh, wit thou hast, save where thou needest it!

Dionysus

Whereso it most imports, there is my wit!—
Nay, peace! Abide till he who hasteth from
The mountain side with news, for thee, be come,
We will not fly, but wait on thy command.

Enter suddenly and in haste a MESSENGER *from
the Mountain*

Messenger

Great Pentheus, Lord of all this Theban land,
I come from high Kithæron, where the frore
Snow spangles gleam and cease not evermore. . . .

Pentheus

And what of import may thy coming bring?

Messenger

I have seen the Wild White Women there, O King,
Whose fleet limbs darted arrow-like but now
From Thebes away, and come to tell thee how
They work strange deeds and passing marvel. Yet
I first would learn thy pleasure. Shall I set
My whole tale forth, or veil the stranger part?
Yea, Lord, I fear the swiftness of thy heart,
Thine edgèd wrath and more than royal soul.

Pentheus

Thy tale shall nothing scathe thee.—Tell the whole.
It skills not to be wroth with honesty.
Nay, if thy news of them be dark, 'tis he
Shall pay it, who bewitched and led them on.

Messenger

Our herded kine were moving in the dawn
Up to the peaks, the greyest, coldest time,
When the first rays steal earthward, and the rime
Yields, when I saw three bands of them. The one
Autonoë led, one Ino, one thine own
Mother, Agâvê. There beneath the trees
Sleeping they lay, like wild things flung at ease
In the forest; one half sinking on a bed
Of deep pine greenery; one with careless head
Amid the fallen oak leaves; all most cold
In purity—not as thy tale was told
Of wine-cups and wild music and the chase
For love amid the forest's loneliness.
Then rose the Queen Agâvê suddenly
Amid her band, and gave the God's wild cry,
"Awake, ye Bacchanals! I hear the sound

Of hornèd kine. Awake ye!"—Then, all round,
Alert, the warm sleep fallen from their eyes,
A marvel of swift ranks I saw them rise,
Dames young and old, and gentle maids unwed
Among them. O'er their shoulders first they shed
Their tresses, and caught up the fallen fold
Of mantles where some clasp had loosened hold,
And girt the dappled fawn-skins in with long
  Quick snakes that hissed and writhed with quivering tongue.
And one a young fawn held, and one a wild
Wolf cub, and fed them with white milk, and smiled
In love, young mothers with a mother's breast
And babes at home forgotten! Then they pressed
Wreathed ivy round their brows, and oaken sprays
And flowering bryony. And one would raise
Her wand and smite the rock, and straight a jet
Of quick bright water came. Another set
Her thyrsus in the bosomed earth, and there
Was red wine that the God sent up to her,
A darkling fountain. And if any lips
Sought whiter draughts, with dipping finger-tips
They pressed the sod, and gushing from the ground
Came springs of milk. And reed-wands ivy-crowned
Ran with sweet honey, drop by drop.—O King,
Hadst thou been there, as I, and seen this thing,
With prayer and most high wonder hadst thou gone
To adore this God whom now thou rail'st upon!

  Howbeit, the kine-wardens and shepherds straight
Came to one place, amazed, and held debate;
And one being there who walked the streets and scanned
The ways of speech, took lead of them whose hand
Knew but the slow soil and the solemn hill,
And flattering spoke, and asked: "Is it your will,
Masters, we stay the mother of the King,
Agâvê, from her lawless worshipping,
And win us royal thanks?"—And this seemed good

To all; and through the branching underwood
We hid us, cowering in the leaves. And there
Through the appointed hour they made their prayer
And worship of the Wand, with one accord
Of heart and cry—"Iacchos, Bromios, Lord,
God of God born!"—And all the mountain felt,
And worshipped with them; and the wild things knelt
And ramped and gloried, and the wilderness
Was filled with moving voices and dim stress.

   Soon, as it chanced, beside my thicket-close
The Queen herself passed dancing, and I rose
And sprang to seize her. But she turned her face
Upon me: "Ho, my rovers of the chase,
My wild White Hounds, we are hunted! Up, each rod,
And follow, follow, for our Lord and God!"
Thereat, for fear they tear us, all we fled
Amazed; and on, with hand unweaponèd,
They swept toward our herds that browsed the green
Hill grass. Great uddered kine then hadst thou seen
Bellowing in sword-like hands that cleave and tear,
A live steer riven asunder, and the air
Tossed with rent ribs or limbs of cloven tread,
And flesh upon the branches, and a red
Rain from the deep green pines. Yea, bulls of pride,
Horns swift to rage, were fronted and aside
Flung stumbling, by those multitudinous hands
Dragged pitilessly. And swifter were the bands
Of garbèd flesh and bone unbound withal
Than on thy royal eyes the lids may fall.

   Then on like birds, by their own speed upborne,
They swept toward the plains of waving corn
That lie beside Asopus' banks, and bring
To Thebes the rich fruit of her harvesting.
On Hysiæ and Erythræ that lie nursed
Amid Kithæron's bowering rocks, they burst
Destroying, as a foeman's army comes.
They caught up little children from their homes,

High on their shoulders, babes unheld, that swayed
And laughed and fell not; all a wreck they made;
Yea, bronze and iron did shatter, and in play
Struck hither and thither, yet no wound had they;
Caught fire from out the hearths, yea, carried hot
Flames in their tresses and were scorchèd not!

The village folk in wrath took spear and sword,
And turned upon the Bacchæ. Then, dread Lord,
The wonder was. For spear nor barbèd brand
Could scathe nor touch the damsels; but the Wand,
The soft and wreathèd wand their white hands sped,
Blasted those men and quelled them, and they fled
Dizzily. Sure some God was in these things!

And the holy women back to those strange springs
Returned, that God had sent them when the day
Dawned, on the upper heights; and washed away
The stain of battle. And those girdling snakes
Hissed out to lap the water-drops from cheeks
And hair and breast.
                    Therefore I counsel thee,
O King, receive this Spirit, whoe'er he be,
To Thebes in glory. Greatness manifold
Is all about him; and the tale is told
That this is he who first to man did give
The grief-assuaging vine. Oh, let him live;
For if he die, then Love herself is slain,
And nothing joyous in the world again!

Leader

Albeit I tremble, and scarce may speak my thought
To a king's face, yet will I hide it not.
Dionyse is God, no God more true nor higher!

Pentheus

It bursts hard by us, like a smothered fire,
This frenzy of Bacchic women! All my land
Is made their mock.—This needs an iron hand!

Ho, Captain! Quick to the Electran Gate;
Bid gather all my men-at-arms thereat;
Call all that spur the charger, all who know
To wield the orbèd targe or bend the bow;
We march to war!—'Fore God, shall women dare
Such deeds against us? 'Tis too much to bear!

Dionysus

Thou mark'st me not, O King, and holdest light
My solemn words; yet, in thine own despite,
I warn thee still. Lift thou not up thy spear
Against a God, but hold thy peace, and fear
His wrath! He will not brook it, if thou fright
His Chosen from the hills of their delight.

Pentheus

Peace, thou! And if for once thou hast slipped thy chain,
Give thanks!—Or shall I knot thine arms again?

Dionysus

Better to yield Him prayer and sacrifice
Than kick against the pricks, since Dionyse
Is God, and thou but mortal.

Pentheus

      That will I!
Yea, sacrifice of women's blood, to cry
His name through all Kithæron!

Dionysus

       Ye shall fly,
All, and abase your shields of bronzen rim
Before their wands.

Pentheus

     There is no way with him,
This stranger that so dogs us! Well or ill
I may entreat him, he must babble still!

Dionysus

Wait, good my friend! These crooked matters may
Even yet be straightened.
> [PENTHEUS *has started as though to seek his army at the gate.*

Pentheus

     Aye, if I obey
Mine own slaves' will; how else?

Dionysus

        Myself will lead
The damsels hither, without sword or steed.

Pentheus

How now?—This is some plot against me!

Dionysus

        What
Dost fear? Only to save thee do I plot.

Pentheus

It is some compact ye have made, whereby
To dance these hills for ever!

Dionysus

     Verily,
That is my compact, plighted with my Lord!

Pentheus (*turning from him*)

Ho, armourers! Bring forth my shield and sword!—
And thou, be silent!

Dionysus
(*after regarding him fixedly, speaks with resignation*)
    Ah!—Have then thy will!

THE BACCHÆ   405

> [*He fixes his eyes upon* PENTHEUS *again, while
> the armourers bring out his armour; then
> speaks in a tone of command.*]

Man, thou wouldst fain behold them on the hill
Praying!

Pentheus

(*who during the rest of this scene, with a few exceptions,
simply speaks the thoughts that* DIONYSUS *puts into
him, losing power over his own mind*)

      That would I, though it cost me all
The gold of Thebes!

Dionysus

               So much? Thou art quick to fall
To such great longing.

Pentheus

(*somewhat bewildered at what he has said*)
                   Aye; 'twould grieve me much
To see them flown with wine.

Dionysus

                   Yet cravest thou such
A sight as would much grieve thee?

Pentheus

                   Yes; I fain
Would watch, ambushed among the pines.

Dionysus

                 'Twere vain
To hide. They soon will track thee out.

Pentheus

               Well said!
'Twere best done openly.

Dionysus

                Wilt thou be led
By me, and try the venture?

Pentheus

                Aye, indeed!
Lead on. Why should we tarry?

Dionysus

                First we need
A rich and trailing robe of fine linen
To gird thee.

Pentheus

       Nay; am I a woman, then,
And no man more?

Dionysus

            Wouldst have them slay thee dead?
No man may see their mysteries.

Pentheus

                Well said!—
I marked thy subtle temper long ere now.

Dionysus

'Tis Dionyse that prompteth me.

Pentheus

                And how
Mean'st thou the further plan?

Dionysus

                First take thy way
Within. I will array thee.

Pentheus

           What array?
The woman's? Nay, I will not.

Dionysus

                            Doth it change
So soon, all thy desire to see this strange
Adoring?

Pentheus

      Wait! What garb wilt thou bestow
About me?

Dionysus

      First a long tress dangling low
Beneath thy shoulders.

Pentheus

      Aye, and next?

Dionysus

                          The said
Robe, falling to thy feet; and on thine head
A snood.

Pentheus

      And after? Hast thou aught beyond?

Dionysus

Surely; the dappled fawn-skin and the wand.

Pentheus (*after a struggle with himself*)

Enough! I cannot wear a robe and snood.

Dionysus

Wouldst liefer draw the sword and spill men's blood?

Pentheus (*again doubting*)

True, that were evil.—Aye; 'tis best to go
First to some place of watch.

Dionysus

                          Far wiser so,
Than seek by wrath wrath's bitter recompense.

Pentheus

What of the city streets? Canst lead me hence
Unseen of any?

Dionysus

            Lonely and untried
Thy path from hence shall be, and I thy guide!

Pentheus

I care for nothing, so these Bacchanals
Triumph not against me! . . . Forward to my halls
Within!—I will ordain what seemeth best.

Dionysus

So be it, O King! 'Tis mine to obey thine hest,
Whate'er it be.

Pentheus

(*after hesitating once more and waiting*)
                Well, I will go—perchance
To march and scatter them with serried lance,
Perchance to take thy plan. . . . I know not yet.
                      [*Exit* Pentheus *into the Castle.*

Dionysus

Damsels, the lion walketh to the net!
He finds his Bacchæ now, and sees and dies,
And pays for all his sin!—O Dionyse,
This is thine hour and thou not far away.
Grant us our vengeance!—First, O Master, stay
The course of reason in him, and instil
A foam of madness. Let his seeing will,

Which ne'er had stooped to put thy vesture on,
Be darkened, till the deed is lightly done.
Grant likewise that he find through all his streets
Loud scorn, this man of wrath and bitter threats
That made Thebes tremble, led in woman's guise.
  I go to fold that robe of sacrifice
On Pentheus, that shall deck him to the dark,
His mother's gift!—So shall he learn and mark
God's true Son, Dionyse, in fulness God,
Most fearful, yet to man most soft of mood.
      [*Exit* DIONYSUS, *following* PENTHEUS *into the Castle.*

Chorus

Some Maidens

Will they ever come to me, ever again,
    The long, long dances,
On through the dark till the dim stars wane?
Shall I feel the dew on my throat, and the stream
Of wind in my hair? Shall our white feet gleam
    In the dim expanses?
Oh, feet of a fawn to the greenwood fled,
    Alone in the grass and the loveliness;
Leap of the hunted, no more in dread,
    Beyond the snares and the deadly press:
Yet a voice still in the distance sounds,
A voice and a fear and a haste of hounds;
O wildly labouring, fiercely fleet,
    Onward yet by river and glen . . .
Is it joy or terror, ye storm-swift feet? . . .
    To the dear lone lands untroubled of men,
Where no voice sounds, and amid the shadowy green
The little things of the woodland live unseen.

What else is Wisdom? What of man's endeavour
    Or God's high grace, so lovely and so great?
    To stand from fear set free, to breathe and wait;

To hold a hand uplifted over Hate;
And shall not Loveliness be loved for ever?

Others

O Strength of God, slow art thou and still,
    Yet failest never!
On them that worship the Ruthless Will,
On them that dream, doth His judgment wait.
Dreams of the proud man, making great
    And greater ever,
Things which are not of God. In wide
    And devious coverts, hunter-wise,
He coucheth Time's unhasting stride,
    Following, following, him whose eyes
Look not to Heaven. For all is vain,
The pulse of the heart, the plot of the brain,
That striveth beyond the laws that live.
And is thy Faith so much to give,
Is it so hard a thing to see
That the Spirit of God, whate'er it be,
The Law that abides and changes not, ages long,
The Eternal and Nature-born—these things be strong?

What else is Wisdom? What of man's endeavour
    Or God's high grace, so lovely and so great?
    To stand from fear set free, to breathe and wait;
    To hold a hand uplifted over Hate;
And shall not Loveliness be loved for ever?

Leader

    Happy he, on the weary sea,
Who hath fled the tempest and won the haven.
    Happy whoso hath risen, free,
Above his striving. For strangely graven
    Is the orb of life, that one and another
    In gold and power may outpass his brother.
    And men in their millions float and flow

And seethe with a million hopes as leaven;
    And they win their Will, or they miss their Will,
    And the hopes are dead or are pined for still;
        But whoe'er can know,
        As the long days go,
That To Live is happy, hath found his Heaven!

    Re-enter DIONYSUS *from the Castle*

Dionysus

O eye that cravest sights thou must not see,
O heart athirst for that which slakes not! Thee,
Pentheus, I call; forth and be seen, in guise
Of woman, Mænad, saint of Dionyse,
To spy upon His Chosen and thine own
Mother!

    [*Enter* PENTHEUS, *clad like a Bacchanal, and strangely excited, a spirit of Bacchic madness overshadowing him.*

        Thy shape, methinks, is like to one
Of Cadmus' royal maids!

Pentheus

            Yea; and mine eye
Is bright! Yon sun shines twofold in the sky,
Thebes twofold and the Wall of Seven Gates. . . .
And is it a Wild Bull this, that walks and waits
Before me? There are horns upon thy brow!
What art thou, man or beast? For surely now
The Bull is on thee!

Dionysus

            He who erst was wrath,
Goes with us now in gentleness. He hath
Unsealed thine eyes to see what thou shouldst see.

Pentheus

Say; stand I not as Ino stands, or she
Who bore me?

Dionysus

                When I look on thee, it seems
I see their very selves!—But stay; why streams
That lock abroad, not where I laid it, crossed
Under the coif?

Pentheus

          I did it, as I tossed
My head in dancing, to and fro, and cried
His holy music!

Dionysus (*tending him*)

              It shall soon be tied
Aright. 'Tis mine to tend thee. . . . Nay, but stand
With head straight.

Pentheus

             In the hollow of thy hand
I lay me. Deck me as thou wilt.

Dionysus

                    Thy zone
Is loosened likewise; and the folded gown
Not evenly falling to the feet.

Pentheus

              'Tis so,
By the right foot. But here, methinks, they flow
In one straight line to the heel.

Dionysus (*while tending him*)

                  And if thou prove
Their madness true, aye, more than true, what love
And thanks hast thou for me?

Pentheus (not listening to him)

                                     In my right hand
Is it, or thus, that I should bear the wand,
To be most like to them?

Dionysus

                                 Up let it swing
In the right hand, timed with the right foot's spring. . .
'Tis well thy heart is changed!

Pentheus (more wildly)

                                  What strength is this!
Kithæron's steeps and all that in them is—
How sayst thou?—Could my shoulders lift the whole?

Dionysus

Surely thou canst, and if thou wilt! Thy soul,
Being once so sick, now stands as it should stand.

Pentheus

Shall it be bars of iron? Or this bare hand
And shoulder to the crags, to wrench them down?

Dionysus

Wouldst wreck the Nymphs' wild temples, and the brown
Rocks, where Pan pipes at noonday?

Pentheus

                                    Nay; not I!
Force is not well with women. I will lie
Hid in the pine-brake.

Dionysus

                              Even as fits a spy
On holy and fearful things, so shalt thou lie!

Pentheus (*with a laugh*)

They lie there now, methinks—the wild birds, caught
By love among the leaves, and fluttering not!

Dionysus

It may be. That is what thou goest to see,
Aye, and to trap them—so they trap not thee!

Pentheus

Forth through the Thebans' town! I am their king,
Aye, their one Man, seeing I dare this thing!

Dionysus

Yea, thou shalt bear their burden, thou alone;
Therefore thy trial awaiteth thee!—But on;
With me into thine ambush shalt thou come
Unscathed; then let another bear thee home!

Pentheus

The Queen, my mother.

Dionysus

Marked of every eye.

Pentheus

For that I go!

Dionysus

Thou shalt be borne on high!

Pentheus

That were like pride!

Dionysus

Thy mother's hands shall share
Thy carrying.

THE BACCHÆ

Pentheus

Nay; I need not such soft care!

Dionysus

So soft?

Pentheus

Whate'er it be, I have earned it well!
[*Exit* PENTHEUS *towards the Mountain.*

Dionysus

Fell, fell art thou; and to a doom so fell
Thou walkest, that thy name from South to North
Shall shine, a sign for ever!—Reach thou forth
Thine arms, Agâvê, now, and ye dark-browed
Cadmeian sisters! Greet this prince so proud
To the high ordeal, where save God and me,
None walks unscathed!—The rest this day shall see.
[*Exit* DIONYSUS, *following* PENTHEUS.

Chorus

Some Maidens

O hounds raging and blind,
  Up by the mountain road,
Sprites of the maddened mind,
  To the wild Maids of God;
Fill with your rage their eyes,
  Rage at the rage unblest,
Watching in woman's guise,
  The spy upon God's Possessed.

A Bacchanal

Who shall be first to mark
  Eyes in the rock that spy,
Eyes in the pine-tree dark—
  Is it his mother?—and cry:

"Lo, what is this that comes,
 Haunting, troubling still,
Even in our heights, our homes,
 The wild Maids of the Hill?
What flesh bare this child?
 Never on woman's breast
Changeling so evil smiled;
 Man is he not, but Beast!
Loin-shape of the wild,
 Gorgon-breed of the waste!"

All the Chorus

Hither for doom and deed!
 Hither with lifted sword,
 Justice, Wrath of the Lord,
Come in our visible need!
Smite till the throat shall bleed,
Smite till the heart shall bleed,
Him, the tyrannous, lawless, Godless, Echîon's earth-born
 seed!

Other Maidens

Tyrannously hath he trod;
 Marched him, in Law's despite,
Against thy Light, O God,
 Yea, and thy Mother's Light;
Girded him, falsely bold,
 Blinded in craft, to quell
And by man's violence hold
 Things unconquerable.

A Bacchanal

A strait pitiless mind
 Is death unto godliness;
And to feel in humankind
 Life, and a pain the less.
Knowledge, we are not foes!
 I seek thee diligently;

But the world with a great wind blows,
    Shining, and not from thee;
Blowing to beautiful things,
    On, amid dark and light,
Till Life, through the trammellings
    Of Laws that are not the Right,
Breaks, clean and pure, and sings
    Glorying to God in the height!

All the Chorus

Hither for doom and deed!
    Hither with lifted sword,
    Justice, Wrath of the Lord,
Come in our visible need!
Smite till the throat shall bleed,
Smite till the heart shall bleed,
Him, the tyrannous, lawless, Godless, Echîon's earth-born seed!

Leader

Appear, appear, whatso thy shape or name,
    O Mountain Bull, Snake of the Hundred Heads,
    Lion of Burning Flame!
O God, Beast, Mystery, come! Thy mystic maids
Are hunted!—Blast their hunter with thy breath,
    Cast o'er his head thy snare;
And laugh aloud and drag him to his death,
    Who stalks thy herded madness in its lair!

Enter hastily a MESSENGER *from the Mountain, pale and distraught*

Messenger

Woe to the house once blest in Hellas! Woe
To thee, old King Sidonian, who didst sow
The dragon-seed on Ares' bloody lea!
Alas, even thy slaves must weep for thee!

Leader

News from the mountain?—Speak! How hath it sped?

Messenger

Pentheus, my king, Echîon's son, is dead!

Leader

All hail, God of the Voice,
Manifest evermore!

Messenger

What sayst thou?—And how strange thy tone, as though
In joy at this my master's overthrow!

Leader

With fierce joy I rejoice,
Child of a savage shore;
For the chains of my prison are broken, and the dread
where I cowered of yore!

Messenger

And deem'st thou Thebes so beggared, so forlorn
Of manhood, as to sit beneath thy scorn?

Leader

Thebes hath o'er me no sway!
None save Him I obey,
Dionysus, Child of the Highest, Him I obey and adore!

Messenger

One can forgive thee!—Yet 'tis no fair thing,
Maids, to rejoice in a man's suffering.

Leader

Speak of the mountain side!
Tell us the doom he died,
The sinner smitten to death, even where his sin was sore!

Messenger

We climbed beyond the utmost habitings
Of Theban shepherds, passed Asopus' springs,
And struck into the land of rock on dim
Kithæron—Pentheus, and, attending him,
I, and the Stranger who should guide our way.
Then first in a green dell we stopped, and lay,
Lips dumb and feet unmoving, warily
Watching, to be unseen and yet to see.

 A narrow glen it was, by crags o'ertowered,
Torn through by tossing waters, and there lowered
A shadow of great pines over it. And there
The Mænad maidens sate; in toil they were,
Busily glad. Some with an ivy chain
Tricked a worn wand to toss its locks again;
Some, wild in joyance, like young steeds set free,
Made answering songs of mystic melody.

 But my poor master saw not the great band
Before him. "Stranger," cried he, "where we stand
Mine eyes can reach not these false saints of thine.
Mount we the bank, or some high-shouldered pine,
And I shall see their follies clear!" At that
There came a marvel. For the Stranger straight
Touched a great pine-tree's high and heavenward crown,
And lower, lower, lower, urged it down
To the herbless floor. Round like a bending bow,
Or slow wheel's rim a joiner forces to,
So in those hands that tough and mountain stem
Bowed slow—oh, strength not mortal dwelt in them!—
To the very earth. And there he set the King,
And slowly, lest it cast him in its spring,
Let back the young and straining tree, till high
It towered again amid the towering sky;
And Pentheus in the branches! Well, I ween,
He saw the Mænads then, and well was seen!
For scarce was he aloft, when suddenly

There was no Stranger any more with me,
But out of Heaven a Voice—oh, what voice else?—
'Twas He that called! "Behold, O damosels,
I bring ye him who turneth to despite
Both me and ye, and darkeneth my great Light.
'Tis yours to avenge!" So spake he, and there came
'Twixt earth and sky a pillar of high flame.
And silence took the air, and no leaf stirred
In all the forest dell. Thou hadst not heard
In that vast silence any wild thing's cry.
And up they sprang; but with bewildered eye,
Agaze and listening, scarce yet hearing true.
Then came the Voice again. And when they knew
Their God's clear call, old Cadmus' royal brood,
Up, like wild pigeons startled in a wood,
On flying feet they came, his mother blind,
Agâvê, and her sisters, and behind
All the wild crowd, more deeply maddened then,
Through the angry rocks and torrent-tossing glen,
Until they spied him in the dark pine-tree:
Then climbed a crag hard by and furiously
Some sought to stone him, some their wands would fling
Lance-wise aloft, in cruel targeting.
But none could strike. The height o'ertopped their rage,
And there he clung, unscathed, as in a cage
Caught. And of all their strife no end was found.
Then, "Hither," cried Agâvê; "stand we round
And grip the stem, my Wild Ones, till we take
This climbing cat-o'-the-mount! He shall not make
A tale of God's high dances!" Out then shone
Arm upon arm, past count, and closed upon
The pine, and gripped; and the ground gave, and down
It reeled. And that high sitter from the crown
Of the green pine-top, with a shrieking cry
Fell, as his mind grew clear, and there hard by
Was horror visible. 'Twas his mother stood
O'er him, first priestess of those rites of blood.

He tore the coif, and from his head away
Flung it, that she might know him, and not slay
To her own misery. He touched the wild
Cheek, crying: "Mother, it is I, thy child,
Thy Pentheus, born thee in Echîon's hall!
Have mercy, Mother! Let it not befall,
Through sin of mine, that thou shouldst slay thy son!"

   But she, with lips afoam and eyes that run
Like leaping fire, with thoughts that ne'er should be
On earth, possessed by Bacchios utterly,
Stays not nor hears. Round his left arm she put
Both hands, set hard against his side her foot,
Drew . . . and the shoulder severed!—not by might
Of arm, but easily, as the God made light
Her hand's essay. And at the other side
Was Ino rending; and the torn flesh cried,
And on Autonoë pressed, and all the crowd
Of ravening arms. Yea, all the air was loud
With groans that faded into sobbing breath,
Dim shrieks, and joy, and triumph-cries of death.
And here was borne a severed arm, and there
A hunter's booted foot; white bones lay bare
With rending; and swift hands ensanguinèd
Tossed as in sport the flesh of Pentheus dead.

   His body lies afar. The precipice
Hath part, and parts in many an interstice
Lurk of the tangled woodland—no light quest
To find. And, ah, the head! Of all the rest,
His mother hath it, pierced upon a wand,
As one might pierce a lion's, and through the land,
Leaving her sisters in their dancing place,
Bears it on high! Yea, to these walls her face
Was set, exulting in her deed of blood,
Calling upon her Bromios, her God,
Her Comrade, Fellow-Render of the Prey,
Her All-Victorious, to whom this day
She bears in triumph . . . her own broken heart!

For me, after that sight, I will depart
Before Agâvê comes.—Oh, to fulfil
God's laws, and have no thought beyond His will,
Is man's best treasure. Aye, and wisdom true,
Methinks, for things of dust to cleave unto!

[*The* MESSENGER *departs into the Castle.*

Chorus

Some Maidens

Weave ye the dance, and call
    Praise to God!
Bless ye the Tyrant's fall!
    Down is trod
Pentheus, the Dragon's Seed!
Wore he the woman's weed?
Clasped he his death indeed,
    Clasped the rod?

A Bacchanal

Yea, the wild ivy lapt him, and the doomed
Wild Bull of Sacrifice before him loomed!

Others

Ye who did Bromios scorn,
    Praise Him the more,
Bacchanals, Cadmus-born;
    Praise with sore
Agony, yea, with tears!
Great are the gifts he bears!
Hands that a mother rears
    Red with gore!

Leader

But stay, Agâvê cometh! And her eyes
Make fire around her, reeling! Ho, the prize
Cometh! All hail, O Rout of Dionyse!

[*Enter from the Mountain* Agâvê, *mad, and to all seeming wondrously happy, bearing the head of* Pentheus *in her hand. The* Chorus Maidens *stand horror-struck at the sight; the* Leader, *also horror-struck, strives to accept it and rejoice in it as the God's deed.*

Agâvê
Ye from the lands of Morn!

Leader
Call me not; I give praise!

Agâvê
Lo, from the trunk new-shorn
Hither a Mountain Thorn
Bear we! O Asia-born
  Bacchanals, bless this chase!

Leader
I see. Yea; I see.
Have I not welcomed thee?

Agâvê (*very calmly and peacefully*)
He was young in the wildwood:
Without nets I caught him!
Nay; look without fear on
The Lion; I have ta'en him!

Leader
Where in the wildwood?
Whence have ye brought him?

Agâvê
Kithæron. . . .

Leader
          Kithæron?

Agâvê

The Mountain hath slain him!

Leader

Who first came nigh him?

Agâvê

I, I, 'tis confessèd!
And they named me there by him
  Agâvê the Blessèd!

Leader

Who was next in the band on him?

Agâvê

The daughters . . .

Leader

   The daughters?

Agâvê

Of Cadmus laid hand on him.
  But the swift hand that slaughters
Is mine; mine is the praise!
Bless ye this day of days!
  [*The* LEADER *tries to speak, but is not able;*
    AGÂVÊ *begins gently stroking the head.*

Agâvê

Gather ye now to the feast!

Leader

Feast!—O miserable!

Agâvê

See, it falls to his breast,
Curling and gently tressed,

THE BACCHÆ

    The hair of the Wild Bull's crest—
    The young steer of the fell!

Leader

    Most like a beast of the wild
    That head, those locks defiled.

Agâvê (*lifting up the head, more excitedly*)

    He wakened his Mad Ones,
      A Chase-God, a wise God!
        He sprang them to seize this!
        He preys where his band preys.

Leader (*brooding, with horror*)

    In the trail of thy Mad Ones
    Thou tearest thy prize, God!

Agâvê

Dost praise it?

Leader

          I praise this?

Agâvê

Ah, soon shall the land praise!

Leader

And Pentheus, O Mother,
    Thy child?

Agâvê

        He shall cry on
My name as none other,
    Bless the spoils of the Lion!

Leader

Aye, strange is thy treasure!

Agâvê

And strange was the taking!

Leader

Thou art glad?

Agâvê

Beyond measure;
Yea, glad in the breaking
Of dawn upon all this land,
By the prize, the prize of my hand!

Leader

Show then to all the land, unhappy one,
The trophy of this deed that thou hast done!

Agâvê

Ho, all ye men that round the citadel
And shining towers of ancient Thêbê dwell,
Come! Look upon this prize, this lion's spoil,
That we have taken—yea, with our own toil,
We, Cadmus' daughters! Not with leathern-set
Thessalian javelins, not with hunter's net,
Only white arms and swift hands' bladed fall.
Why make ye much ado, and boast withal
Your armourers' engines? See, these palms were bare
That caught the angry beast, and held, and tare
The limbs of him! . . . Father! . . . Go, bring to me
My father! . . . Aye, and Pentheus, where is he,
My son? He shall set up a ladder-stair
Against this house, and in the triglyphs there
Nail me this lion's head, that gloriously
I bring ye, having slain him—I, even I!

[*She goes through the crowd towards the Castle, showing the head and looking for a place to hang it. Enter from the Mountain* CADMUS, *with attendants, bearing the body of* PENTHEUS *on a bier.*]

Cadmus

On, with your awful burden. Follow me,
Thralls, to his house, whose body grievously
With many a weary search at last in dim
Kithæron's glens I found, torn limb from limb,
And through the intervening forest weed
Scattered.—Men told me of my daughters' deed,
When I was just returned within these walls,
With grey Teiresias, from the Bacchanals.
And back I hied me to the hills again
To seek my murdered son. There saw I plain
Actæon's mother, ranging where he died,
Autonoë; and Ino by her side,
Wandering ghastly in the pine-copses.
  Agâvê was not there. The rumour is
She cometh fleet-foot hither.—Ah! 'Tis true;
A sight I scarce can bend mine eyes unto.

Agâvê

(*turning from the Palace and seeing him*)
My father, a great boast is thine this hour.
Thou hast begotten daughters, high in power
And valiant above all mankind—yea, all
Valiant, though none like me! I have let fall
The shuttle by the loom, and raised my hand
For higher things, to slay from out thy land
Wild beasts! See, in mine arms I bear the prize,
That nailed above these portals it may rise
To show what things thy daughters did! Do thou
Take it, and call a feast. Proud art thou now
And highly favoured in our valiancy!

Cadmus

O depth of grief, how can I fathom thee
Or look upon thee!—Poor, poor blood-stained hand!
Poor sisters!—A fair sacrifice to stand
Before God's altars, daughter; yea, and call
Me and my citizens to feast withal!
  Nay, let me weep—for thine affliction most,
Then for mine own. All, all of us are lost,
Not wrongfully, yet is it hard, from one
Who might have loved—our Bromios, our own!

Agâvê

How crabbèd and how scowling in the eyes
Is man's old age!—Would that my son likewise
Were happy of his hunting, in my way,
When with his warrior bands he will essay
The wild beast!—Nay, his valiance is to fight
With God's will! Father, thou shouldst set him right. . . .
Will no one bring him hither, that mine eyes
May look on his, and show him this my prize!

Cadmus

Alas, if ever ye can know again
The truth of what ye did, what pain of pain
That truth shall bring! Or were it best to wait
Darkened for evermore, and deem your state
Not misery, though ye know no happiness?

Agâvê

What seest thou here to chide, or not to bless?

Cadmus (after hesitation, resolving himself)

Raise me thine eyes to yon blue dome of air!

Agâvê

'Tis done. What dost thou bid me seek for there?

Cadmus
Is it the same, or changèd in thy sight?

Agâvê
More shining than before, more heavenly bright!

Cadmus
And that wild tremour, is it with thee still?

Agâvê (*troubled*)
I know not what thou sayest; but my will
Clears, and some change cometh, I know not how.

Cadmus
Canst hearken then, being changed, and answer now?

Agâvê
I have forgotten something; else I could.

Cadmus
What husband led thee of old from mine abode?

Agâvê
Echîon, whom men named the Child of Earth.

Cadmus
And what child in Echîon's house had birth?

Agâvê
Pentheus, of my love and his father's bred.

Cadmus
Thou bearest in thine arms an head—what head?

Agâvê
(*beginning to tremble, and not looking at what she carries*)
A lion's—so they all said in the chase.

Cadmus

Turn to it now—'tis no long toil—and gaze.

Agâvê

Ah! But what is it? What am I carrying here?

Cadmus

Look once upon it full, till all be clear!

Agâvê

I see . . . most deadly pain! Oh, woe is me!

Cadmus

Wears it the likeness of a lion to thee?

Agâvê

No; 'tis the head—O God!—of Pentheus, this!

Cadmus

Blood-drenched ere thou wouldst know him! Aye, 'tis his.

Agâvê

Who slew him?—How came I to hold this thing?

Cadmus

O cruel Truth, is this thine home-coming?

Agâvê

Answer! My heart is hanging on thy breath!

Cadmus

'Twas thou.—Thou and thy sisters wrought his death.

Agâvê

In what place was it? His own house, or where?

Cadmus

Where the dogs tore Actæon, even there.

Agâvê

Why went he to Kithæron? What sought he?

Cadmus

To mock the God and thine own ecstasy.

Agâvê

But how should we be on the hills this day?

Cadmus

Being mad! A spirit drove all the land that way.

Agâvê

'Tis Dionyse hath done it! Now I see.

Cadmus (earnestly)

Ye wronged Him! Ye denied His deity!

Agâvê (turning from him)

Show me the body of the son I love!

Cadmus (leading her to the bier)

'Tis here, my child. Hard was the quest thereof.

Agâvê

Laid in due state?
[*As there is no answer, she lifts the veil of the bier, and sees.*

Oh, if I wrought a sin,
'Twas mine! What portion had my child therein?

Cadmus

He made him like to you, adoring not
The God; who therefore to one bane hath brought

You and this body, wrecking all our line,
And me. Aye, no man-child was ever mine;
And now this first-fruit of the flesh of thee,
Sad woman, foully here and frightfully
Lies murdered! Whom the house looked up unto,
[*Kneeling by the body.*
O Child, my daughter's child! who heldest true
My castle walls; and to the folk a name
Of fear thou wast; and no man sought to shame
My grey beard, when they knew that thou wast there,
Else had they swift reward!—And now I fare
Forth in dishonour, outcast, I, the great
Cadmus, who sowed the seed-rows of this state
Of Thebes, and reaped the harvest wonderful.
O my belovèd, though thy heart is dull
In death, O still belovèd, and alway
Belovèd! Nevermore, then, shalt thou lay
Thine hand to this white beard, and speak to me,
Thy "Mother's Father"; ask, "Who wrongeth thee?
Who stints thine honour, or with malice stirs
Thine heart? Speak, and I smite thine injurers!"
But now—woe, woe, to me and thee also,
Woe to thy mother and her sisters, woe
Alway! Oh, whoso walketh not in dread
Of Gods, let him but look on this man dead!

Leader

Lo, I weep with thee. 'Twas but due reward
God sent on Pentheus; but for thee . . . 'tis hard.

Agâvê

My father, thou canst see the change in me,

* * * * *
* * * * *

[*A page or more has here been torn out of the MS. from which all our copies of "The Bacchæ" are derived. It evidently contained a speech of Agâvê (followed presumably*

by *some words of the Chorus*), *and an appearance of*
DIONYSUS *upon a cloud. He must have pronounced judgment upon the Thebans in general, and especially upon the daughters of* CADMUS, *have justified his own action, and declared his determination to establish his godhead. Where the MS. begins again, we find him addressing* CADMUS.]

* * * * *

Dionysus

* * * * *
* * * * *

And tell of Time, what gifts for thee he bears,
What griefs and wonders in the winding years.
For thou must change and be a Serpent Thing
Strange, and beside thee she whom thou didst bring
Of old to be thy bride from Heaven afar,
Harmonia, daughter of the Lord of War.
Yea, and a chariot of kine—so spake
The word of Zeus—thee and thy Queen shall take
Through many lands, Lord of a wild array
Of orient spears. And many towns shall they
Destroy beneath thee, that vast horde, until
They touch Apollo's dwelling, and fulfil
Their doom, back driven on stormy ways and steep.
Thee only and thy spouse shall Ares keep,
And save alive to the Islands of the Blest.
 Thus speaketh Dionysus, Son confessed
Of no man but of Zeus!—Ah, had ye seen
Truth in the hour ye would not, all had been
Well with ye, and the Child of God your friend!

Agâvê

Dionysus, we beseech thee! We have sinned!

Dionysus

Too late! When there was time, ye knew me not!

Agâvê

We have confessed. Yet is thine hand too hot.

Dionysus

Ye mocked me, being God; this is your wage.

Agâvê

Should God be like a proud man in his rage?

Dionysus

'Tis as my sire, Zeus, willed it long ago.

Agâvê (*turning from him almost with disdain*)

Old man, the word is spoken; we must go.

Dionysus

And seeing ye must, what is it that ye wait?

Cadmus

Child, we are come into a deadly strait,
All; thou, poor sufferer, and thy sisters twain,
And my sad self. Far off to barbarous men,
A grey-haired wanderer, I must take my road.
And then the oracle, the doom of God,
That I must lead a raging horde far-flown
To prey on Hellas; lead my spouse, mine own
Harmonia, Ares' child, discorporate
And haunting forms, dragon and dragon-mate,
Against the tombs and altar-stones of Greece,
Lance upon lance behind us; and not cease
From toils, like other men, nor dream, nor past
The foam of Acheron find my peace at last.

Agâvê

Father! And I must wander far from thee!

Cadmus

O Child, why wilt thou reach thine arms to me,
As yearns the milk-white swan, when old swans die?

Agâvê

Where shall I turn me else? No home have I.

Cadmus

I know not; I can help thee not.

Agâvê

Farewell, O home, O ancient tower!
Lo, I am outcast from my bower,
And leave ye for a worser lot.

Cadmus

Go forth, go forth to misery,
The way Actæon's father went!

Agâvê

Father, for thee my tears are spent.

Cadmus

Nay, Child, 'tis I must weep for thee;

For thee and for thy sisters twain!

Agâvê

On all this house, in bitter wise,
Our Lord and Master, Dionyse,
Hath poured the utter dregs of pain!

Dionysus

In bitter wise, for bitter was the shame
Ye did me, when Thebes honoured not my name.

Agâvê

Then lead me where my sisters be;
　　Together let our tears be shed,
　　Our ways be wandered; where no red
Kithæron waits to gaze on me;

Nor I gaze back; no thyrsus stem,
　　Nor song, nor memory in the air.
　　Oh, other Bacchanals be there,
Not I, not I, to dream of them!
　　[AGÂVÊ *with her group of attendants goes out on the side away from the Mountain.* DIONYSUS *rises upon the Cloud and disappears.*

Chorus

There be many shapes of mystery.
And many things God makes to be,
　　Past hope or fear.
And the end men looked for cometh not,
And a path is there where no man thought.
　　So hath it fallen here.　　　　　　[*Exeunt.*

THE FROGS
OF ARISTOPHANES

TRANSLATED BY
B. B. ROGERS

INTRODUCTORY NOTE

ARISTOPHANES, the greatest of comic writers in Greek and, in the opinion of many, in any language, is the only one of the Attic comedians any of whose works has survived in complete form. He was born in Athens about the middle of the fifth century B.C., and had his first comedy produced when he was so young that his name was withheld on account of his youth. He is credited with over forty plays, eleven of which survive, along with the names and fragments of some twenty-six others. His satire deals with political, religious, and literary topics, and with all its humor and fancy is evidently the outcome of profound conviction and a genuine patriotism. The Attic comedy was produced at the festivals of Dionysus, which were marked by great license, and to this, rather than to the individual taste of the poet, must be ascribed the undoubted coarseness of many of the jests. Aristophanes seems, indeed, to have been regarded by his contemporaries as a man of noble character. He died shortly after the production of his "Plutus," in 388 B.C.

"The Frogs" was produced the year after the death of Euripides, and laments the decay of Greek tragedy which Aristophanes attributed to that writer. It is an admirable example of the brilliance of his style, and of that mingling of wit and poetry with rollicking humor and keen satirical point which is his chief characteristic. Here, as elsewhere, he stands for tradition against innovation of all kinds, whether in politics, religion, or art. The hostility to Euripides displayed here and in several other plays, like his attacks on Socrates, is a result of this attitude of conservatism. The present play is notable also as a piece of elaborate if not overserious literary criticism from the pen of a great poet.

THE FROGS

OF ARISTOPHANES

DRAMATIS PERSONÆ

The God Dionysus	Xanthias, *his slave*	Æschylus
Euripides	Heracles	Pluto
Charon	Æacus, *house porter to Pluto*	A Corpse
A Maidservant of Persephone	A Landlady in Hades	
Plathane, *her partner*	A Chorus of Frogs	
A Chorus of Initiated Persons		

Attendants at a Funeral; Women worshipping Iacchus; Servants of Pluto, &c.

Xanthias

SHALL I crack any of those old jokes, master,
At which the audience never fail to laugh?
 Dionysus. Aye, what you will, except *I'm getting crushed:*
Fight shy of that: I'm sick of that already.
 Xan. Nothing else smart? *Dio.* Aye, save *my shoulder's aching.*
 Xan. Come now, that comical joke? *Dio.* With all my heart.
Only be careful not to shift your pole,
And— *Xan.* What? *Dio.* And vow that you've a belly-ache.
 Xan. May I not say I'm overburdened so
That if none ease me, I must ease myself?
 Dio. For mercy's sake, not till I'm going to vomit.
 Xan. What! must I bear these burdens, and not make
One of the jokes Ameipsias and Lycis
And Phrynichus, in every play they write,
Put in the mouths of all their burden-bearers?
 Dio. Don't make them; no! I tell you when I see
Their plays, and hear those jokes, I come away
More than a twelvemonth older than I went.
 Xan. O, thrice unlucky neck of mine, which now
Is *getting crushed*, yet must not crack its joke!

Dio. Now is not this fine pampered insolence
When I myself, Dionysus, son of—Pipkin,
Toil on afoot, and let this fellow ride,
Taking no trouble, and no burden bearing?
  Xan. What, don't I bear? *Dio.* How can you when you're riding?
  Xan. Why, I bear these. *Dio.* How? *Xan.* Most unwillingly.
  Dio. Does not the donkey bear the load you're bearing?
  Xan. Not what I bear myself: by Zeus, not he.
  Dio. How can you bear, when you are borne yourself?
  Xan. Don't know: but anyhow *my shoulder's aching.*
  Dio. Then since you say the donkey helps you not,
You lift him up and carry him in turn.
  Xan. O, hang it all! why didn't I fight at sea?
You should have smarted bitterly for this.
  Dio. Get down, you rascal; I've been trudging on
Till now I've reached the portal, where I'm going
First to turn in. Boy! Boy! I say there, Boy!
  Heracles. Who banged the door? How like a prancing Centaur
He drove against it! Mercy o' me, what's this?
  Dio. Boy. *Xan.* Yes. *Dio.* Did you observe? *Xan.* What? *Dio.* How alarmed
He is. *Xan.* Aye, truly, lest you've lost your wits.
  Her. O, by Demeter, I can't choose but laugh.
Biting my lips won't stop me. Ha! ha! ha!
  Dio. Pray you, come hither, I have need of you.
  Her. I vow I can't help laughing, I can't help it.
A lion's hide upon a yellow silk,
A club and buskin! What's it all about?
Where were you going? *Dio.* I was serving lately
Aboard the—Cleisthenes. *Her.* And fought? *Dio.* And sank
More than a dozen of the enemy's ships.
  Her. You two? *Dio.* We two. *Her.* And then I awoke, and lo!
  Dio. There as, on deck, I'm reading to myself
The "Andromeda," a sudden pang of longing
Shoots through my heart, you can't conceive how keenly.
  Her. How big a pang? *Dio.* A small one, Molon's size.
  Her. Caused by a woman? *Dio.* No. *Her.* A boy? *Dio.* No, no.

Her. A man? *Dio.* Ah! ah! *Her.* Was it for Cleisthenes?
  Dio. Don't mock me, brother; on my life I am
In a bad way: such fierce desire consumes me.
  Her. Aye, little brother? how? *Dio.* I can't describe it.
But yet I'll tell you in a riddling way.
Have you e'er felt a sudden lust for soup?
  Her. Soup! Zeus-a-mercy, yes, ten thousand times.
  Dio. Is the thing clear, or must I speak again?
  Her. Not of the soup: I'm clear about the soup.
  Dio. Well, just that sort of pang devours my heart
For lost Euripides. *Her.* A dead man too.
  Dio. And no one shall persuade me not to go
After the man. *Her.* Do you mean below, to Hades?
  Dio. And lower still, if there's a lower still.
  Her. What on earth for? *Dio.* I want a genuine poet,
"For some are not, and those that are, are bad."
  Her. What! does not Iophon live? *Dio.* Well, he's the sole
Good thing remaining, if even he is good.
For even of that I'm not exactly certain.
  Her. If go you must, there's Sophocles—he comes
Before Euripides—why not take *him*?
  Dio. Not till I've tried if Iophon's coin rings true
When he's alone, apart from Sophocles.
Besides, Euripides, the crafty rogue,
Will find a thousand shifts to get away,
But *he* was easy here, is easy there.
  Her. But Agathon, where is he? *Dio.* He has gone and left us.
A genial poet, by his friends much missed.
  Her. Gone where? *Dio.* To join the blessed in their banquets.
  Her. But what of Xenocles? *Dio.* O, he be hanged!
  Her. Pythangelus? *Xan.* But never a word of me,
Not though my shoulder's chafed so terribly.
  Her. But have you not a shoal of little songsters,
Tragedians by the myriad, who can chatter
A furlong faster than Euripides?
  Dio. Those be mere vintage-leavings, jabberers, choirs
Of swallow-broods, degraders of their art,

Who get one chorus, and are seen no more,
The Muses' love once gained. But, O my friend,
Search where you will, you'll never find a true
Creative genius, uttering startling things.

   Her. Creative? how do you mean? *Dio.* I mean a man
Who'll dare some novel venturesome conceit,
Air, Zeus's chamber, or *Time's foot,* or this:
*'Twas not my mind that swore: my tongue committed
A little perjury on its own account.*

   Her. You like that style? *Dio.* Like it? I dote upon it.
   Her. I vow it's ribald nonsense, and you know it.
   Dio. "Rule not my mind": you've got a house to mind.
   Her. Really and truly, though, 'tis paltry stuff.
   Dio. Teach me to dine! *Xan.* But never a word of me.
   Dio. But tell me truly—'twas for this I came
Dressed up to mimic you—what friends received
And entertained you when you went below
To bring back Cerberus, in case I need them.
And tell me too the havens, fountains, shops,
Roads, resting-places, stews, refreshment rooms,
Towns, lodgings, hostesses, with whom were found
The fewest bugs. *Xan.* But never a word of me.

   Her. You are really game to go? *Dio.* O, drop that, can't you?
And tell me this: of all the roads you know,
Which is the quickest way to get to Hades?
I want one not too warm, nor yet too cold.

   Her. Which shall I tell you first? which shall it be?
There's one by rope and bench: you launch away
And—hang yourself. *Dio.* No, thank you: that's too stifling.

   Her. Then there's a track, a short and beaten cut,
By pestle and mortar. *Dio.* Hemlock, do you mean?

   Her. Just so. *Dio.* No, that's too deathly cold a way;
You have hardly started ere your shins get numbed.

   Her. Well, would you like a steep and swift descent?
   Dio. Aye, that's the style: my walking powers are small.
   Her. Go down to the Cerameicus. *Dio.* And do what?

Her. Climb to the tower's top pinnacle— *Dio.* And then?
Her. Observe the torch-race started, and when all
The multitude is shouting *Let them go,*
Let yourself go. *Dio.* Go whither? *Her.* To the ground.
Dio. O, that would break my brain's two envelopes.
I'll not try that. *Her.* Which *will* you try? *Dio.* The way
You went yourself. *Her.* A parlous voyage that,
For first you'll come to an enormous lake
Of fathomless depth. *Dio.* And how am I to cross?
Her. An ancient mariner will row you over
In a wee boat, *so* big. The fare's two obols.
Dio. Fie! The power two obols have, the whole world through!
How came they thither? *Her.* Theseus took them down.
And next you'll see great snakes and savage monsters
In tens of thousands. *Dio.* You needn't try to scare me,
I'm going to go. *Her.* Then weltering seas of filth
And ever-rippling dung: and plunged therein,
Whoso has wronged the stranger here on earth,
Or robbed his boy-love of the promised pay,
Or swinged his mother, or profanely smitten
His father's cheek, or sworn an oath forsworn,
Or copied out a speech of Morsimus.
Dio. There too, perdie, should *he* be plunged, whoe'er
Has danced the sword-dance of Cinesias.
Her. And next the breath of flutes will float around you,
And glorious sunshine, such as ours, you'll see,
And myrtle groves, and happy bands who clap
Their hands in triumph, men and women too.
Dio. And who are they? *Her.* The happy mystic bands,
Xan. And I'm the donkey in the mystery show.
But I'll not stand it, not one instant longer.
Her. Who'll tell you everything you want to know.
You'll find them dwelling close beside the road
You are going to travel, just at Pluto's gate.
And fare thee well, my brother. *Dio.* And to you
Good cheer. (*To Xan.*) Now, sirrah, pick you up the traps.
Xan. Before I've put them down? *Dio.* And quickly too.

Xan. No, prithee, no; but hire a body, one
They're carrying out, on purpose for the trip.
   Dio. If I can't find one? *Xan.* Then I'll take them. *Dio.* Good.
And see! they are carrying out a body now.
Hallo! you there, you deadman, are you willing
To carry down our little traps to Hades?
   Corpse. What are they? *Dio.* These. *Corp.* Two drachmas for
      the job?
   Dio. Nay, that's too much. *Corp.* Out of the pathway, you!
   Dio. Beshrew thee, stop: maybe we'll strike a bargain.
   Corp. Pay me two drachmas, or it's no use talking.
   Dio. One and a half. *Corp.* I'd liefer live again!
   Xan. How absolute the knave is! He be hanged!
I'll go myself. *Dio.* You're the right sort, my man.
Now to the ferry. *Charon.* Yoh, up! lay her to.
   Xan. Whatever's that? *Dio.* Why, that's the lake, by Zeus,
Whereof he spake, and yon's the ferry-boat.
   Xan. Poseidon, yes, and that old fellow's Charon.
   Dio. Charon! O welcome, Charon! welcome, Charon!
   Char. Who's for the Rest from every pain and ill?
Who's for the Lethe's plain? the Donkey-shearings?
Who's for Cerberia? Tænarum? or the Ravens?
   Dio. I. *Char.* Hurry in. *Dio.* But where are you going really?
In truth to the Ravens? *Char.* Aye, for your behoof.
Step in. *Dio.* (*To Xan.*) Now, lad. *Char.* A slave? I take no slave,
Unless he has fought for his body-rights at sea.
   Xan. I couldn't go. I'd got the eye-disease.
   Char. Then fetch a circuit round about the lake.
   Xan. Where must I wait? *Char.* Beside the Withering stone,
Hard by the Rest. *Dio.* You understand? *Xan.* Too well.
O, what ill omen crossed me as I started!
   Char. (*To Dio.*) Sit to the oar. (*Calling.*) Who else for the boat?
      Be quick.
(*To Dio.*) Hi! what are you doing? *Dio.* What am I doing? Sitting
On to the oar. You told me to, yourself.
   Char. Now sit you there, you little Potgut. *Dio.* So?
   Char. Now stretch your arms full length before you. *Dio.* So?

Char. Come, don't keep fooling; plant your feet, and now
Pull with a will. *Dio.* Why, how am *I* to pull?
I'm not an oarsman, seaman, Salaminian.
I can't! *Char.* You can. Just dip your oar in once,
You'll hear the loveliest timing songs. *Dio.* What from?
 Char. Frog-swans, most wonderful. *Dio.* Then give the word.
 Char. Heave ahoy! heave ahoy!
 Frogs. Brekekekex, ko-ax, ko-ax!
Brekekekex, ko-ax, ko-ax!
We children of the fountain and the lake,
    Let us wake
Our full choir-shout, as the flutes are ringing out,
    Our symphony of clear-voiced song.
The song we used to love, in the Marshland up above,
    In praise of Dionysus to produce,
    Of Nysæan Dionysus, son of Zeus,
When the revel-tipsy throng, all crapulous and gay,
To our precinct reeled along on the holy
        Pitcher day.
Brekekekex, ko-ax, ko-ax.
 Dio. O, dear! O, dear! now I declare
I've got a bump upon my rump.
 Fr. Brekekekex, ko-ax, ko-ax.
 Dio. But you, perchance, don't care.
 Fr. Brekekekex, ko-ax, ko-ax.
 Dio. Hang you, and your ko-axing too!
There's nothing but ko-ax with you.
 Fr. That is right, Mr. Busybody, right!
For the Muses of the lyre love us well;
And hornfoot Pan who plays on the pipe his jocund lays;
And Apollo, Harper bright, in our Chorus takes delight;
For the strong reed's sake which I grow within my lake
    To be girdled in his lyre's deep shell.
        Brekekekex, ko-ax, ko-ax.
 Dio. My hands are blistered very sore;
My stern below is sweltering so,
'Twill soon, I know, upturn and roar

Brekekekex, ko-ax, ko-ax.
O tuneful race, O, pray give o'er,
O, sing no more. *Fr.* Ah, no! ah, no!
Loud and louder our chant must flow.
Sing if ever ye sang of yore,
When in sunny and glorious days
Through the rushes and marsh-flags springing
On we swept, in the joy of singing
Myriad-diving roundelays.
Or when fleeing the storm, we went
Down to the depths, and our choral song
Wildly raised to a loud and long
Bubble-bursting accompaniment.
   Fr. and *Dio.* Brekekekex, ko-ax, ko-ax.
   Dio. This timing song I take from you.
   Fr. That's a dreadful thing to do.
   Dio. Much more dreadful, if I row
Till I burst myself, I trow.
   Fr. and *Dio.* Brekekekex, ko-ax, ko-ax.
   Dio. Go, hang yourselves; for what care I?
   Fr. All the same we'll shout and cry,
Stretching all our throats with song,
Shouting, crying, all day long,
   Fr. and *Dio.* Brekekekex, ko-ax, ko-ax.
   Dio. In this you'll never, never win.
   Fr. This you shall not beat us in.
   Dio. No, nor ye prevail o'er me.
Never! never! I'll my song
Shout, if need be, all day long,
Until I've learned to master your ko-ax.
Brekekekex, ko-ax, ko-ax.
I thought I'd put a stop to your ko-ax.
   Char. Stop! Easy! Take the oar and push her to.
Now pay your fare and go. *Dio.* Here 'tis: two obols.
Xanthias! where's Xanthias? Is it Xanthias there?
   Xan. Hoi, hoi! *Dio.* Come hither. *Xan.* Glad to meet you,
     master.

Dio. What have you there? *Xan.* Nothing but filth and darkness.
Dio. But tell me, did you see the parricides
And perjured folk he mentioned? *Xan.* Didn't you?
Dio. Poseidon, yes. Why, look! (*Pointing to the audience.*) I see them now.
What's the next step? *Xan.* We'd best be moving on.
This is the spot where Heracles declared
Those savage monsters dwell. *Dio.* O, hang the fellow!
That's all his bluff: he thought to scare me off,
The jealous dog, knowing my plucky ways.
There's no such swaggerer lives as Heracles.
Why, I'd like nothing better than to achieve
Some bold adventure, worthy of our trip.
Xan. I know you would. Hallo! I hear a noise.
Dio. Where? what? *Xan.* Behind us, there. *Dio.* Get you behind.
Xan. No, it's in front. *Dio.* Get you in front directly.
Xan. And now I see the most ferocious monster.
Dio. O, what's it like? *Xan.* Like everything by turns.
Now it's a bull: now it's a mule: and now
The loveliest girl. *Dio.* O, where? I'll go and meet her.
Xan. It's ceased to be a girl: it's a dog now.
Dio. It is Empusa! *Xan.* Well, its face is all
Ablaze with fire. *Dio.* Has it a copper leg?
Xan. A copper leg? yes, one; and one of cow dung.
Dio. O, whither shall I flee? *Xan.* O, whither I?
Dio. My priest, protect me, and we'll sup together.
Xan. King Heracles, we're done for. *Dio.* O, forbear,
Good fellow, call me anything but that.
Xan. Well, then, Dionysus. *Dio.* O, that's worse again.
Xan. (*To the Spectre.*) Aye, go thy way. O master, here, come here.
Dio. O, what's up now? *Xan.* Take courage; all's serene.
And, like Hegelochus, we now may say,
"Out of the storm there comes a new fine wether."
Empusa's gone. *Dio.* Swear it. *Xan.* By Zeus she is.

Dio. Swear it again. *Xan.* By Zeus. *Dio.* Again. *Xan.* By Zeus.
O, dear, O, dear, how pale I grew to see her,
But *he* from fright has yellowed me all over.
   Dio. Ah me, whence fall these evils on my head?
Who is the god to blame for my destruction?
Air, Zeus's chamber, or the Foot of Time?

(A flute is played behind the scenes.)

   Dio. Hist! *Xan.* What's the matter? *Dio.* Didn't you hear it?
      Xan. What?
   Dio. The breath of flutes. *Xan.* Aye, and a whiff of torches
Breathed o'er me too; a very mystic whiff.
   Dio. Then crouch we down, and mark what's going on.
   Chorus. (*In the distance.*)   O Iacchus!
                    O Iacchus! O Iacchus!
   Xan. I have it, master: 'tis those blessed Mystics,
Of whom he told us, sporting hereabouts.
They sing the Iacchus which Diagoras made.
   Dio. I think so too: we had better both keep quiet
And so find out exactly what it is.

(The calling forth of Iacchus.)

   Chor. O Iacchus! power excelling, here in stately temples
      dwelling,
     O Iacchus! O Iacchus!
     Come to tread this verdant level,
     Come to dance in mystic revel,
     Come whilst round thy forehead hurtles
     Many a wreath of fruitful myrtles,
     Come with wild and saucy paces
     Mingling in our joyous dance,
Pure and holy, which embraces all the charms of all the Graces,
     When the mystic choirs advance.
   Xan. Holy and sacred queen, Demeter's daughter,
O, what a jolly whiff of pork breathed o'er me!
   Dio. Hist! and perchance you'll get some tripe yourself.

THE FROGS

(The welcome to Iacchus.)

Chor. Come, arise, from sleep awaking, come the fiery torches shaking,
O Iacchus! O Iacchus!
Morning Star that shinest nightly.
Lo, the mead is blazing brightly,
Age forgets its years and sadness,
Agèd knees curvet for gladness,
Lift thy flashing torches o'er us,
Marshal all thy blameless train,
Lead, O, lead the way before us; lead the lovely youthful Chorus
To the marshy flowery plain.

(The warning-off of the profane.)

All evil thoughts and profane be still: far hence, far hence from our choirs depart,
Who knows not well what the Mystics tell, or is not holy and pure of heart;
Who ne'er has the noble revelry learned, or danced the dance of the Muses high;
Or shared in the Bacchic rites which old bull-eating Cratinus's words supply;
Who vulgar coarse buffoonery loves, though all untimely the jests they make;
Or lives not easy and kind with all, or kindling faction forbears to slake,
But fans the fire, from a base desire some pitiful gain for himself to reap;
Or takes, in office, his gifts and bribes, while the city is tossed on the stormy deep;
Who fort or fleet to the foe betrays; or, a vile Thorycion, ships away
Forbidden stores from Ægina's shores, to Epidaurus across the Bay
Transmitting oar-pads and sails and tar, that curst collector of five per cents;
The knave who tries to procure supplies for the use of the enemy's armaments;

The Cyclian singer who dares befoul the Lady Hecate's wayside shrine;
The public speaker who once lampooned in our Bacchic feasts would, with heart malign,
Keep nibbling away the Comedians' pay;—to these I utter my warning cry,
I charge them once, I charge them twice, I charge them thrice, that they draw not nigh
To the sacred dance of the mystic choir. But YE, my comrades, awake the song,
The night-long revels of joy and mirth which ever of right to our feast belong.

(*The start of the procession.*)

Advance, true hearts, advance!
On to the gladsome bowers,
On to the sward, with flowers
    Embosomed bright!
March on with jest, and jeer, and dance,
Full well ye've supped to-night.

(*The processional hymn to Persephone.*)

March, chanting loud your lays,
Your hearts and voices raising,
The Saviour goddess praising
    Who vows she'll still
Our city save to endless days,
Whate'er Thorycion's will.

Break off the measure, and change the time; and now with chanting and hymns adorn
Demeter, goddess mighty and high, the harvest-queen, the giver of corn.

(*The processional hymn to Demeter.*)

O Lady, over our rites presiding,
Preserve and succour thy choral throng,

And grant us all, in thy help confiding,
To dance and revel the whole day long;
AND MUCH in earnest, and much in jest,
Worthy thy feast, may we speak therein.
And when we have bantered and laughed our best,
The victor's wreath be it ours to win.

Call we now the youthful god, call him hither without delay,
Him who travels amongst his chorus, dancing along on the Sacred
  Way.

(*The processional hymn to Iacchus.*)

O, come with the joy of thy festival song,
O, come to the goddess, O, mix with our throng
Untired, though the journey be never so long.
  O Lord of the frolic and dance,
  Iacchus, beside me advance!
For fun, and for cheapness, our dress thou hast rent,
Through thee we may dance to the top of our bent,
Reviling, and jeering, and none will resent.
  O Lord of the frolic and dance,
  Iacchus, beside me advance!
A sweet pretty girl I observed in the show,
Her robe had been torn in the scuffle, and lo,
There peeped through the tatters a bosom of snow.
  O Lord of the frolic and dance,
  Iacchus, beside me advance!

Dio. Wouldn't I like to follow on, and try
A little sport and dancing? *Xan.* Wouldn't I?

(*The banter at the bridge of Cephisus.*)

Chor.   Shall we all a merry joke
          At Archedemus poke,
Who has not cut his guildsmen yet, though seven years old;
          Yet up among the dead
          He is demagogue and head,
And contrives the topmost place of the rascaldom to hold?

                    And Cleisthenes, they say,
                    Is among the tombs all day,
Bewailing for his lover with a lamentable whine.
                    And Callias, I'm told,
                    Has become a sailor bold,
And casts a lion's hide o'er his members feminine.
    Dio.   Can any of you tell
              Where Pluto here may dwell?
For we, sirs, are two strangers who were never here before.
    Chor.   O, then no further stray,
              Nor again inquire the way,
For know that ye have journeyed to his very entrance-door.
    Dio.   Take up the wraps, my lad.
    Xan.   Now is not this too bad?
Like "Zeus's Corinth," he "the wraps" keeps saying o'er and o'er.

    Chor. Now wheel your sacred dances through the glade with
              flowers bedight,
All ye who are partakers of the holy festal rite;
And I will with the women and the holy maidens go
Where they keep the nightly vigil, an auspicious light to show.

            (*The departure for the Thriasian Plain*)
                    Now haste we to the roses,
                    And the meadows full of posies,
                    Now haste we to the meadows
                            In our own old way,
                    In choral dances blending,
                    In dances never ending,
                    Which only for the holy
                            The Destinies array.
                    O happy mystic chorus,
                    The blessed sunshine o'er us
                    On us alone is smiling,
                            In its soft sweet light:
                    On us who strove for ever

> With holy, pure endeavour,
> Alike by friend and stranger
> To guide our steps aright.

Dio. What's the right way to knock? I wonder how
The natives here are wont to knock at doors.
 Xan. No dawdling: taste the door. You've got, remember,
The lion-hide and pride of Heracles.
 Dio. Boy! Boy! *Æacus.* Who's there? *Dio.* I, Heracles the
   strong!
 Æac. O you most shameless desperate ruffian, you!
O villain, villain, arrant vilest villain!
Who seized our Cerberus by the throat, and fled,
And ran, and rushed, and bolted, haling off
The dog, my charge! But now I've got thee fast.
So close the Styx's inky-hearted rock,
The blood-bedabbled peak of Acheron
Shall hem thee in: the hell-hounds of Cocytus
Prowl round thee; whilst the hundred-headed Asp
Shall rive thy heartstrings: the Tartesian Lamprey
Prey on thy lungs: and those Tithrasian Gorgons
Mangle and tear thy kidneys, mauling them,
Entrails and all, into one bloody mash.
I'll speed a running foot to fetch them hither.
 Xan. Hallo! what now? *Dio.* I've done it: call the god.
 Xan. Get up, you laughing-stock; get up directly,
Before you're seen. *Dio.* What, *I* get up? I'm fainting.
Please dab a sponge of water on my heart.
 Xan. Here! *Dio.* Dab it, you. *Xan.* Where? O ye golden gods,
Lies your heart THERE? *Dio.* It got so terrified
It fluttered down into my stomach's pit.
 Xan. Cowardliest of gods and men! *Dio.* The cowardliest? I?
What, I, who asked you for a sponge, a thing
A coward never would have done! *Xan.* What then?
 Dio. A coward would have lain there wallowing;
But I stood up, and wiped myself withal.

Xan. Poseidon! quite heroic. *Dio.* 'Deed I think so.
But weren't *you* frightened at those dreadful threats
And shoutings? *Xan.* Frightened? Not a bit. I cared not.

Dio. Come then, if you're so *very* brave a man,
Will you be I, and take the hero's club
And lion's skin, since you're so monstrous plucky?
And I'll be now the slave, and bear the luggage.

Xan. Hand them across. I cannot choose but take them.
And now observe the Xanthio-heracles
If I'm a coward and a sneak like you.

Dio. Nay, you're the rogue from Melite's own self.
And I'll pick up and carry on the traps.

Maid. O, welcome, Heracles! come in, sweetheart.
My Lady, when they told her, set to work,
Baked mighty loaves, boiled two or three tureens
Of lentil soup, roasted a prime ox whole,
Made rolls and honey-cakes. So come along.

Xan. (*Declining.*) You are too kind. *Maid.* I will not let you go.
I will not LET you! Why, she's stewing slices
Of juicy bird's-flesh, and she's making comfits,
And tempering down her richest wine. Come, dear,
Come along in. *Xan.* (*Still declining.*) Pray thank her. *Maid.* O, you're jesting,
I shall not let you off: there's such a lovely
Flute-girl all ready, and we've two or three
Dancing-girls also. *Xan.* Eh! what! Dancing-girls?

Maid. Young budding virgins, freshly tired and trimmed.
Come, dear, come in. The cook was dishing up
The cutlets, and they are bringing in the tables.

Xan. Then go you in, and tell those dancing-girls
Of whom you spake, I'm coming in Myself.
Pick up the traps, my lad, and follow me.

Dio. Hi! stop! you're not in earnest, just because
I dressed you up, in fun, as Heracles?
Come, don't keep fooling, Xanthias, but lift
And carry in the traps yourself. *Xan.* Why! what!
You are never going to strip me of these togs

You gave me! *Dio.* Going to? No, I'm doing it now.
Off with that lion-skin. *Xan.* Bear witness all,
The Gods shall judge between us. *Dio.* Gods, indeed!
Why, how could *you* (the vain and foolish thought!)
A slave, a mortal, act Alcmena's son?
  Xan. All right, then, take them; maybe, if God will,
You'll soon require my services again.

Chor. This is the part of a dexterous clever
   Man with his wits about him ever,
   One who has travelled the world to see;
   Always to shift, and to keep through all
   Close to the sunny side of the wall;
   Not like a pictured block to be,
   Standing always in one position;
   Nay, but to veer, with expedition,
   And ever to catch the favouring breeze,
   This is the part of a shrewd tactician,
   This is to be a—THERAMENES!
Dio. Truly an exquisite joke 'twould be,
   Him with a dancing-girl to see,
   Lolling at ease on Milesian rugs;
   Me, like a slave, beside him standing,
   Aught that he wants to his lordship handing;
   Then as the damsel fair he hugs,
   Seeing me all on fire to embrace her,
   He would perchance (for there's no man baser),
   Turning him round like a lazy lout,
   Straight on my mouth deliver a facer,
   Knocking my ivory choirmen out.

Hostess. O Plathane! Plathane! Here's that naughty man,
That's he who got into our tavern once,
And ate up sixteen loaves. *Plathane.* O, so he is!
The very man. *Xan.* Bad luck for somebody!
  Hos. O, and, besides, those twenty bits of stew,
Half-obol pieces. *Xan.* Somebody's going to catch it!

Hos. That garlic too. *Dio.* Woman, you're talking nonsense.
You don't know what you're saying. *Hos.* O, you thought
I shouldn't know you with your buskins on!
Ah, and I've not yet mentioned all that fish,
No, nor the new-made cheese: he gulped it down,
Baskets and all, unlucky that we were.
And when I just alluded to the price,
He looked so fierce, and bellowed like a bull.
   Xan. Yes, that's his way: that's what he always does.
   Hos. O, and he drew his sword, and seemed quite mad.
   Pla. O, that he did. *Hos.* And terrified us so
We sprang up to the cockloft, she and I.
Then out he hurled, decamping with the rugs.
   Xan. That's his way too; but something must be done.
   Hos. Quick, run and call my patron Cleon here!
   Pla. O, if you meet him, call Hyperbolus!
We'll pay you out to-day. *Hos.* O filthy throat,
O, how I'd like to take a stone, and hack
Those grinders out with which you chawed my wares.
   Pla. I'd like to pitch you in the deadman's pit.
   Hos. I'd like to get a reaping-hook and scoop
That gullet out with which you gorged my tripe.
But I'll to Cleon: he'll soon serve his writs;
He'll twist it out of you to-day, he will.
   Dio. Perdition seize me, if I don't love Xanthias.
   Xan. Aye, aye, I know your drift: stop, stop that talking.
I won't be Heracles. *Dio.* O, don't say so,
Dear, darling Xanthias. *Xan.* Why, how can I,
A slave, a mortal, act Alcmena's son!
   Dio. Aye, aye, I know you are vexed, and I deserve it,
And if you pummel me, I won't complain.
But if I strip you of these togs again,
Perdition seize myself, my wife, my children,
And, most of all, that blear-eyed Archedemus.
   Xan. That oath contents me: on those terms I take them.

   Chor. Now that at last you appear once more,
Wearing the garb that at first you wore,

Wielding the club and the tawny skin,
Now it is yours to be up and doing,
Glaring like mad, and your youth renewing,
Mindful of him whose guise you are in.
If, when caught in a bit of a scrape, you
Suffer a word of alarm to escape you,
Showing yourself but a feckless knave,
Then will your master at once undrape you,
Then you'll again be the toiling slave.

Xan. There, I admit, you have given to me a
Capital hint, and the like idea,
Friends, had occurred to myself before.
Truly if anything good befell
He would be wanting, I know full well,
Wanting to take to the togs once more.
Nevertheless, while in these I'm vested,
Ne'er shall you find me craven-crested,
No, for a dittany look I'll wear,
Aye, and methinks it will soon be tested:
Hark! how the portals are rustling there.

Æac. Seize the dog-stealer, bind him, pinion him,
Drag him to justice! *Dio.* Somebody's going to catch it.
  Xan. (*Striking out.*) Hands off! get away! stand back! *Æac.* Eh?
     You're for fighting?
Ho! Ditylas, Sceblyas, and Pardocas,
Come hither, quick; fight me this sturdy knave.
  Dio. Now isn't it a shame the man should strike,
And he a thief besides? *Æac.* A monstrous shame!
  Dio. A regular burning shame! *Xan.* By the Lord Zeus,
If ever I was here before, if ever
I stole one hair's-worth from you, let me die!
And now I'll make you a right noble offer:
Arrest my lad: torture him as you will,
And if you find I'm guilty, take and kill me.
  Æac. Torture him, how? *Xan.* In any mode you please.
Pile bricks upon him: stuff his nose with acid:
Flay, rack him, hoist him; flog him with a scourge

Of prickly bristles: only not with this,
A soft-leaved onion, or a tender leek.
 Æac. A fair proposal. If I strike too hard
And maim the boy, I'll make you compensation.
 Xan. I shan't require it. Take him out and flog him.
 Æac. Nay, but I'll do it here before your eyes.
Now then, put down the traps, and mind you speak
The truth, young fellow. *Dio.* (*In agony.*) Man! don't torture ME!
I am a god. You'll blame yourself hereafter
If you touch ME. *Æac.* Hillo! What's that you are saying?
 Dio. I say I'm Bacchus, son of Zeus, a god,
And *he's* the slave. *Æac.* You hear him? *Xan.* Hear him? Yes.
All the more reason you should flog him well.
For if he is a god, he won't perceive it.
 Dio. Well, but you say that you're a god yourself.
So why not *you* be flogged as well as I?
 Xan. A fair proposal. And be this the test:
Whichever of us two you first behold
Flinching or crying out—he's not the god.
 Æac. Upon my word you're quite the gentleman,
You're all for right and justice. Strip then, both.
 Xan. How can you test us fairly? *Æac.* Easily,
I'll give you blow for blow. *Xan.* A good idea.
We're ready! Now! (*Æacus strikes him*) see if you catch me flinch-
  ing.
 Æac. I struck you. *Xan.* (*Incredulously.*) No! *Æac.* Well, it
  seems "no," indeed.
Now then I'll strike the other. (*Strikes Dio.*) *Dio.* Tell me when.
 Æac. I struck you. *Dio.* Struck me? Then why didn't I sneeze?
 Æac. Don't know, I'm sure. I'll try the other again.
 Xan. And quickly too. Good gracious! *Æac.* Why "good
  gracious"?
Not hurt you, did I? *Xan.* No, I merely thought of
The Diomeian feast of Heracles.
 Æac. A holy man! 'Tis now the other's turn.
 Dio. Hi! Hi! *Æac.* Hallo! *Dio.* Look at those horsemen, look!
 Æac. But why these tears? *Dio.* There's such a smell of onions.

Æac. Then you don't mind it? *Dio.* (*Cheerfully.*) Mind it?
  Not a bit.
Æac. Well, I must go to the other one again.
Xan. O! O! *Æac.* Hallo! *Xan.* Do, pray, pull out this thorn.
Æac. What does it mean? 'Tis this one's turn again.
Dio. (*Shrieking.*) Apollo! Lord! (*Calmly*) of Delos and of
  Pytho.
Xan. He flinched! You heard him? *Dio.* Not at all; a jolly
Verse of Hipponax flashed across my mind.
Xan. You don't half do it: cut his flanks to pieces.
Æac. By Zeus, well thought on. Turn your belly here.
Dio. (*Screaming.*) Poseidon! *Xan.* There! he's flinching. *Dio.*
  (*Singing*) Who dost reign
Amongst the Ægean peaks and creeks
And o'er the deep blue main.
Æac. No, by Demeter, still I can't find out
Which is the god, but come ye both indoors;
My lord himself and Persephassa there,
Being gods themselves, will soon find out the truth.
Dio. Right! right! I only wish you had thought of that
Before you gave me those tremendous whacks.

Chor. Come, Muse, to our mystical Chorus, O, come to the joy
  of my song,
O, see on the benches before us that countless and wonderful throng,
Where wits by the thousand abide, with more than a Cleophon's
  pride—
On the lips of that foreigner base, of Athens the bane and disgrace,
There is shrieking, his kinsman by race,
The garrulous swallow of Thrace;
From that perch of exotic descent,
Rejoicing her sorrow to vent,
She pours, to her spirit's content, a nightingale's woful lament
That e'en though the voting be equal, his ruin will soon be the
  sequel.

Well it suits the holy Chorus evermore with counsel wise
To exhort and teach the city; this we therefore now advise—

End the townsmen's apprehensions; equalize the rights of all;
If by Phrynichus's wrestlings some perchance sustained a fall,
Yet to these 'tis surely open, having put away their sin,
For their slips and vacillations pardon at your hands to win.
Give your brethren back their franchise. Sin and shame it were that slaves,
Who have once with stern devotion fought your battle on the waves,
Should be straightway lords and masters, yea, Platæans fully blown—
Not that this deserves our censure; there I praise you; there alone
Has the city, in her anguish, policy and wisdom shown—
Nay, but these, of old accustomed on our ships to fight and win
(They, their fathers too before them), these, our very kith and kin,
You should likewise, when they ask you, pardon for their single sin.
O, by nature best and wisest, O, relax your jealous ire,
Let us all the world as kinsfolk and as citizens acquire,
All who on our ships will battle well and bravely by our side.
If we cocker up our city, narrowing her with senseless pride,
Now when she is rocked and reeling in the cradles of the sea,
Here again will after ages deem we acted brainlessly.

And O, if I'm able to scan the habits and life of a man
Who shall rue his iniquities soon! not long shall that little baboon,
That Cleigenes shifty and small, the wickedest bath-man of all
Who are lords of the earth—which is brought from the isle of Cimolus, and wrought
With nitre and lye into soap—
Not long shall he vex us, I hope.
And this the unlucky one knows,
Yet ventures a peace to oppose,
And being addicted to blows, he carries a stick as he goes,
Lest while he is tipsy and reeling, some robber his cloak should be stealing.

Often has it crossed my fancy, that the city loves to deal
With the very best and noblest members of her commonweal,
Just as with our ancient coinage, and the newly minted gold.
Yea, for these, our sterling pieces, all of pure Athenian mould,

All of perfect die and metal, all the fairest of the fair,
All of workmanship unequalled, proved and valued everywhere
Both amongst our own Hellenes and Barbarians far away,
These we use not: but the worthless pinchbeck coins of yesterday,
Vilest die and basest metal, now we always use instead.
Even so, our sterling townsmen, nobly born and nobly bred,
Men of worth and rank and mettle, men of honourable fame,
Trained in every liberal science, choral dance, and manly game,
These we treat with scorn and insult, but the strangers newliest
      come,
Worthless sons of worthless fathers, pinchbeck townsmen, yellowy
      scum,
Whom in earlier days the city hardly would have stooped to use
Even for her scapegoat victims, these for every task we choose.
O unwise and foolish people, yet to mend your ways begin;
Use again the good and useful: so hereafter, if ye win
'Twill be due to this your wisdom: if ye fall, at least 'twill be
Not a fall that brings dishonour, falling from a worthy tree.

    Æac. By Zeus the Saviour, quite the gentleman
Your master is. *Xan.* Gentleman? I believe you.
He's all for wine and women, is my master.
    Æac. But not to have flogged you, when the truth came out
That you, the slave, were passing off as master!
    Xan. He'd get the worst of that. *Æac.* Bravo! that's spoken
Like a true slave: that's what I love myself.
    Xan. You love it, do you? *Æac.* Love it? I'm entranced
When I can curse my lord behind his back.
    Xan. How about grumbling, when you have felt the stick,
And scurry out of doors? *Æac.* That's jolly too.
    Xan. How about prying? *Æac.* That beats everything!
    Xan. Great Kin-god Zeus! And what of overhearing
Your master's secrets? *Æac.* What? I'm mad with joy.
    Xan. And blabbing them abroad? *Æac.* O, heaven and earth!
When I do that, I can't contain myself.
    Xan. Phœbus Apollo! clap your hand in mine,
Kiss and be kissed: and prithee tell me this,

Tell me by Zeus, our rascaldom's own god,
What's all that noise within? What means this hubbub
And row? *Æac.* That's Æschylus and Euripides.

Xan. Eh? *Æac.* Wonderful, wonderful things are going on.
The dead are rioting, taking different sides.

Xan. Why, what's the matter? *Æac.* There's a custom here
With all the crafts, the good and noble crafts,
That the chief master of his art in each
Shall have his dinner in the assembly hall,
And sit by Pluto's side. *Xan.* I understand.

Æac. Until another comes, more wise than he
In the same art: then must the first give way.

Xan. And how has this disturbed our Æschylus?

Æac. 'Twas he that occupied the tragic chair,
As, in his craft, the noblest. *Xan.* Who does now?

Æac. But when Euripides came down, he kept
Flourishing off before the highwaymen,
Thieves, burglars, parricides—these form our mob
In Hades—till with listening to his twists
And turns, and pleas and counterpleas, they went
Mad on the man, and hailed him first and wisest:
Elate with this, he claimed the tragic chair
Where Æschylus was seated. *Xan.* Wasn't he pelted?

Æac. Not he: the populace clamoured out to try
Which of the twain was wiser in his art.

Xan. You mean the rascals? *Æac.* Aye, as high as heaven!

Xan. But were there none to side with Æschylus?

Æac. Scanty and sparse the good, (*Regards the audience*) the
same as here.

Xan. And what does Pluto now propose to do?

Æac. He means to hold a tournament, and bring
Their tragedies to the proof. *Xan.* But Sophocles,
How came not he to claim the tragic chair?

Æac. Claim it? Not he! When *he* came down, he kissed
With reverence Æschylus, and clasped his hand,
And yielded willingly the chair to him.
But now he's going, says Cleidemides,

To sit third man: and then if Æschylus win,
He'll stay content: if not, for his art's sake,
He'll fight to the death against Euripides.
 Xan. Will it come off? *Æac.* O, yes, by Zeus, directly.
And then, I hear, will wonderful things be done,
The art poetic will be weighed in scales.
 Xan. What! weigh out tragedy, like butcher's meat?
 Æac. Levels they'll bring, and measuring-tapes for words,
And moulded oblongs. *Xan.* Is it bricks they are making?
 Æac. Wedges and compasses: for Euripides
Vows that he'll test the dramas, word by word.
 Xan. Æschylus chafes at this, I fancy. *Æac.* Well,
He lowered his brows, upglaring like a bull.
 Xan. And who's to be the judge? *Æac.* There came the rub.
Skilled men were hard to find: for with the Athenians
Æschylus, somehow, did not hit it off.
 Xan. Too many burglars, I expect he thought.
 Æac. And all the rest, he said, were trash and nonsense
To judge poetic wits. So then at last
They chose your lord, an expert in the art.
But go we in: for when our lords are bent
On urgent business, that means blows for us.

 Chor. O, surely with terrible wrath will the thunder-voiced monarch be filled,
When he sees his opponent beside him, the tonguester, the artifice-skilled,
Stand, whetting his tusks for the fight! O, surely, his eyes, rolling fell,
  Will with terrible madness be fraught!
O, then will be charging of plume-waving words with their wild-floating mane,
And then will be whirling of splinters, and phrases smoothed down with the plane,
When the man would the grand-stepping maxims, the language gigantic, repel
  Of the hero-creator of thought.

There will his shaggy-born crest upbristle for anger and woe,
Horribly frowning and growling, his fury will launch at the foe
Huge-clamped masses of words, with exertion Titanic uptearing
      Great ship-timber planks for the fray.
But here will the tongue be at work, uncoiling, word-testing, refining,
Sophist-creator of phrases, dissecting, detracting, maligning,
Shaking the envious bits, and with subtle analysis paring
      The lung's large labour away.

Euripides. Don't talk to me; I won't give up the chair,
I say I am better in the art than he.
   Dio. You hear him, Æschylus: why don't you speak?
   Eur. He'll do the grand at first, the juggling trick
He used to play in all his tragedies.
   Dio. Come, my fine fellow; pray, don't talk too big.
   Eur. I know the man, I've scanned him through and through,
A savage-creating stubborn-pulling fellow,
Uncurbed, unfettered, uncontrolled of speech,
Unperiphrastic, bombastiloquent.
   Æschylus. Hah! sayest thou so, child of the garden quean!
And this to ME, thou chattery-babble-collector,
Thou pauper-creating rags-and-patches-stitcher?
Thou shalt abye it dearly! *Dio.* Pray, be still;
Nor heat thy soul to fury, Æschylus.
   Æsch. Not till I've made you see the sort of man
This cripple-maker is who crows so loudly.
   Dio. Bring out a ewe, a black-fleeced ewe, my boys:
Here's a typhoon about to burst upon us.
   Æsch. Thou picker-up of Cretan monodies,
Foisting thy tales of incest on the stage—
   Dio. Forbear, forbear, most honoured Æschylus;
And you, my poor Euripides, begone,
If you are wise, out of this pitiless hail,
Lest with some heady word he crack your skull
And batter out your brain—less Telephus.
And not with passion, Æschylus, but calmly
Test and be tested. 'Tis not meet for poets

To scold each other, like two baking-girls.
But you go roaring like an oak on fire.
   Eur. I'm ready, I! I don't draw back one bit.
I'll lash or, if he will, let him lash first
The talk, the lays, the sinews of a play:
Aye, and my Peleus, aye, and Æolus,
And Meleager, aye, and Telephus.
   Dio. And what do *you* propose? Speak, Æschylus.
   Æsch. I could have wished to meet him otherwhere.
We fight not here on equal terms. *Dio.* Why not?
   Æsch. My poetry survived me: his died with him:
He's got it here, all handy to recite.
Howbeit, if so you wish it, so we'll have it.
   Dio. O, bring me fire, and bring me frankincense.
I'll pray, or e'er the clash of wits begin,
To judge the strife with high poetic skill.
Meanwhile (*To the Chorus*) invoke the Muses with a song.

   Chor. O Muses, the daughters divine of Zeus, the immaculate Nine,
Who gaze from your mansions serene on intellects subtle and keen,
When down to the tournament lists, in bright-polished wit they descend,
With wrestling and turnings and twists in the battle of words to contend,
O, come and behold what the two antagonist poets can do,
Whose mouths are the swiftest to teach grand language and filings of speech:
For now of their wits is the sternest encounter commencing in earnest.

   Dio. Ye two, put up your prayers before ye start.
   Æsch. Demeter, mistress, nourisher of my soul,
O, make me worthy of thy mystic rites!
   Dio. (*To Eur.*) Now put on incense, you. *Eur.* Excuse me, no;
My vows are paid to other gods than these.
   Dio. What, a new coinage of your own? *Eur.* Precisely.

Dio. Pray then to them, those private gods of yours.
Eur. Ether, my pasture, volubly rolling tongue,
Intelligent wit and critic nostrils keen,
O, well and neatly may I trounce his plays!

   Chor. We also are yearning from these to be learning
        Some stately measure, some majestic grand
        Movement telling of conflicts nigh.
        Now for battle arrayed they stand,
        Tongues embittered, and anger high.
        Each has got a venturesome will,
        Each an eager and nimble mind;
        One will wield, with artistic skill,
        Clear-cut phrases, and wit refined;
        Then the other, with words defiant,
        Stern and strong, like an angry giant
        Laying on with uprooted trees,
        Soon will scatter a world of these
        Superscholastic subtleties.

  Dio. Now then, commence your arguments, and mind you both display
True wit, not metaphors, nor things which any fool could say.
  Eur. As for myself, good people all, I'll tell you by-and-by
My own poetic worth and claims; but first of all I'll try
To show how this portentous quack beguiled the silly fools
Whose tastes were nurtured, ere he came, in Phrynichus's schools.
He'd bring some single mourner on, seated and veiled, 'twould be
Achilles, say, or Niobe—the face you could not see—
An empty show of tragic woe, who uttered not one thing.
  Dio. 'Tis true. *Eur.* Then in the Chorus came, and rattled off a string
Of four continuous lyric odes: the mourner never stirred.
  Dio. I liked it too. I sometimes think that I those mutes preferred
To all your chatterers nowadays. *Eur.* Because, if you must know,
You were an ass. *Dio.* An ass, no doubt: what made him do it though?

Eur. That was his quackery, don't you see, to set the audience guessing
When Niobe would speak; meanwhile, the drama was progressing.
Dio. The rascal, how he took me in! 'Twas shameful, was it not?
(*To Æsch.*) What makes you stamp and fidget so? *Eur.* He's catching it so hot.
So when he had humbugged thus awhile, and now his wretched play
Was halfway through, a dozen words, great wild-bull words, he'd say,
Fierce Bugaboos, with bristling crests, and shaggy eyebrows too,
Which not a soul could understand. *Æsch.* O, heavens! *Dio.* Be quiet, do.
Eur. But not one single word was clear. *Dio.* St! don't your teeth be gnashing.
Eur. 'Twas all Scamanders, moated camps, and griffin-eagles flashing
In burnished copper on the shields, chivalric-precipice-high
Expressions, hard to comprehend. *Dio.* Aye, by the Powers, and I
Full many a sleepless night have spent in anxious thought, because
I'd find the tawny cock-horse out, what sort of bird it was!
Æsch. It was a sign, you stupid dolt, engraved the ships upon.
Dio. Eryxis I supposed it was, Philoxenus's son.
Eur. Now really should a cock be brought into a tragic play?
Æsch. You enemy of gods and men, what was *your* practice, pray?
Eur. No cock-horse in *my* plays, by Zeus, no goat-stag there you'll see,
Such figures as are blazoned forth in Median tapestry.
When first I took the art from you, bloated and swoln, poor thing,
With turgid gasconading words and heavy dieting,
First I reduced and toned her down, and made her slim and neat
With wordlets and with exercise and poultices of beet,
And next a dose of chatterjuice, distilled from books, I gave her,
And monodies she took, with sharp Cephisophon for flavour.
I never used haphazard words, or plunged abruptly in;
Who entered first explained at large the drama's origin
And source. *Dio.* Its source, I really trust, was better than your own.

    Eur. Then from the very opening lines no idleness was shown;
The mistress talked with all her might, the servant talked as much,
The master talked, the maiden talked, the beldame talked. *Æsch.*
           For such
An outrage was not death your due? *Eur.* No, by Apollo, no:
That was my democratic way. *Dio.* Ah, let that topic go.
Your record is not there, my friend, particularly good.
    Eur. Then next I taught all these to speak. *Æsch.* You did so, and
        I would
That ere such mischief you had wrought, your very lungs had
        split.
    Eur. Canons of verse I introduced, and neatly chiselled wit;
To look, to scan: to plot, to plan: to twist, to turn, to woo:
On all to spy; in all to pry. *Æsch.* You did: I say so too.
    Eur. I showed them scenes of common life, the things we know
        and see,
Where any blunder would at once by all detected be.
I never blustered on, or took their breath and wits away
By Cycnuses or Memnons clad in terrible array,
With bells upon their horses' heads, the audience to dismay.
Look at *his* pupils, look at mine: and there the contrast view.
Uncouth Megænetus is his, and rough Phormisius too;
Great long-beard-lance-and-trumpet-men, flesh-tearers with the pine:
But natty smart Theramenes, and Cleitophon are mine.
    Dio. Theramenes? a clever man and wonderfully sly:
Immerse him in a flood of ills, he'll soon be high and dry,
"A Kian with a kappa, sir, not Chian with a chi."
    Eur. I taught them all these knowing ways
        By chopping logic in my plays,
        And making all my speakers try
        To reason out the How and Why.
        So now the people trace the springs,
        The sources, and the roots of things,
        And manage all their households too
        Far better than they used to do,
        Scanning and searching *What's amiss?*
        And, *Why was that?* And, *How is this?*

Dio. Aye, truly, never now a man
  Comes home, but he begins to scan;
  And to his household loudly cries,
  Why, where's my pitcher? What's the matter?
  'Tis dead and gone my last year's platter.
  Who gnawed these olives? Bless the sprat,
  Who nibbled off the head of that?
  And where's the garlic vanished, pray,
  I purchased only yesterday?
  —Whereas, of old, our stupid youths
  Would sit, with open mouths and eyes,
  Like any dull-brained Mammacouths.

Chor. "All this thou beholdest, Achilles our boldest."
  And what wilt thou reply? Draw tight the rein
  Lest that fiery soul of thine
  Whirl thee out of the listed plain,
  Past the olives, and o'er the line.
  Dire and grievous the charge he brings.
  See thou answer him, noble heart,
  Not with passionate bickerings.
  Shape thy course with a sailor's art,
  Reef the canvas, shorten the sails,
  Shift them edgewise to shun the gales.
  When the breezes are soft and low,
  Then, well under control, you'll go
  Quick and quicker to strike the foe.
O first of all the Hellenic bards high loftily-towering verse to rear,
And tragic phrase from the dust to raise, pour forth thy fountain
    with right good cheer.

Æsch. My wrath is hot at this vile mischance, and my spirit revolts
    at the thought that I
Must bandy words with a fellow like *him:* but lest he should vaunt
    that I can't reply—
Come, tell me what are the points for which a noble poet our praise
    obtains.

Eur. For his ready wit, and his counsels sage, and because the
 citizen-folk he trains
To be better townsmen and worthier men. *Æsch.* If then you have
 done the very reverse,
Found noble-hearted and virtuous men, and altered them, each and
 all, for the worse,
Pray what is the meed you deserve to get? *Dio.* Nay, ask not *him*.
 He deserves to die.
 Æsch. For just consider what style of men he received from me,
 great six-foot-high
Heroical souls, who never would blench from a townsman's duties
 in peace or war;
Not idle loafers, or low buffoons, or rascally scamps such as now
 they are,
But men who were breathing spears and helms, and the snow-white
 plume in its crested pride,
The greave, and the dart, and the warrior's heart in its sevenfold
 casing of tough bull-hide.
 Dio. He'll stun me, I know, with his armoury-work; this business
 is going from bad to worse.
 Eur. And how did you manage to make them so grand, exalted,
 and brave with your wonderful verse?
 Dio. Come, Æschylus, answer, and don't stand mute in your self-
 willed pride and arrogant spleen.
 Æsch. A drama I wrote with the War-god filled. *Dio.* Its name?
Æsch. 'Tis the "Seven against Thebes" that I mean,
Which whoso beheld, with eagerness swelled to rush to the battlefield
 there and then.
 Dio. O, that was a scandalous thing you did! You have made the
 Thebans mightier men,
More eager by far for the business of war. Now, therefore, receive
 this punch on the head.
 Æsch. Ah, *ye* might have practised the same yourselves, but ye
 turned to other pursuits instead.
Then next the "Persians" I wrote, in praise of the noblest deed that
 the world can show,
And each man longed for the victor's wreath, to fight and to van-
 quish his country's foe.

Dio. I was pleased, I own, when I heard their moan for old Darius, their great king, dead;
When they smote together their hands, like this, and *Evir alake* the Chorus said.
Æsch. Aye, such are the poet's appropriate works: and just consider how all along
From the very first they have wrought you good, the noble bards, the masters of song.
First, Orpheus taught you religious rites, and from bloody murder to stay your hands:
Musæus healing and oracle lore; and Hesiod all the culture of lands,
The time to gather, the time to plough. And gat not Homer his glory divine
By singing of valour, and honour, and right, and the sheen of the battle-extended line,
The ranging of troops and the arming of men? *Dio.* O, aye, but he didn't teach *that,* I opine,
To Pantacles; when he was leading the show I couldn't imagine what he was at,
He had fastened his helm on the top of his head, he was trying to fasten his plume upon that.
Æsch. But others, many and brave, he taught, of whom was Lamachus, hero true;
And thence my spirit the impress took, and many a lion-heart chief I drew,
Patrocluses, Teucers, illustrious names; for I fain the citizen-folk would spur
To stretch themselves to *their* measure and height, whenever the trumpet of war they hear.
But Phædras and Stheneboeas? No! no harlotry business deformed my plays.
And none can say that ever I drew a love-sick woman in all my days.
Eur. For *you* no lot or portion had got in Queen Aphrodite. *Æsch.* Thank Heaven for that.
But ever on you and yours, my friend, the mighty goddess mightily sat;

Yourself she cast to the ground at last. *Dio.* O, aye, that came uncommonly pat.
You showed how cuckolds are made, and lo, you were struck yourself by the very same fate.
  Eur. But say, you cross-grained censor of mine, how *my* Stheneboeas could harm the state.
  Æsch. Full many a noble dame, the wife of a noble citizen, hemlock took,
And died, unable the shame and sin of your Bellerophon-scenes to brook.
  Eur. Was then, I wonder, the tale I told of Phædra's passionate love untrue?
  Æsch. Not so: but tales of incestuous vice the sacred poet should hide from view,
Nor ever exhibit and blazon forth on the public stage to the public ken.
For boys a teacher at school is found, but we, the poets, are teachers of men.
We are BOUND things honest and pure to speak. *Eur.* And to speak great Lycabettuses, pray,
And massive blocks of Parnassian rocks, is *that* things honest and pure to say?
In human fashion we ought to speak. *Æsch.* Alas, poor witling, and can't you see
That for mighty thoughts and heroic aims, the words themselves must appropriate be?
And grander belike on the ear should strike the speech of heroes and godlike powers,
Since even the robes that invest their limbs are statelier, grander robes than ours.
Such was *my* plan: but when *you* began, you spoilt and degraded it all. *Eur.* How so?
  Æsch. Your kings in tatters and rags you dressed, and brought them on, a beggarly show,
To move, forsooth, our pity and ruth. *Eur.* And what was the harm, I should like to know.
  Æsch. No more will a wealthy citizen now equip for the state a galley of war.

He wraps his limbs in tatters and rags, and whines *he is poor, too poor by far.*
 Dio. But under his rags he is wearing a vest, as woolly and soft as a man could wish.
Let him gull the state, and he's off to the mart; an eager, extravagant buyer of fish.
 Æsch. Moreover, to prate, to harangue, to debate, is now the ambition of all in the state.
Each exercise-ground is in consequence found deserted and empty: to evil repute
Your lessons have brought our youngsters, and taught our sailors to challenge, discuss, and refute
The orders they get from their captains, and yet, when *I* was alive, I protest that the knaves
Knew nothing at all, save for rations to call, and to sing "Rhyppapæ" as they pulled through the waves.
 Dio. And, bedad, to let fly from their sterns in the eye of the fellow who tugged at the undermost oar,
And a jolly young messmate with filth to besmirch, and to land for a filching adventure ashore;
 But now they harangue, and dispute, and won't row,
 And idly and aimlessly float to and fro.
 Æsch. Of what ills is he NOT the creator and cause?
 Consider the scandalous scenes that he draws,
 His bawds, and his panders, his women who give,
  Give birth in the sacredest shrine,
 Whilst others with brothers are wedded and bedded,
  And others opine
 That "not to be living" is truly "to live."
 And therefore our city is swarming to-day
 With clerks and with demagogue-monkeys, who play
 Their jackanape tricks at all times, in all places,
 Deluding the people of Athens; but none
 Has training enough in athletics to run
  With the torch in his hand at the races.
 Dio. By the Powers, you are right! At the Panathenæa
I laughed till I felt like a potsherd to see a
Pale, paunchy young gentleman pounding along,

With his head butting forward, the last of the throng,
In the direst of straits; and, behold, at the gates,
The Ceramites flapped him, and smacked him, and slapped him,
In the ribs, and the loin, and the flank, and the groin,
And still, as they spanked him, he puffed and he panted,
Till at one mighty cuff, he discharged such a puff
  That he blew out his torch and levanted.

 Chor. Dread the battle, and stout the combat, mighty and manifold looms the war.
   Hard to decide in the fight they're waging,
   One like a stormy tempest raging,
One alert in the rally and skirmish, clever to parry and foin and spar.
   Nay, but don't be content to sit
Always in one position only: many the fields for your keen-edged wit.
   On then, wrangle in every way,
   Argue, battle, be flayed and flay,
   Old and new from your stores display,
Yea, and strive with venturesome daring something subtle and neat to say.

Fear ye this, that to-day's spectators lack the grace of artistic lore,
   Lack the knowledge they need for taking
   All the points ye will soon be making?
Fear it not: the alarm is groundless: that, be sure, is the case no more.
   All have fought the campaign ere this:
Each a book of the words is holding; never a single point they'll miss.
   Bright their natures, and now, I ween,
   Newly whetted, and sharp, and keen.
   Dread not any defect of wit,
Battle away without misgiving, sure that the audience, at least, are fit.

 Eur. Well, then, I'll turn me to your prologues now,
Beginning first to test the first beginning
Of this fine poet's plays. Why, he's obscure
Even in the enunciation of the facts.

Dio. Which of them will you test? *Eur.* Many: but first
Give us that famous one from the "Oresteia."
   Dio. St! Silence, all! Now, Æschylus, begin.
   Æsch. Grave Hermes, witnessing a father's power,
Be thou my saviour and mine aid to-day,
For here I come, and hither I return.
   Dio. Any fault there? *Eur.* A dozen faults, and more.
   Dio. Eh! why, the lines are only three in all.
   Eur. But every one contains a score of faults.
   Dio. Now, Æschylus, keep silent; if you don't,
You won't get off with three iambic lines.
   Æsch. Silent for *him!* *Dio.* If *my* advice you'll take.
   Eur. Why, at first starting, here's a fault sky-high.
   Æsch. (*To Dio.*) You see your folly? *Dio.* Have your way; I
     care not.
   Æsch. (*To Eur.*) What is my fault? *Eur.* Begin the lines
     again.
   Æsch. Grave Hermes, witnessing a father's power—
   Eur. And this beside his murdered father's grave
Orestes speaks? *Æsch.* I say not otherwise.
   Eur. Then does he mean that when his father fell
By craft and violence at a woman's hand,
The god of craft was witnessing the deed?
   Æsch. It was not he: it was the Helper Hermes
He called the grave: and this he showed by adding
It was his sire's prerogative he held.
   Eur. Why, this is worse than all. If from his father
He held this office grave, why, then— *Dio.* He was
A graveyard rifler on his father's side.
   Æsch. Bacchus, the wine you drink is stale and fusty.
   Dio. Give him another: (*To Eur.*) you, look out for faults.
   Æsch. Be thou my saviour and mine aid to-day,
For here I come, and hither I return.
   Eur. The same thing twice says clever Æschylus.
   Dio. How twice? *Eur.* Why, just consider: I'll explain.
"I come," says he; and "I return," says he:
It's the same thing, to "come" and to "return."

Dio. Aye, just as if you said, "Good fellow, lend me
A kneading-trough: likewise, a trough to knead in."
  Æsch. It is not so, you everlasting talker,
They're not the same, the words are right enough.
  Dio. How so? inform me how you use the words.
  Æsch. A man, not banished from his home, may "come"
To any land, with no especial chance.
A home-bound exile both "returns" and "comes."
  Dio. O, good, by Apollo!
What do you say, Euripides, to that?
  Eur. I say Orestes never did "return."
He came in secret: nobody recalled him.
  Dio. O, good, by Hermes!
(*Aside.*) I've not the least suspicion what he means.
  Eur. Repeat another line. *Dio.* Aye, Æschylus,
Repeat one instantly: *you*, mark what's wrong.
  *Æsch. Now on this funeral mound I call my father
To hear, to hearken.* *Eur.* There he is again.
To "hear," to "hearken"; the same thing, exactly.
  Dio. Aye, but he's speaking to the dead, you knave,
Who cannot hear us though we call them thrice.
  Æsch. And how do you make *your* prologues? *Eur.* You shall
    hear;
And if you find one single thing said twice,
Or any useless padding, spit upon me.
  Dio. Well, fire away: I'm all agog to hear
Your very accurate and faultless prologues.
  Eur. A happy man was Œdipus at first—
  Æsch. Not so, by Zeus; a most unhappy man,
Who, not yet born nor yet conceived, Apollo
Foretold would be his father's murderer.
How could *he* be a happy man at first?
  Eur. Then he became the wretchedest of men.
  Æsch. Not so, by Zeus; he never ceased to be.
No sooner born, than they exposed the babe
(And that in winter), in an earthen crock,
Lest he should grow a man, and slay his father.

Then with both ankles pierced and swoln, he limped
Away to Polybus: still young, he married
An ancient crone, and her his mother too;
Then scratched out both his eyes. *Dio.* Happy indeed
Had he been Erasinides's colleague!
   Eur. Nonsense; I say my prologues are first-rate.
   Æsch. Nay, then, by Zeus, no longer line by line
I'll maul your phrases: but with heaven to aid
I'll smash your prologues with a bottle of oil.
   Eur. You mine with a bottle of oil? *Æsch.* With only one.
You frame your prologues so that each and all
Fit in with a "bottle of oil," or "coverlet-skin,"
Or "reticule-bag." I'll prove it here, and now.
   Eur. You'll prove it? You? *Æsch.* I will. *Dio.* Well, then,
     begin.
   Eur. Ægyptus, sailing with his fifty sons,
As ancient legends mostly tell the tale,
Touching at Argos, *Æsch.* Lost his bottle of oil.
   Eur. Hang it, what's that? Confound that bottle of oil!
   Dio. Give him another: let him try again.
   Eur. Bacchus, who, clad in fawn-skins, leaps and bounds
With torch and thyrsus in the choral dance
Along Parnassus, *Æsch.* Lost his bottle of oil.
   Dio. Ah me, we are stricken—with that bottle again!
   Eur. Pooh, pooh, that's nothing. I've a prologue here,
He'll never tack his bottle of oil to this:
No man is blest in every single thing.
One is of noble birth, but lacking means.
Another, baseborn, *Æsch.* Lost his bottle of oil.
   Dio. Euripides! *Eur.* Well? *Dio.* Lower your sails, my boy;
This bottle of oil is going to blow a gale.
   Eur. O, by Demeter, I don't care one bit;
Now from his hands I'll strike that bottle of oil.
   Dio. Go on then, go; but ware the bottle of oil.
   Eur. Once Cadmus, quitting the Sidonian town,
Agenor's offspring, *Æsch.* Lost his bottle of oil.
   Dio. O, pray, my man, buy off that bottle of oil,

Or else he'll smash our prologues all to bits.
  Eur. I buy of *him*? *Dio.* If *my* advice you'll take.
  Eur. No, no, I've many a prologue yet to say,
To which he can't tack on his bottle of oil.
Pelops, the son of Tantalus, while driving
His mares to Pisa, Æsch. Lost his bottle of oil.
  Dio. There! he tacked on the bottle of oil again.
O, for heaven's sake, pay him its price, dear boy;
You'll get it for an obol, spick-and-span.
  Eur. Not yet, by Zeus; I've plenty of prologues left.
Œneus once reaping. Æsch. Lost his bottle of oil.
  Eur. Pray let me finish one entire line first.
Œneus once reaping an abundant harvest,
Offering the first fruits, Æsch. Lost his bottle of oil.
  Dio. What, in the act of offering? Fie! Who stole it?
  Eur. O, don't keep bothering! Let him try with this!
Zeus, as by Truth's own voice the tale is told,
  Dio. No, he'll cut in with "Lost his bottle of oil."
Those bottles of oil on all your prologues seem
To gather and grow, like styes upon the eye.
Turn to his melodies now, for goodness' sake.
  Eur. O, I can easily show that he's a poor
Melody-maker; makes them all alike.

> *Chor.* What, O, what will be done!
> Strange to think that he dare
> Blame the bard who has won,
> More than all in our days,
> Fame and praise for his lays,
> Lays so many and fair.
> Much I marvel to hear
> What the charge he will bring
> 'Gainst our tragedy king;
> Yea, for himself do I fear.

  Eur. Wonderful lays! O, yes, you'll see directly.
I'll cut down all his metrical strains to one.
  Dio. And I, I'll take some pebbles, and keep count.

(A slight pause, during which the music of a flute is heard. The music continues to the end of line 1277 as an accompaniment to the recitative.)

    Eur. Lord of Phthia, Achilles, *why, hearing the voice of the hero-dividing,*
    Hah! smiting! approachest thou not to the rescue?
We, by the lake who *abide, are adoring our ancestor Hermes.*
    Hah! smiting! approachest thou not to the rescue?
    Dio. O Æschylus, twice art thou smitten!
    Eur. Hearken to me, great king; yea, hearken, *Atreides, thou noblest of all the Achæans.*
    Hah! smiting! approachest thou not to the rescue?
    Dio. Thrice, Æschylus, thrice art thou smitten!
    Eur. Hush! the bee-wardens are here: they *will quickly the Temple of Artemis open.*
    Hah! smiting! approachest thou not to the rescue?
I will expound (for *I know it*) the omen the chieftains encountered.
    Hah! smiting! approachest thou not to the rescue?
    Dio. O Zeus and King, the terrible lot of smitings!
I'll to the bath: I'm very sure my kidneys
Are quite inflamed and swoln with all these smitings.
    Eur. Wait till you've heard another batch of lays
Culled from his lyre-accompanied melodies.
    Dio. Go on then, go: but no more smitings, please.
    Eur. How the twin-throned powers of *Achæa, the lords of the mighty Hellenes.*
    O phlattothrattophlattothrat!
Sendeth *The Sphinx, the unchancy, the chieftainess bloodhound.*
    O phlattothrattophlattothrat!
Launcheth fierce with brand *and hand the avengers the terrible eagle.*
    O phlattothrattophlattothrat!
So for the swift-*winged hounds of the air he provided a booty.*
    O phlattothrattophlattothrat!
The throng down-bearing on Aias.
    O phlattothrattophlattothrat!

Dio. Whence comes that phlattothrat? From Marathon, or
Where picked you up these cable-twister's strains?
  Æsch. From noblest source for noblest ends I brought them,
Unwilling in the Muses' holy field
The selfsame flowers as Phrynichus to cull.
But *he* from all things rotten draws his lays,
From Carian flutings, catches of Meletus,
Dance-music, dirges. You shall hear directly.
Bring me the lyre. Yet wherefore need a lyre
For songs like these? Where's she that bangs and jangles
Her castanets? Euripides's Muse,
Present yourself: fit goddess for fit verse.
  Dio. The Muse herself can't be a wanton? No!
  Æsch. Halcyons, who by the ever-rippling
    Waves of the sea are babbling,
    Dewing your plumes with the drops that fall
    From wings in the salt spray dabbling.

    Spiders, ever with twir-r-r-r-rling fingers
    Weaving the warp and the woof,
    Little, brittle, network, fretwork,
    Under the coigns of the roof.

    The minstrel shuttle's care.

    Where in the front of the dark-prowed ships
    Yarely the flute-loving dolphin skips.

    Races here and oracles there.

    And the joy of the young vines smiling,
    And the tendril of grapes, care-beguiling.
    O, embrace me, my child, O, embrace me.
  (*To Dio.*) You see this foot? *Dio.* I do.
  Æsch. And this? Dio. And that one too.
  Æsch. (*To Eur.*) You, such stuff who compile,
    Dare my songs to upbraid;

THE FROGS

    You, whose songs in the style
    Of Cyrene's embraces are made.
So much for them: but still I'd like to show
The way in which your monodies are framed.
    "O darkly-light mysterious Night,
    What may this Vision mean,
    Sent from the world unseen
    With baleful omens rife;
    A thing of lifeless life,
    A child of sable night,
    A ghastly curdling sight,
    In black funereal veils,
  With murder, murder in its eyes,
    And great enormous nails?
Light ye the lanterns, my maidens, and dipping your jugs in the stream,
Draw me the dew of the water, and heat it to boiling and steam;
So will I wash me away the ill effects of my dream.
        God of the sea!
        My dream's come true.
        Ho, lodgers, ho,
        This portent view.
    Glyce has vanished, carrying off my cock,
      My cock that crew!
    O Mania, help! O Oreads of the rock,
      Pursue! pursue!
    For I, poor girl, was working within,
    Holding my distaff heavy and full,
    Twir-r-r-r-rling my hand as the threads I spin,
    Weaving an excellent bobbin of wool;
    Thinking, 'To-morrow I'll go to the fair,
    In the dusk of the morn, and be selling it there.'
    But he to the blue upflew, upflew,
    On the lightliest tips of his wings outspread;
    To me he bequeathed but woe, but woe,
    And tears, sad tears, from my eyes o'erflow,
    Which I, the bereaved, must shed, must shed.

>   O children of Ida, sons of Crete,
>   Grasping your bows, to the rescue come;
>   Twinkle about on your restless feet,
>   Stand in a circle around her home.
>   O Artemis, thou maid divine,
>   Dictynna, huntress, fair to see,
>   O, bring that keen-nosed pack of thine,
>   And hunt through all the house with me.
>   O Hecate, with flameful brands,
>   O Zeus's daughter, arm thine hands,
>   Those swiftliest hands, both right and left;
>   Thy rays on Glyce's cottage throw
>   That I serenely there may go
>   And search by moonlight for the theft."

Dio. Enough of both your odes. *Æsch.* Enough for me.
Now would I bring the fellow to the scales.
That, that alone, shall test our poetry now,
And prove whose words are weightiest, his or mine.
  Dio. Then both come hither, since I needs must weigh
The art poetic like a pound of cheese.

>   *Chor.* O, the labour these wits go through!
>   O, the wild, extravagant, new,
>   Wonderful things they are going to do!
>   Who but they would ever have thought of it?
>   Why, if a man had happened to meet me
>   Out in the street, and intelligence brought of it,
>   I should have thought he was trying to cheat me;
>   Thought that his story was false and deceiving.
>   That were a tale I could never believe in.

Dio. Each of you stand beside his scale, $\genfrac{}{}{0pt}{}{\textit{Æsch.}}{\textit{Eur.}}\Big\}$ We're here.
  Dio. And grasp it firmly whilst ye speak your lines,
And don't let go until I cry "Cuckoo."
  $\genfrac{}{}{0pt}{}{\textit{Æsch.}}{\textit{Eur.}}\Big\}$ Ready! *Dio.* Now speak your lines into the scale.
  Eur. *O, that the Argo had not winged her way—*

Æsch. River Spercheius, cattle-grazing haunts—
  Dio. Cuckoo! let go. O, look, by far the lowest
His scale sinks down. *Eur.* Why, how came that about?
  Dio. He threw a river in, like some wool-seller
Wetting his wool, to make it weight the more.
But *you* threw in a light and wingèd word.
  Eur. Come, let him match another verse with mine.
  Dio. Each to his scale. *Æsch.*⎫ We're ready. *Dio.* Speak your lines.
                          Eur. ⎭
  Eur. Persuasion's only shrine is eloquent speech.
  Æsch. Death loves not gifts, alone amongst the gods.
  Dio. Let go, let go. Down goes his scale again.
He threw in Death, the heaviest ill of all.
  Eur. And I Persuasion, the most lovely word.
  Dio. A vain and empty sound, devoid of sense.
Think of some heavier-weighted line of yours,
To drag your scale down: something strong and big.
  Eur. Where have I got one? Where? Let's see. *Dio.* I'll tell you.
"*Achilles threw two singles and a four.*"
Come, speak your lines: this is your last set-to.
  Eur. In his right hand he grasped an iron-clamped mace.
  Æsch. Chariot on chariot, corpse on corpse was hurled.
  Dio. There now! again he has done you. *Eur.* Done me? How?
  Dio. He threw two chariots and two corpses in;
Fivescore Egyptians could not lift that weight.
  Æsch. No more of "line for line"; let him—himself,
His children, wife, Cephisophon—get in,
With all his books collected in his arms,
Two lines of mine shall overweigh the lot.
  Dio. Both are my friends; I can't decide between them:
I don't desire to be at odds with either:
One is so clever, one delights me so.
  Pluto. Then you'll effect nothing for which you came?
  Dio. And how, if I decide? *Pluto.* Then take the winner;
So will your journey not be made in vain.
  Dio. Heaven bless your Highness! Listen, I came down
After a poet. *Eur.* To what end? *Dio.* That so

The city, saved, may keep her choral games.
Now then, whichever of you two shall best
Advise the city, *he* shall come with me.
And first of Alcibiades, let each
Say what he thinks; the city travails sore.
  Eur. What does she think herself about him? *Dio.* What?
She loves, and hates, and longs to have him back.
But give me *your* advice about the man.
  Eur. I loathe a townsman who is slow to aid,
And swift to hurt, his town: who ways and means
Finds for himself, but finds not for the state.
  Dio. Poseidon, but that's smart! (*To Æsch.*) And what say *you?*
  Æsch. 'Twere best to rear no lion in the state:
But having reared, 'tis best to humour him.
  Dio. By Zeus the Saviour, still I can't decide.
One is so clever, and so clear the other.
But once again. Let each in turn declare
What plan of safety for the state ye've got.
  Eur. [First with Cinesias wing Cleocritus,
Then zephyrs waft them o'er the watery plain.
  Dio. A funny sight, I own: but where's the sense?
  Eur. If, when the fleets engage, they, holding cruets,
Should rain down vinegar in the foemen's eyes,]
I know, and I can tell you. *Dio.* Tell away.
  Eur. When things, mistrusted now, shall trusted be,
And trusted things, mistrusted. *Dio.* How! I don't
Quite comprehend. Be clear, and not so clever.
  Eur. If we mistrust those citizens of ours
Whom now we trust, and those employ whom now
We don't employ, the city will be saved.
If on our present tack we fail, we surely
Shall find salvation in the opposite course.
  Dio. Good, O Palamedes! Good, you genius you.
[Is this *your* cleverness or Cephisophon's?
  Eur. This is my own: the cruet-plan was his.]
  Dio. (*To Æsch.*) Now, you. *Æsch.* But tell me whom the city
      uses.

The good and useful? *Dio.* What are you dreaming of?
She hates and loathes them. *Æsch.* Does she love the bad?
  Dio. Not love them, no: she uses them perforce.
  Æsch. How can one save a city such as this,
Whom neither frieze nor woollen tunic suits?
  Dio. O, if to earth you rise, find out some way.
  Æsch. There will I speak: I cannot answer here.
  Dio. Nay, nay; send up your guerdon from below.
  Æsch. When they shall count the enemy's soil their own,
And theirs the enemy's: when they know that ships
Are their true wealth, their so-called wealth delusion.
  Dio. Aye, but the justices suck that down, you know.
  Pluto. Now then, decide. *Dio.* I will; and thus I'll do it:
I'll choose the man in whom my soul delights.
  Eur. O, recollect the gods by whom you swore
You'd take me home again; and choose your friends.
  Dio. 'Twas my tongue swore; my choice is—Æschylus.
  Eur. Hah! what have you done? *Dio.* Done? Given the victor's prize
To Æschylus; why not? *Eur.* And do you dare
Look in my face, after that shameful deed?
  Dio. What's shameful, if the audience think not so?
  Eur. Have you no heart? Wretch, would you leave me dead?
  Dio. Who knows if death be life, and life be death,
And breath be mutton broth, and sleep a sheepskin?
  Pluto. Now, Dionysus, come ye in, *Dio.* What for?
  Pluto. And sup before ye go. *Dio.* A bright idea.
I' faith, I'm nowise indisposed for that.

  Chor.   Blest the man who possesses a
            Keen intelligent mind.
            This full often we find.
            He, the bard of renown,
            Now to earth reascends,
            Goes, a joy to his town,
            Goes, a joy to his friends,
            Just because he possesses a

    Keen intelligent mind.
    RIGHT it is and befitting,
    Not, by Socrates sitting,
    Idle talk to pursue,
    Stripping tragedy-art of
    All things noble and true,
    Surely the mind to school
    Fine-drawn quibbles to seek,
    Fine-set phrases to speak,
    Is but the part of a fool!

Pluto.   Farewell then, Æschylus, great and wise,
    Go, save our state by the maxims rare
    Of thy noble thought; and the fools chastise,
       For many a fool dwells there.
    And *this* to Cleophon give, my friend,
    And *this* to the revenue-raising crew,
    Nicomachus, Myrmex, next I send,
       And *this* to Archenomus too.
    And bid them all that without delay,
    To my realm of the dead they hasten away.
    For if they loiter above, I swear
    I'll come myself and arrest them there.
    And branded and fettered the slaves shall go
    With the vilest rascal in all the town,
    Adeimantus, son of Leucolophus, down,
       Down, down to the darkness below.
Æsch.   I take the mission. This chair of mine
    Meanwhile to Sophocles here commit
    (For I count him next in our craft divine),
       Till I come once more by thy side to sit.
    But as for that rascally scoundrel there,
    That low buffoon, that worker of ill,
       O, let him not sit in my vacant chair,
          Not even against his will.
Pluto.   (*To the Chorus.*) Escort him up with your mystic throngs,
    While the holy torches quiver and blaze.

> Escort him up with his own sweet songs
> And his noble festival lays.

Chor. First, as the poet triumphant is passing away to the light,
Grant him success on his journey, ye powers that are ruling below.
Grant that he find for the city good counsels to guide her aright;
So we at last shall be freed from the anguish, the fear, and the woe,
Freed from the onsets of war. Let Cleophon now and his band
Battle, if battle they must, far away in their own fatherland.

www.ingramcontent.com/pod-product-compliance
Lightning Source LLC
Chambersburg PA
CBHW031305150426
43191CB00005B/79